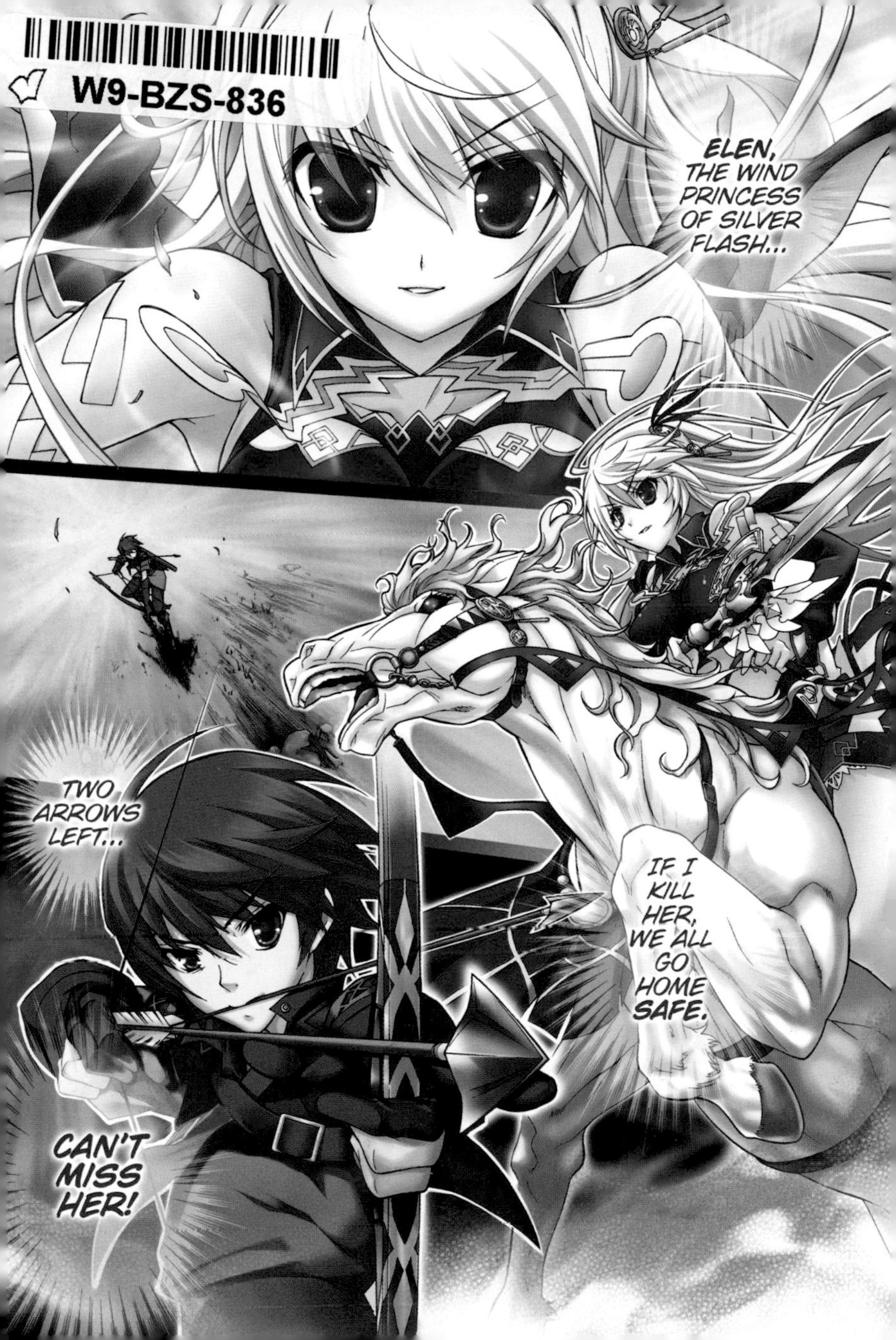
ELEN, THE WIND PRINCESS OF SILVER FLASH...
IF I KILL HER, WE ALL GO HOME SAFE.
TWO ARROWS LEFT...
CAN'T MISS HER!

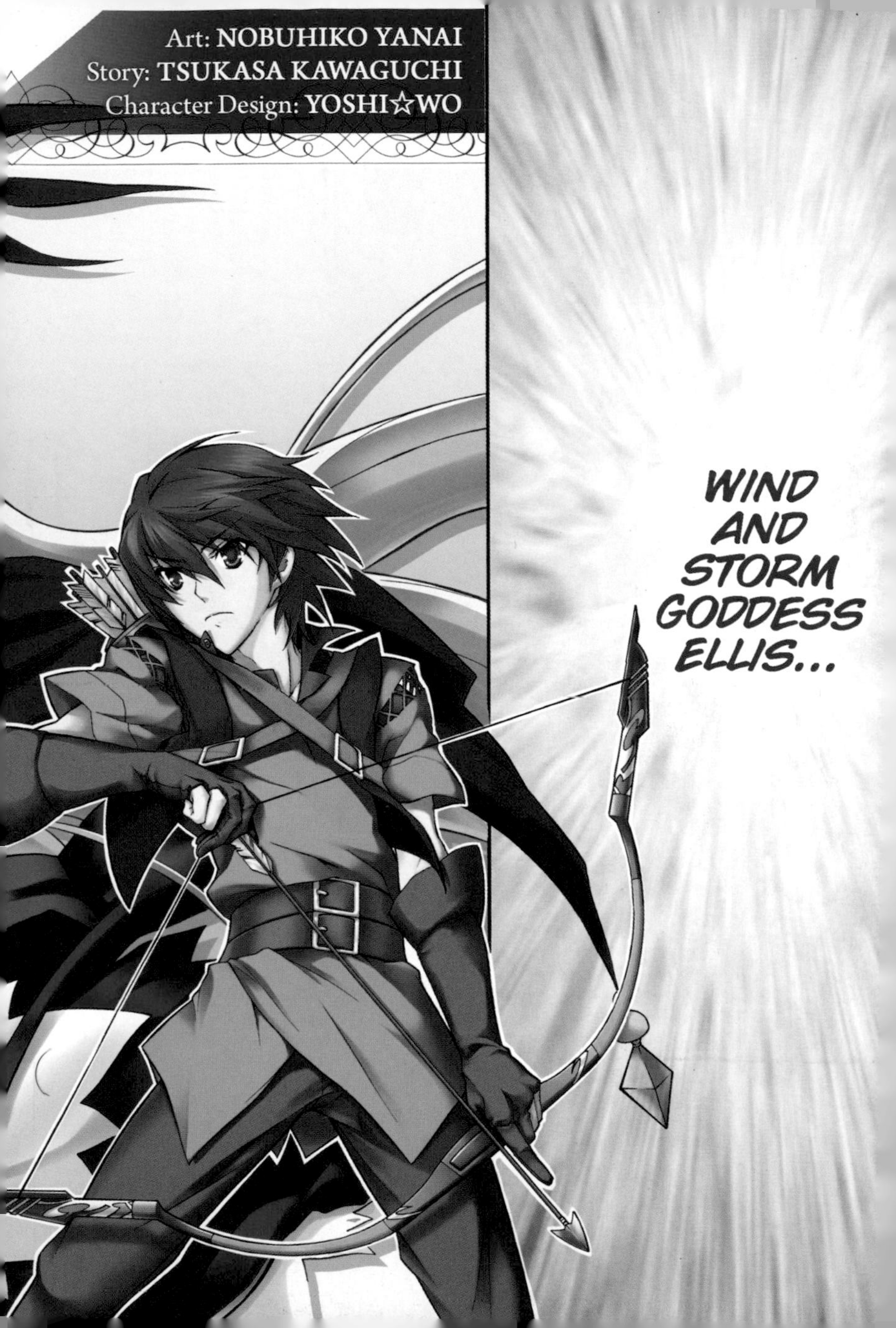
WIND AND STORM GODDESS ELLIS...
Art: NOBUHIKO YANAI
Story: TSUKASA KAWAGUCHI
Character Design: YOSHI☆WO

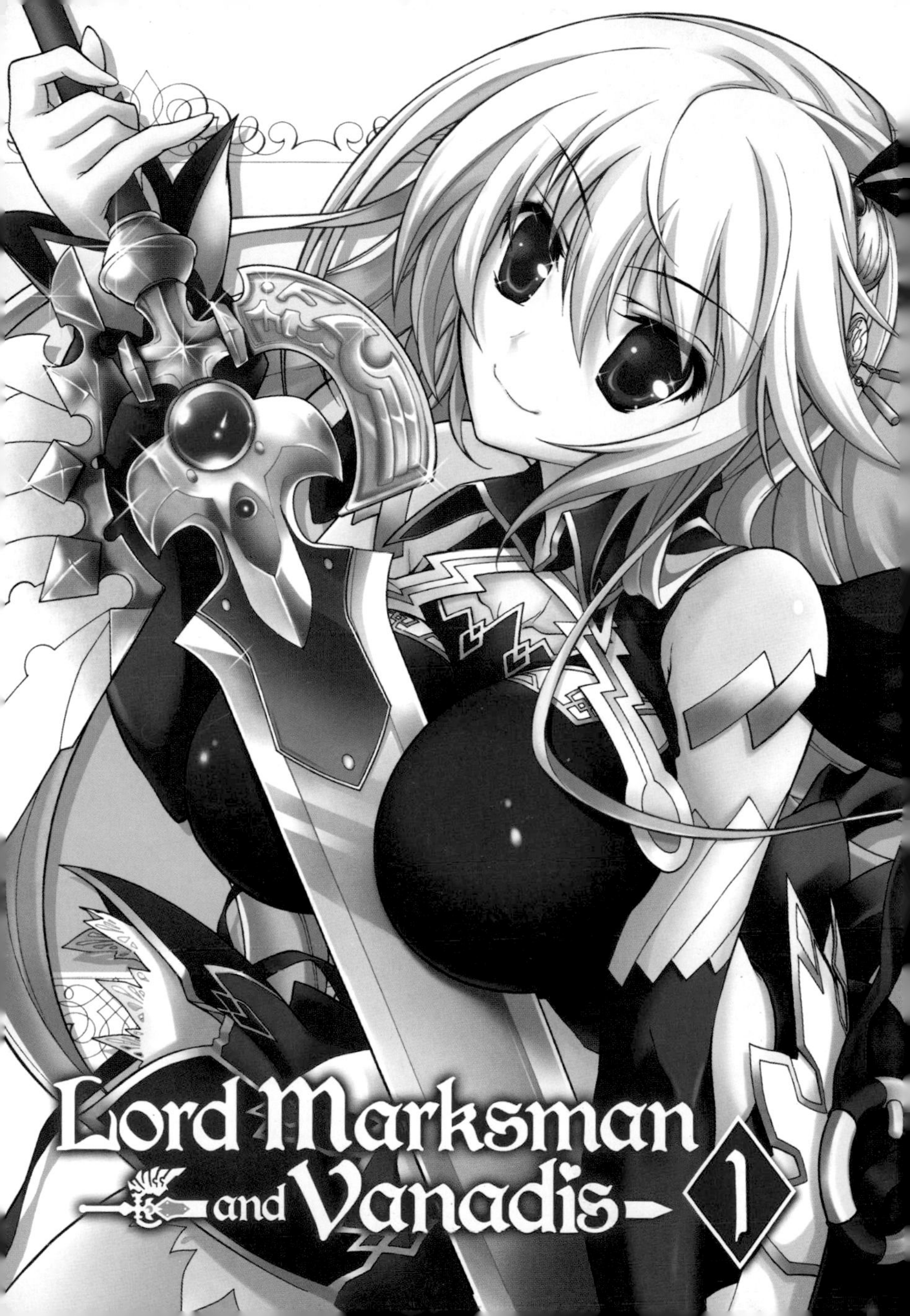
Lord Marksman
and Vanadis
1

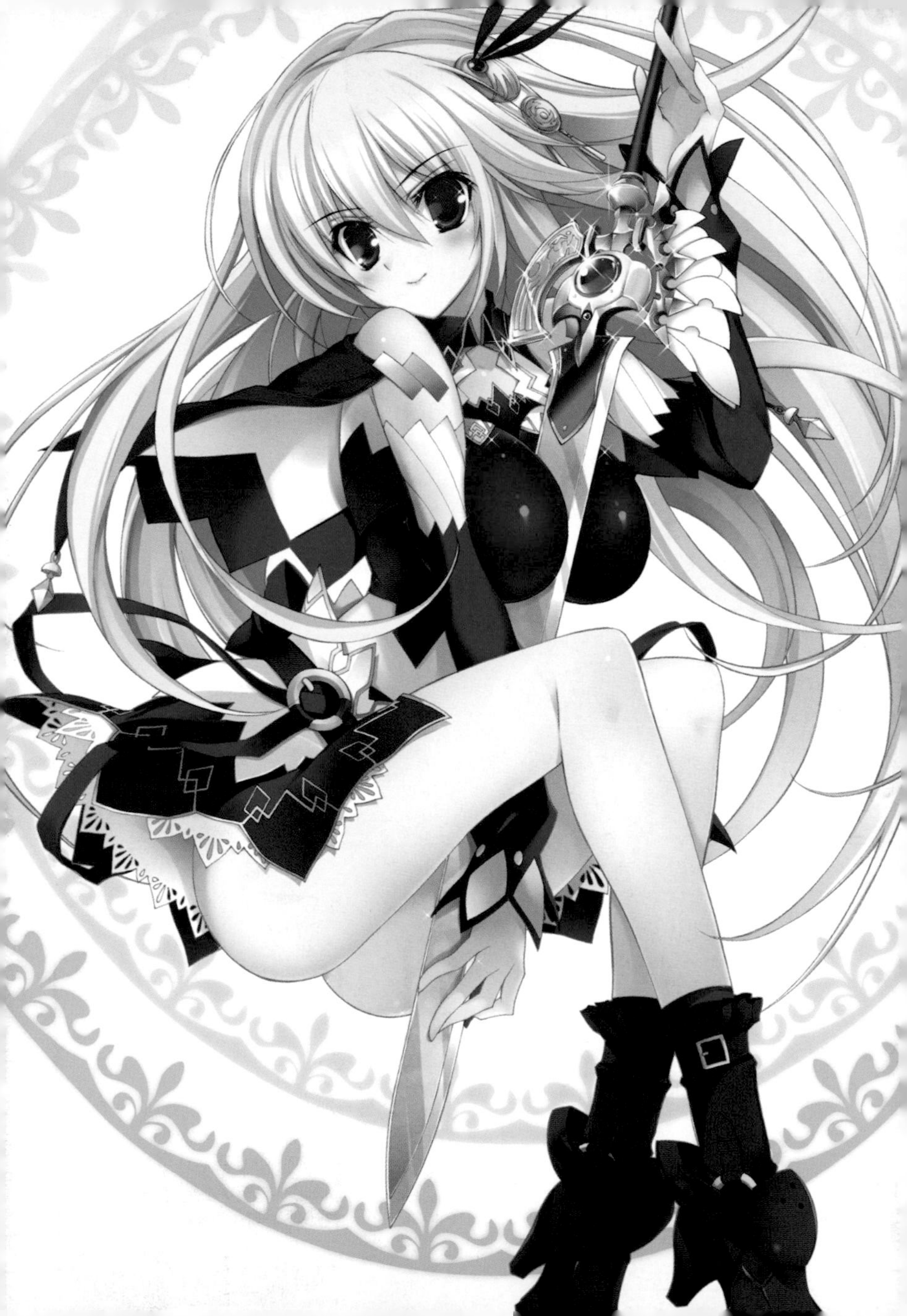

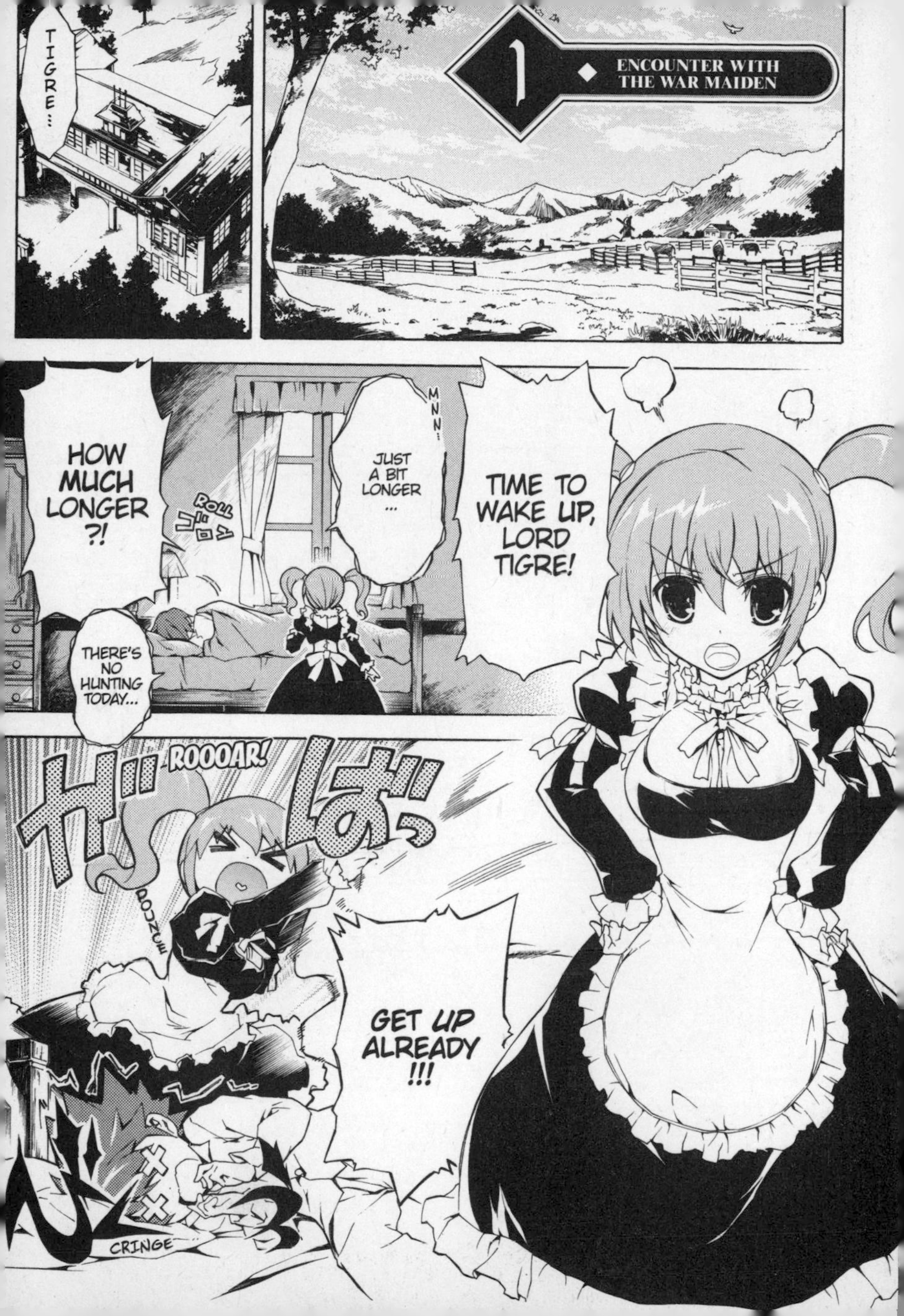
1 ◆ ENCOUNTER WITH THE WAR MAIDEN
TIGRE...
TIME TO WAKE UP, LORD TIGRE!
MNN...
JUST A BIT LONGER...
ROLL
HOW MUCH LONGER?!
THERE'S NO HUNTING TODAY...
GET UP ALREADY!!!
ROOOAR!
POUNCE!!
CRINGE

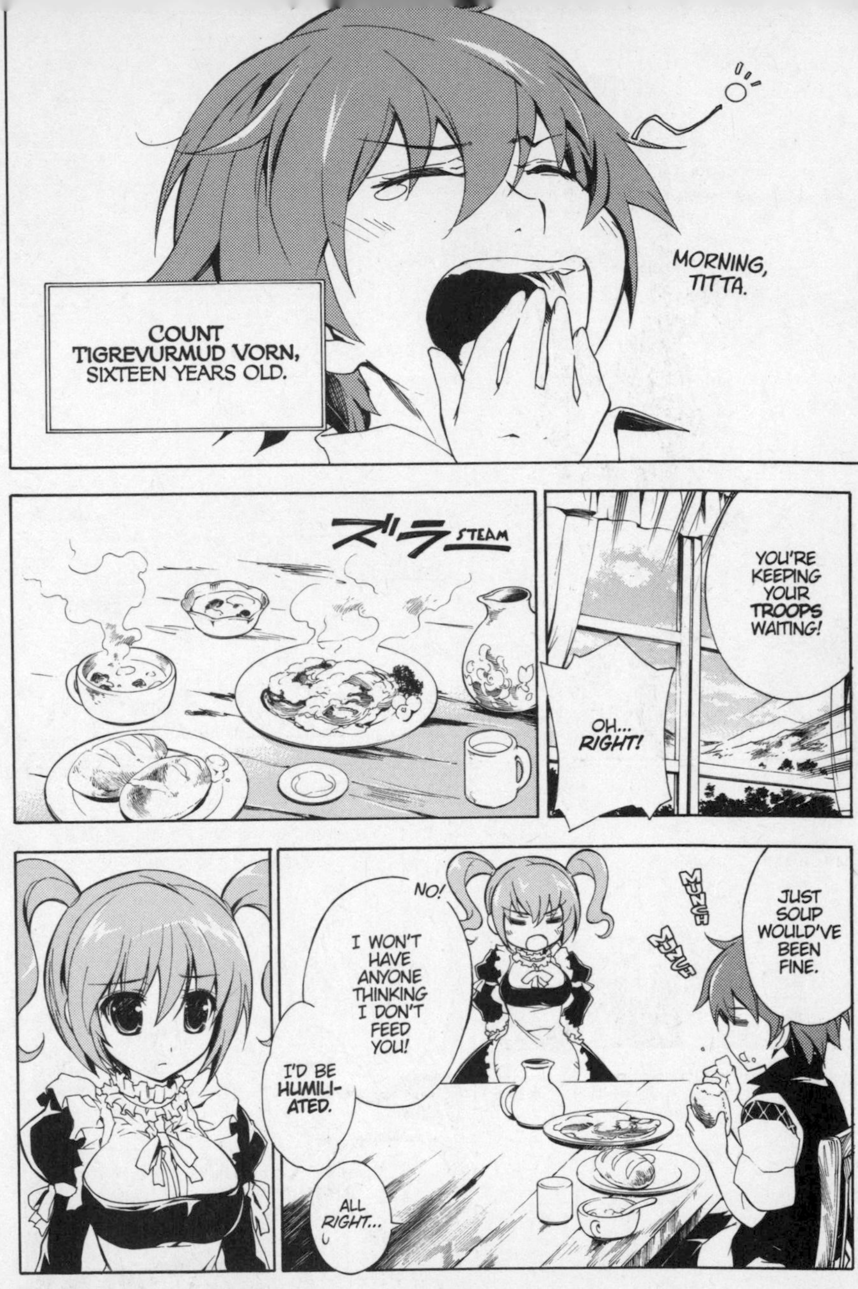
MORNING, TITTA.
COUNT TIGREVURMUD VORN, SIXTEEN YEARS OLD.
YOU'RE KEEPING YOUR TROOPS WAITING!
OH... RIGHT!
ズラ STEAM
JUST SOUP WOULD'VE BEEN FINE.
MUNCH
NO!
I WON'T HAVE ANYONE THINKING I DON'T FEED YOU!
I'D BE HUMILIATED.
ALL RIGHT...

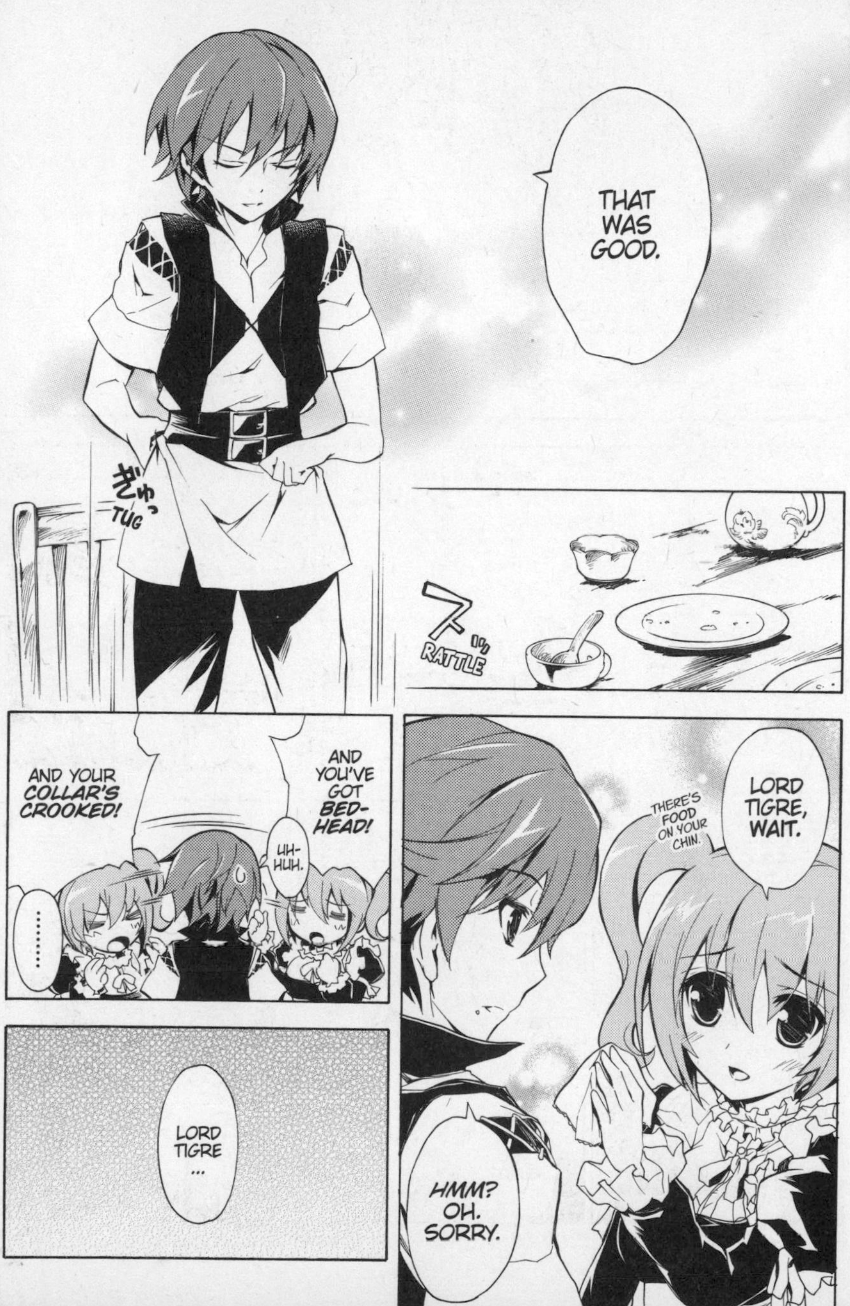
THAT WAS GOOD.
ぎゅっ
TUG
ス
RATTLE
LORD TIGRE, WAIT.
THERE'S FOOD ON YOUR CHIN.
HMM? OH. SORRY.
AND YOU'VE GOT BED-HEAD!
UH-HUH.
AND YOUR COLLAR'S CROOKED!
......
LORD TIGRE ...

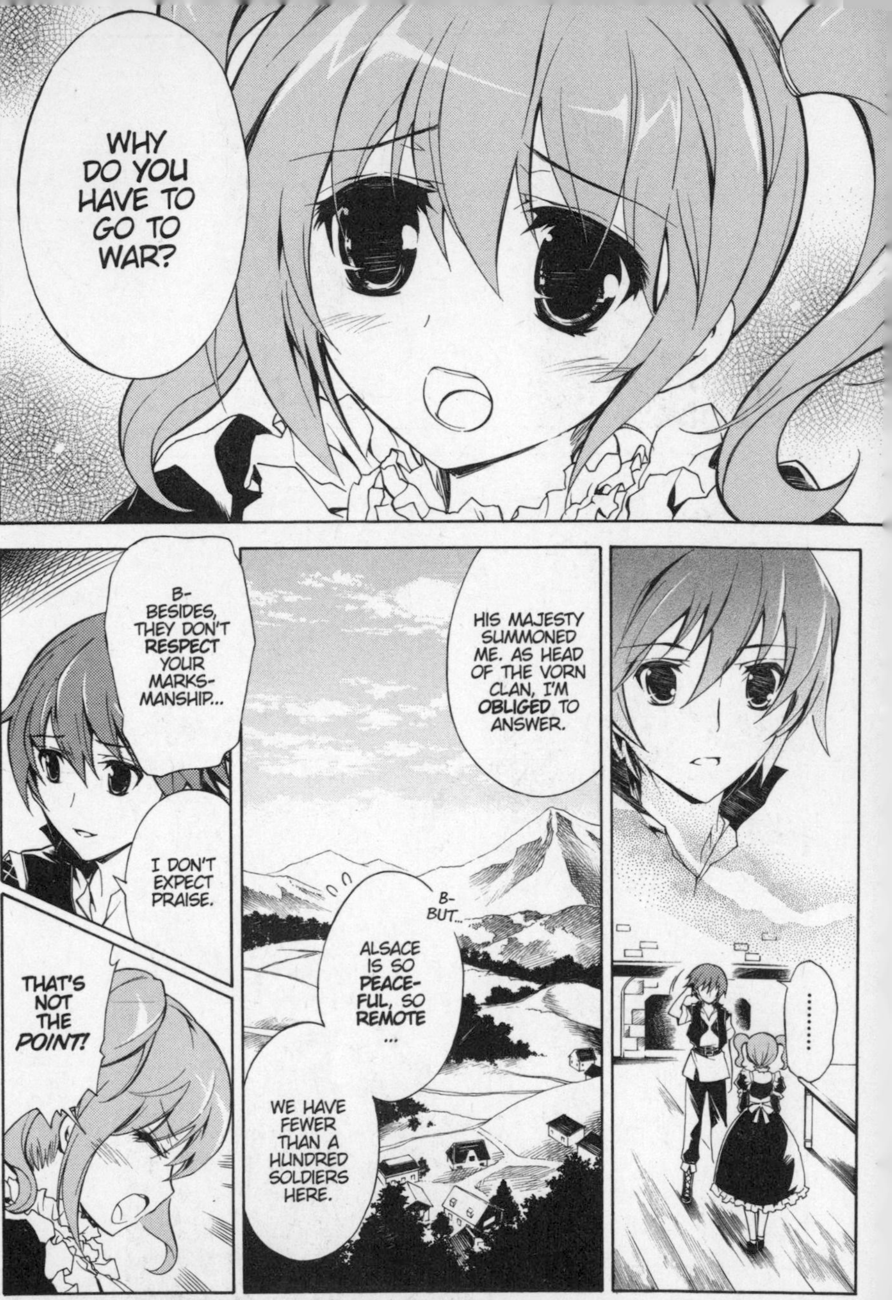
WHY DO YOU HAVE TO GO TO WAR?
HIS MAJESTY SUMMONED ME. AS HEAD OF THE VORN CLAN, I'M **OBLIGED** TO ANSWER.
....
B-BUT...
ALSACE IS SO **PEACEFUL**, SO **REMOTE**...
WE HAVE FEWER THAN A HUNDRED SOLDIERS HERE.
B-BESIDES, THEY DON'T **RESPECT** YOUR MARKSMANSHIP...
I DON'T EXPECT PRAISE.
THAT'S NOT THE ***POINT!***

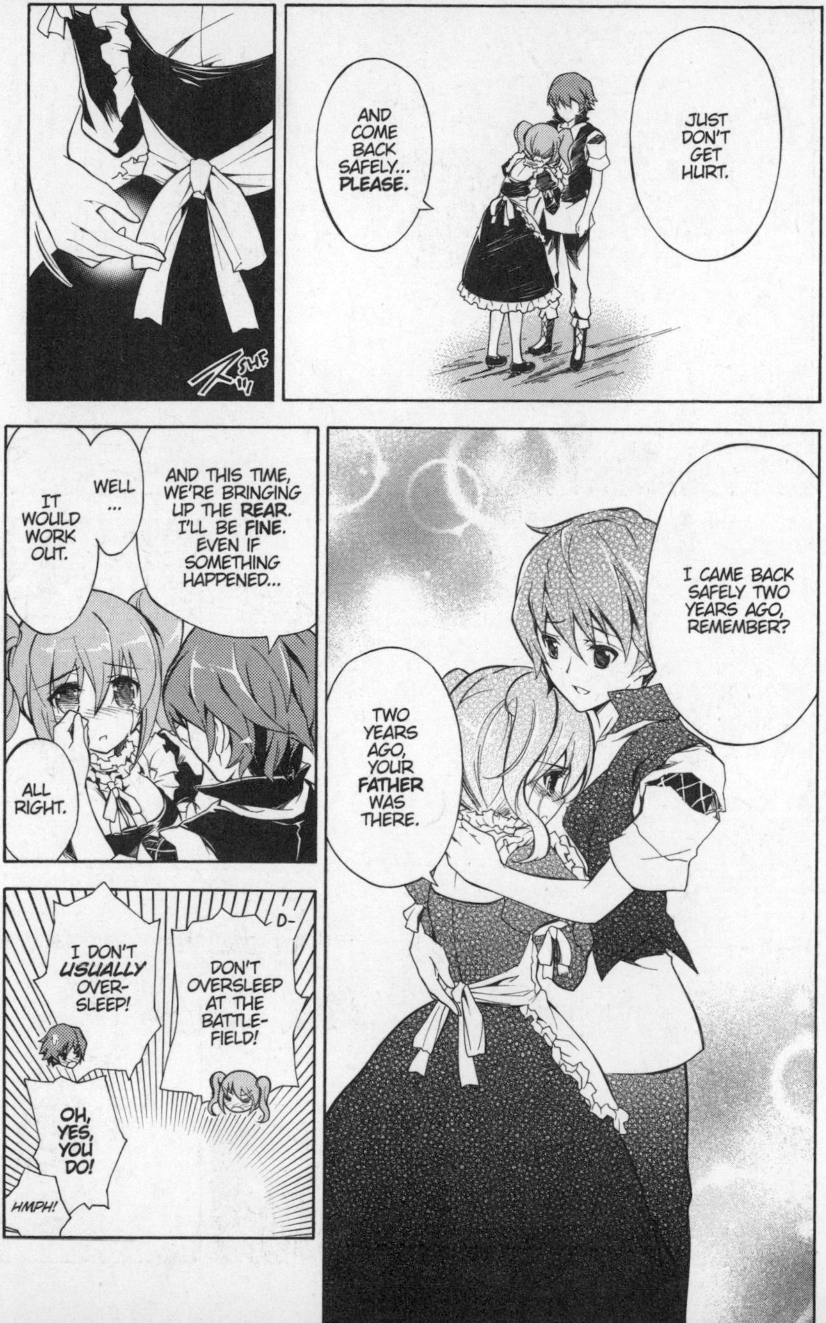
JUST DON'T GET HURT.
AND COME BACK SAFELY... PLEASE.
SHF
I CAME BACK SAFELY TWO YEARS AGO, REMEMBER?
TWO YEARS AGO, YOUR FATHER WAS THERE.
AND THIS TIME, WE'RE BRINGING UP THE REAR. I'LL BE FINE. EVEN IF SOMETHING HAPPENED...
WELL ...
IT WOULD WORK OUT.
ALL RIGHT.
D-
DON'T OVERSLEEP AT THE BATTLEFIELD!
I DON'T USUALLY OVERSLEEP!
OH, YES, YOU DO!
HMPH!

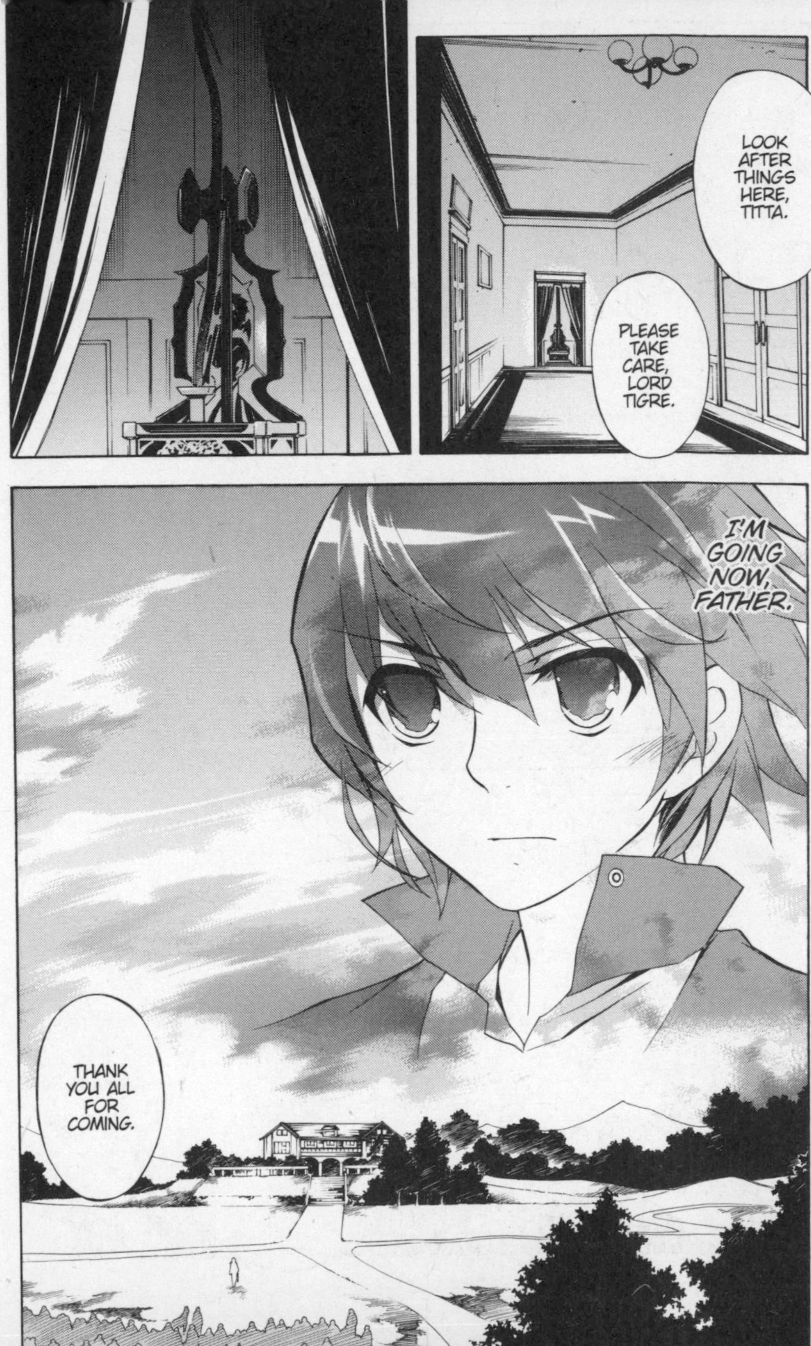
LOOK AFTER THINGS HERE, TITTA.
PLEASE TAKE CARE, LORD TIGRE.
I'M GOING NOW, FATHER.
THANK YOU ALL FOR COMING.

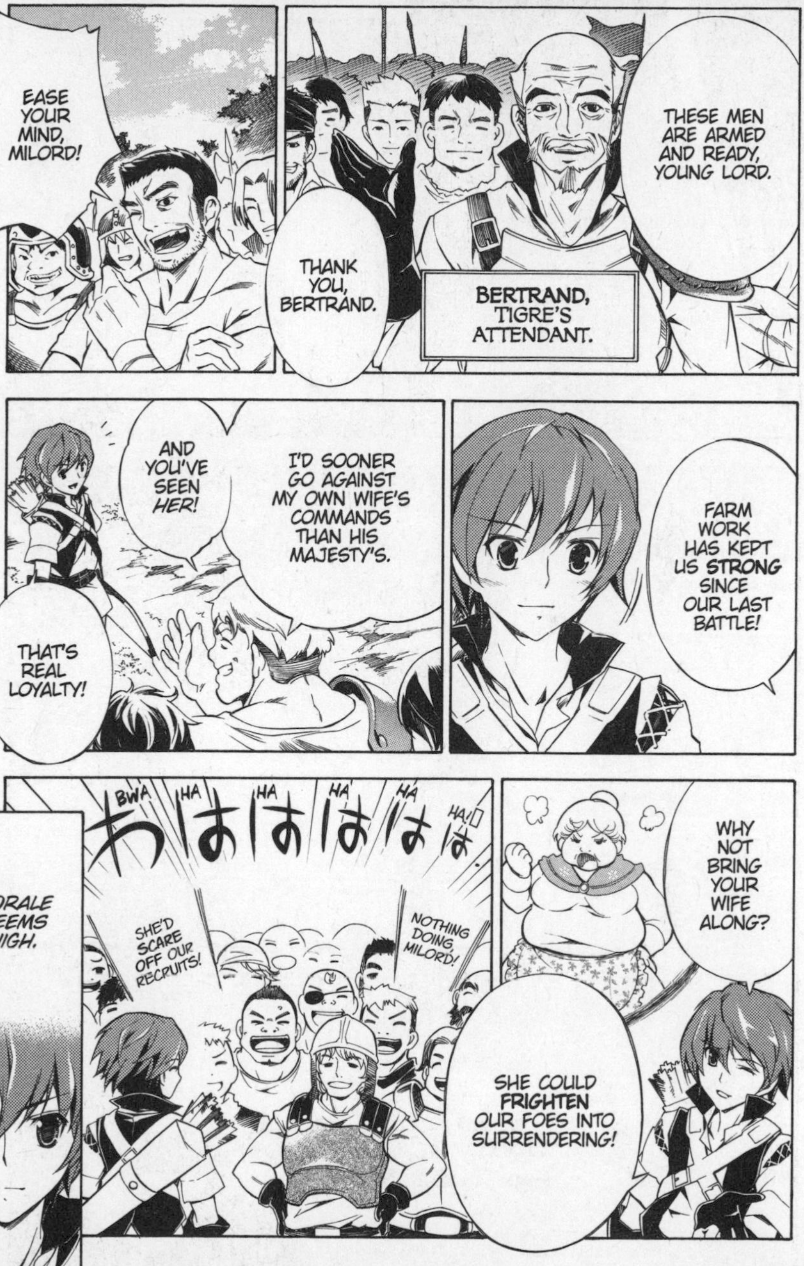
THESE MEN ARE ARMED AND READY, YOUNG LORD.
BERTRAND, TIGRE'S ATTENDANT.
THANK YOU, BERTRAND.
EASE YOUR MIND, MILORD!
FARM WORK HAS KEPT US STRONG SINCE OUR LAST BATTLE!
I'D SOONER GO AGAINST MY OWN WIFE'S COMMANDS THAN HIS MAJESTY'S.
AND YOU'VE SEEN HER!
THAT'S REAL LOYALTY!
WHY NOT BRING YOUR WIFE ALONG?
SHE COULD FRIGHTEN OUR FOES INTO SURRENDERING!
BWA HA HA HA HA HA!
NOTHING DOING, MILORD!
SHE'D SCARE OFF OUR RECRUITS!
MORALE SEEMS HIGH.

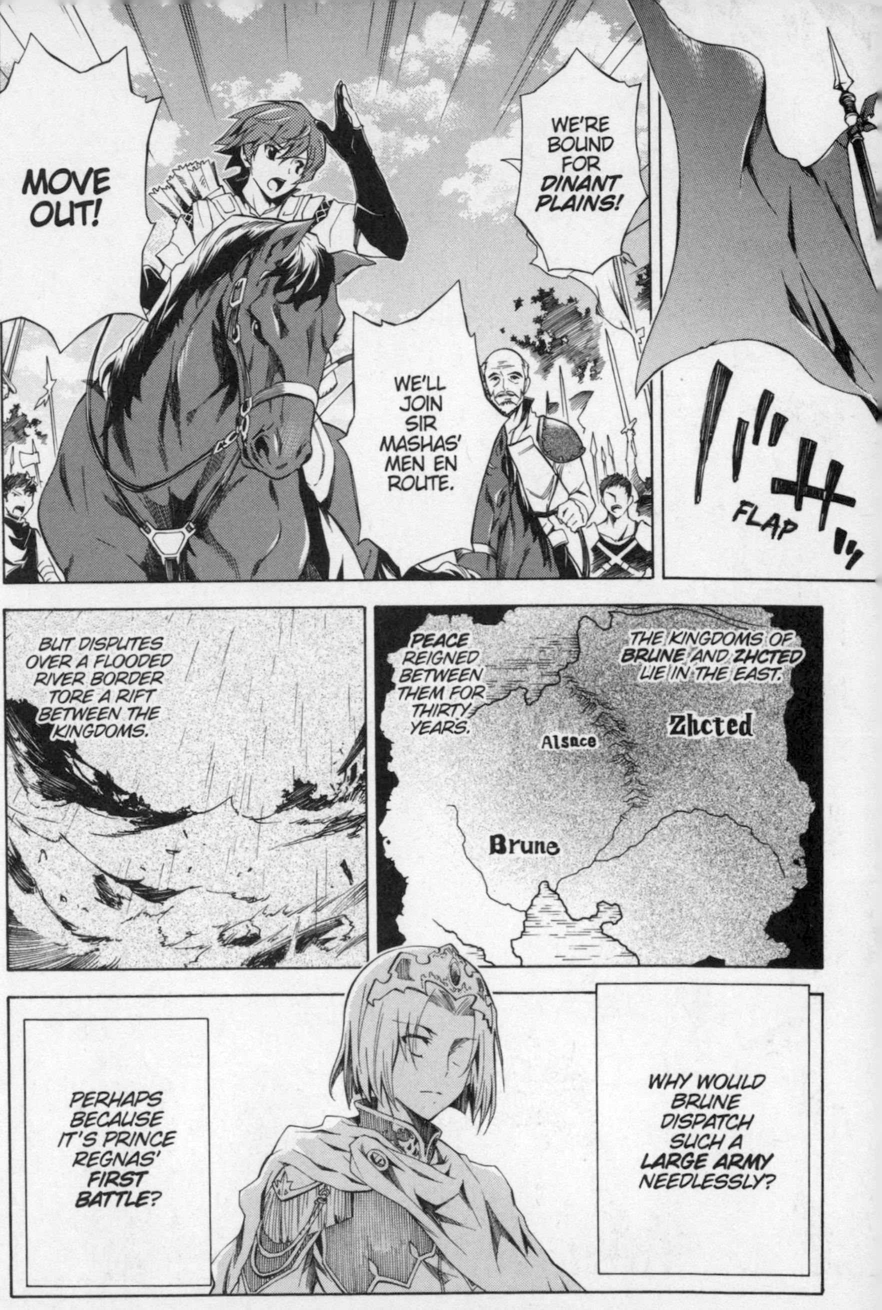
FLAP
WE'RE BOUND FOR DINANT PLAINS!
MOVE OUT!
WE'LL JOIN SIR MASHAS' MEN EN ROUTE.
THE KINGDOMS OF BRUNE AND ZHCTED LIE IN THE EAST.
PEACE REIGNED BETWEEN THEM FOR THIRTY YEARS.
Zhcted
Alsace
Brune
BUT DISPUTES OVER A FLOODED RIVER BORDER TORE A RIFT BETWEEN THE KINGDOMS.
WHY WOULD BRUNE DISPATCH SUCH A LARGE ARMY NEEDLESSLY?
PERHAPS BECAUSE IT'S PRINCE REGNAS' FIRST BATTLE?

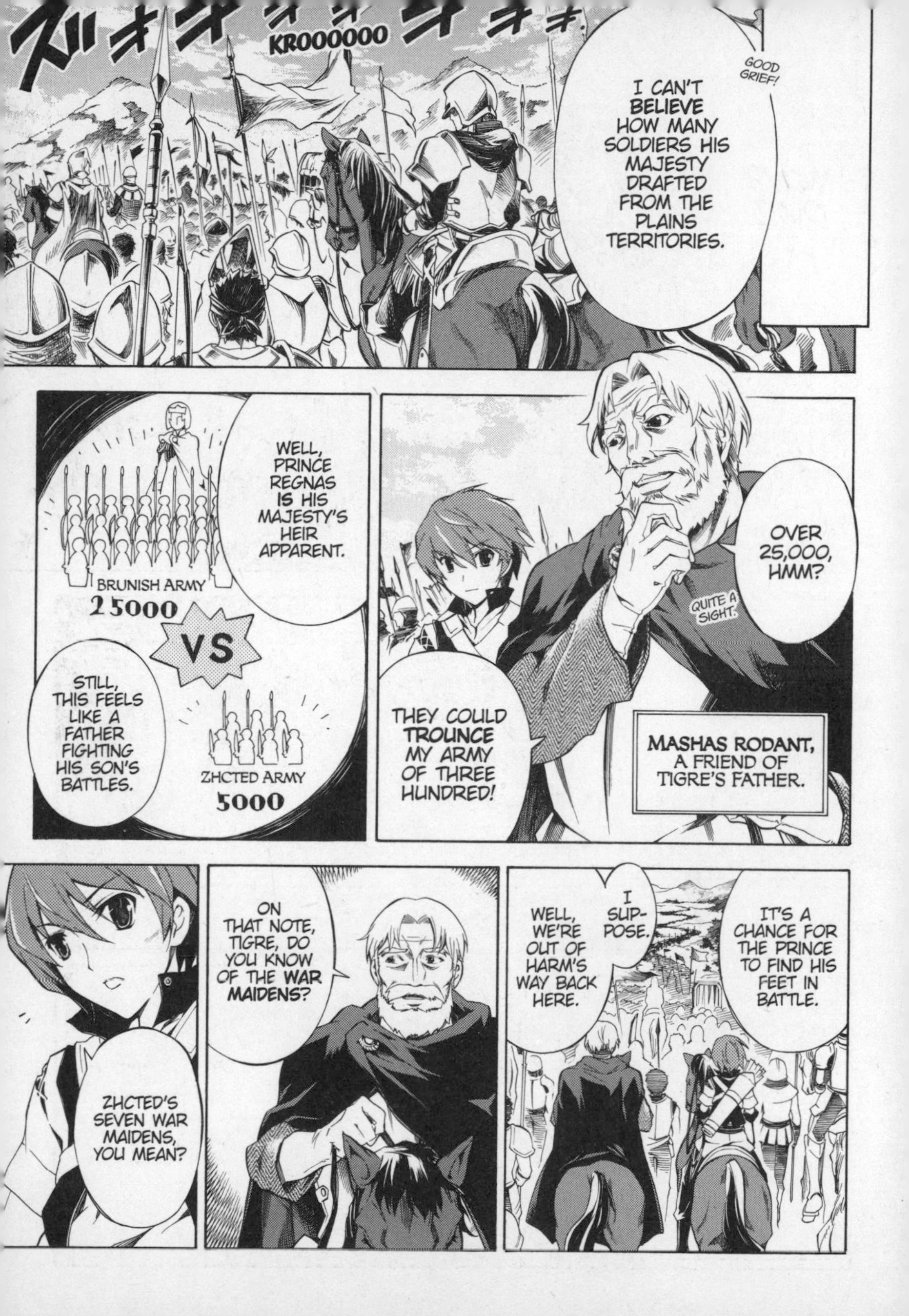
GOOD GRIEF!
I CAN'T BELIEVE HOW MANY SOLDIERS HIS MAJESTY DRAFTED FROM THE PLAINS TERRITORIES.
KROOOOOO
OVER 25,000, HMM?
QUITE A SIGHT.
MASHAS RODANT, A FRIEND OF TIGRE'S FATHER.
THEY COULD TROUNCE MY ARMY OF THREE HUNDRED!
WELL, PRINCE REGNAS IS HIS MAJESTY'S HEIR APPARENT.
BRUNISH ARMY 25000
VS
STILL, THIS FEELS LIKE A FATHER FIGHTING HIS SON'S BATTLES.
ZHCTED ARMY 5000
IT'S A CHANCE FOR THE PRINCE TO FIND HIS FEET IN BATTLE.
I SUP-POSE.
WELL, WE'RE OUT OF HARM'S WAY BACK HERE.
ON THAT NOTE, TIGRE, DO YOU KNOW OF THE WAR MAIDENS?
ZHCTED'S SEVEN WAR MAIDENS, YOU MEAN?

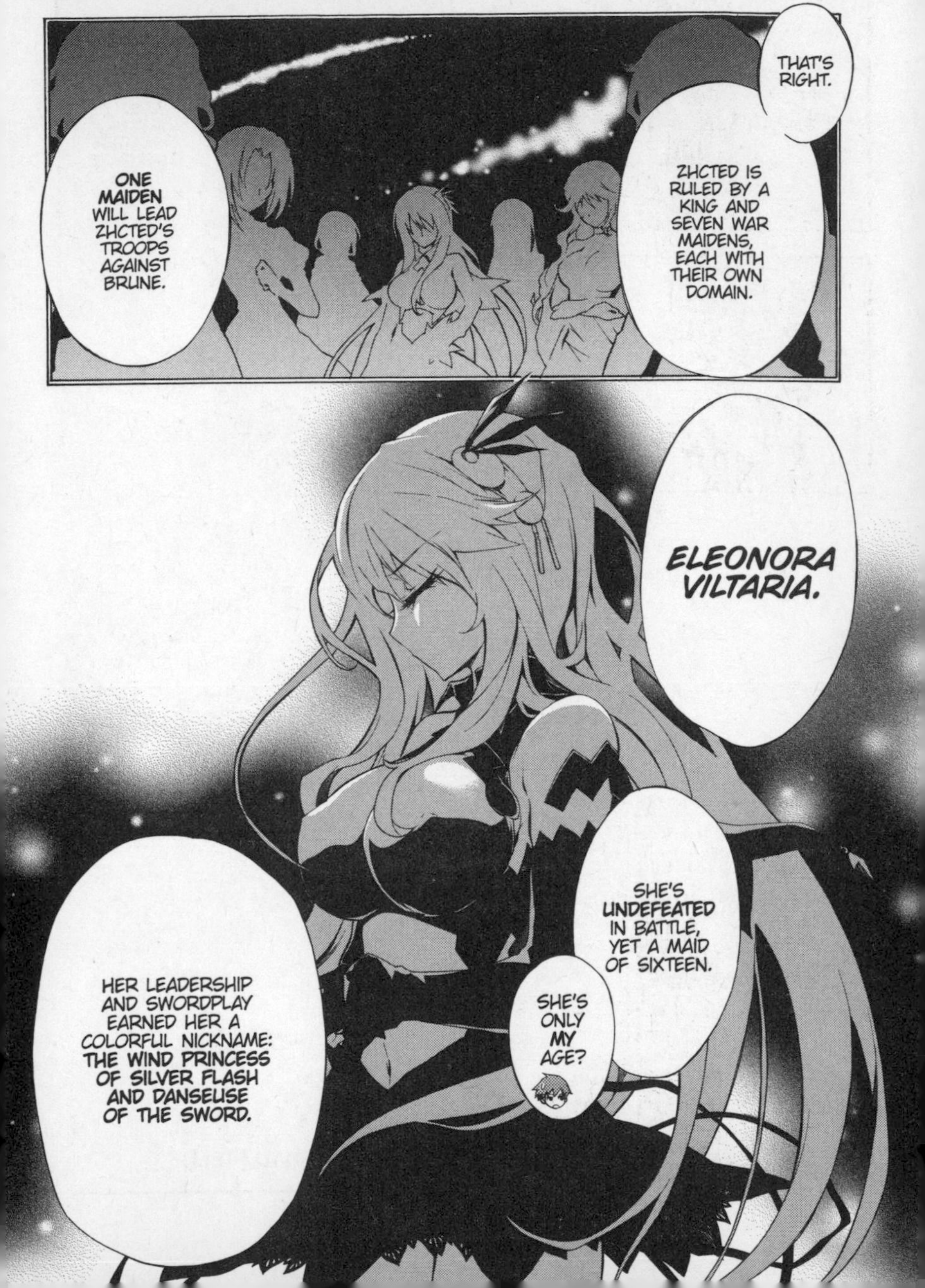
THAT'S RIGHT.
ZHCTED IS RULED BY A KING AND SEVEN WAR MAIDENS, EACH WITH THEIR OWN DOMAIN.
ONE MAIDEN WILL LEAD ZHCTED'S TROOPS AGAINST BRUNE.
ELEONORA VILTARIA.
SHE'S UNDEFEATED IN BATTLE, YET A MAID OF SIXTEEN.
SHE'S ONLY MY AGE?
HER LEADERSHIP AND SWORDPLAY EARNED HER A COLORFUL NICKNAME: THE WIND PRINCESS OF SILVER FLASH AND DANSEUSE OF THE SWORD.

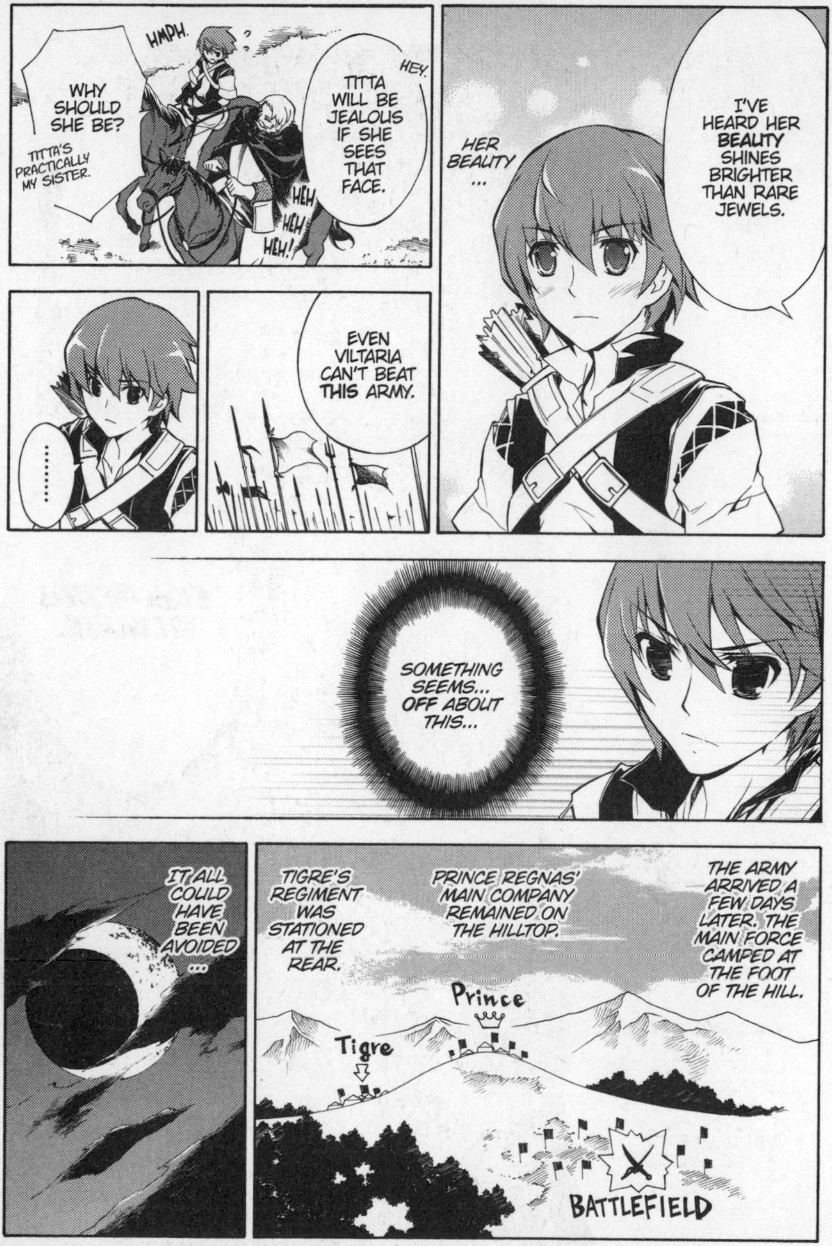
I'VE HEARD HER BEAUTY SHINES BRIGHTER THAN RARE JEWELS.
HER BEAUTY ...
HEY.
TITTA WILL BE JEALOUS IF SHE SEES THAT FACE.
HEH HEH HEH!
HMPH.
WHY SHOULD SHE BE?
TITTA'S PRACTICALLY MY SISTER.
EVEN VILTARIA CAN'T BEAT THIS ARMY.
......
SOMETHING SEEMS... OFF ABOUT THIS...
THE ARMY ARRIVED A FEW DAYS LATER. THE MAIN FORCE CAMPED AT THE FOOT OF THE HILL.
PRINCE REGNAS' MAIN COMPANY REMAINED ON THE HILLTOP.
TIGRE'S REGIMENT WAS STATIONED AT THE REAR.
Prince
Tigre
BATTLEFIELD
IT ALL COULD HAVE BEEN AVOIDED ...

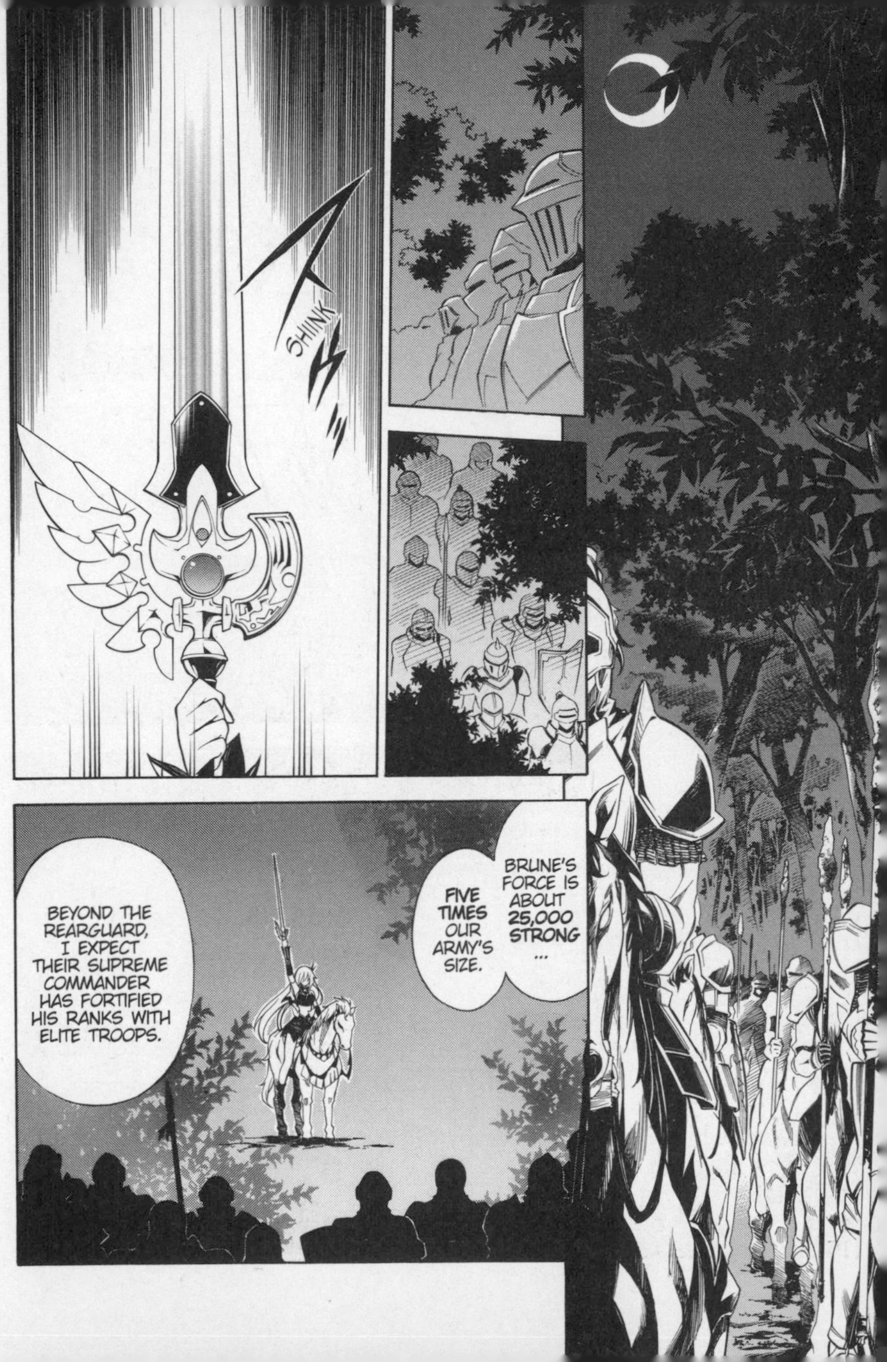
SHINK
BRUNE'S FORCE IS ABOUT 25,000 STRONG...
FIVE TIMES OUR ARMY'S SIZE.
BEYOND THE REARGUARD, I EXPECT THEIR SUPREME COMMANDER HAS FORTIFIED HIS RANKS WITH ELITE TROOPS.

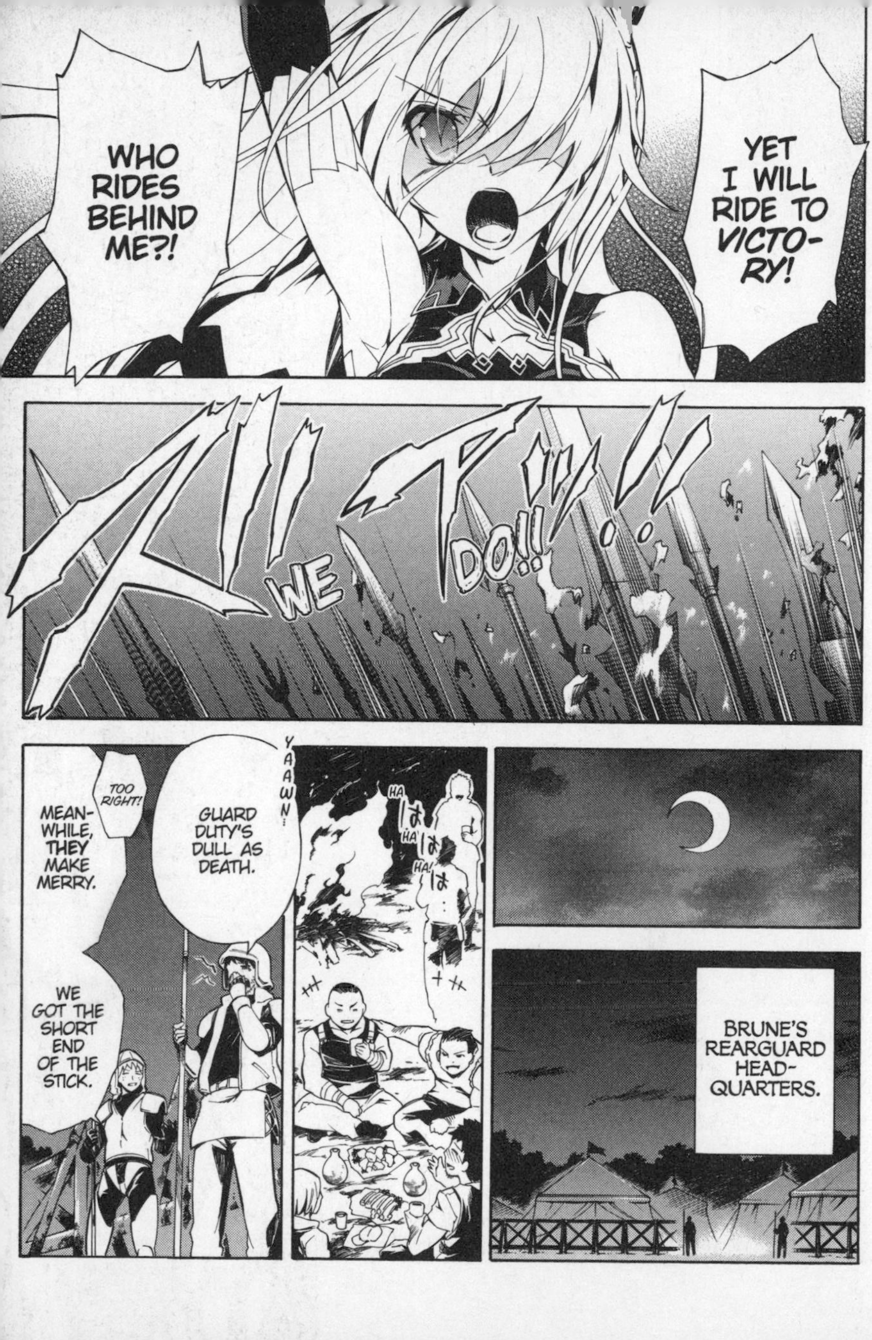
YET I WILL RIDE TO VICTO-RY!
WHO RIDES BEHIND ME?!
WE DO!!
BRUNE'S REARGUARD HEAD-QUARTERS.
HA は HA は HA! は
YAAAWN...
GUARD DUTY'S DULL AS DEATH.
TOO RIGHT!
MEAN-WHILE, THEY MAKE MERRY.
WE GOT THE SHORT END OF THE STICK.

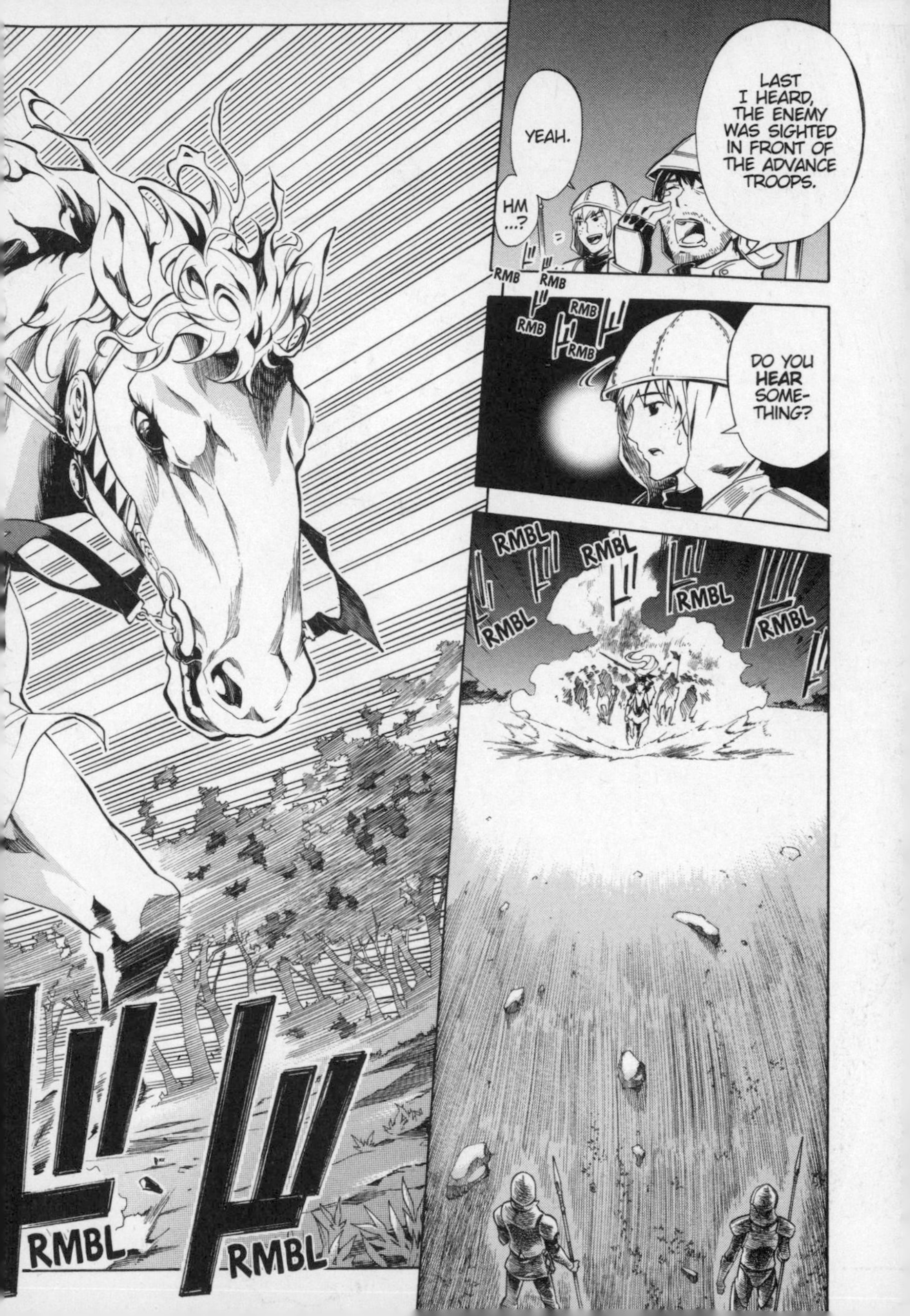
LAST I HEARD, THE ENEMY WAS SIGHTED IN FRONT OF THE ADVANCE TROOPS.
YEAH.
HM ...?
RMB
RMB
RMB
RMB
RMB
DO YOU HEAR SOMETHING?
RMBL
RMBL
RMBL
RMBL
RMBL
RMBL
RMBL

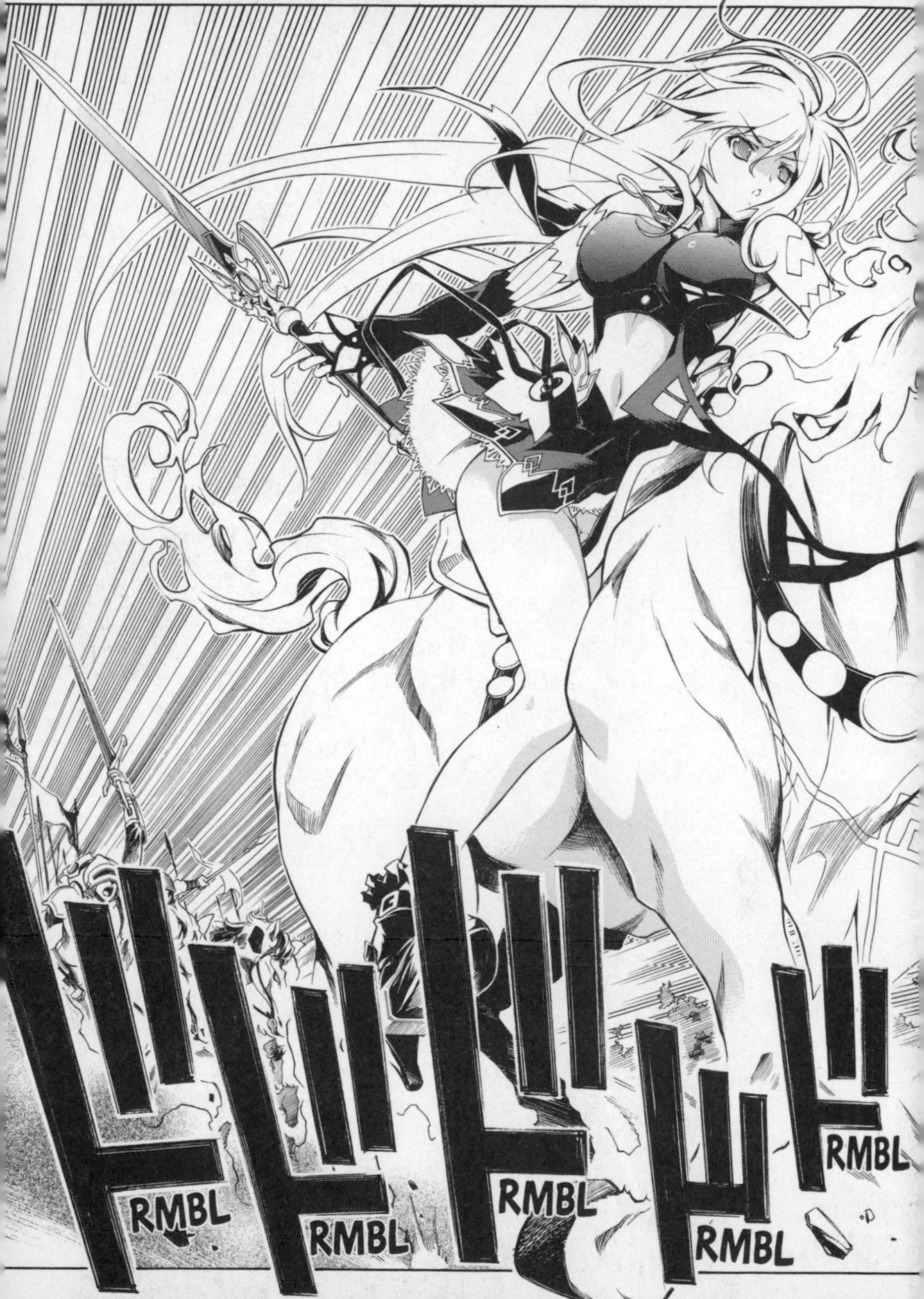
RMBL
RMBL
RMBL
RMBL
RMBL

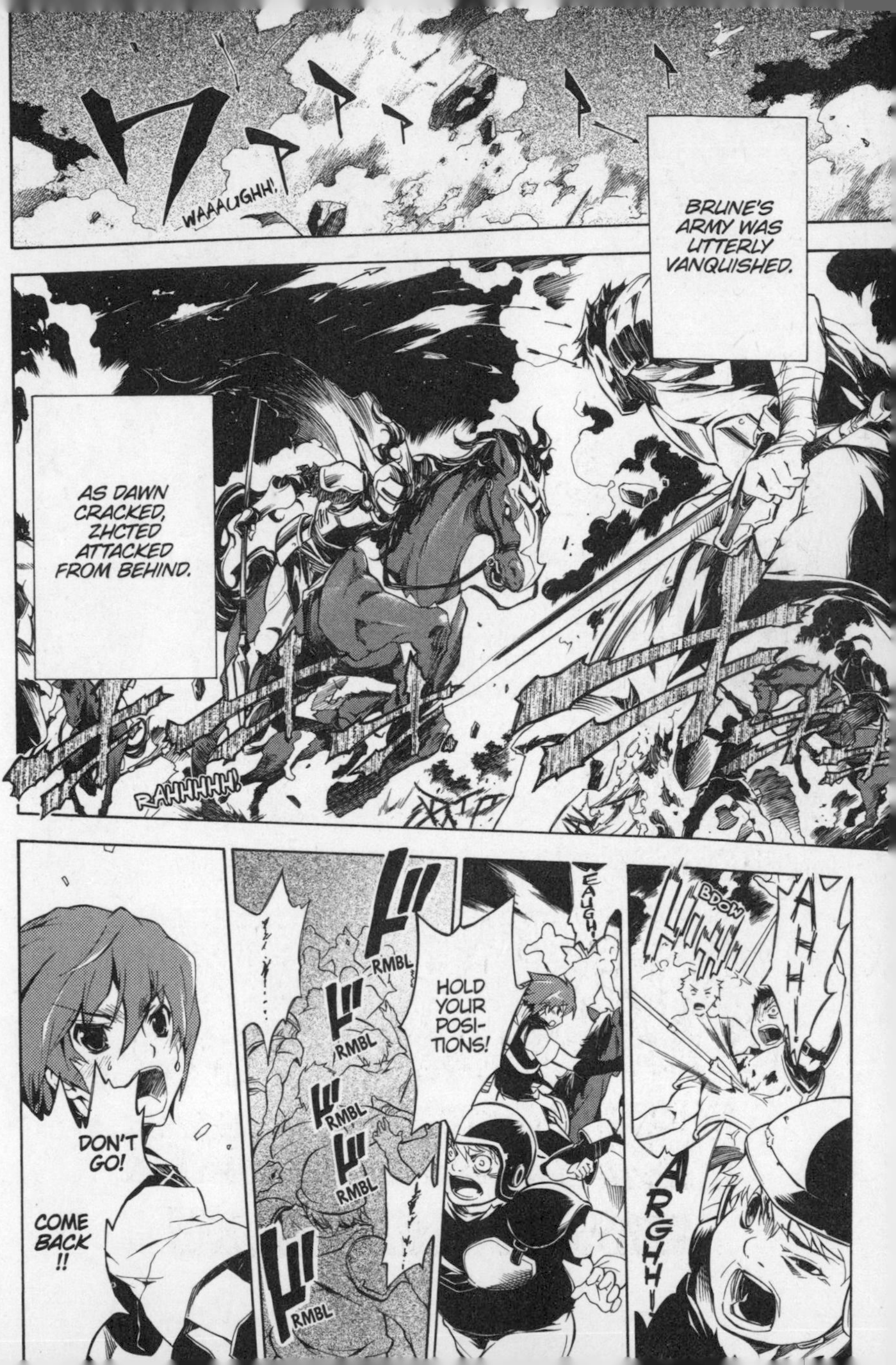

WAAAUGHH!
BRUNE'S ARMY WAS UTTERLY VANQUISHED.
AS DAWN CRACKED, ZHCTED ATTACKED FROM BEHIND.
RAHHHHH!
BDOW
ARGHH!
EAUGH!
HOLD YOUR POSI-TIONS!
RMBL
RMBL
RMBL
RMBL
RMBL
DON'T GO!
COME BACK!!

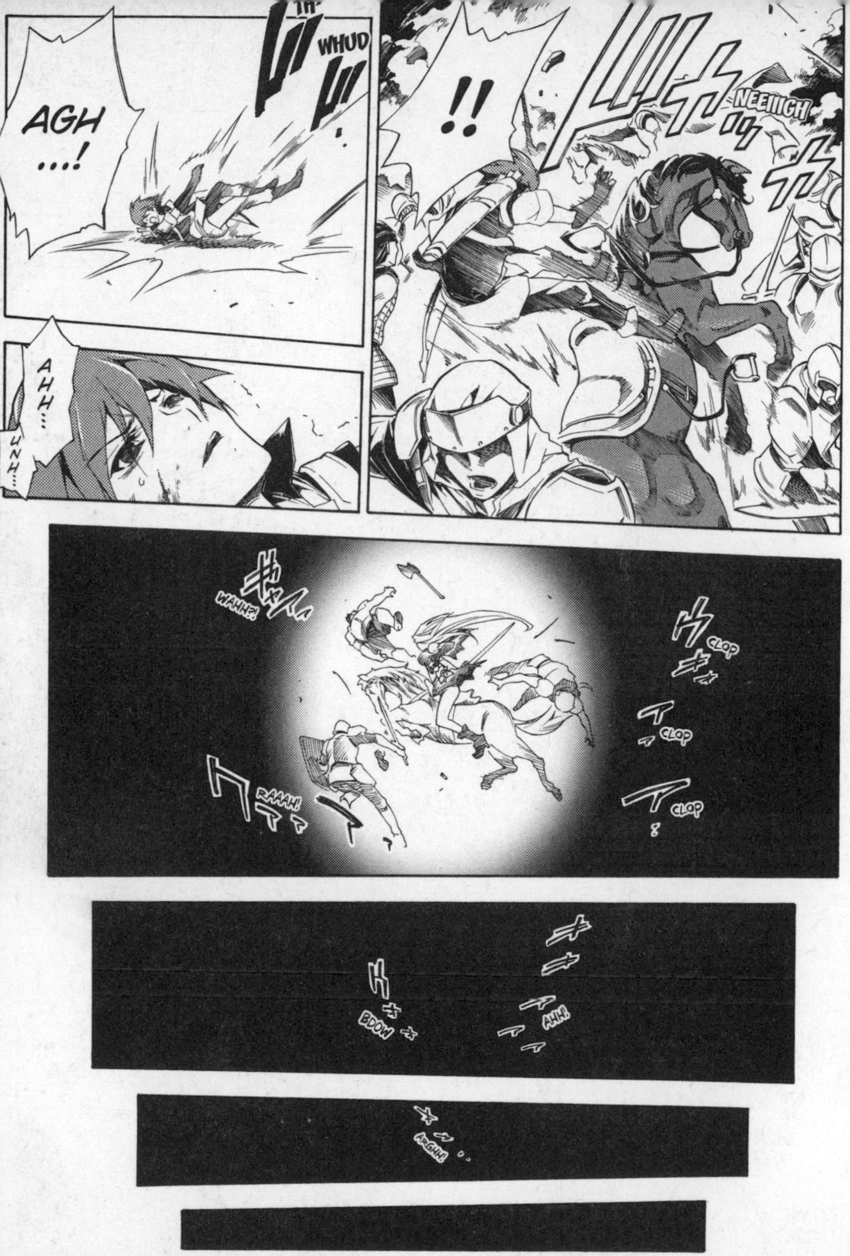
!!
NEEIIIGH
WHUD
AGH ...!
AHH...
UNH...
CLOP
CLOP
CLOP
WAHH!
RAAAH!
AHH!
BDOW
ARGHH!

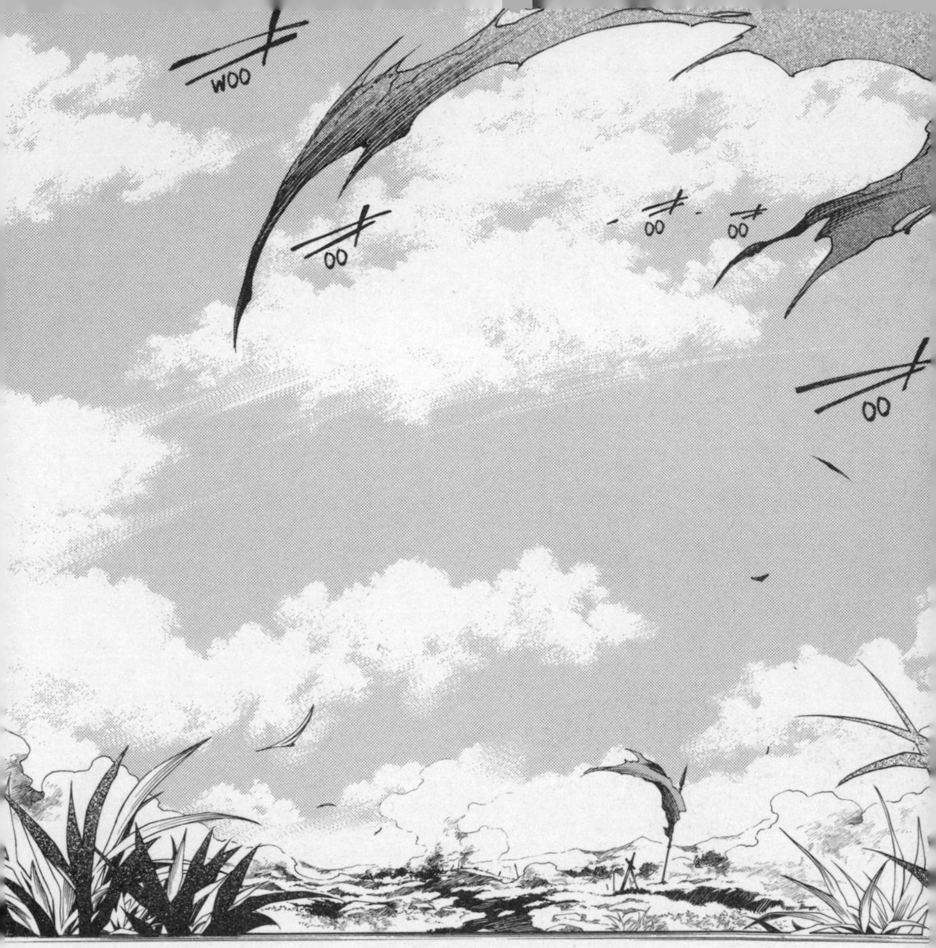
WOO
OO
OO
OO
OO
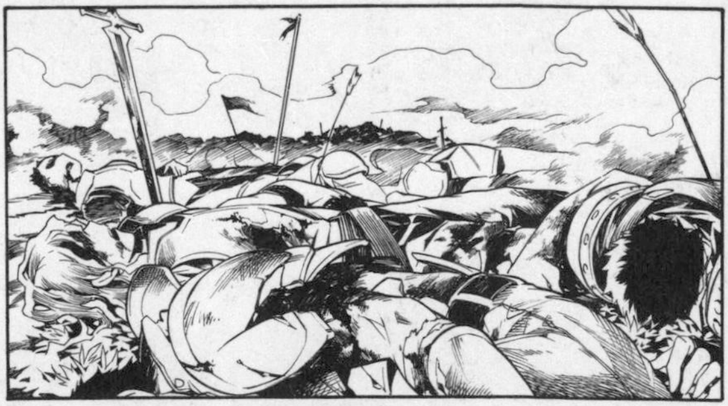
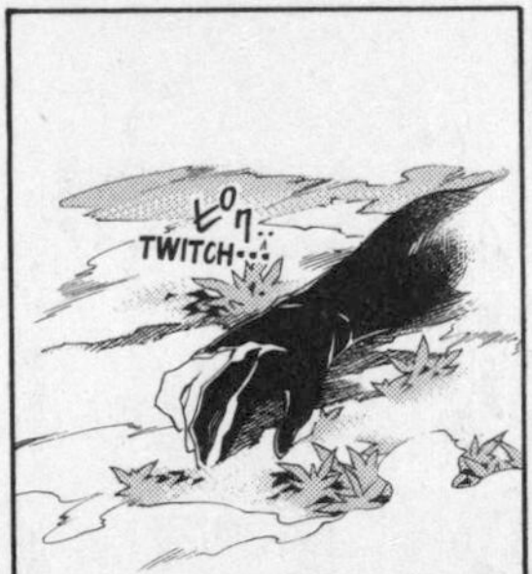
TWITCH...

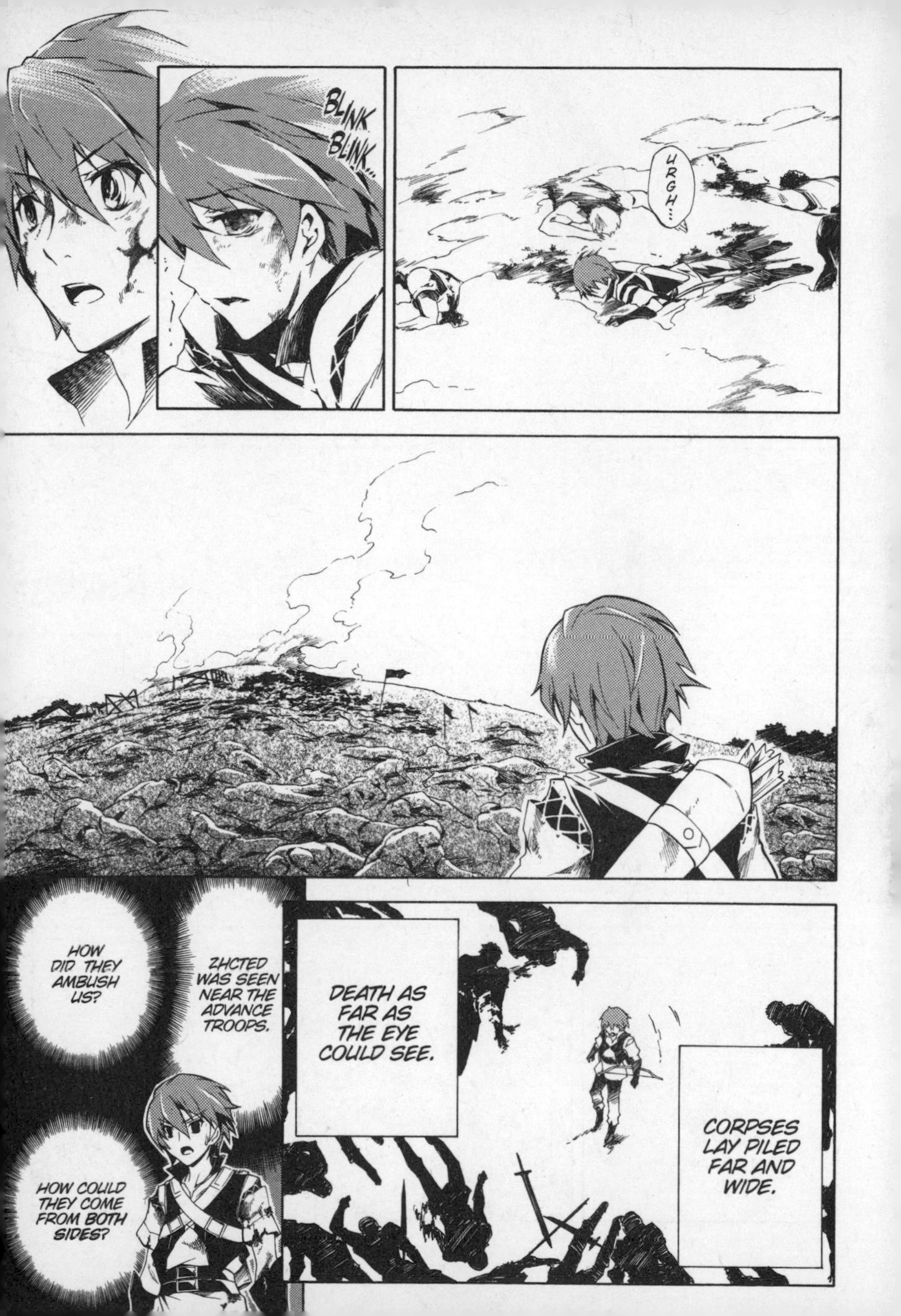
URGH...
BLINK BLINK...
DEATH AS FAR AS THE EYE COULD SEE.
CORPSES LAY PILED FAR AND WIDE.
ZHCTED WAS SEEN NEAR THE ADVANCE TROOPS.
HOW DID THEY AMBUSH US?
HOW COULD THEY COME FROM BOTH SIDES?

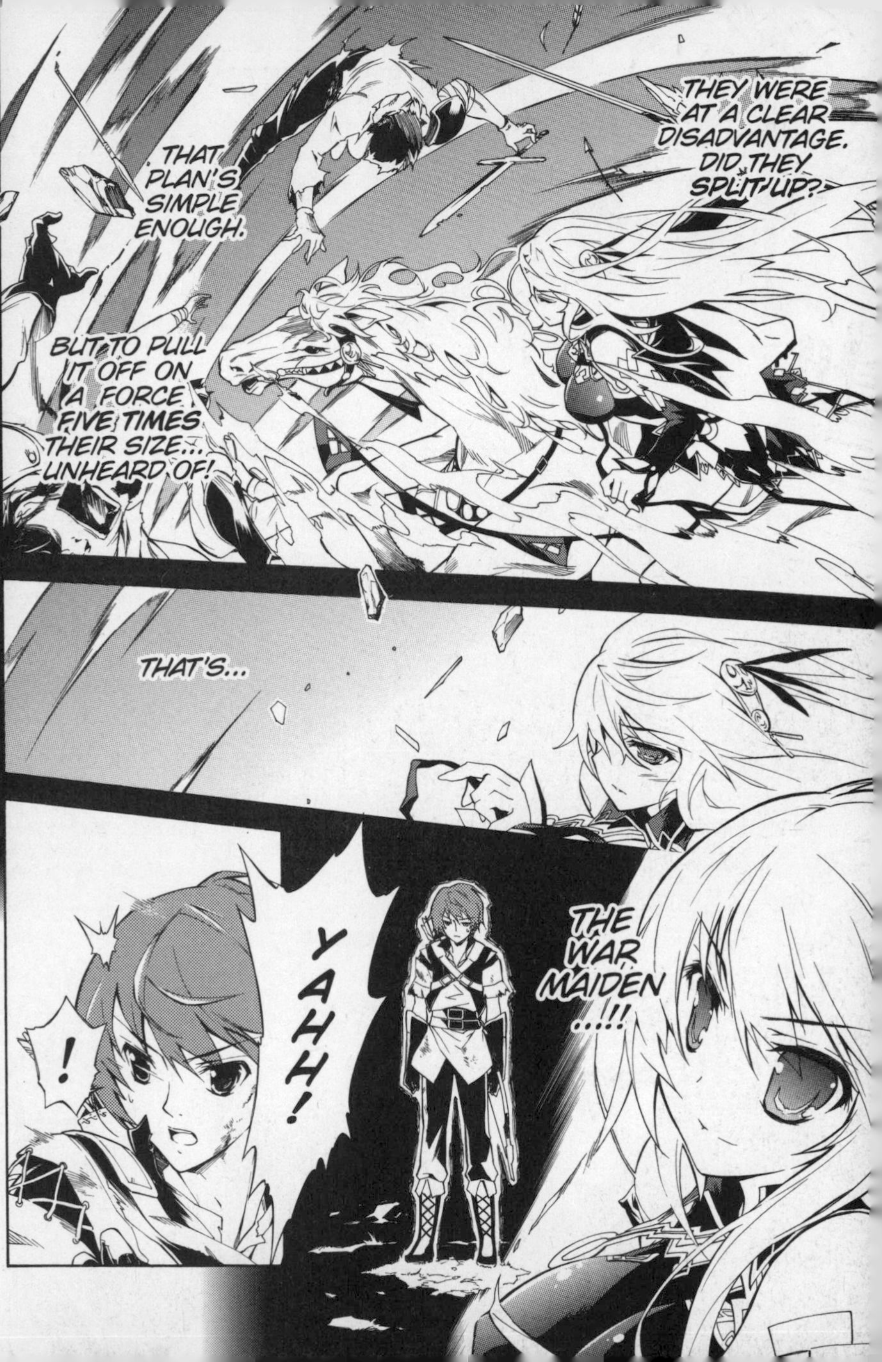
THEY WERE AT A CLEAR DISADVANTAGE. DID THEY SPLIT UP?
THAT PLAN'S SIMPLE ENOUGH.
BUT TO PULL IT OFF ON A FORCE FIVE TIMES THEIR SIZE... UNHEARD OF!
THAT'S...
THE WAR MAIDEN...!!
YAHH!
!

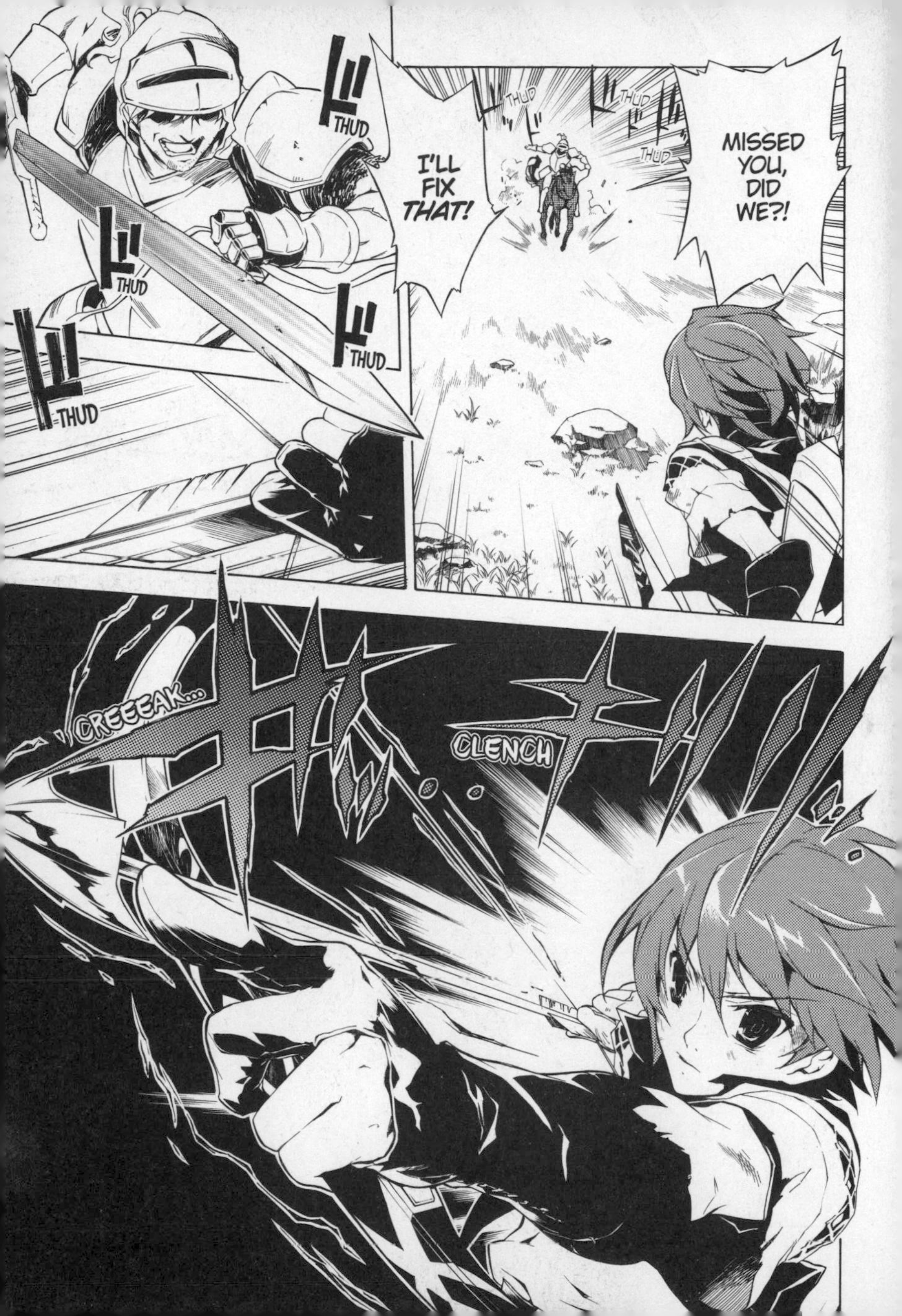
MISSED YOU, DID WE?!
THUD
THUD
THUD
I'LL FIX THAT!
THUD
THUD
THUD
THUD
CLENCH
CREEEAK...

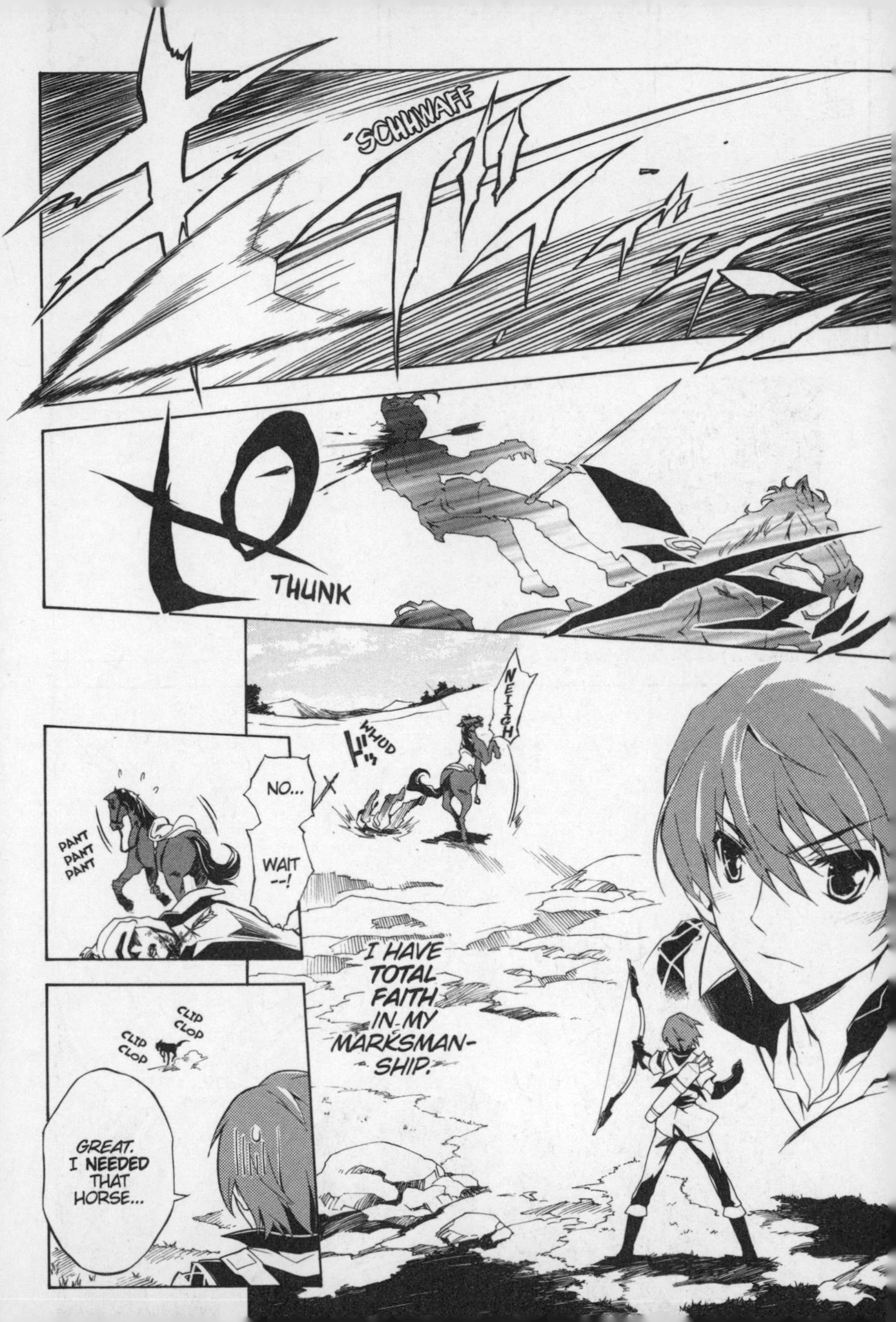
SCHHWAFF
THUNK
NEIGH
WHUD
I HAVE TOTAL FAITH IN MY MARKSMANSHIP.
PANT PANT PANT
NO...
WAIT --!
CLIP CLOP CLIP CLOP
GREAT. I NEEDED THAT HORSE...

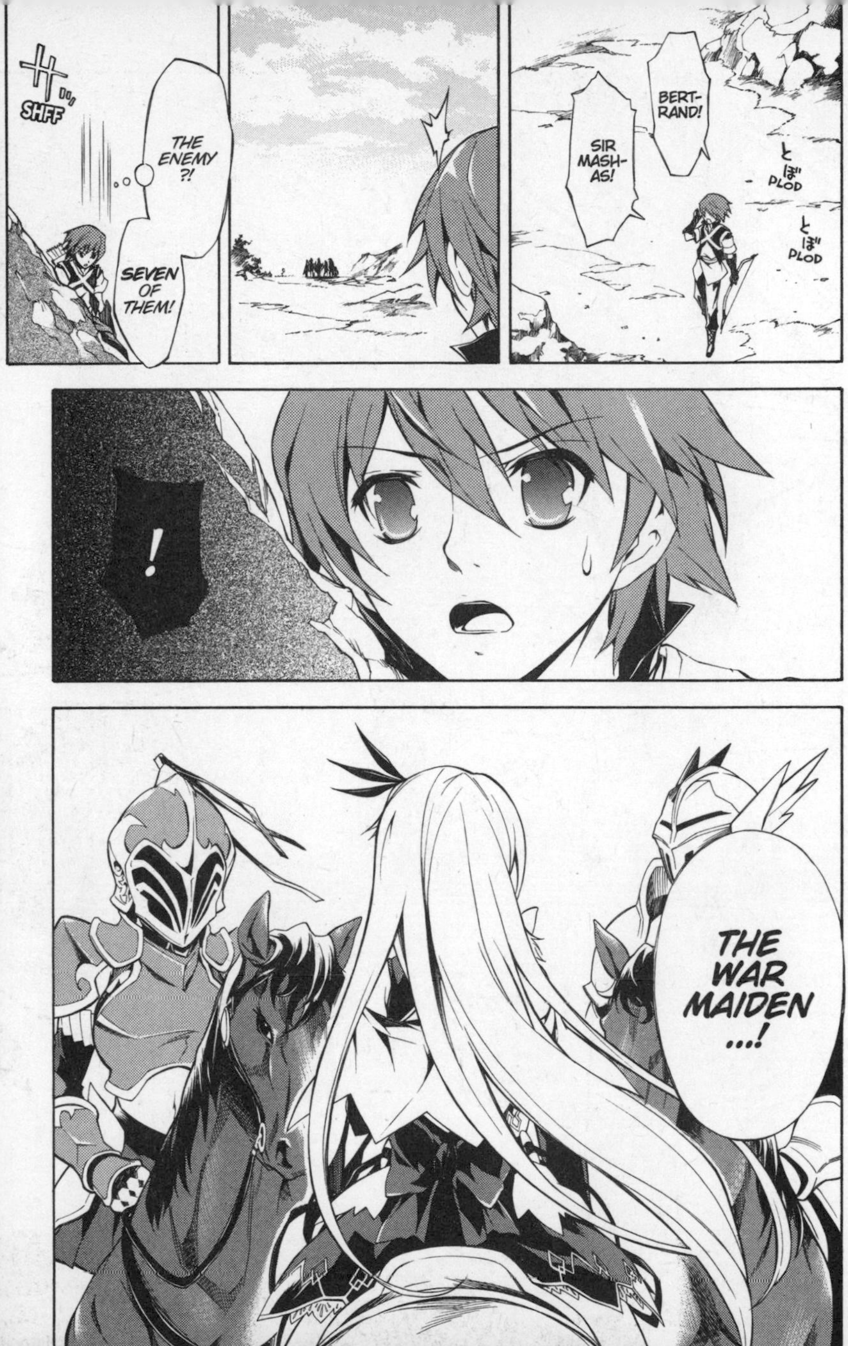
BERT-RAND!
SIR MASH-AS!
とぼ PLOD
とぼ PLOD
SHFF
THE ENEMY ?!
SEVEN OF THEM!
!
THE WAR MAIDEN ...!

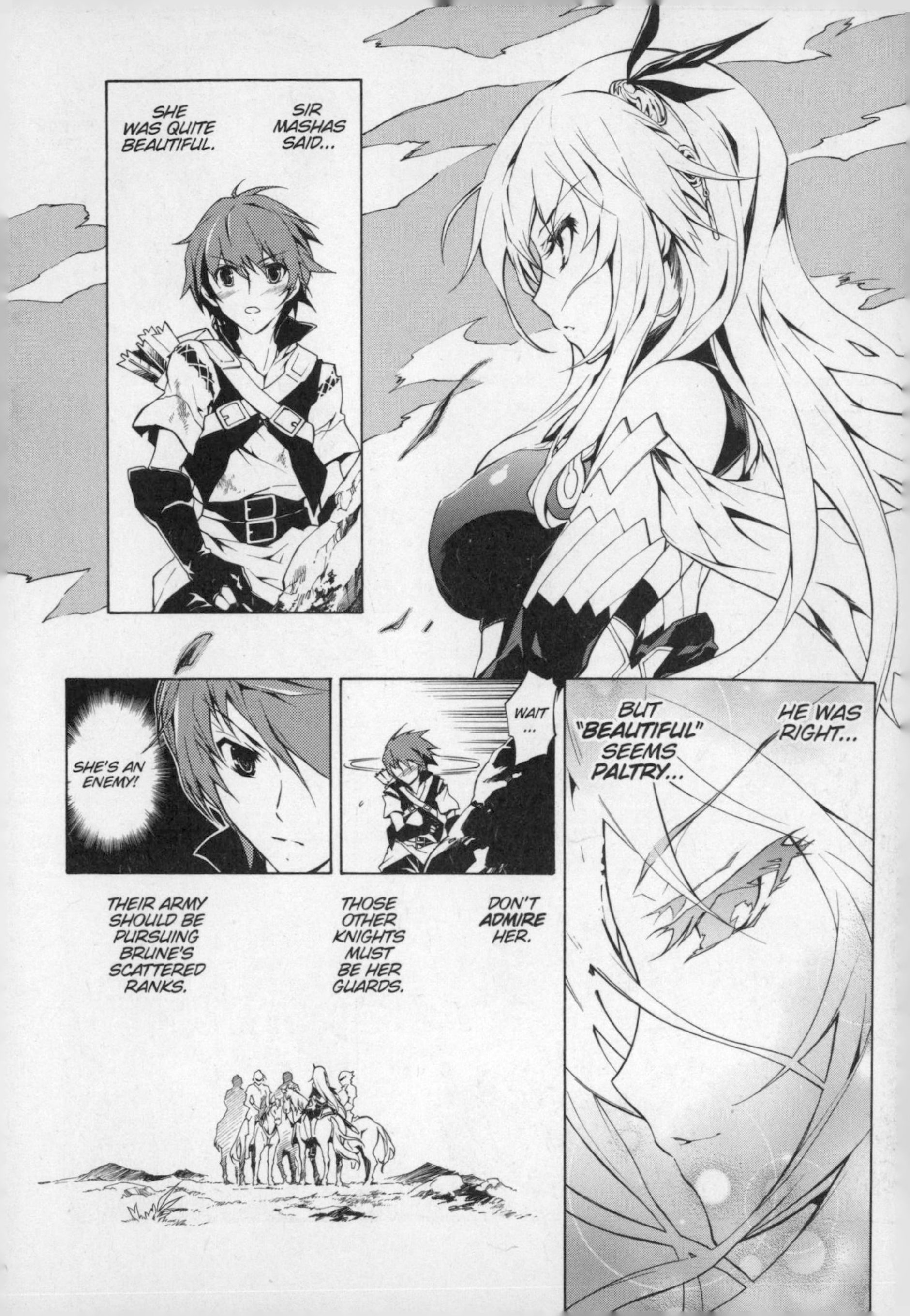
SIR MASHAS SAID...
SHE WAS QUITE BEAUTIFUL.
HE WAS RIGHT...
BUT "BEAUTIFUL" SEEMS PALTRY...
WAIT ...
SHE'S AN ENEMY!
DON'T ADMIRE HER.
THOSE OTHER KNIGHTS MUST BE HER GUARDS.
THEIR ARMY SHOULD BE PURSUING BRUNE'S SCATTERED RANKS.

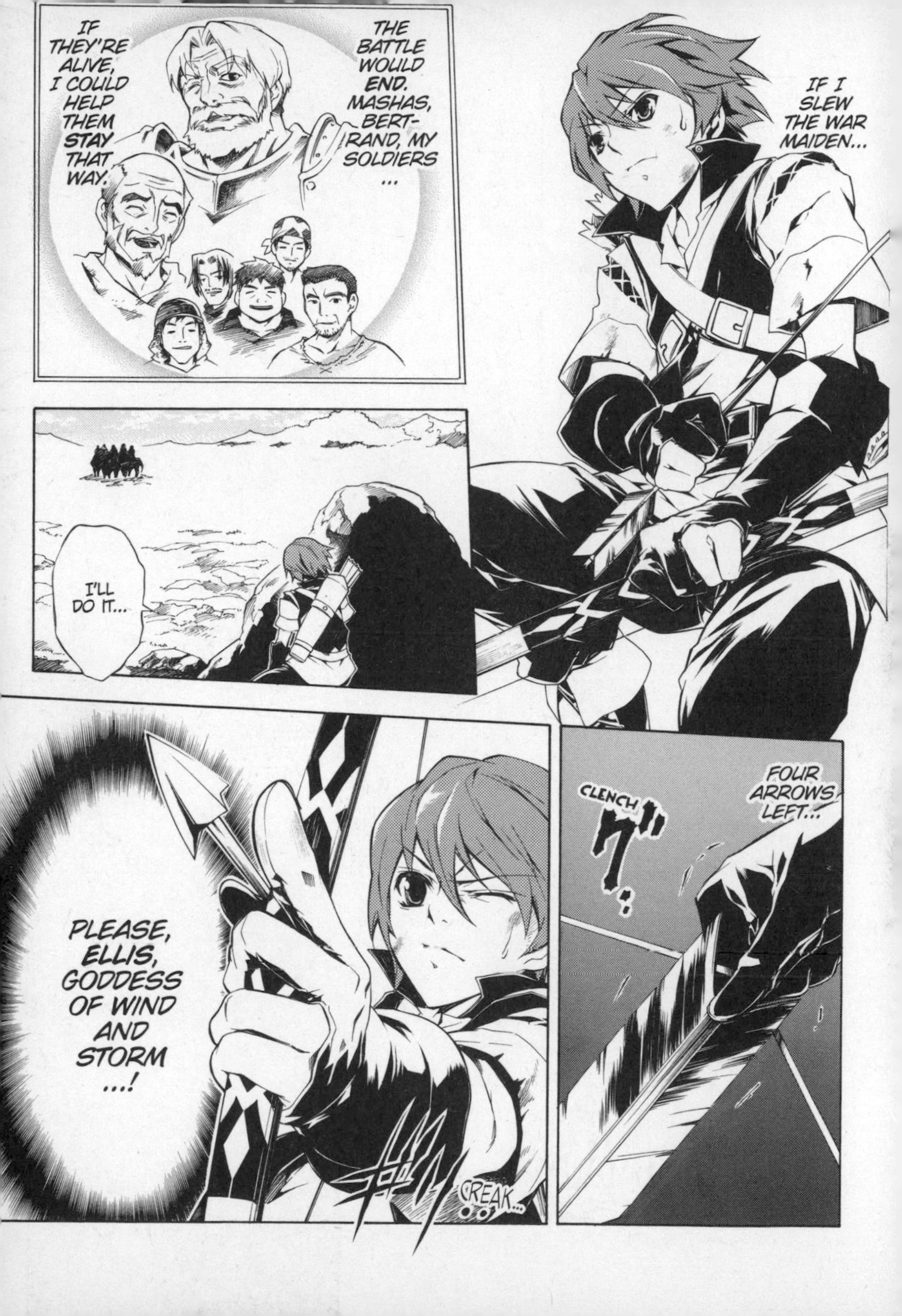
IF I SLEW THE WAR MAIDEN...
THE BATTLE WOULD END. MASHAS, BERT-RAND, MY SOLDIERS ...
IF THEY'RE ALIVE, I COULD HELP THEM STAY THAT WAY.
I'LL DO IT...
FOUR ARROWS LEFT...
CLENCH
PLEASE, ELLIS, GODDESS OF WIND AND STORM ...!
CREAK...

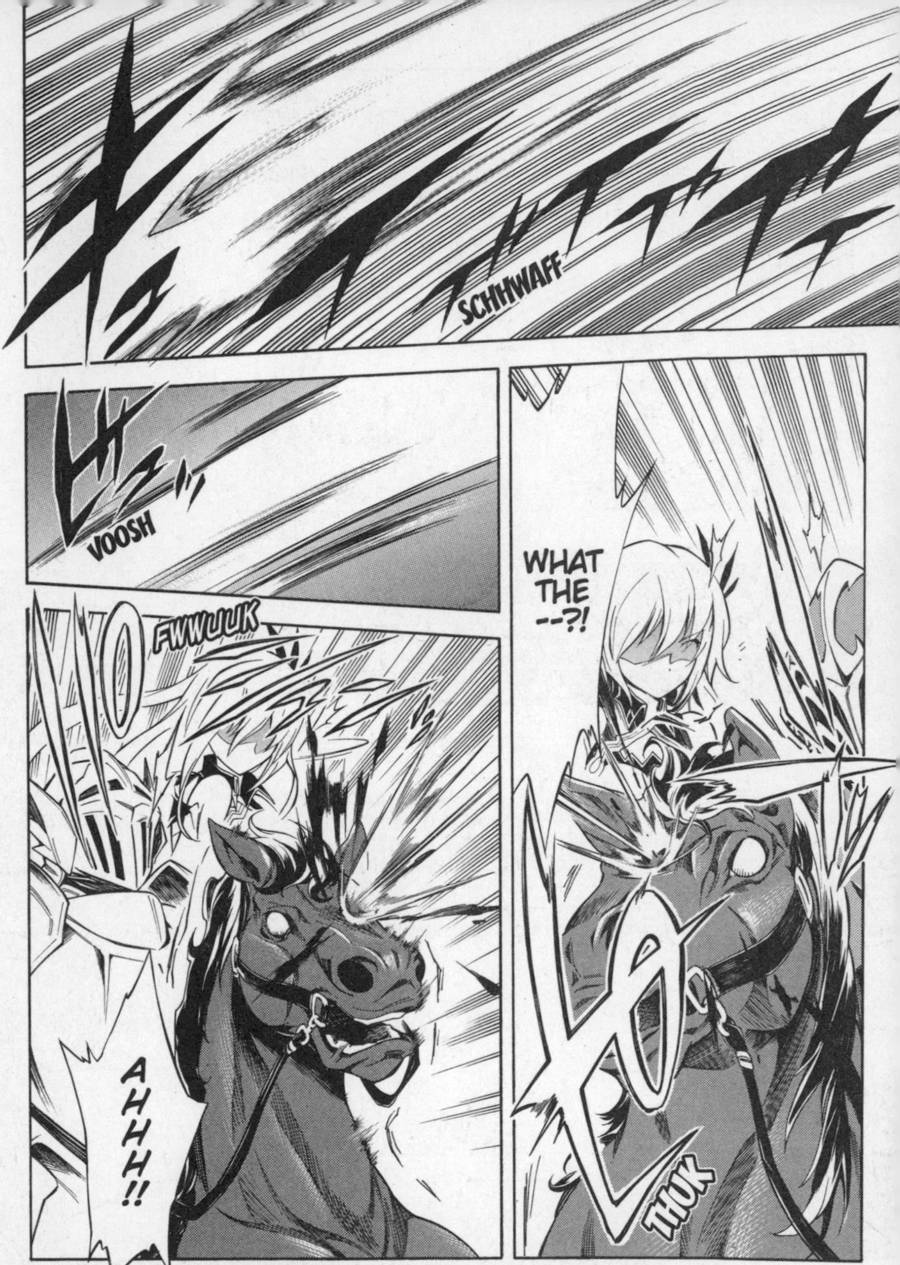
SCHHWAFF
WHAT THE --?!
THUK
VOOSH
FWWUUK
AHHH!!

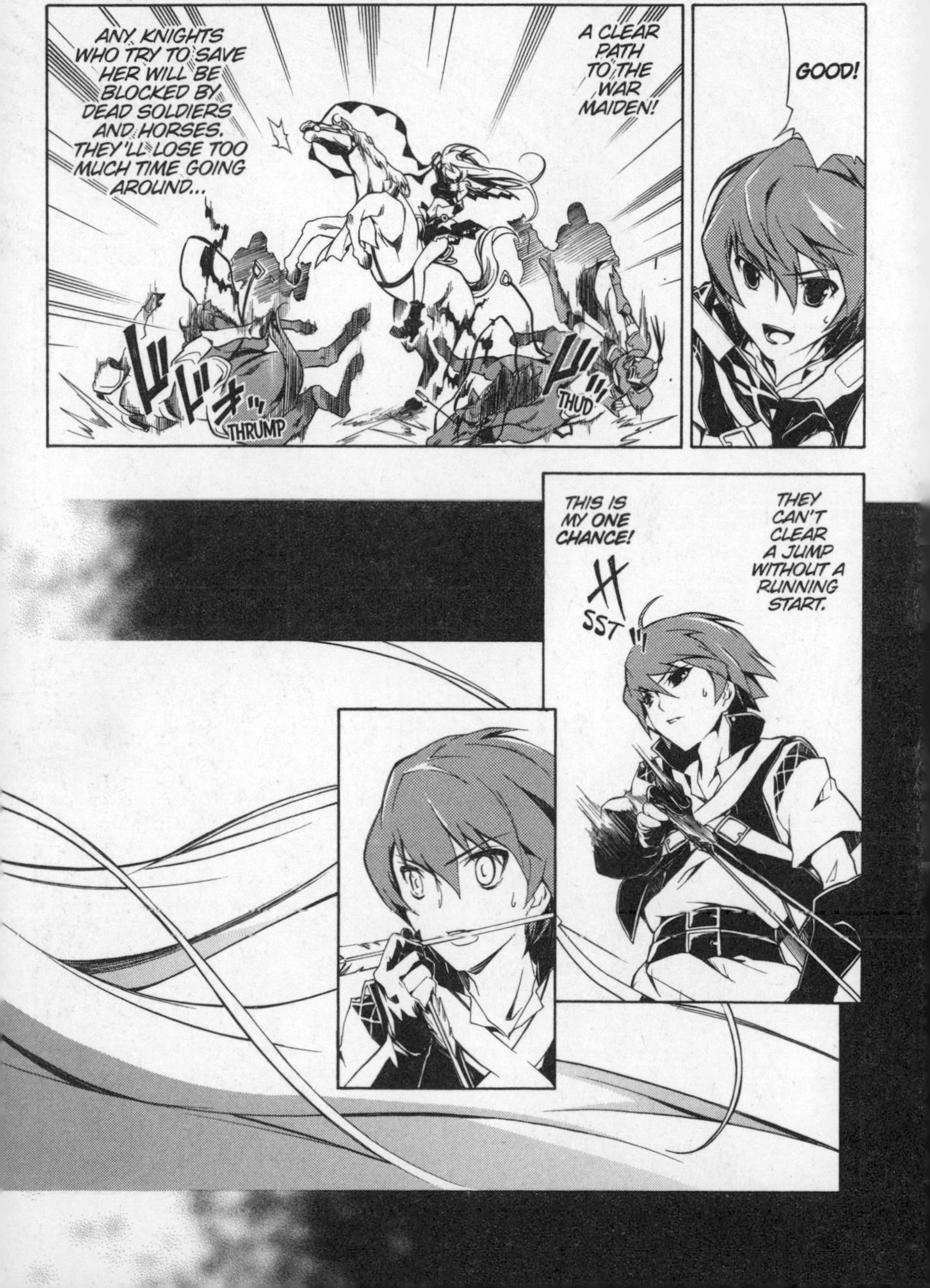
GOOD!
A CLEAR PATH TO THE WAR MAIDEN!
ANY KNIGHTS WHO TRY TO SAVE HER WILL BE BLOCKED BY DEAD SOLDIERS AND HORSES. THEY'LL LOSE TOO MUCH TIME GOING AROUND...
THUD
THRUMP
THEY CAN'T CLEAR A JUMP WITHOUT A RUNNING START.
THIS IS MY ONE CHANCE!
SST

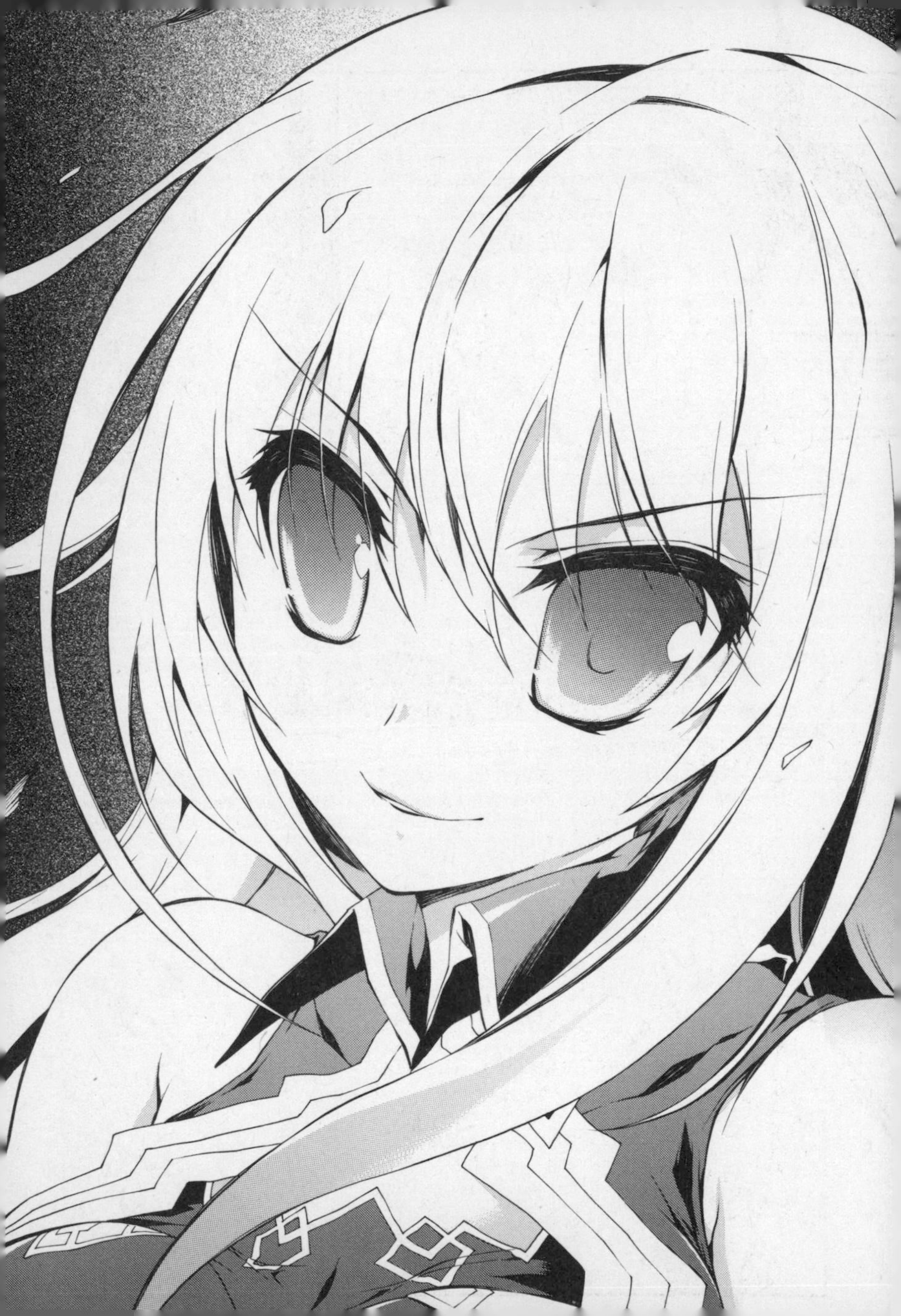

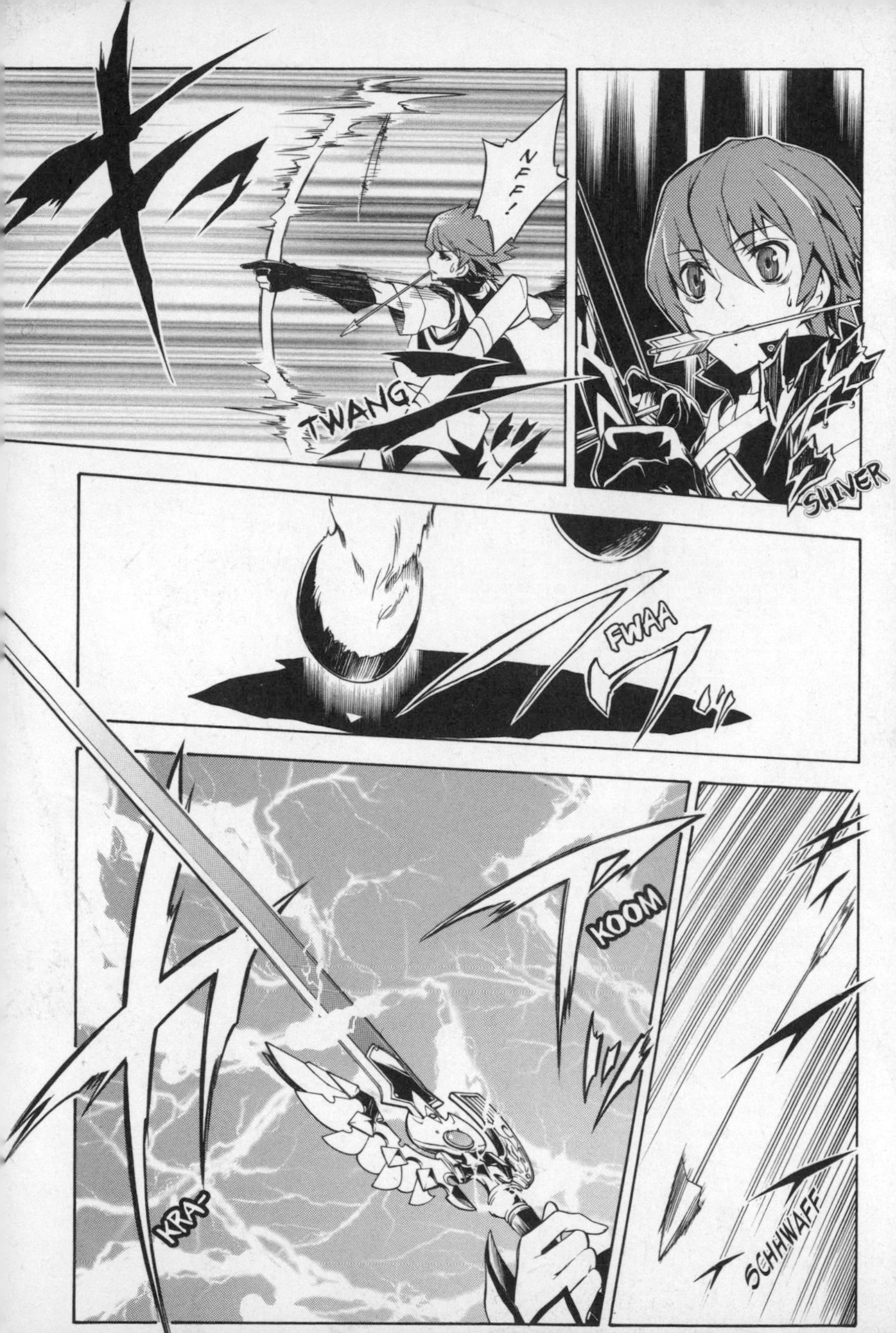
SHIVER
NFF!
TWANG
FWAA
SCHWAFF
KOOM
KRA-

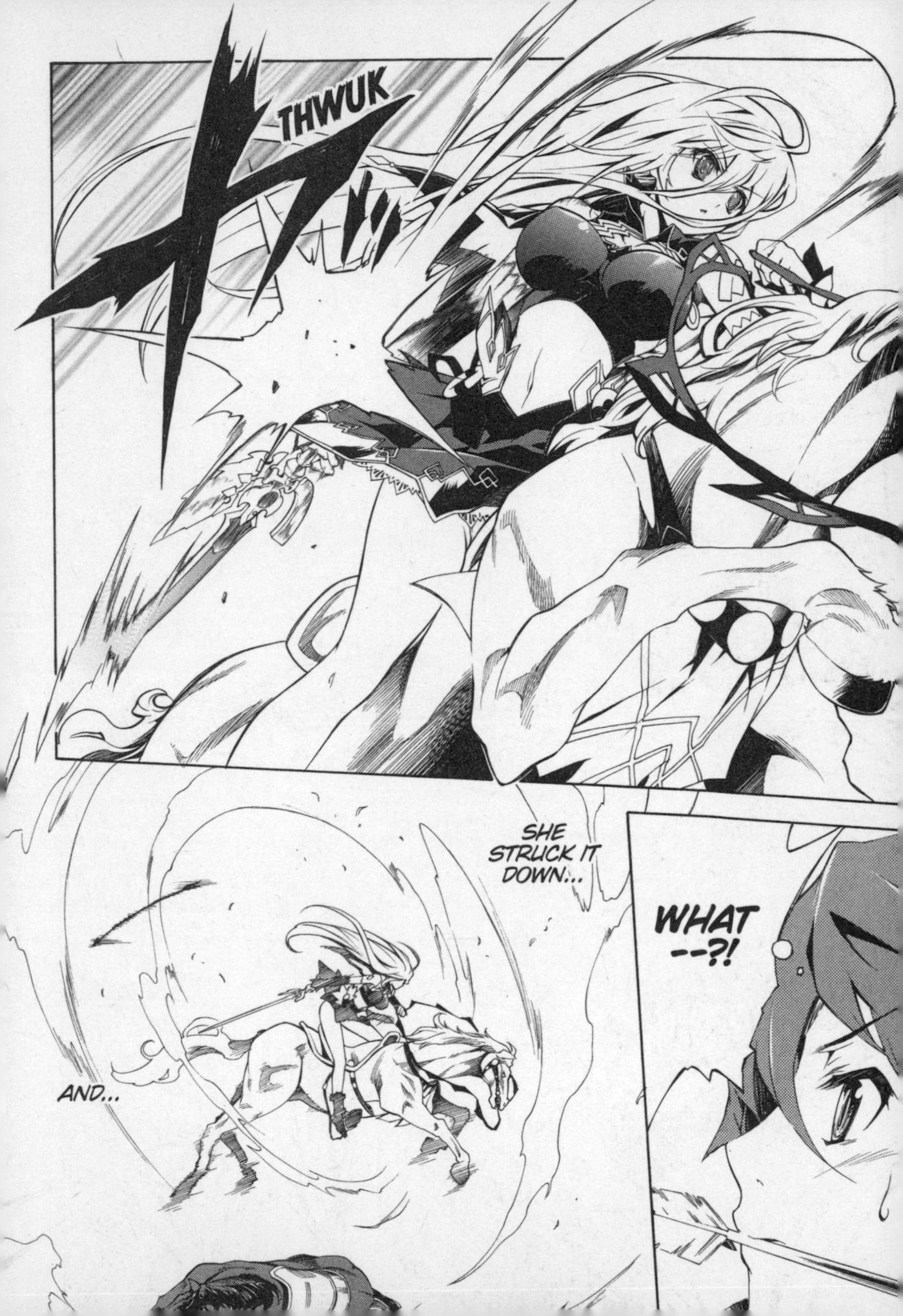
THWUK
WHAT --?!
SHE STRUCK IT DOWN...
AND...

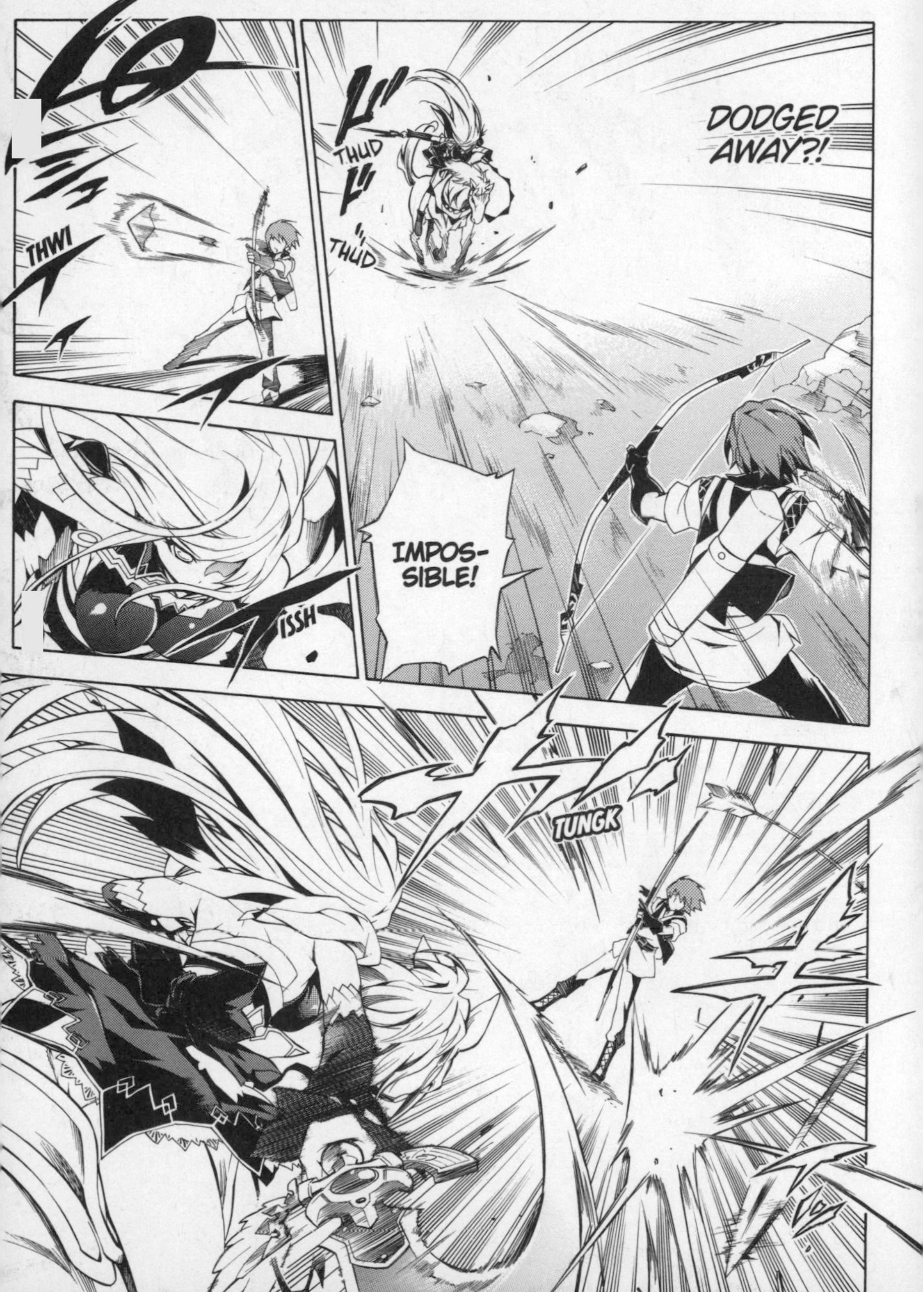
DODGED AWAY?!
THUD
THUD
IMPOS-SIBLE!
THWI
ISSH
TUNGK

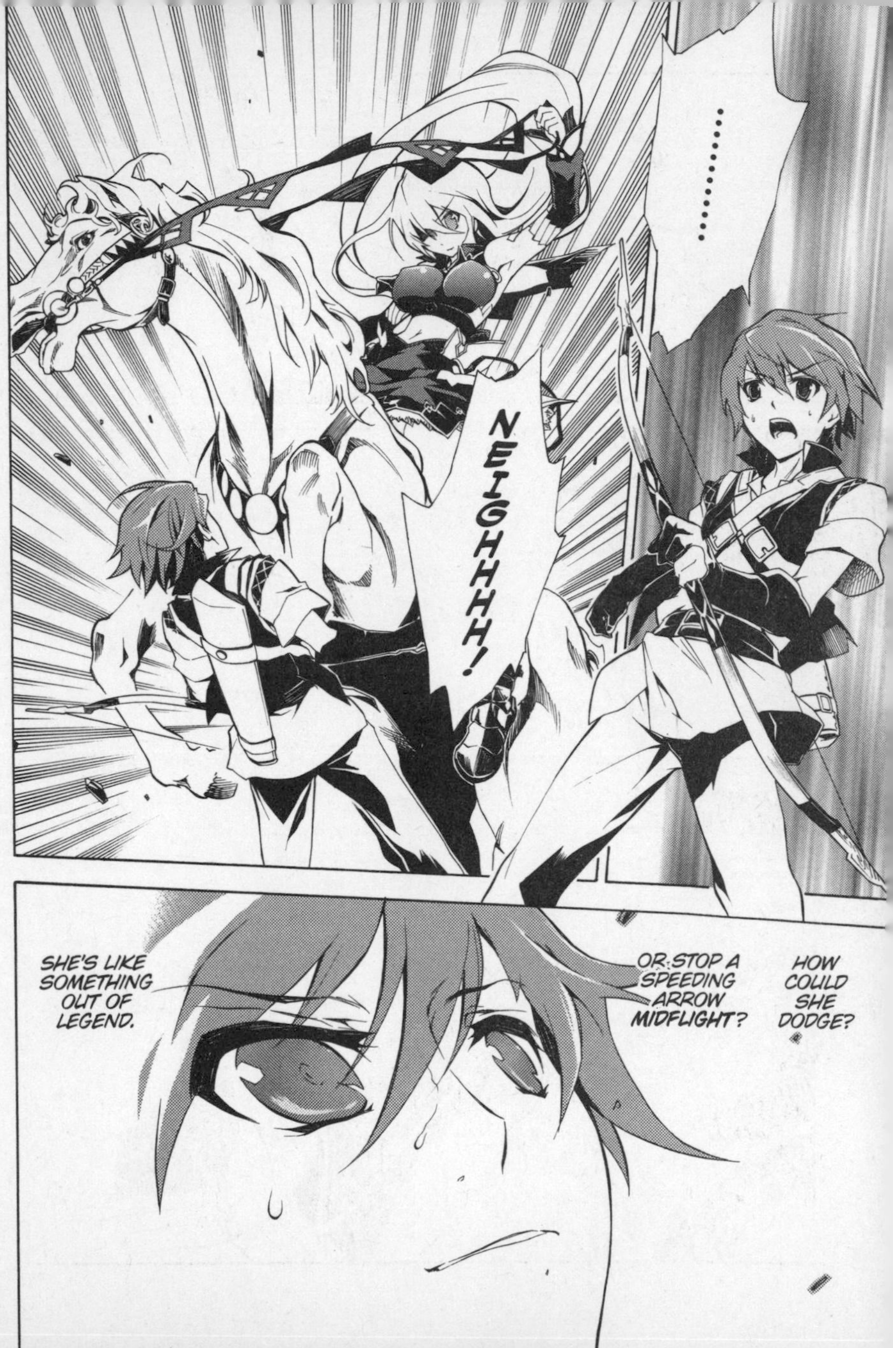
......
NEIGHHHHH!
HOW COULD SHE DODGE?
OR STOP A SPEEDING ARROW MIDFLIGHT?
SHE'S LIKE SOMETHING OUT OF LEGEND.

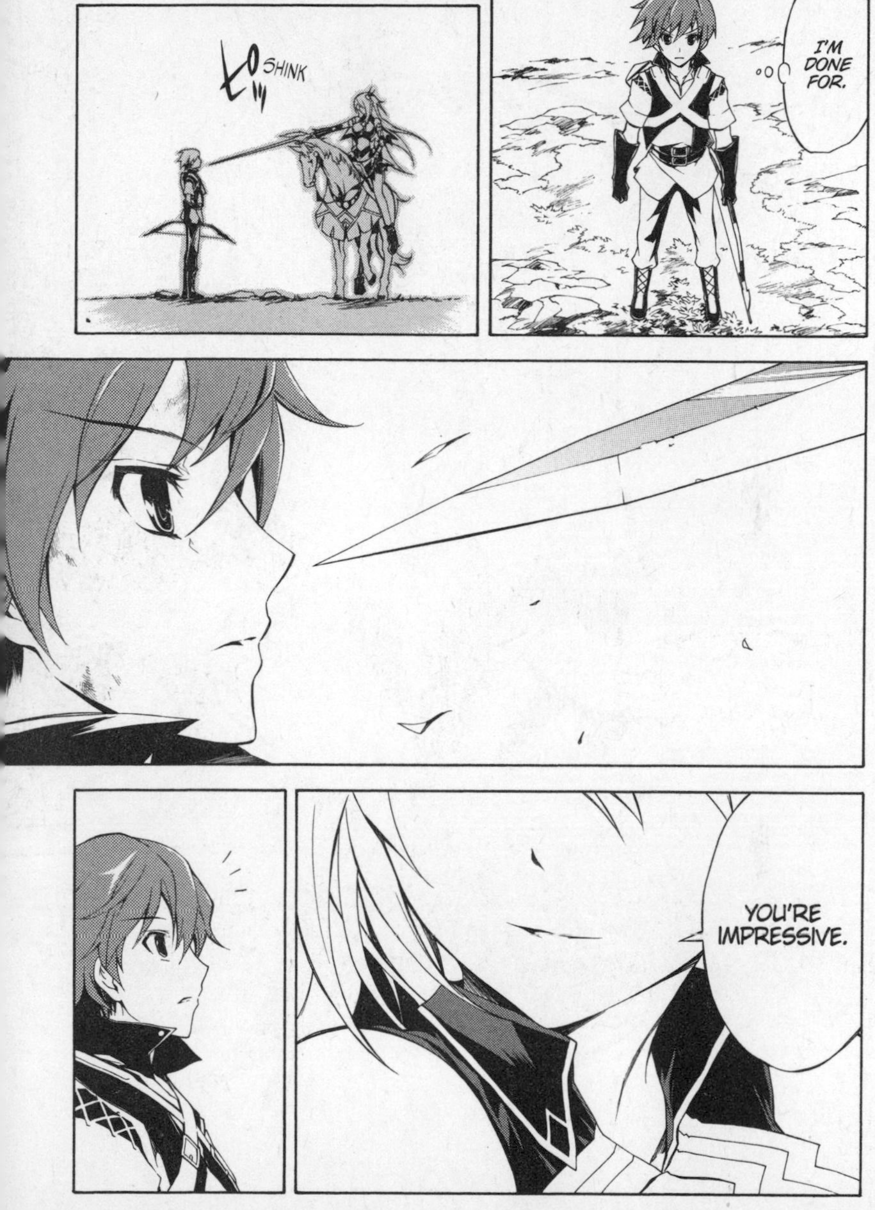
I'M DONE FOR.
SHINK
YOU'RE IMPRESSIVE.

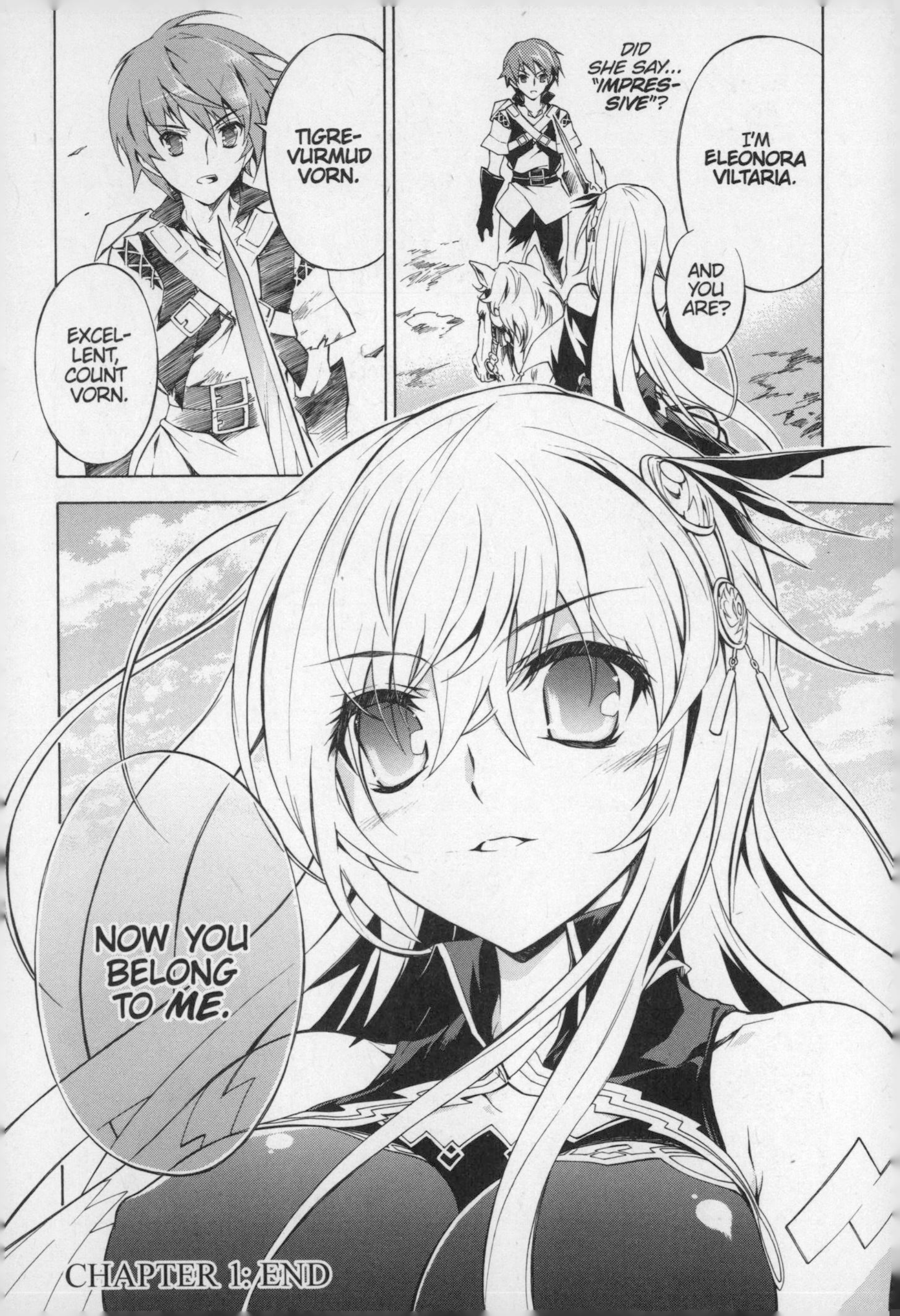
DID SHE SAY... "IMPRESSIVE"?
I'M ELEONORA VILTARIA.
AND YOU ARE?
TIGREVURMUD VORN.
EXCELLENT, COUNT VORN.
NOW YOU BELONG TO ME.
CHAPTER 1: END

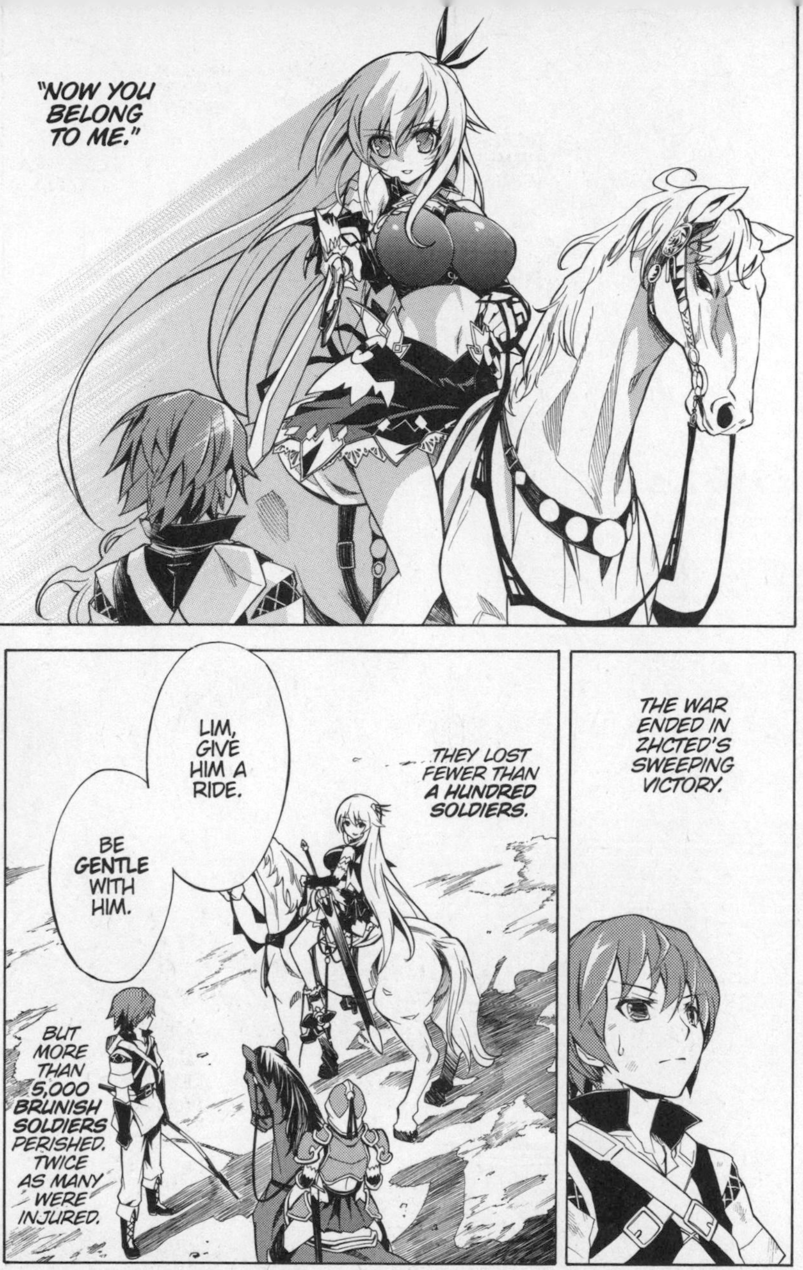
"NOW YOU BELONG TO ME."
THE WAR ENDED IN ZHCTED'S SWEEPING VICTORY.
THEY LOST FEWER THAN A HUNDRED SOLDIERS.
LIM, GIVE HIM A RIDE.
BE GENTLE WITH HIM.
BUT MORE THAN 5,000 BRUNISH SOLDIERS PERISHED. TWICE AS MANY WERE INJURED.

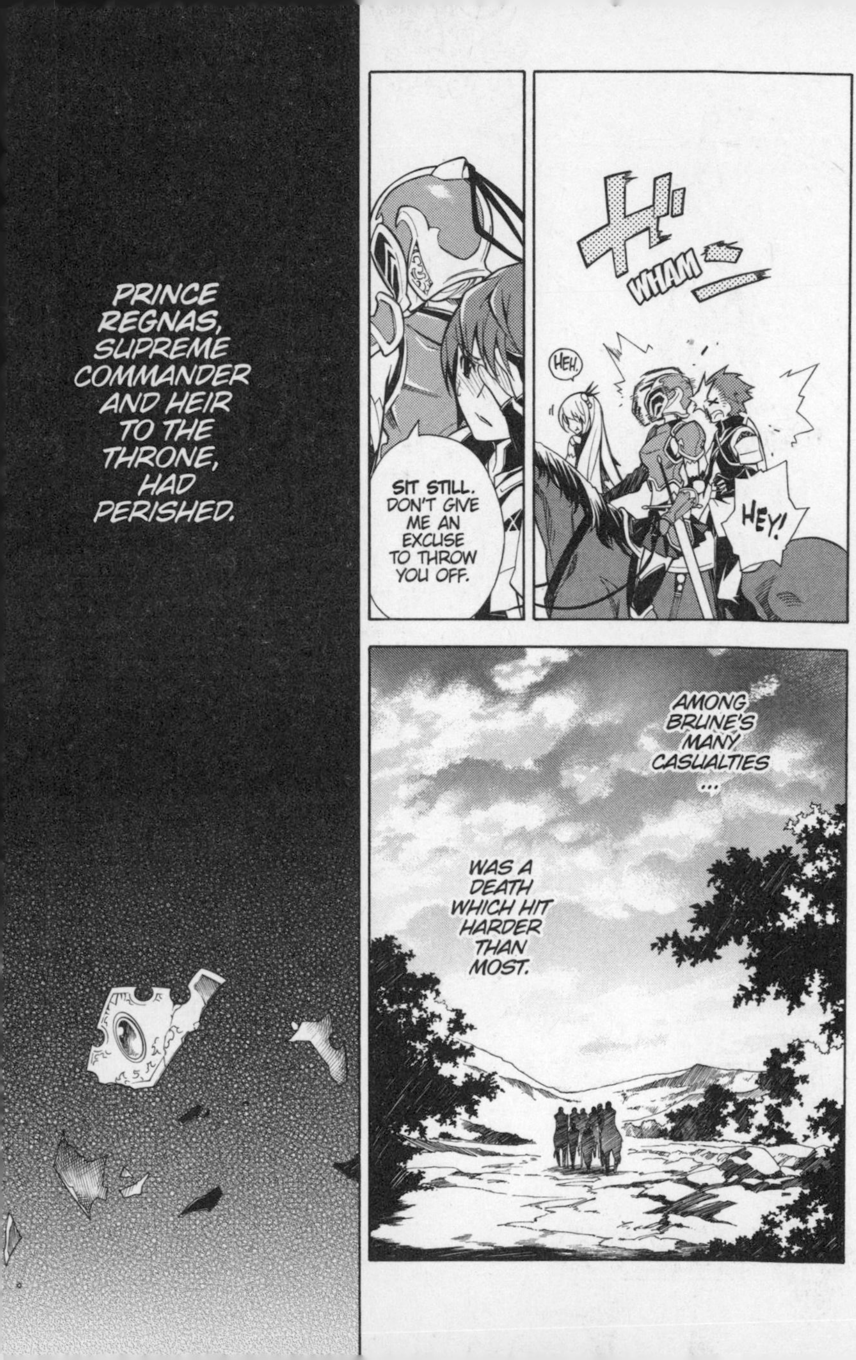
WHAM
HEH.
HEY!
SIT STILL. DON'T GIVE ME AN EXCUSE TO THROW YOU OFF.
AMONG BRUNE'S MANY CASUALTIES...
WAS A DEATH WHICH HIT HARDER THAN MOST.
PRINCE REGNAS, SUPREME COMMANDER AND HEIR TO THE THRONE, HAD PERISHED.

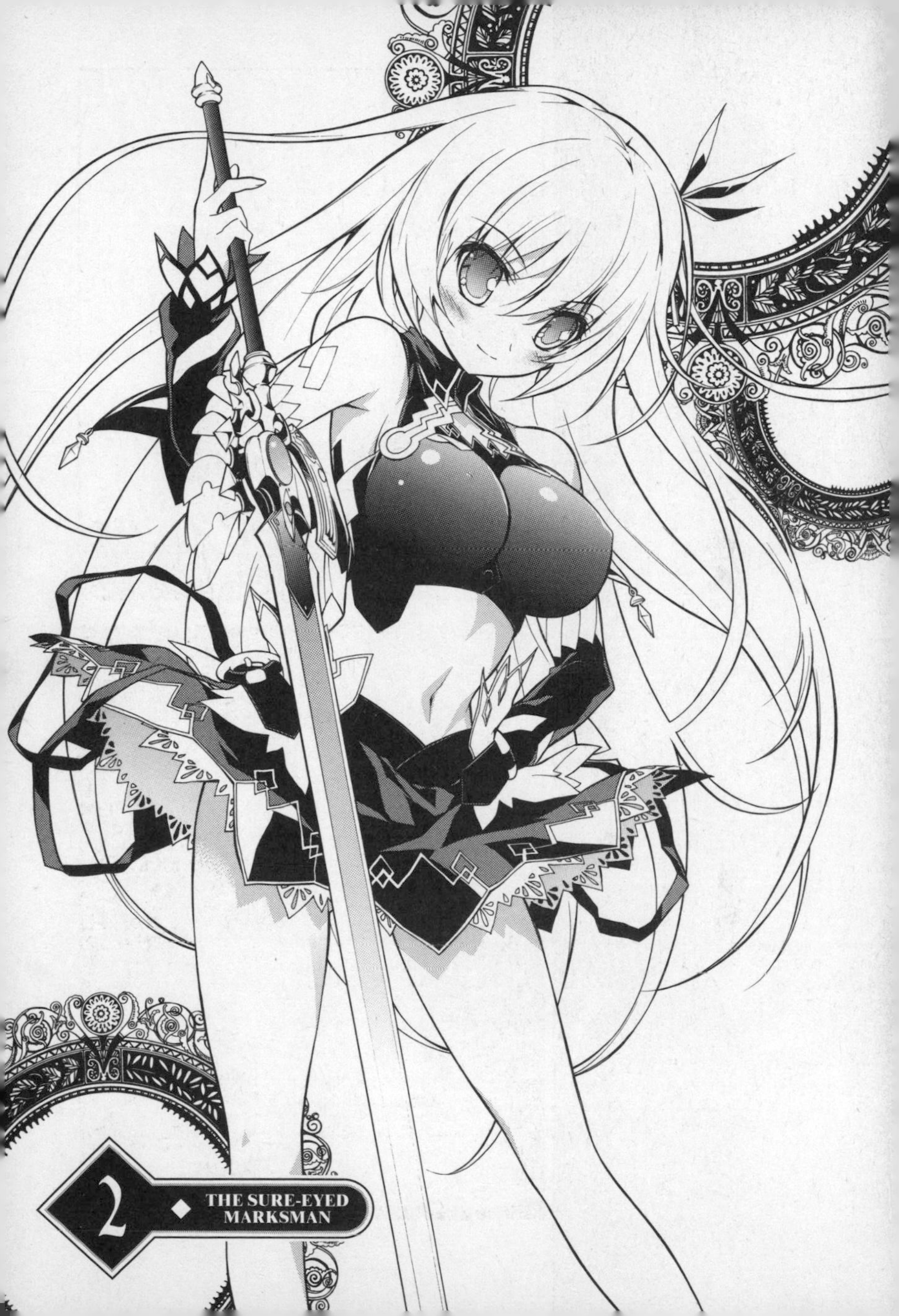

2 ◆ THE SURE-EYED MARKSMAN

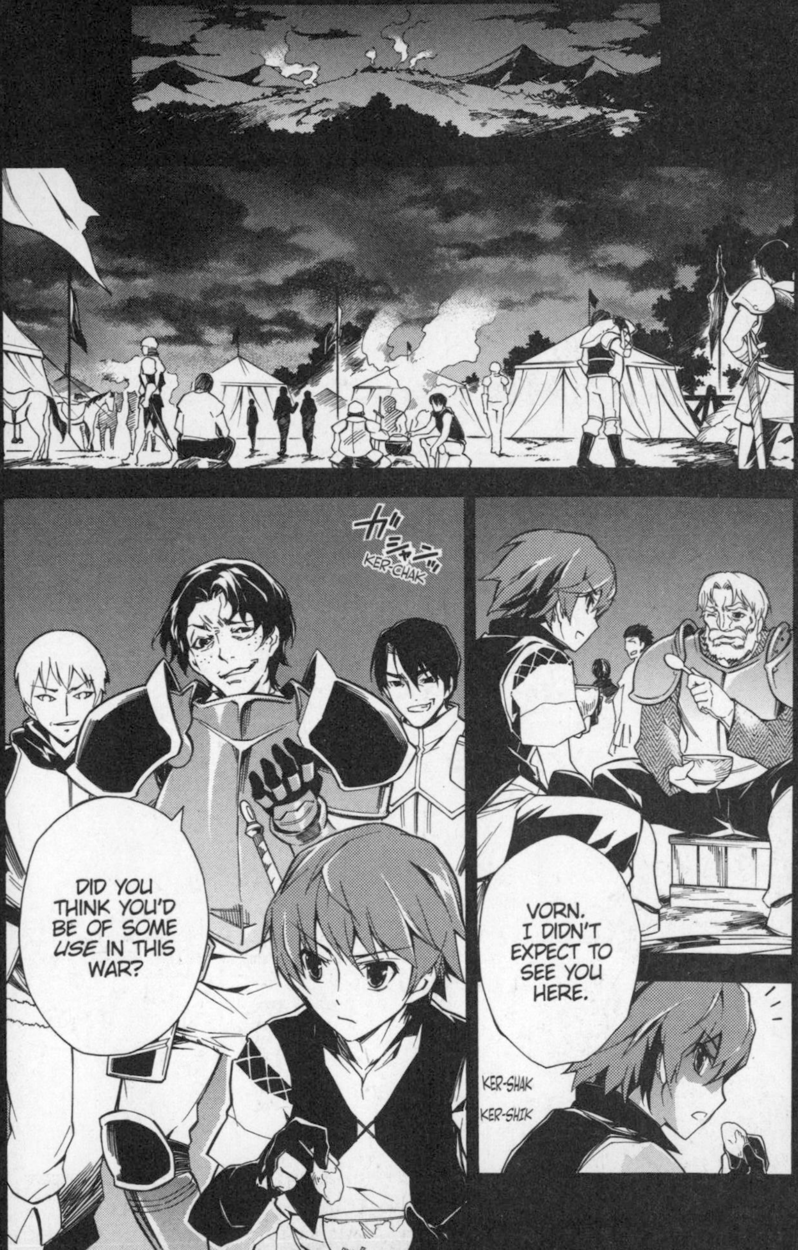
VORN. I DIDN'T EXPECT TO SEE YOU HERE.
KER-SHAK
KER-SHIK
ガシャン
KER-CHAK
DID YOU THINK YOU'D BE OF SOME *USE* IN THIS WAR?

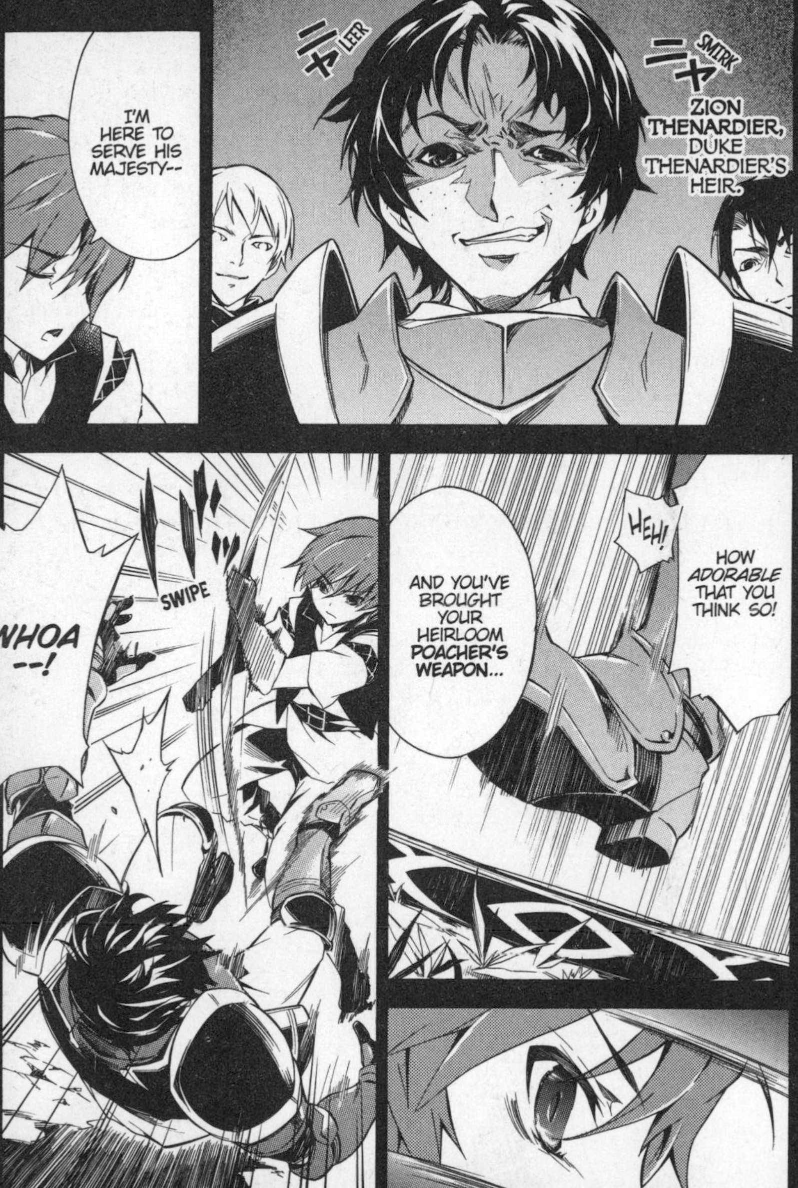
ニヤ LEER
ニヤ SMIRK
ZION THENARDIER, DUKE THENARDIER'S HEIR.
I'M HERE TO SERVE HIS MAJESTY--
HEH!
HOW *ADORABLE* THAT YOU THINK SO!
AND YOU'VE BROUGHT YOUR HEIRLOOM POACHER'S WEAPON...
SWIPE
WHOA --!

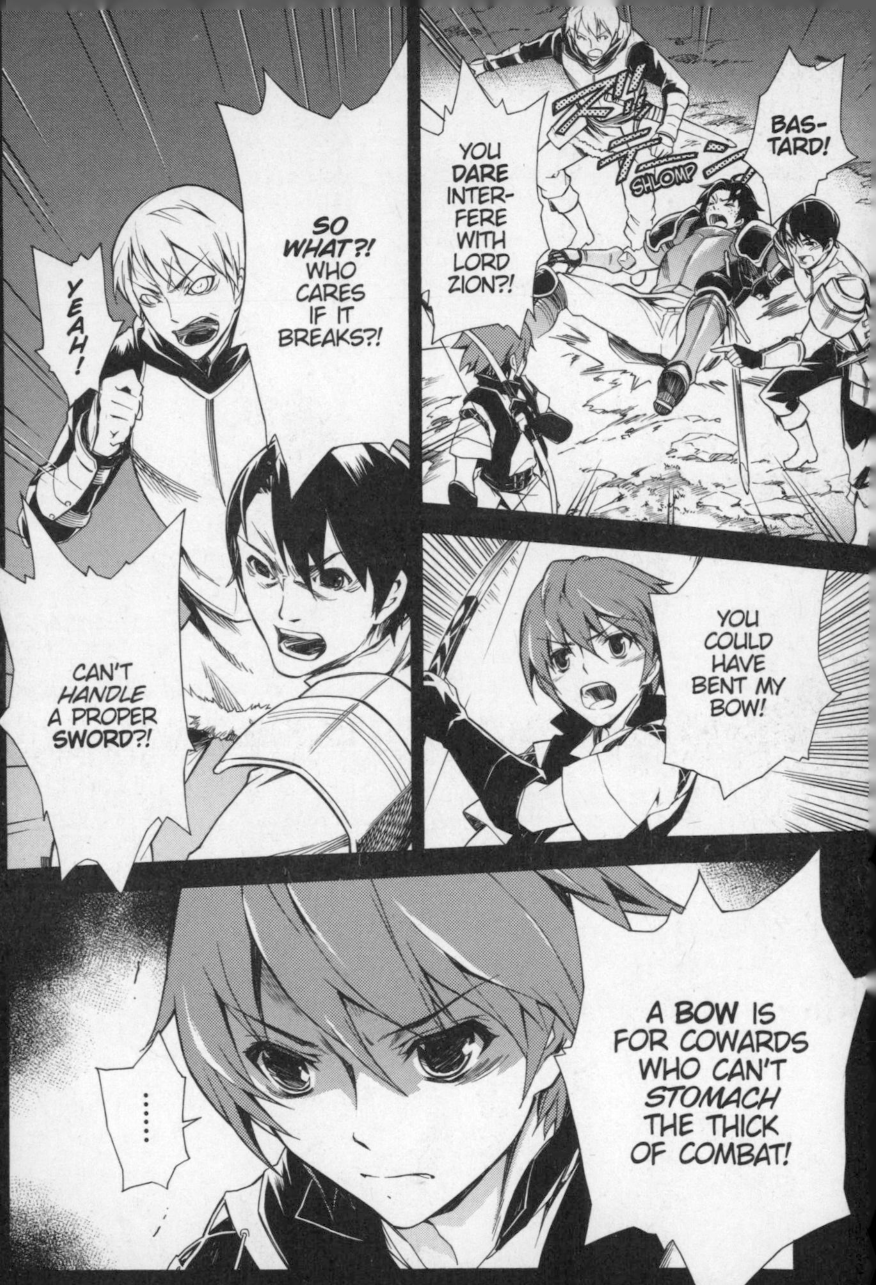
BASTARD!
YOU DARE INTERFERE WITH LORD ZION?!
SHLOMP
YOU COULD HAVE BENT MY BOW!
SO WHAT?! WHO CARES IF IT BREAKS?!
YEAH!
CAN'T HANDLE A PROPER SWORD?!
A BOW IS FOR COWARDS WHO CAN'T STOMACH THE THICK OF COMBAT!
......

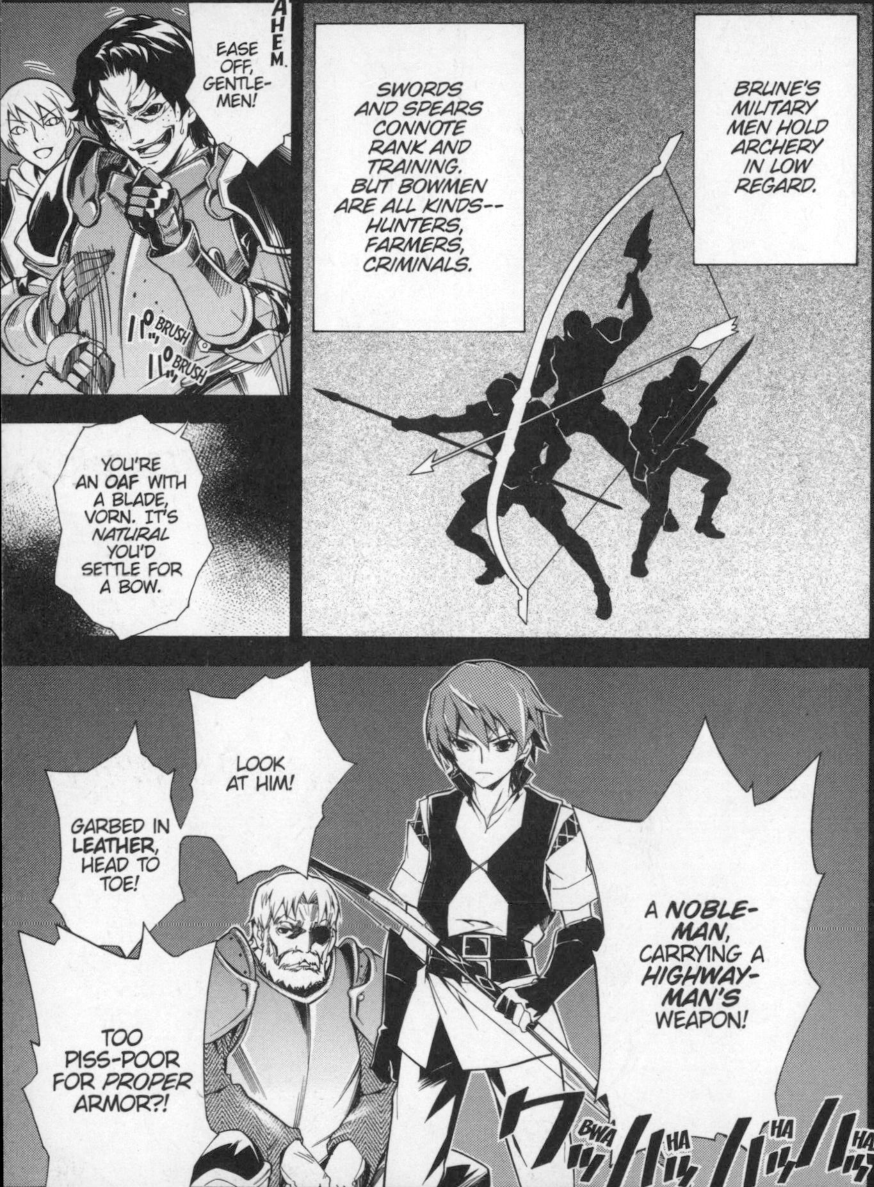
BRUNE'S MILITARY MEN HOLD ARCHERY IN LOW REGARD.
SWORDS AND SPEARS CONNOTE RANK AND TRAINING. BUT BOWMEN ARE ALL KINDS--HUNTERS, FARMERS, CRIMINALS.
AHEM.
EASE OFF, GENTLE-MEN!
BRUSH
BRUSH
YOU'RE AN OAF WITH A BLADE, VORN. IT'S *NATURAL* YOU'D SETTLE FOR A BOW.
A *NOBLE-MAN*, CARRYING A *HIGHWAY-MAN'S* WEAPON!
LOOK AT HIM!
GARBED IN *LEATHER*, HEAD TO TOE!
TOO PISS-POOR FOR *PROPER* ARMOR?!
BWA HA HA HA!

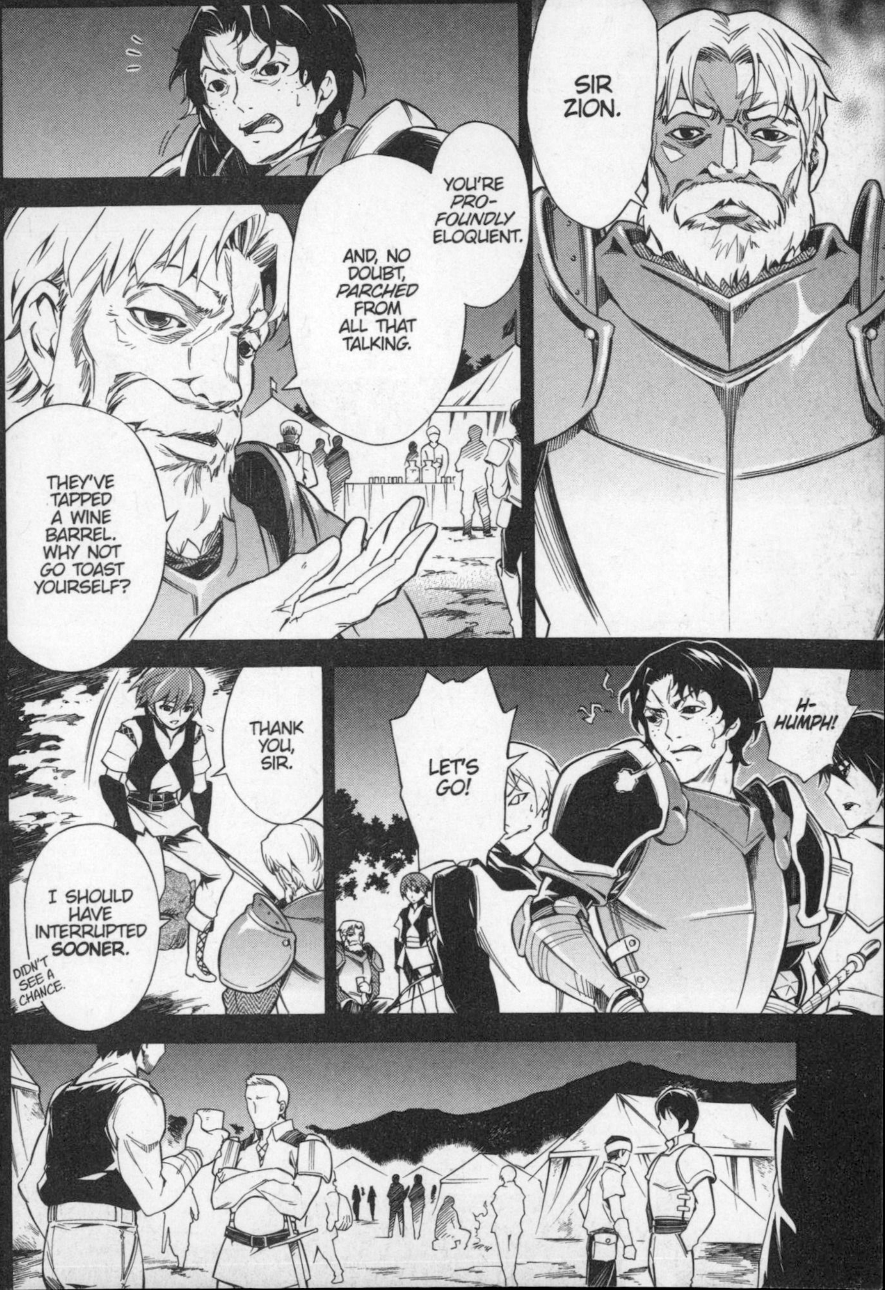
SIR ZION.
YOU'RE PRO-FOUNDLY ELOQUENT.
AND, NO DOUBT, PARCHED FROM ALL THAT TALKING.
THEY'VE TAPPED A WINE BARREL. WHY NOT GO TOAST YOURSELF?
H-HUMPH!
LET'S GO!
THANK YOU, SIR.
I SHOULD HAVE INTERRUPTED SOONER.
DIDN'T SEE A CHANCE.

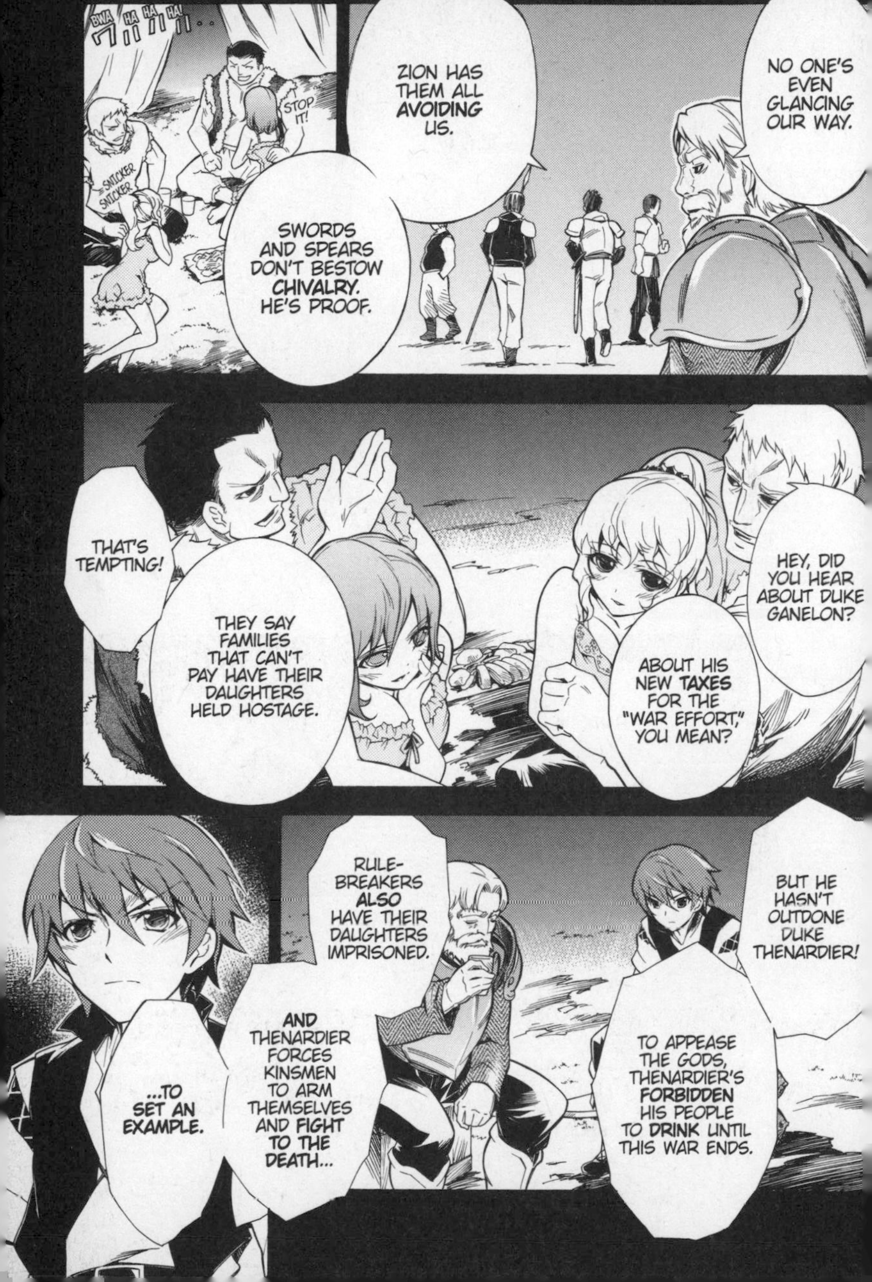
NO ONE'S EVEN GLANCING OUR WAY.
ZION HAS THEM ALL **AVOIDING** US.
SWORDS AND SPEARS DON'T BESTOW **CHIVALRY.** HE'S PROOF.
BWA HA HA HA!
STOP IT!
SNICKER SNICKER
HEY, DID YOU HEAR ABOUT DUKE GANELON?
ABOUT HIS NEW **TAXES** FOR THE "WAR EFFORT," YOU MEAN?
THEY SAY FAMILIES THAT CAN'T PAY HAVE THEIR DAUGHTERS HELD HOSTAGE.
THAT'S TEMPTING!
BUT HE HASN'T OUTDONE DUKE THENARDIER!
TO APPEASE THE GODS, THENARDIER'S **FORBIDDEN** HIS PEOPLE TO **DRINK** UNTIL THIS WAR ENDS.
RULE-BREAKERS **ALSO** HAVE THEIR DAUGHTERS IMPRISONED.
AND THENARDIER FORCES KINSMEN TO ARM THEMSELVES AND **FIGHT** TO THE **DEATH...**
...TO SET AN EXAMPLE.

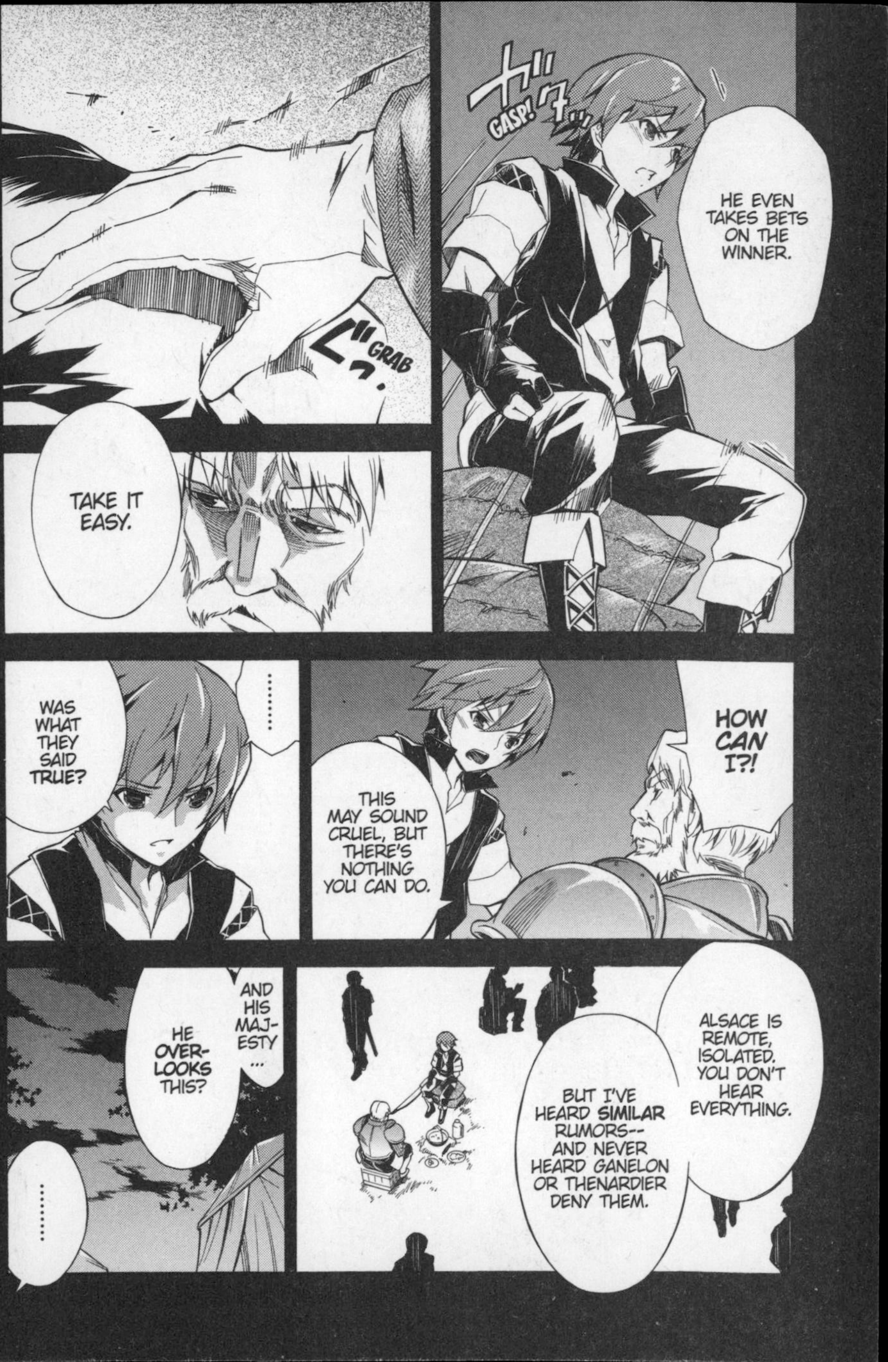
GASP!
HE EVEN TAKES BETS ON THE WINNER.
GRAB
TAKE IT EASY.
HOW CAN I?!
THIS MAY SOUND CRUEL, BUT THERE'S NOTHING YOU CAN DO.
......
WAS WHAT THEY SAID TRUE?
ALSACE IS REMOTE, ISOLATED. YOU DON'T HEAR EVERYTHING.
BUT I'VE HEARD **SIMILAR** RUMORS-- AND NEVER HEARD GANELON OR THENARDIER DENY THEM.
AND HIS MAJESTY...
HE OVERLOOKS THIS?
......

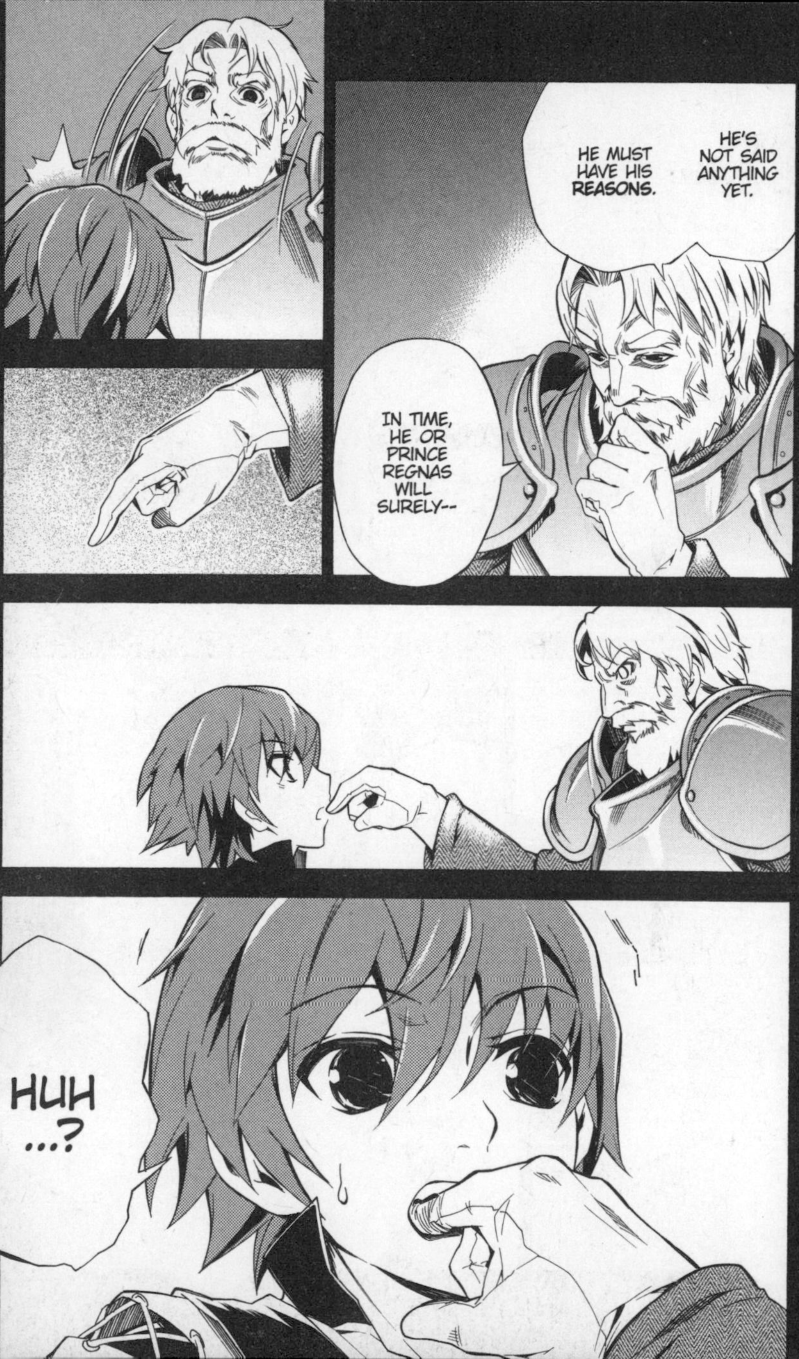
HE'S NOT SAID ANYTHING YET.
HE MUST HAVE HIS REASONS.
IN TIME, HE OR PRINCE REGNAS WILL SURELY--
HUH ...?

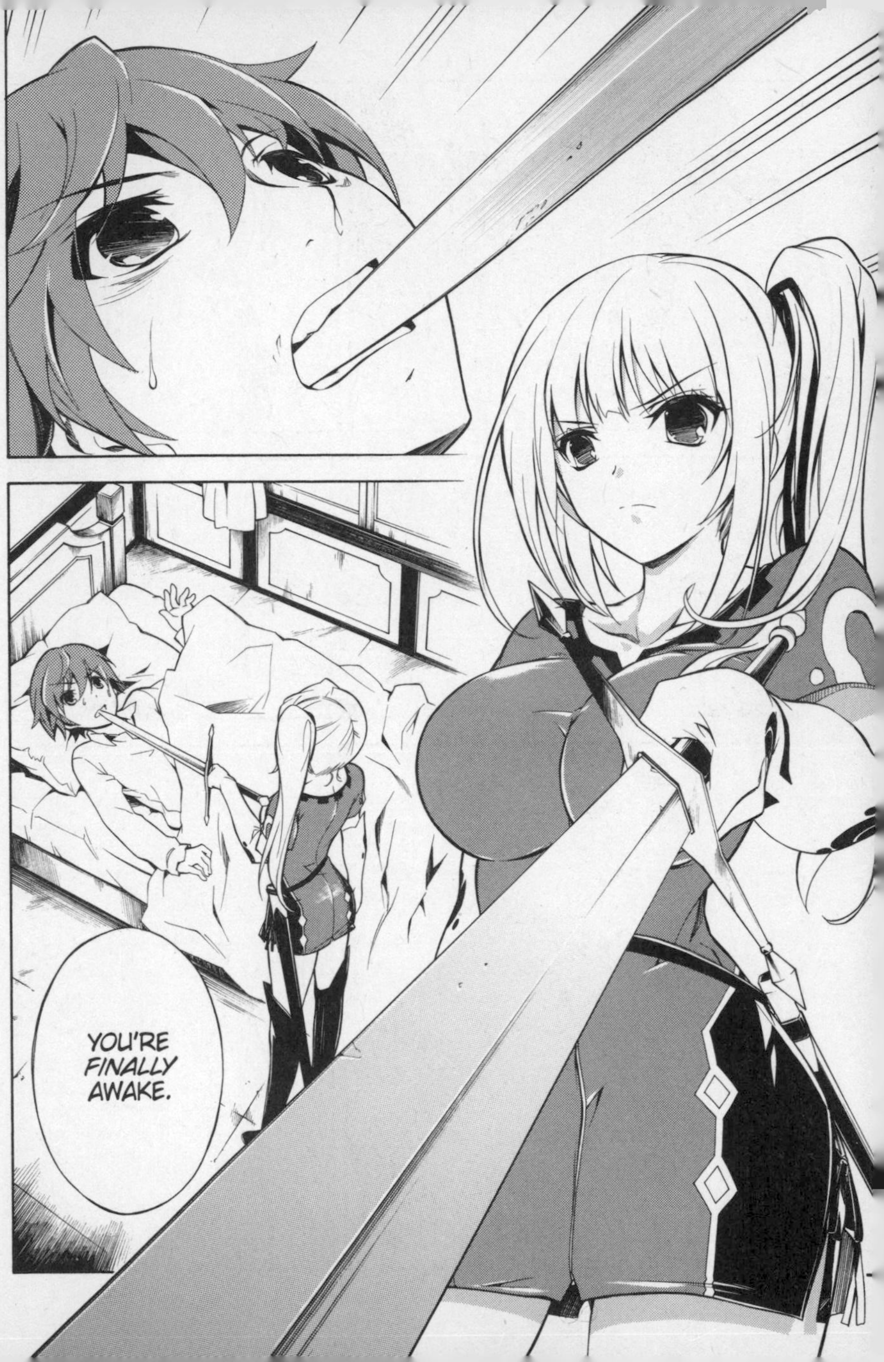
YOU'RE FINALLY AWAKE.

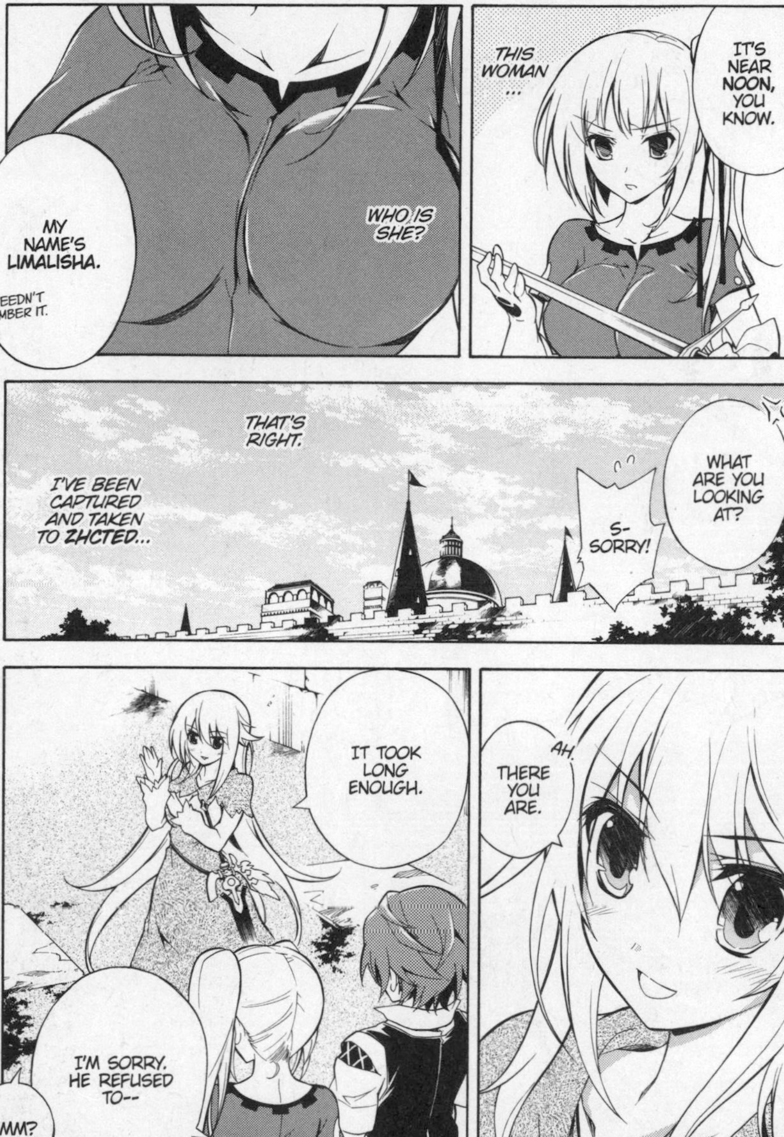
IT'S NEAR NOON, YOU KNOW.
THIS WOMAN ...
WHO IS SHE?
MY NAME'S LIMALISHA.
YOU NEEDN'T REMEMBER IT.
WHAT ARE YOU LOOKING AT?
S-SORRY!
THAT'S RIGHT.
I'VE BEEN CAPTURED AND TAKEN TO ZHCTED...
AH. THERE YOU ARE.
IT TOOK LONG ENOUGH.
I'M SORRY. HE REFUSED TO--
HMM?

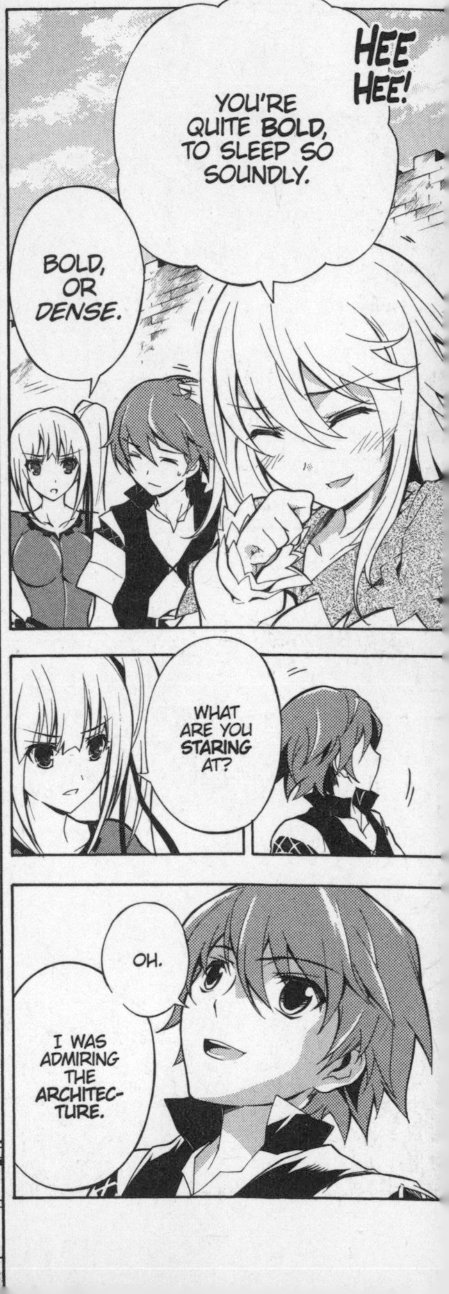
HEE HEE!
YOU'RE QUITE BOLD, TO SLEEP SO SOUNDLY.
BOLD, OR DENSE.
WHAT ARE YOU STARING AT?
OH.
I WAS ADMIRING THE ARCHITEC-TURE.

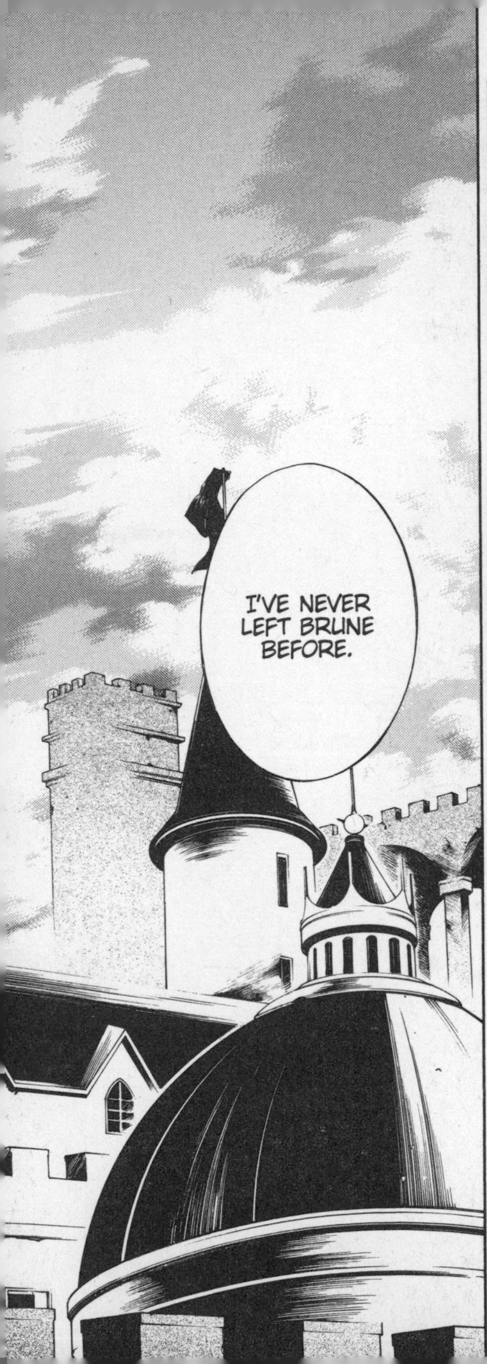
I'VE NEVER LEFT BRUNE BEFORE.

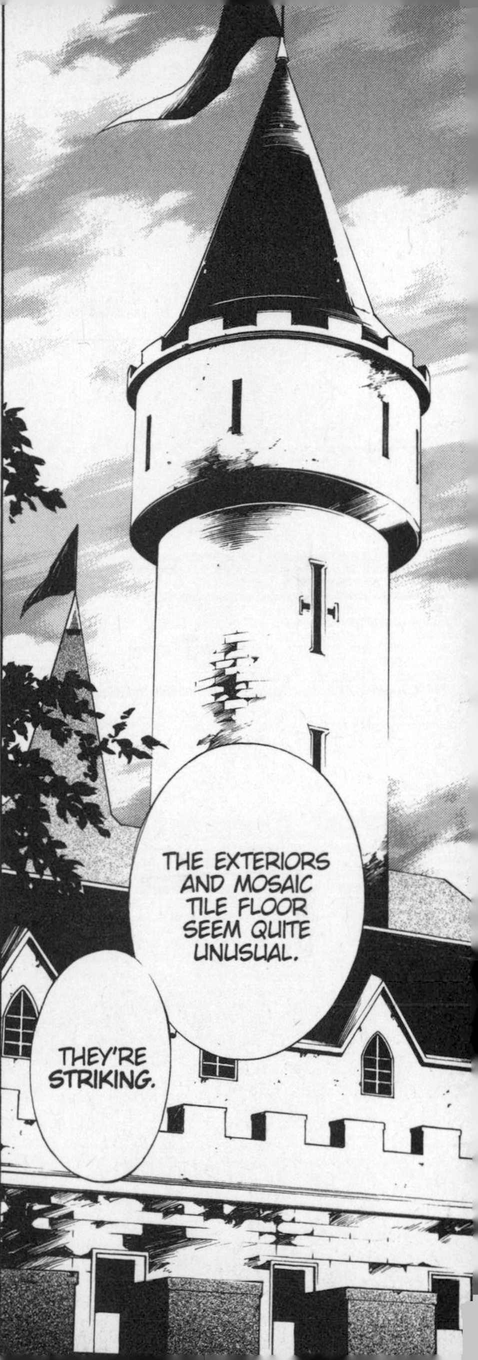
THE EXTERIORS AND MOSAIC TILE FLOOR SEEM QUITE UNUSUAL.
THEY'RE STRIKING.

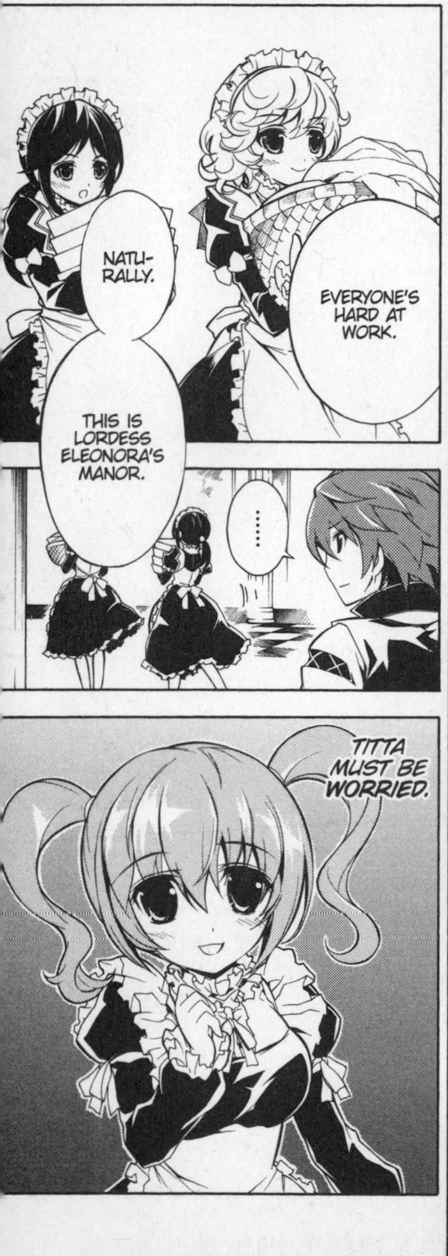
EVERYONE'S HARD AT WORK.
NATU-RALLY.
THIS IS LORDESS ELEONORA'S MANOR.
......
TITTA MUST BE WORRIED.

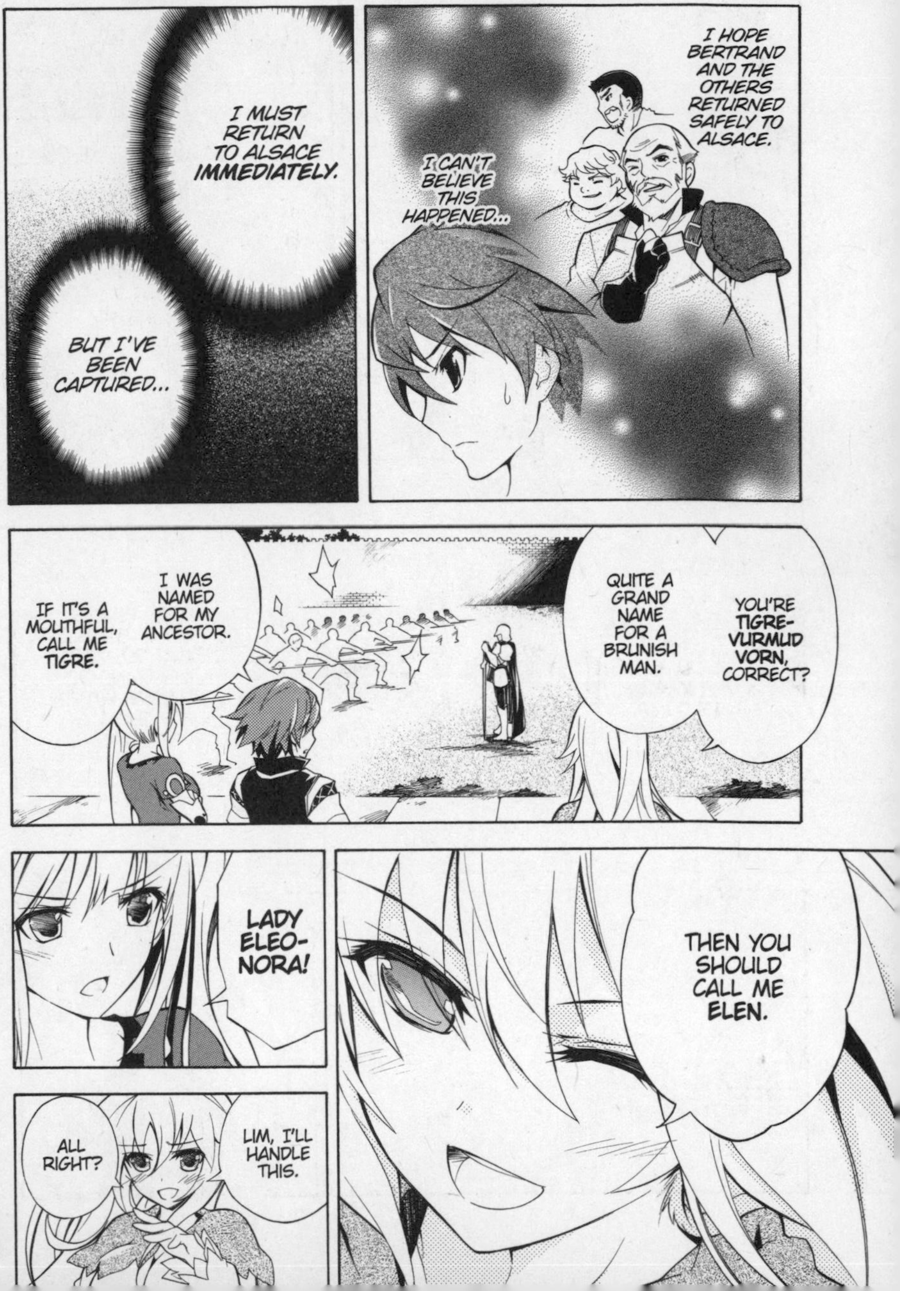
I HOPE BERTRAND AND THE OTHERS RETURNED SAFELY TO ALSACE.
I CAN'T BELIEVE THIS HAPPENED...
I MUST RETURN TO ALSACE IMMEDIATELY.
BUT I'VE BEEN CAPTURED...
YOU'RE TIGRE-VURMUD VORN, CORRECT?
QUITE A GRAND NAME FOR A BRUNISH MAN.
I WAS NAMED FOR MY ANCESTOR.
IF IT'S A MOUTHFUL, CALL ME TIGRE.
THEN YOU SHOULD CALL ME ELEN.
LADY ELEONORA!
LIM, I'LL HANDLE THIS.
ALL RIGHT?

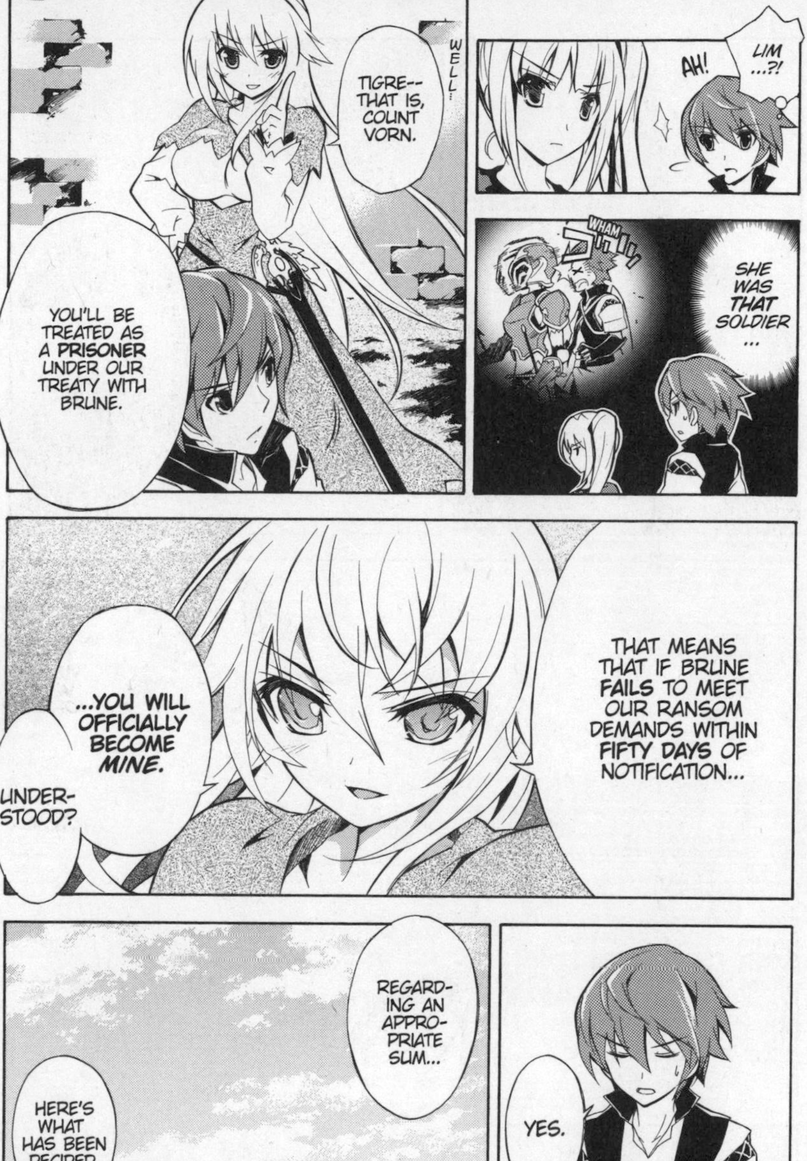
LIM ...?!
AH!
WHAM
SHE WAS THAT SOLDIER ...
WELL...
TIGRE-- THAT IS, COUNT VORN.
YOU'LL BE TREATED AS A PRISONER UNDER OUR TREATY WITH BRUNE.
THAT MEANS THAT IF BRUNE FAILS TO MEET OUR RANSOM DEMANDS WITHIN FIFTY DAYS OF NOTIFICATION...
...YOU WILL OFFICIALLY BECOME MINE.
UNDER-STOOD?
YES.
REGARD-ING AN APPRO-PRIATE SUM...
HERE'S WHAT HAS BEEN DECIDED.

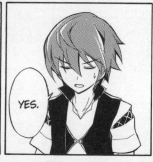

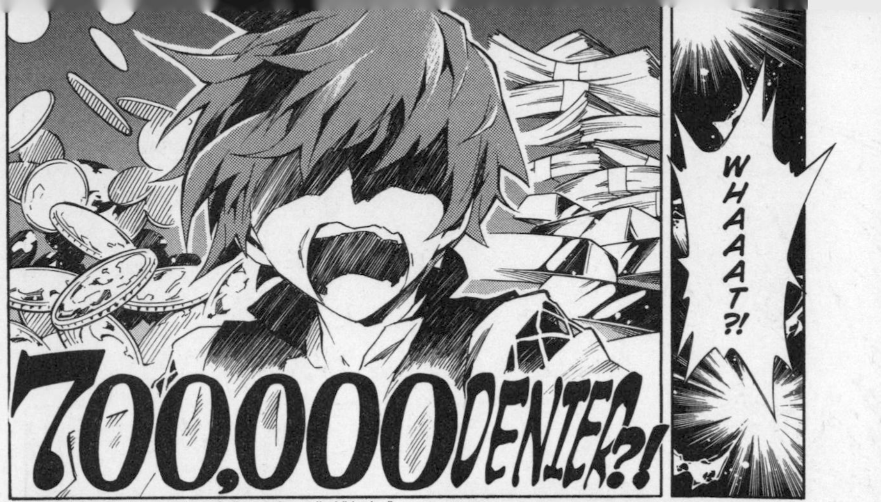
WHAAAT?!
700,000 DENIER?!

※Brune's currency consists of silver coins called "denier."

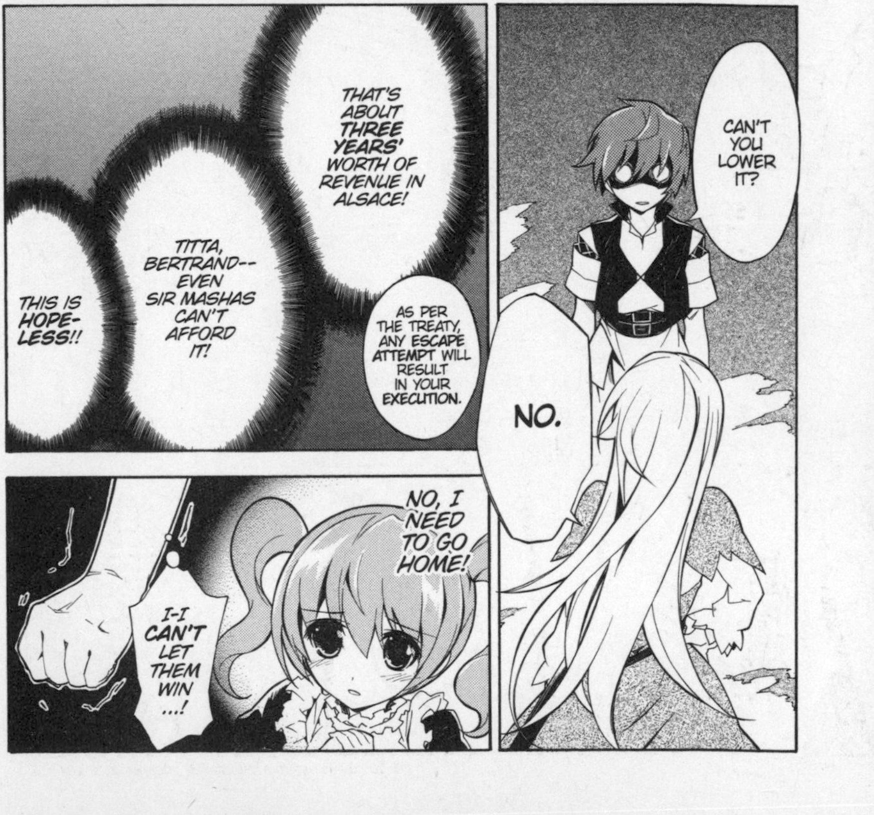
CAN'T YOU LOWER IT?
NO.
THAT'S ABOUT THREE YEARS' WORTH OF REVENUE IN ALSACE!
AS PER THE TREATY, ANY ESCAPE ATTEMPT WILL RESULT IN YOUR EXECUTION.
TITTA, BERTRAND-- EVEN SIR MASHAS CAN'T AFFORD IT!
THIS IS HOPE-LESS!!
NO, I NEED TO GO HOME!
I-I CAN'T LET THEM WIN ...!

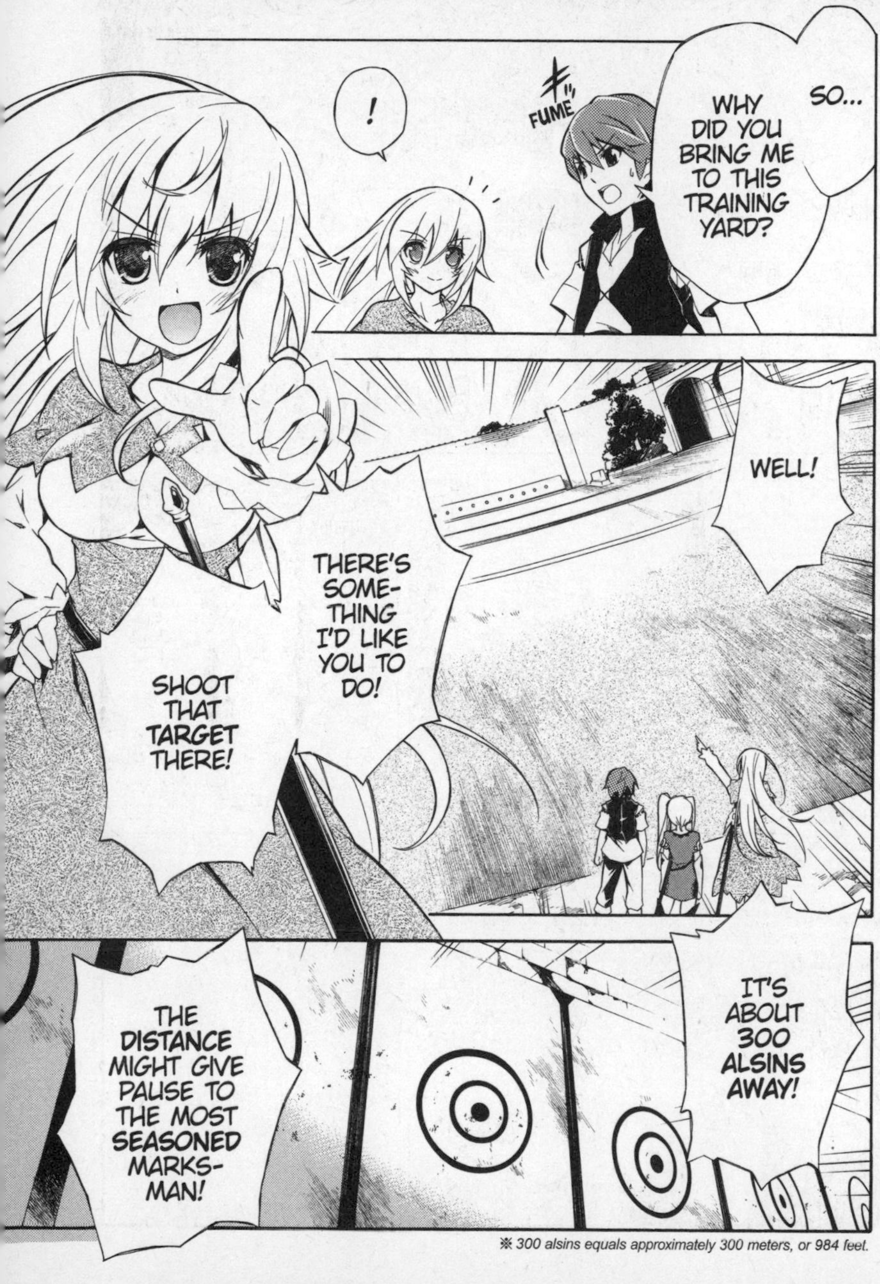
SO...
WHY DID YOU BRING ME TO THIS TRAINING YARD?
FUME
!
WELL!
THERE'S SOME-THING I'D LIKE YOU TO DO!
SHOOT THAT TARGET THERE!
IT'S ABOUT 300 ALSINS AWAY!
THE DISTANCE MIGHT GIVE PAUSE TO THE MOST SEASONED MARKS-MAN!

※ *300 alsins equals approximately 300 meters, or 984 feet.*

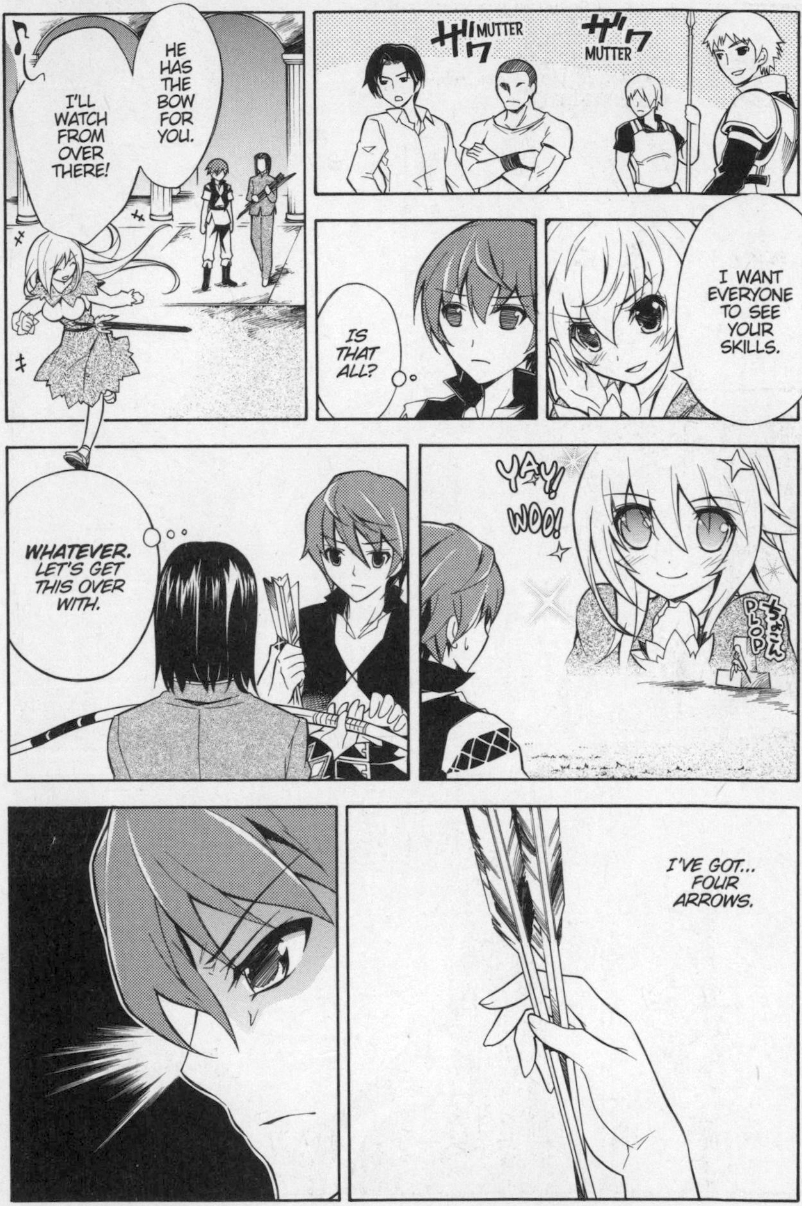
ザワ MUTTER
ザワ MUTTER
I WANT EVERYONE TO SEE YOUR SKILLS.
IS THAT ALL?
HE HAS THE BOW FOR YOU.
I'LL WATCH FROM OVER THERE!
YAY! WOO!
ちょこん PLOP
WHATEVER. LET'S GET THIS OVER WITH.
I'VE GOT... FOUR ARROWS.

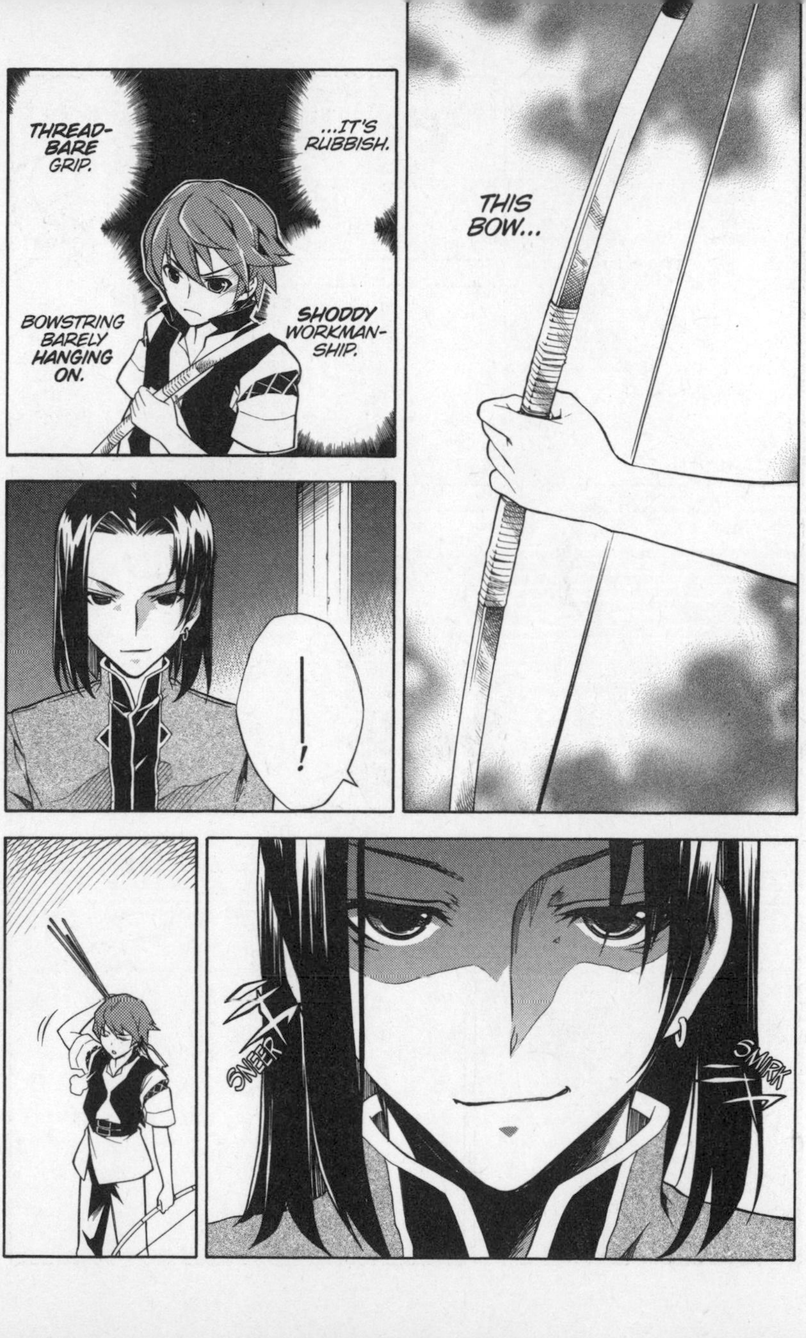
THIS BOW...
...IT'S RUBBISH.
THREAD-BARE GRIP.
SHODDY WORKMAN-SHIP.
BOWSTRING BARELY HANGING ON.
—!
SMIRK
SNEER

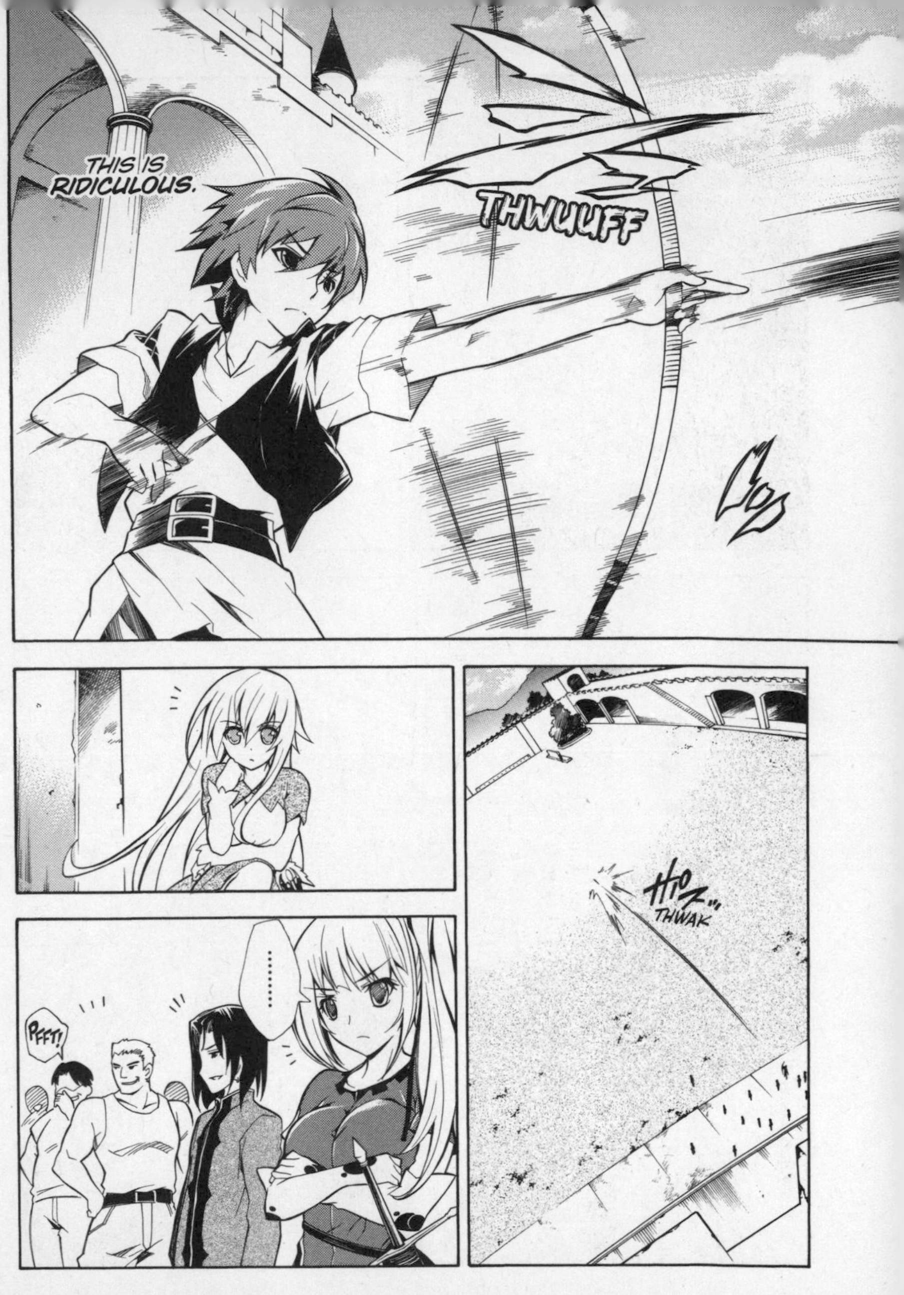
THIS IS RIDICULOUS.
THWUUFF
THWAK
......
PFFT!

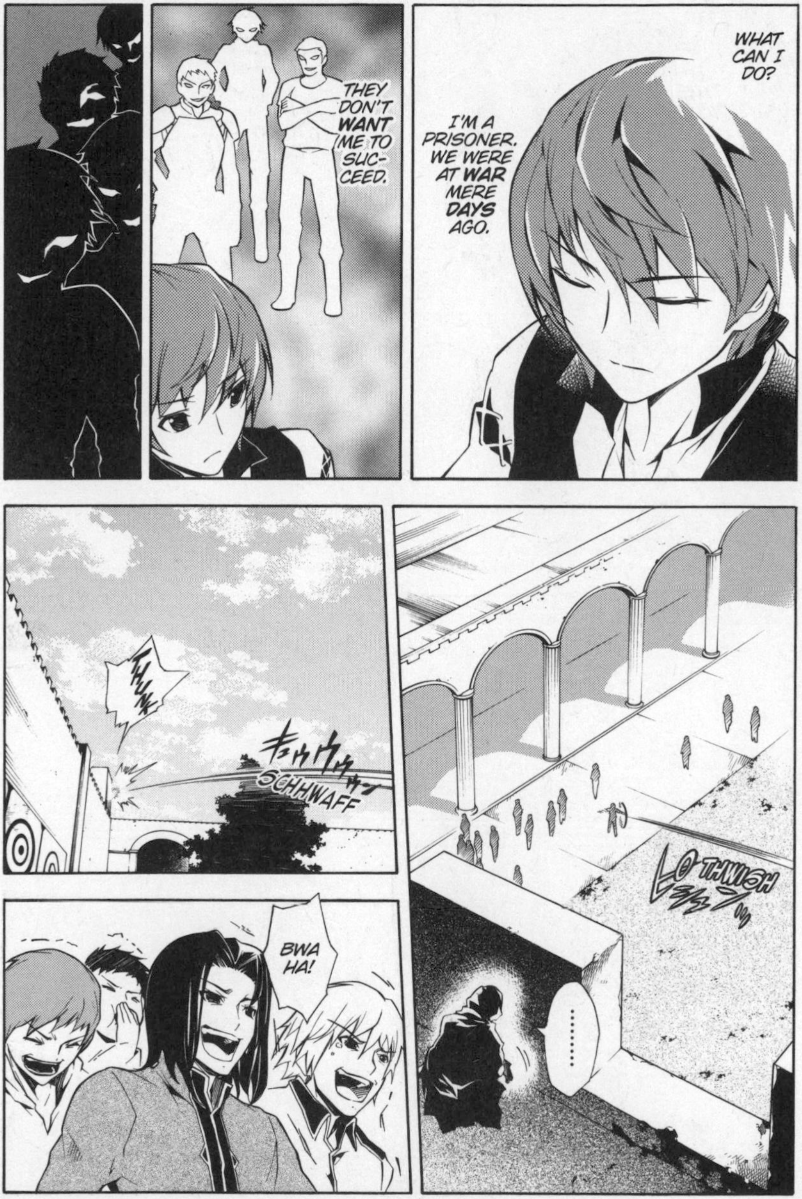
WHAT CAN I DO?
I'M A PRISONER. WE WERE AT WAR MERE DAYS AGO.
THEY DON'T WANT ME TO SUC-CEED.
THWISH
......
THUNK
SCHHWAFF
BWA HA!

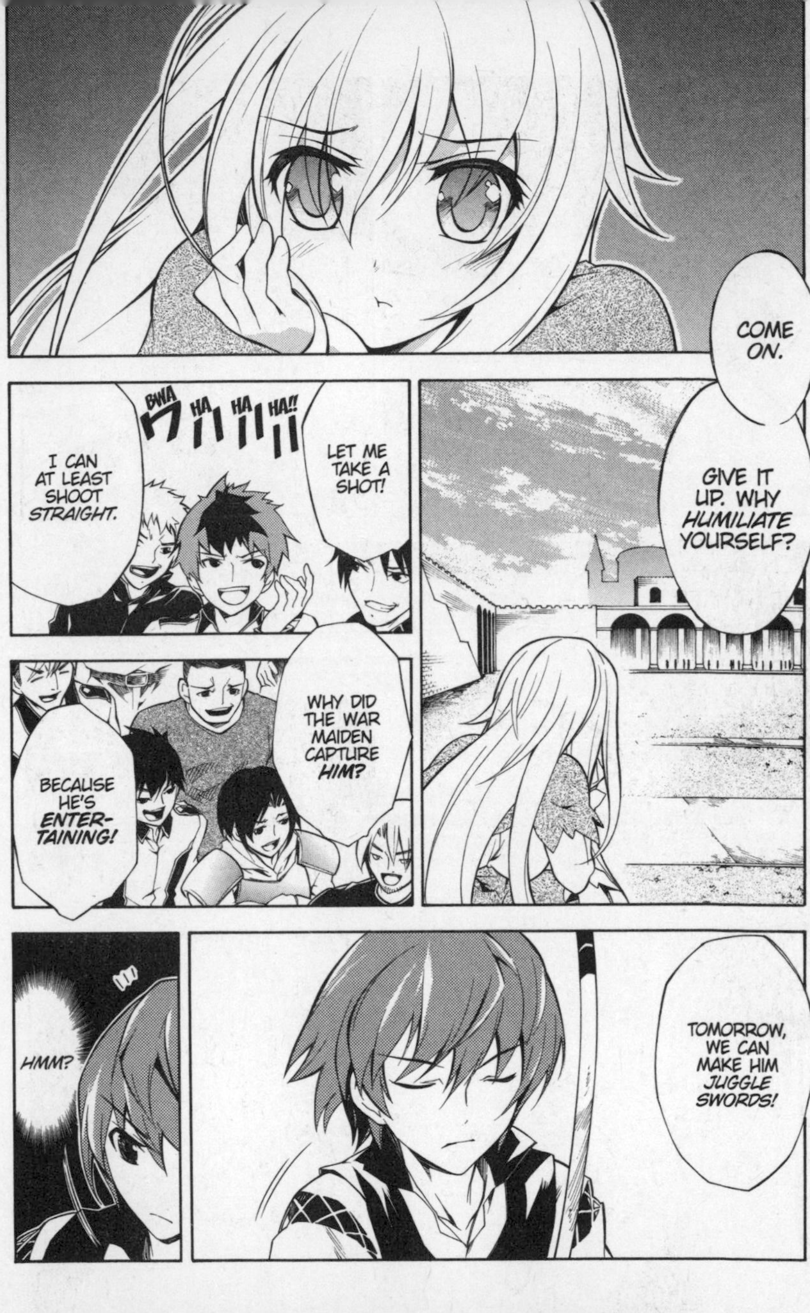
COME ON.
GIVE IT UP. WHY *HUMILIATE* YOURSELF?
LET ME TAKE A SHOT!
BWA HA HA HA!!
I CAN AT LEAST SHOOT *STRAIGHT.*
WHY DID THE WAR MAIDEN CAPTURE *HIM?*
BECAUSE HE'S *ENTERTAINING!*
TOMORROW, WE CAN MAKE HIM *JUGGLE SWORDS!*
HMM?

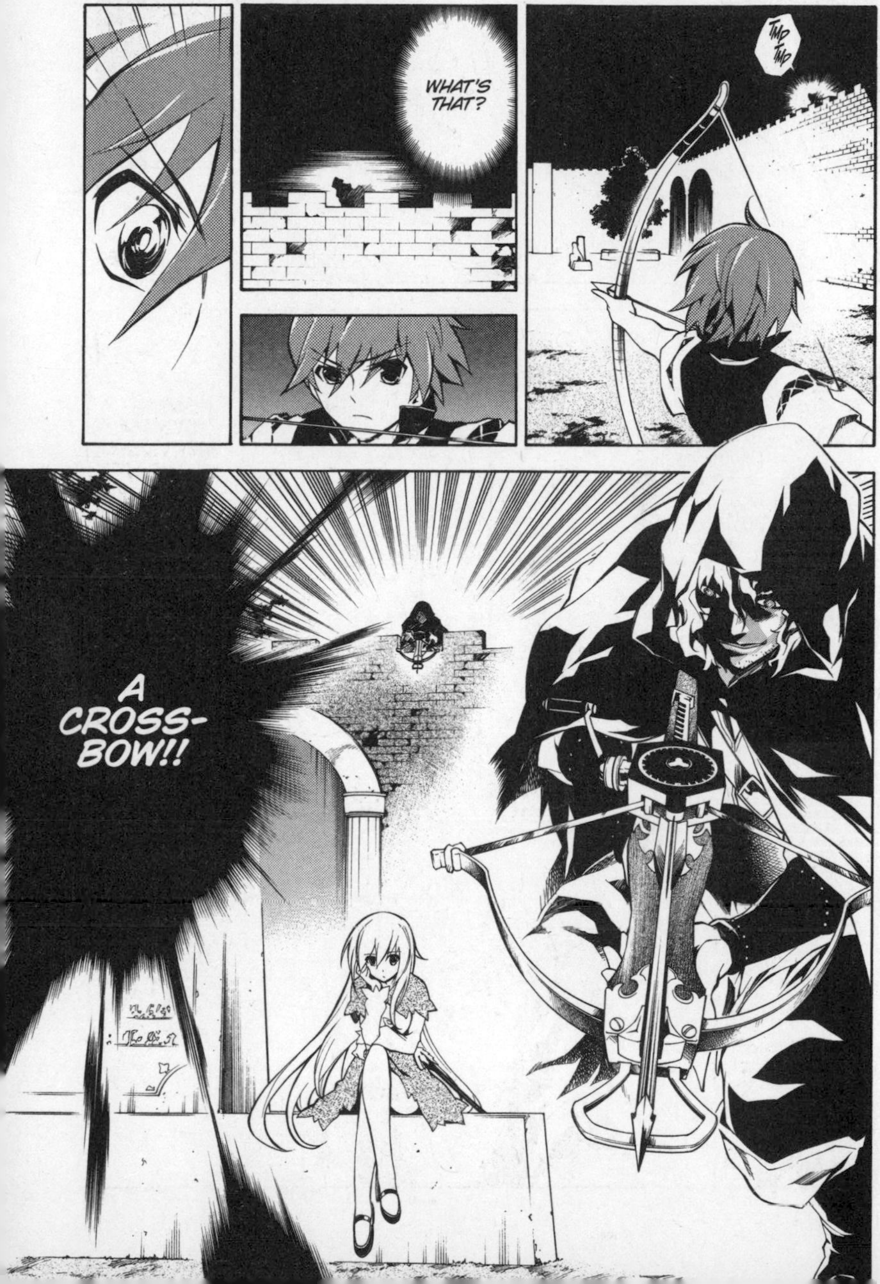
TMP TMP
WHAT'S THAT?
A CROSS-BOW!!

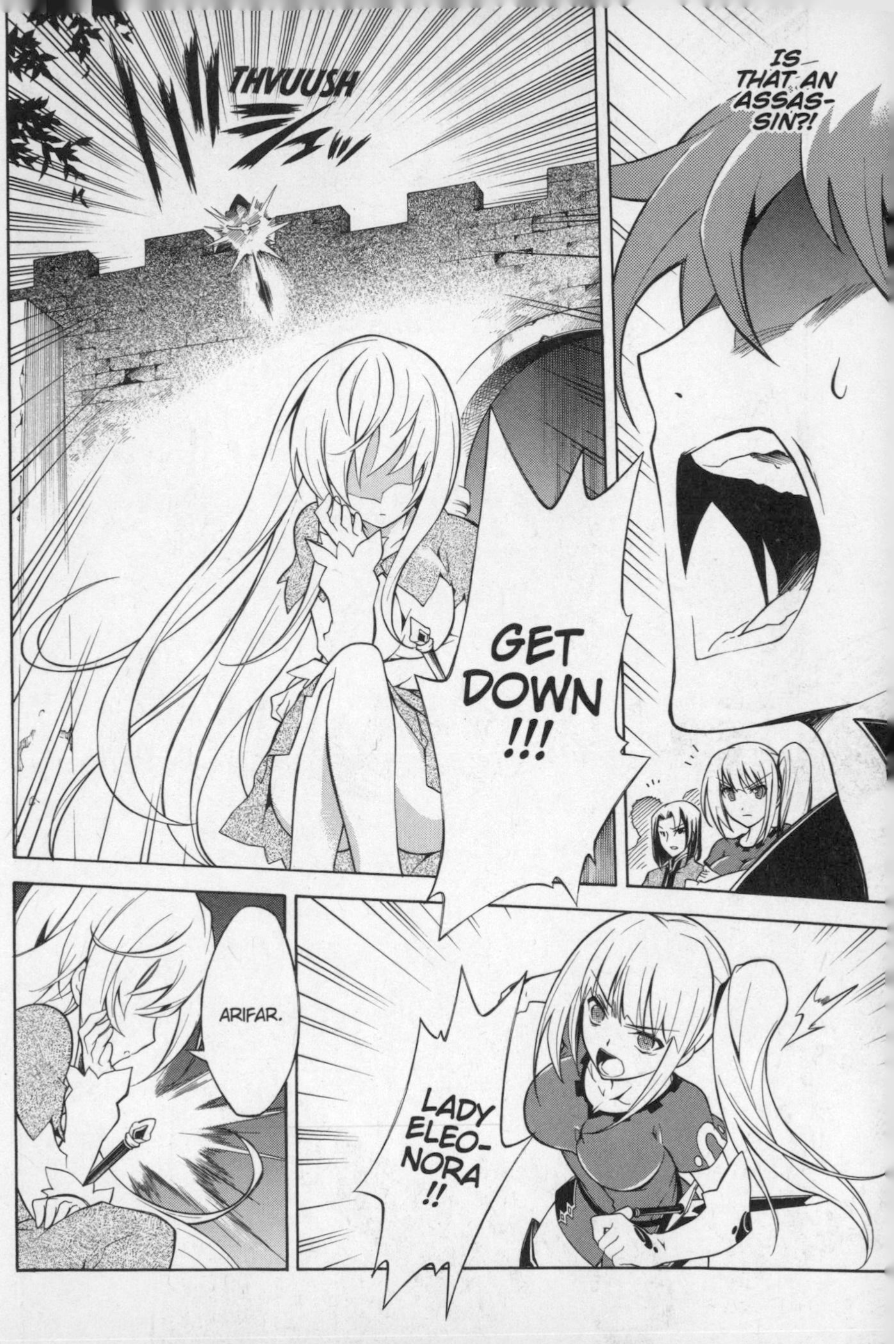
IS THAT AN ASSAS-SIN?!
GET DOWN !!!
THVUUSH
LADY ELEO-NORA !!
ARIFAR.

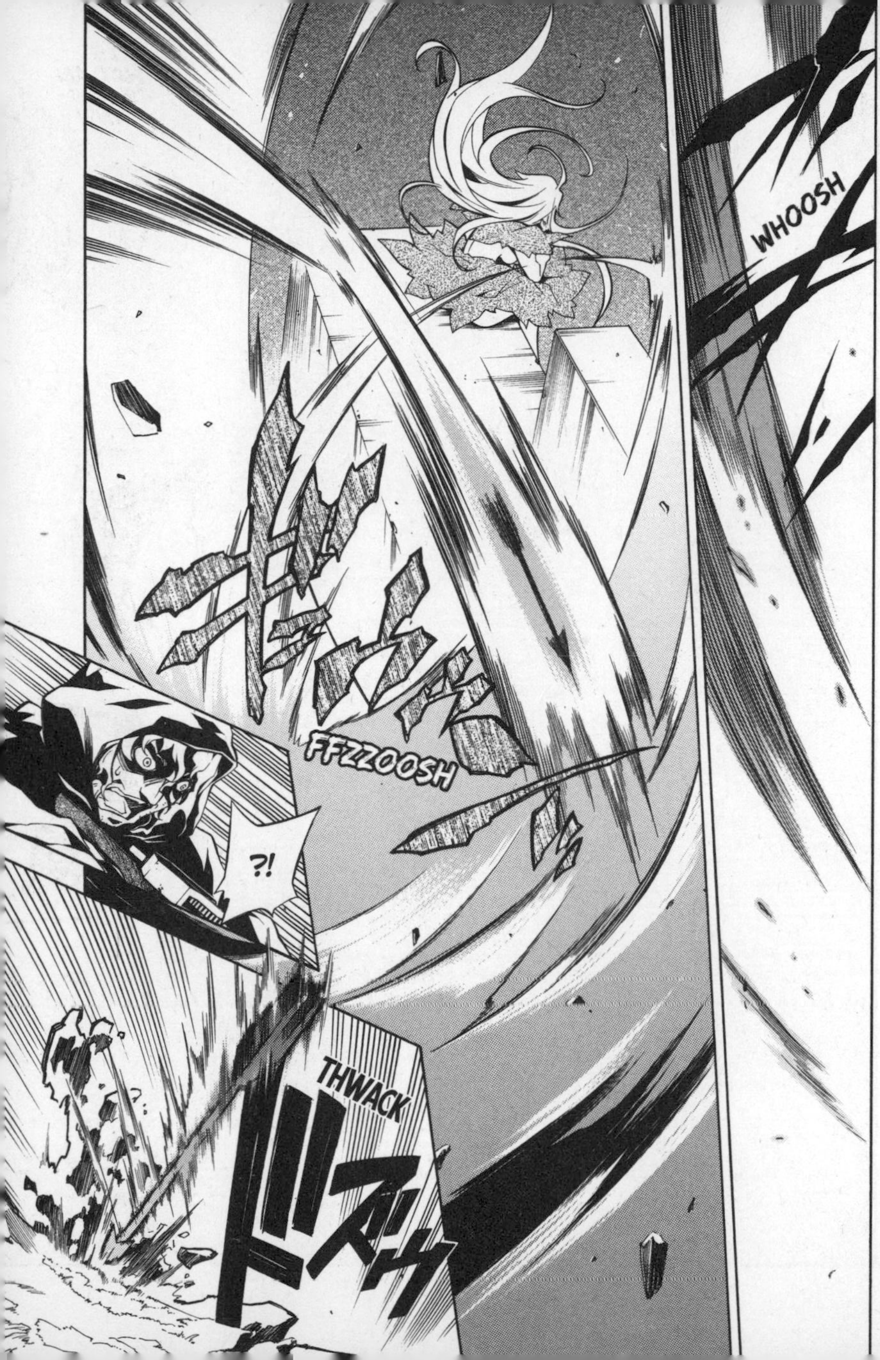
WHOOSH
FFZZOOSH
?!
THWACK

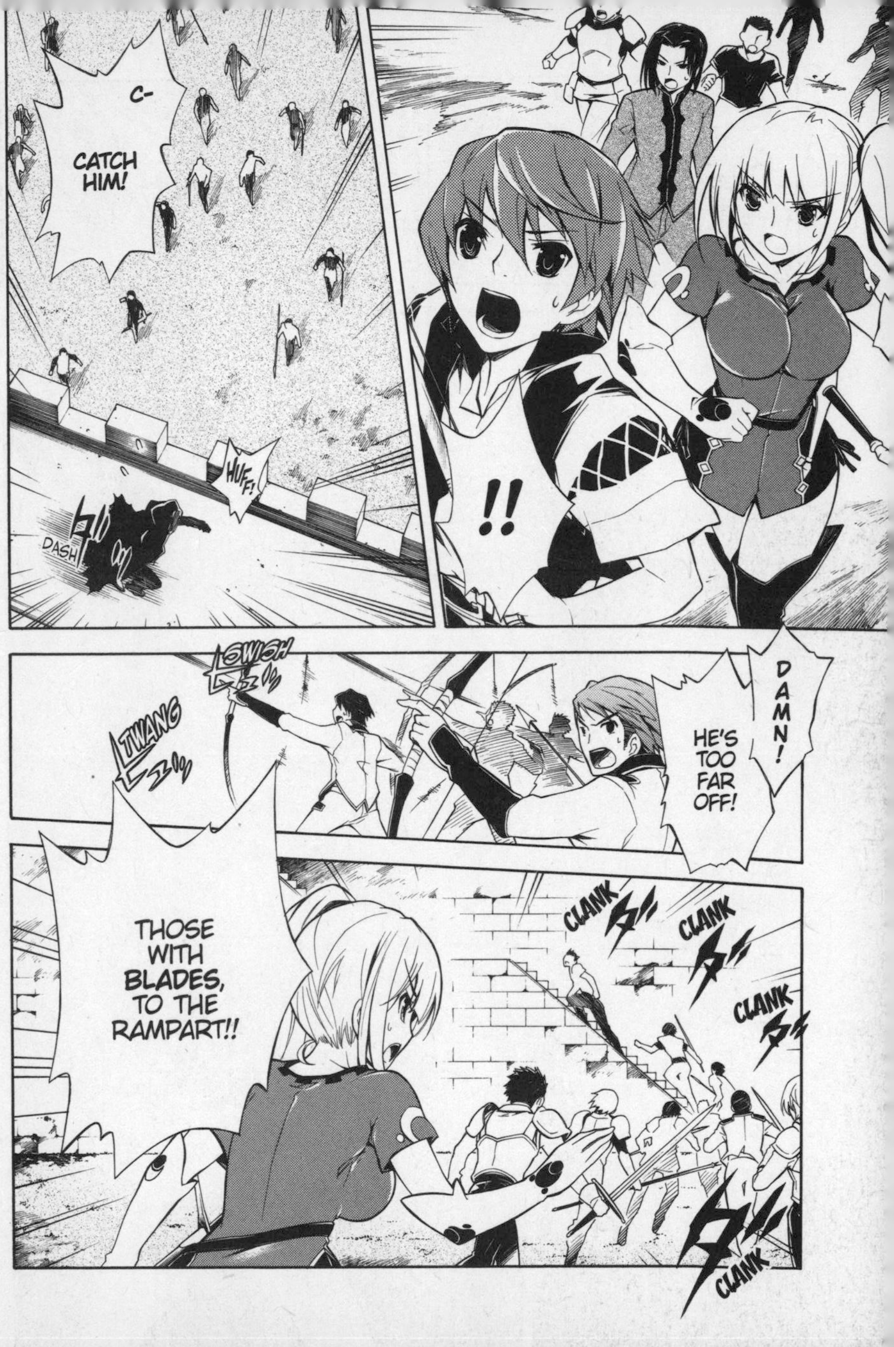
!!
C-
CATCH HIM!
HUFF!
DASH
DAMN!
HE'S TOO FAR OFF!
SWISH
TWANG
CLANK
CLANK
CLANK
THOSE WITH BLADES, TO THE RAMPART!!
CLANK

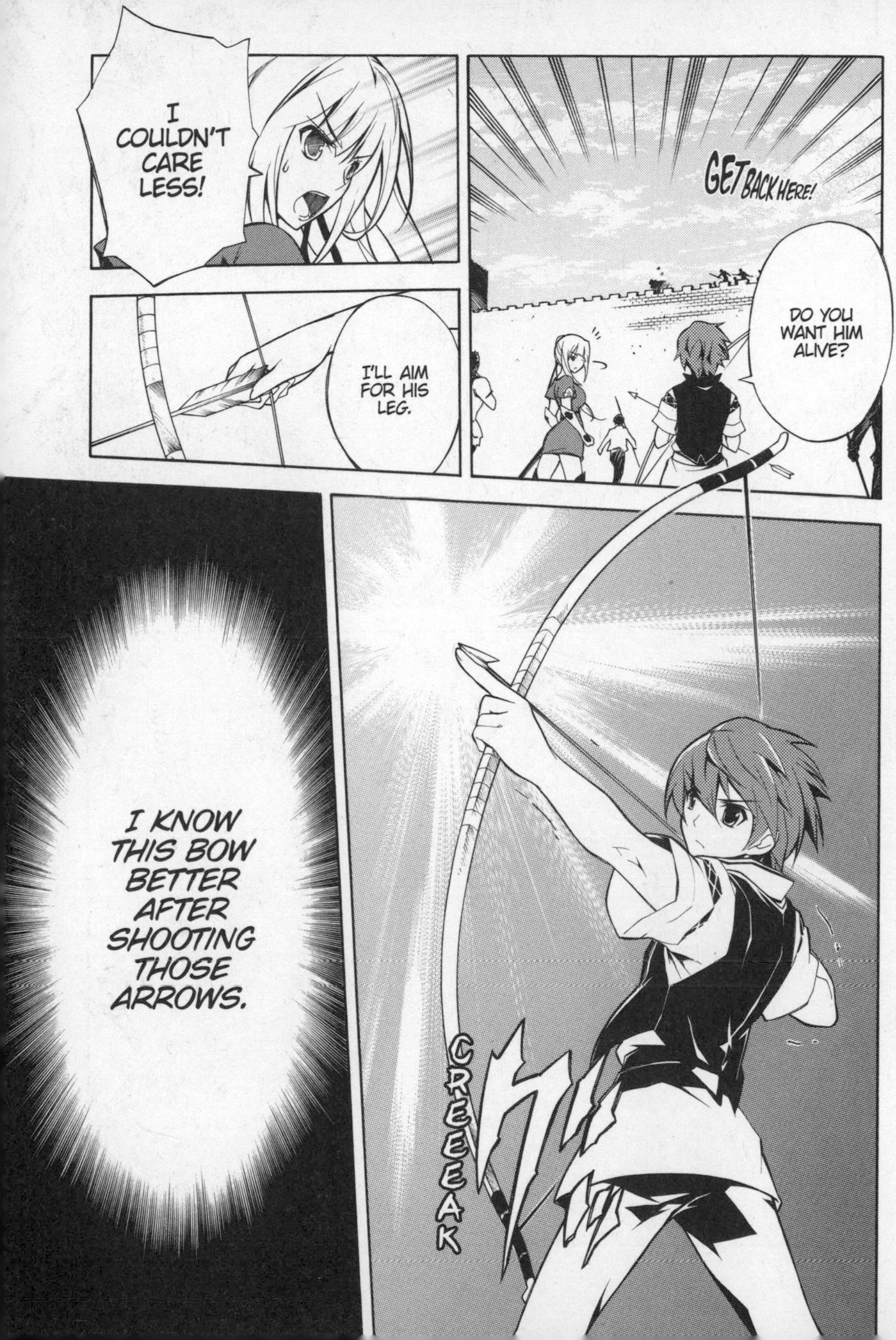
GET BACK HERE!
DO YOU WANT HIM ALIVE?
I COULDN'T CARE LESS!
I'LL AIM FOR HIS LEG.
CREEEAK
I KNOW THIS BOW BETTER AFTER SHOOTING THOSE ARROWS.

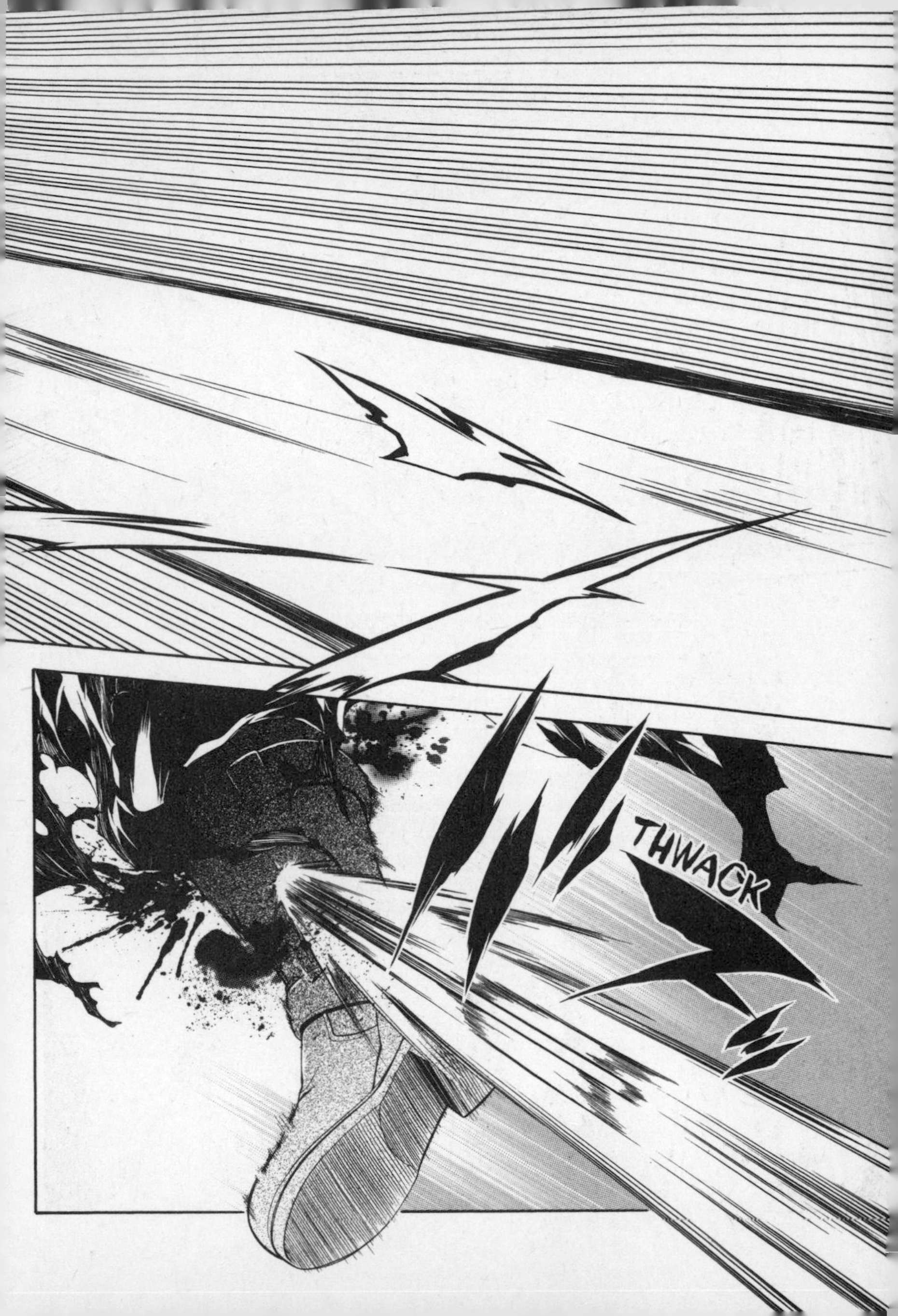
THWACK

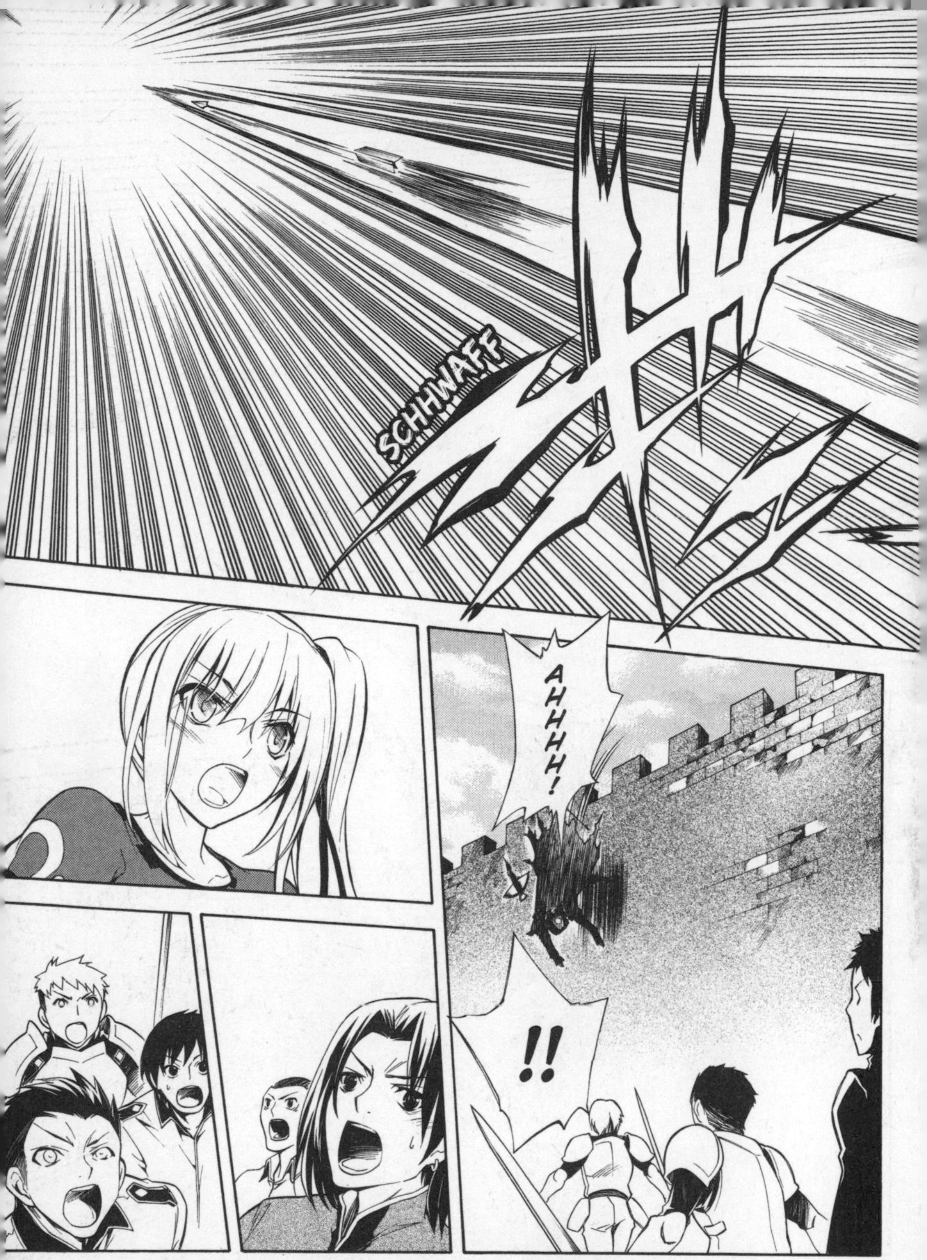
SCHWAFF
AHHHHH!
!!

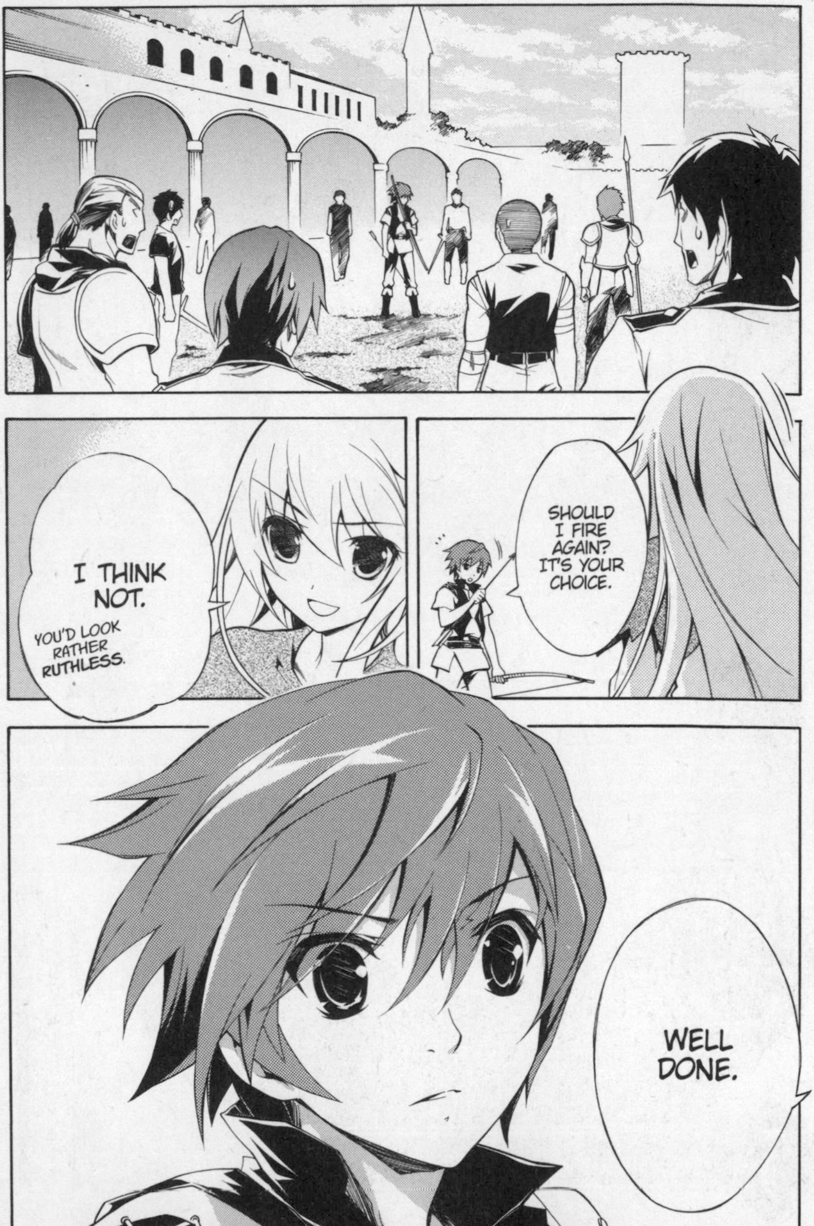
SHOULD I FIRE AGAIN? IT'S YOUR CHOICE.
I THINK NOT.
YOU'D LOOK RATHER RUTHLESS.
WELL DONE.
CHAPTER 2: END

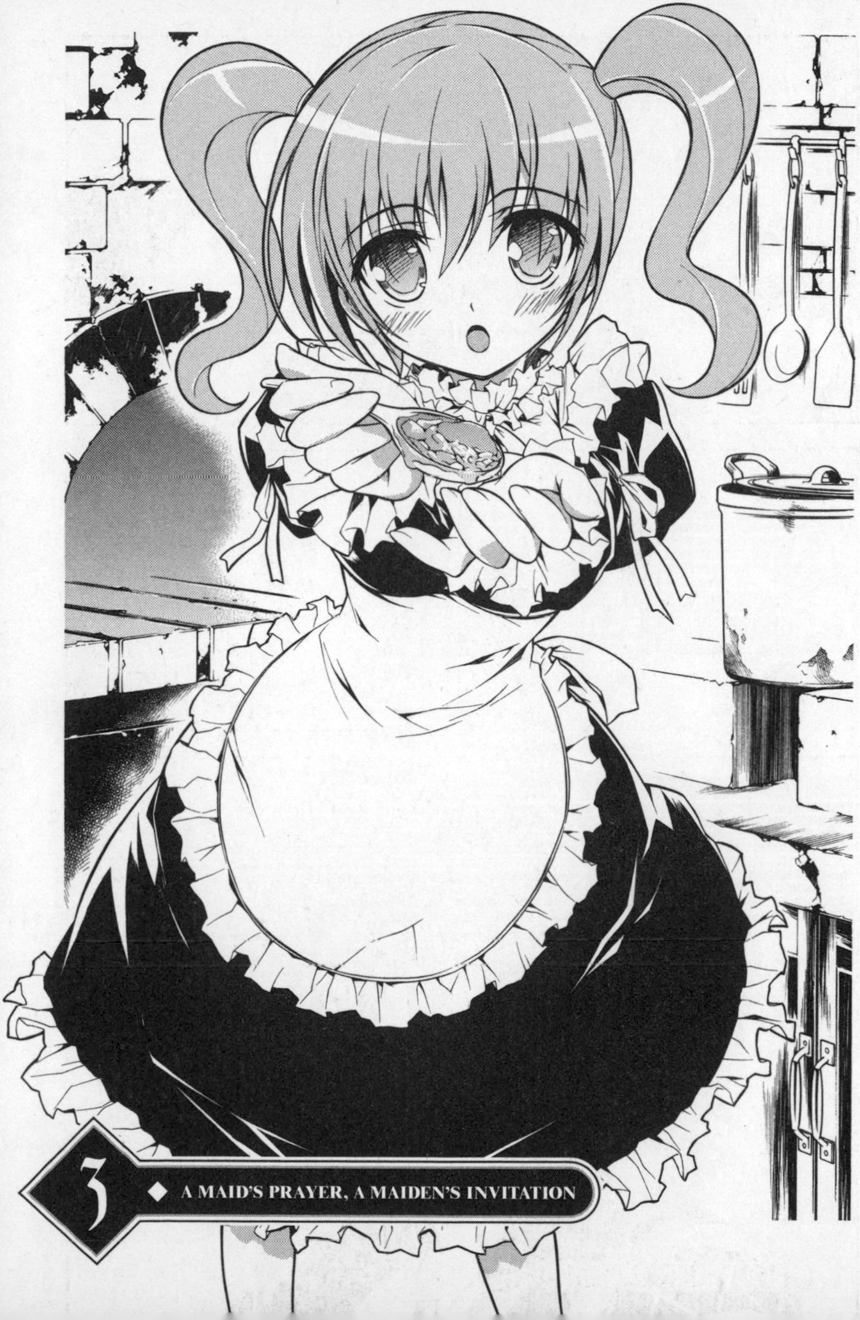

3
A MAID'S PRAYER, A MAIDEN'S INVITATION

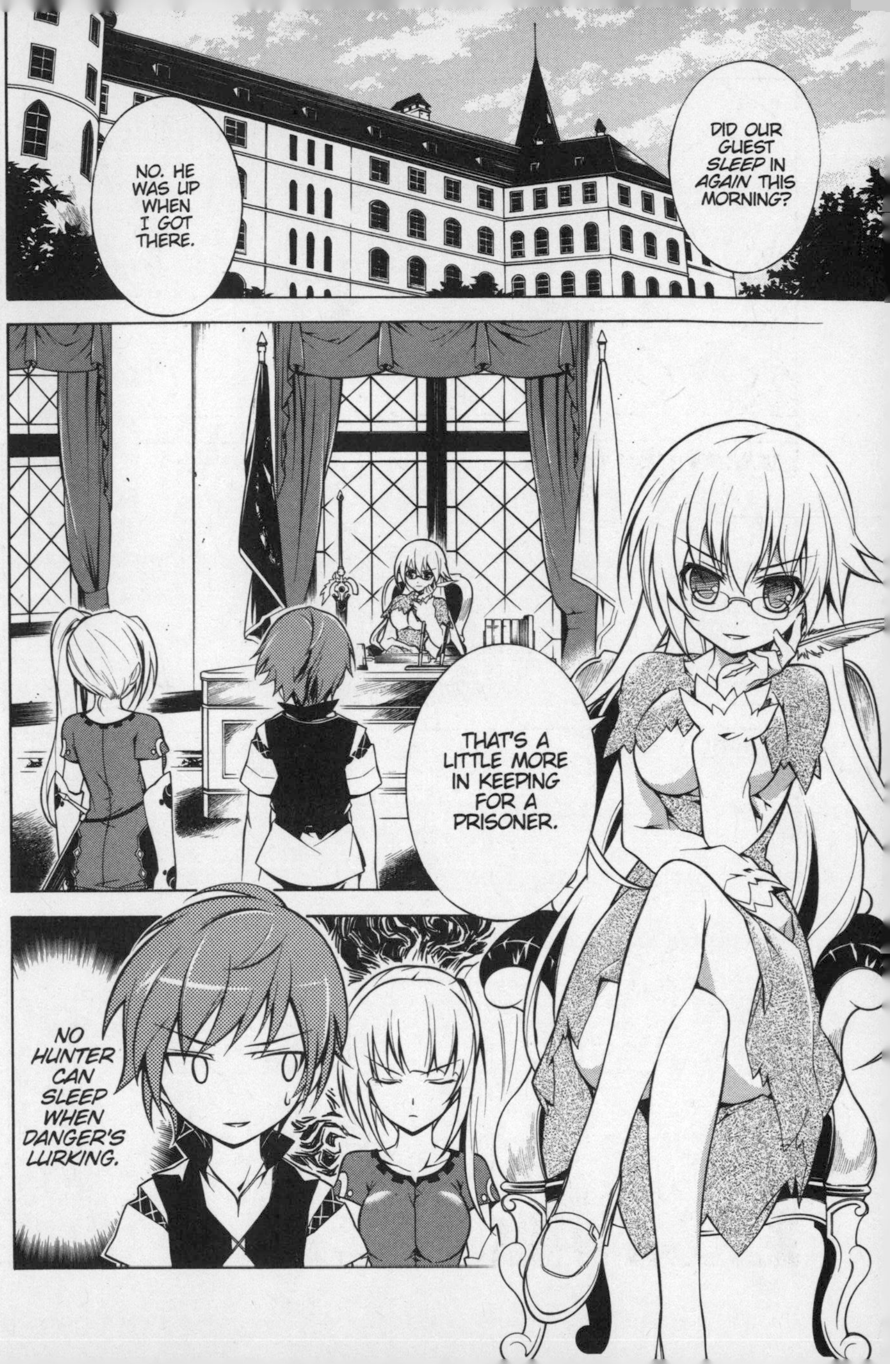
DID OUR GUEST SLEEP IN AGAIN THIS MORNING?
NO. HE WAS UP WHEN I GOT THERE.
THAT'S A LITTLE MORE IN KEEPING FOR A PRISONER.
NO HUNTER CAN SLEEP WHEN DANGER'S LURKING.

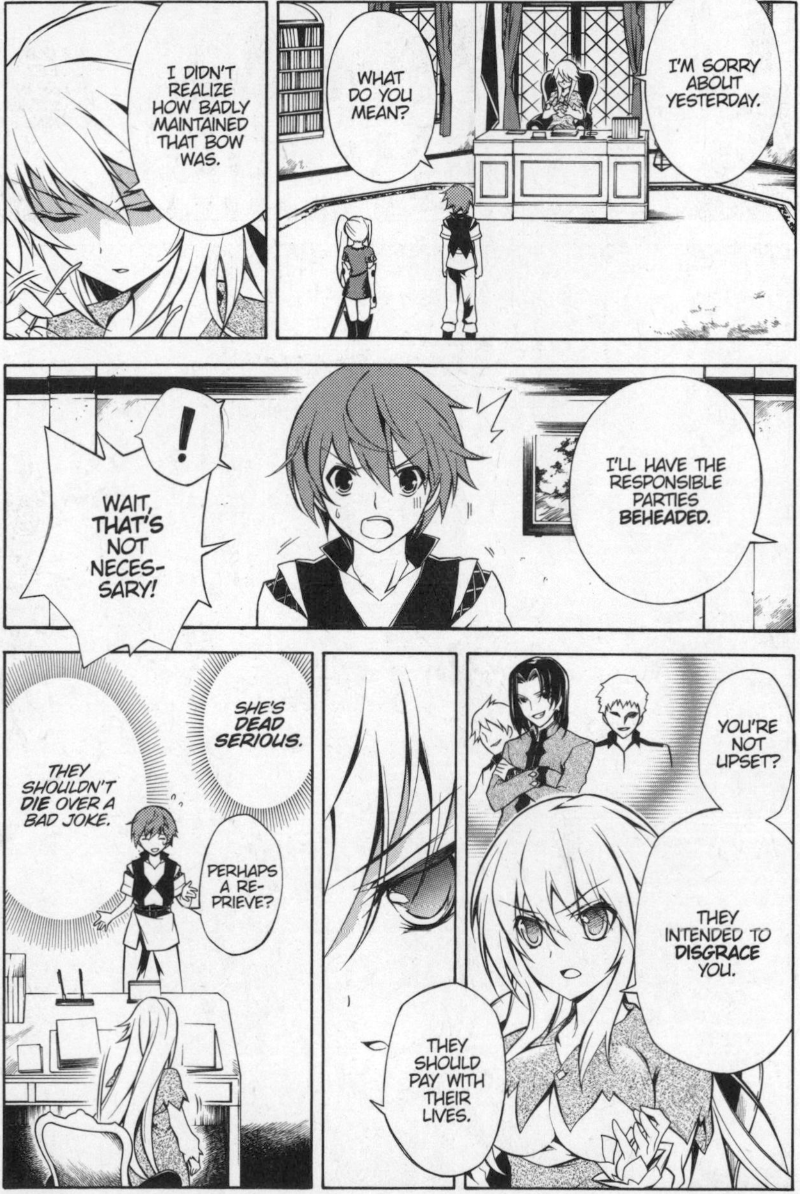
I'M SORRY ABOUT YESTERDAY.
WHAT DO YOU MEAN?
I DIDN'T REALIZE HOW BADLY MAINTAINED THAT BOW WAS.
I'LL HAVE THE RESPONSIBLE PARTIES BEHEADED.
!
WAIT, THAT'S NOT NECESSARY!
YOU'RE NOT UPSET?
THEY INTENDED TO DISGRACE YOU.
THEY SHOULD PAY WITH THEIR LIVES.
SHE'S DEAD SERIOUS.
PERHAPS A REPRIEVE?
THEY SHOULDN'T DIE OVER A BAD JOKE.

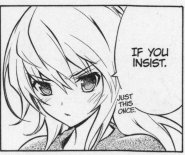

IF YOU INSIST.
JUST THIS ONCE.
ON THAT NOTE...
WHY TEST MY MARKS-MANSHIP AT ALL?
YOUR PRESENCE HERE HAS RAISED EYEBROWS.
LADY ELEONORA HAS NEVER BROUGHT HOME A CAPTIVE BEFORE.
IS THAT TRUE?
A FOOLISH RUMOR HAS CROPPED UP AMONGST THE SOLDIERS.
THEY SAY I FELL IN LOVE WITH YOU AT FIRST SIGHT.
IN LOVE?!

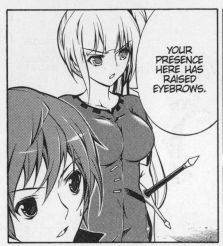

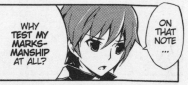

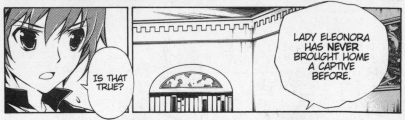

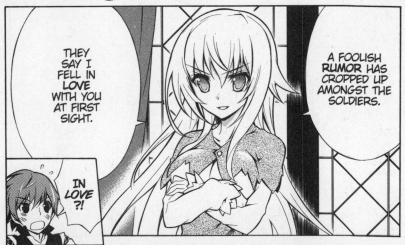

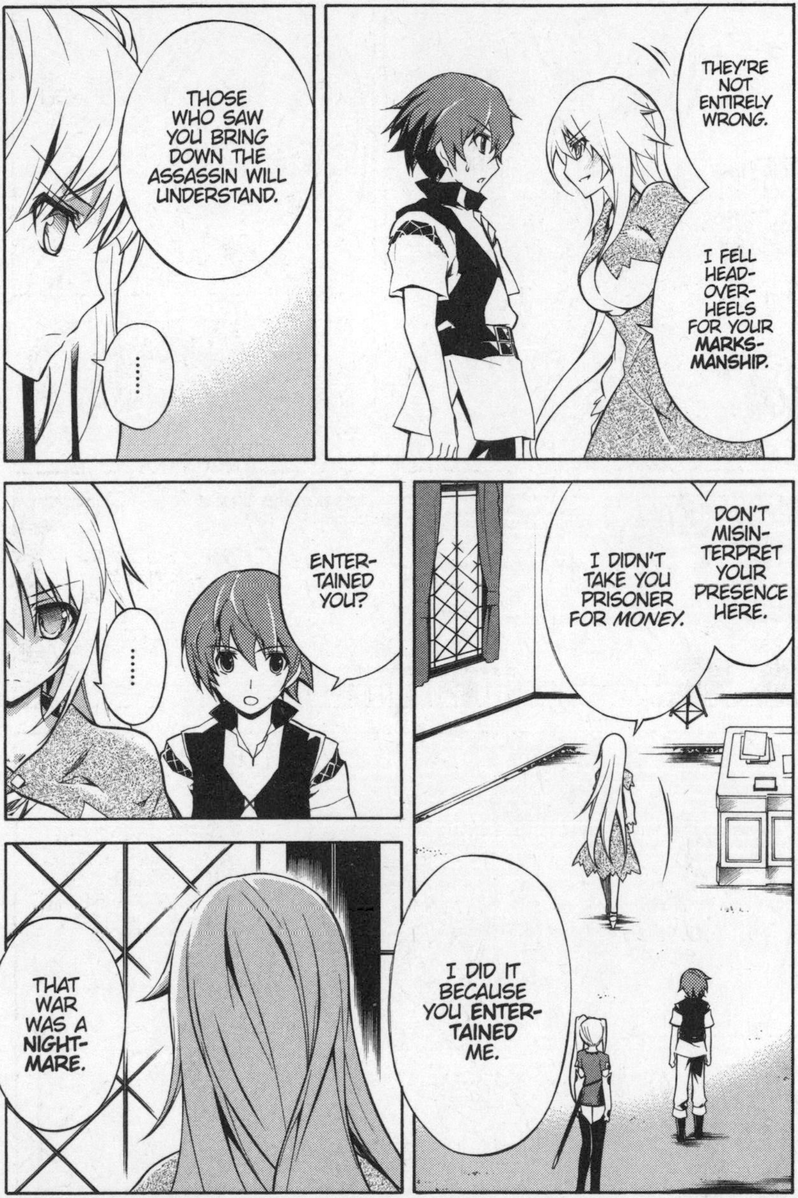

THEY'RE NOT ENTIRELY WRONG.
I FELL HEAD-OVER-HEELS FOR YOUR MARKSMANSHIP.
THOSE WHO SAW YOU BRING DOWN THE ASSASSIN WILL UNDERSTAND.
......
DON'T MISINTERPRET YOUR PRESENCE HERE.
I DIDN'T TAKE YOU PRISONER FOR *MONEY*.
I DID IT BECAUSE YOU ENTERTAINED ME.
ENTERTAINED YOU?
......
THAT WAR WAS A NIGHTMARE.

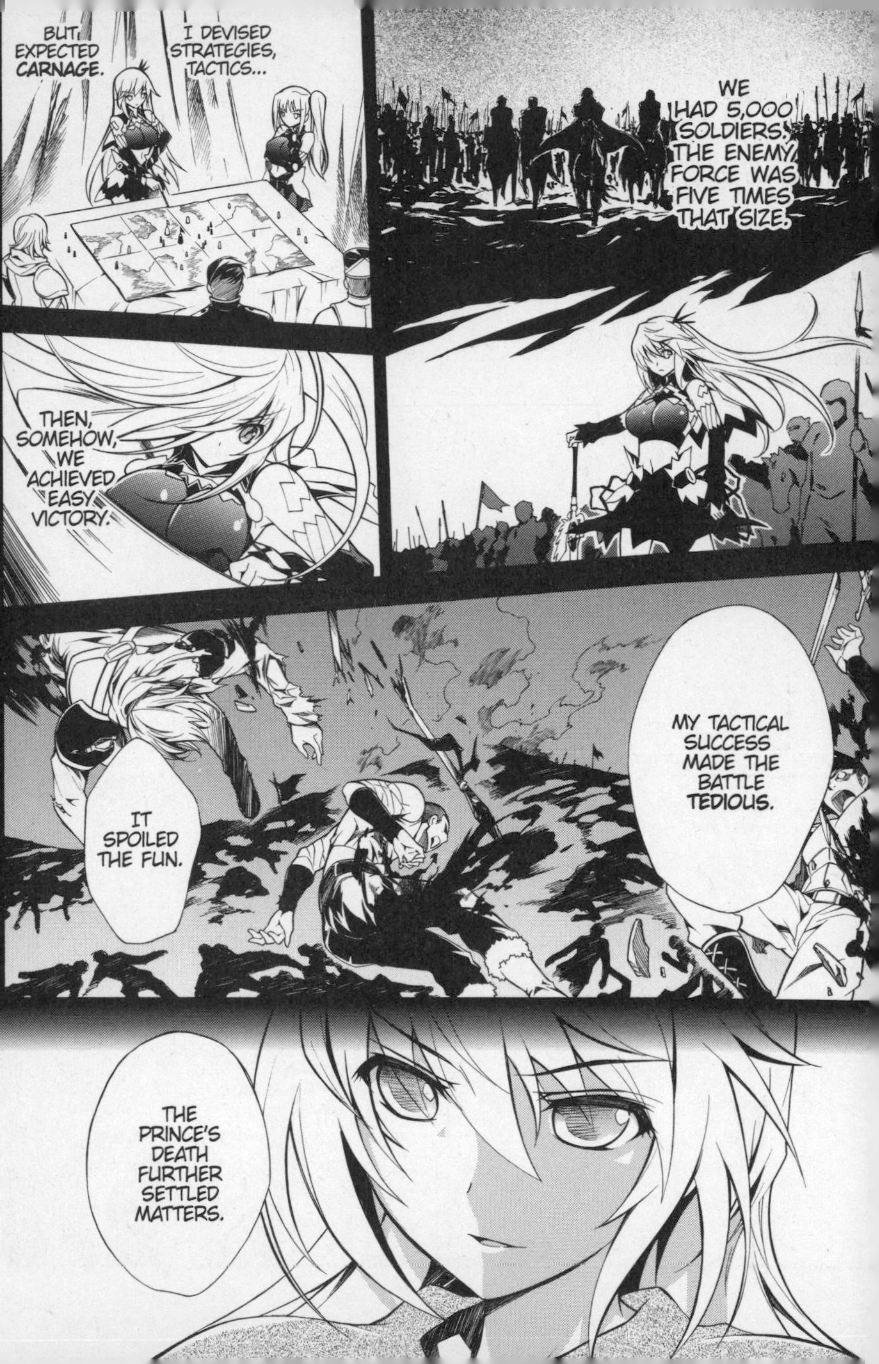
WE HAD 5,000 SOLDIERS. THE ENEMY FORCE WAS FIVE TIMES THAT SIZE.
I DEVISED STRATEGIES, TACTICS...
BUT EXPECTED CARNAGE.
THEN, SOMEHOW, WE ACHIEVED EASY VICTORY.
MY TACTICAL SUCCESS MADE THE BATTLE TEDIOUS.
IT SPOILED THE FUN.
THE PRINCE'S DEATH FURTHER SETTLED MATTERS.

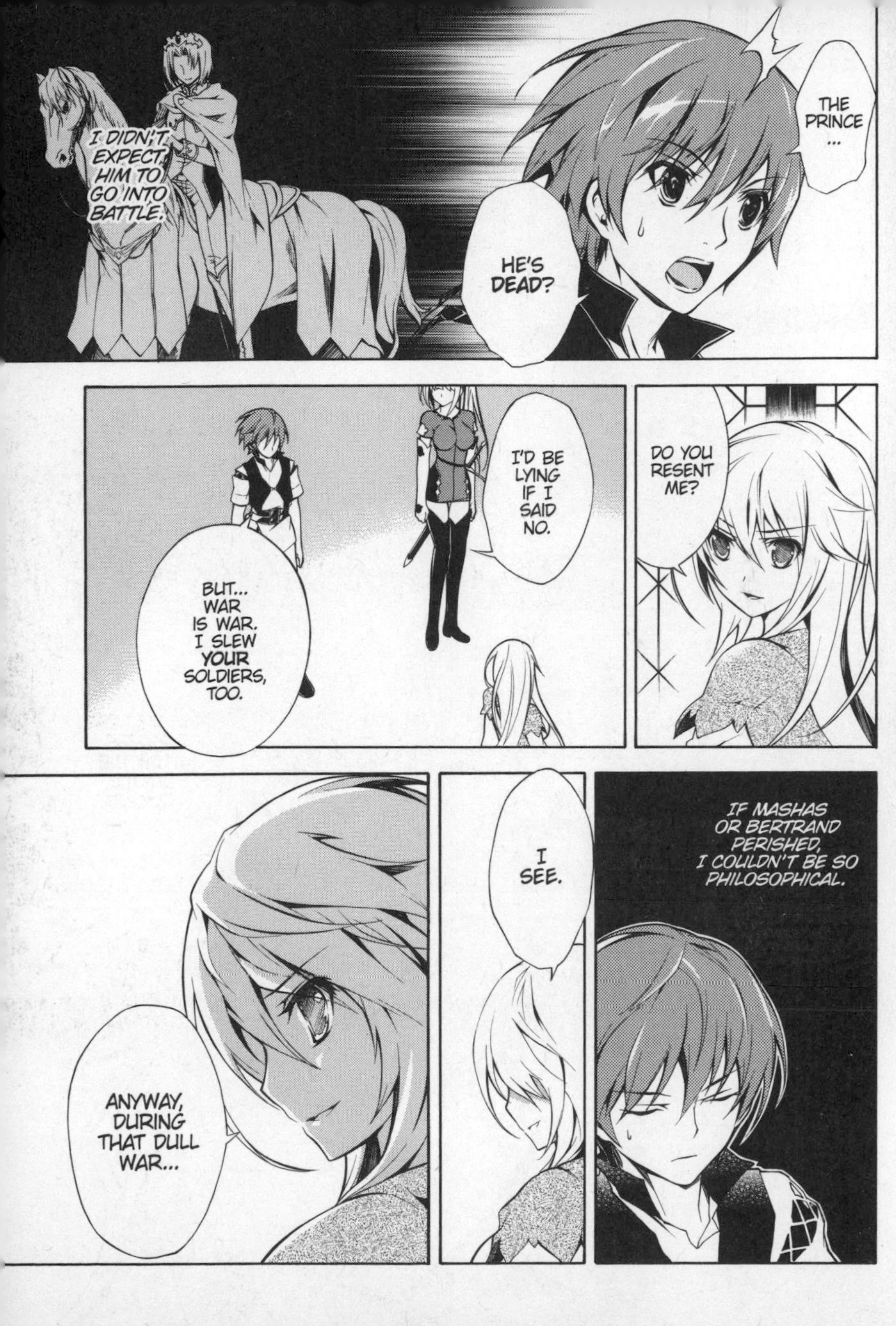
THE PRINCE...
HE'S DEAD?
I DIDN'T EXPECT HIM TO GO INTO BATTLE.
DO YOU RESENT ME?
I'D BE LYING IF I SAID NO.
BUT... WAR IS WAR. I SLEW YOUR SOLDIERS, TOO.
IF MASHAS OR BERTRAND PERISHED, I COULDN'T BE SO PHILOSOPHICAL.
I SEE.
ANYWAY, DURING THAT DULL WAR...

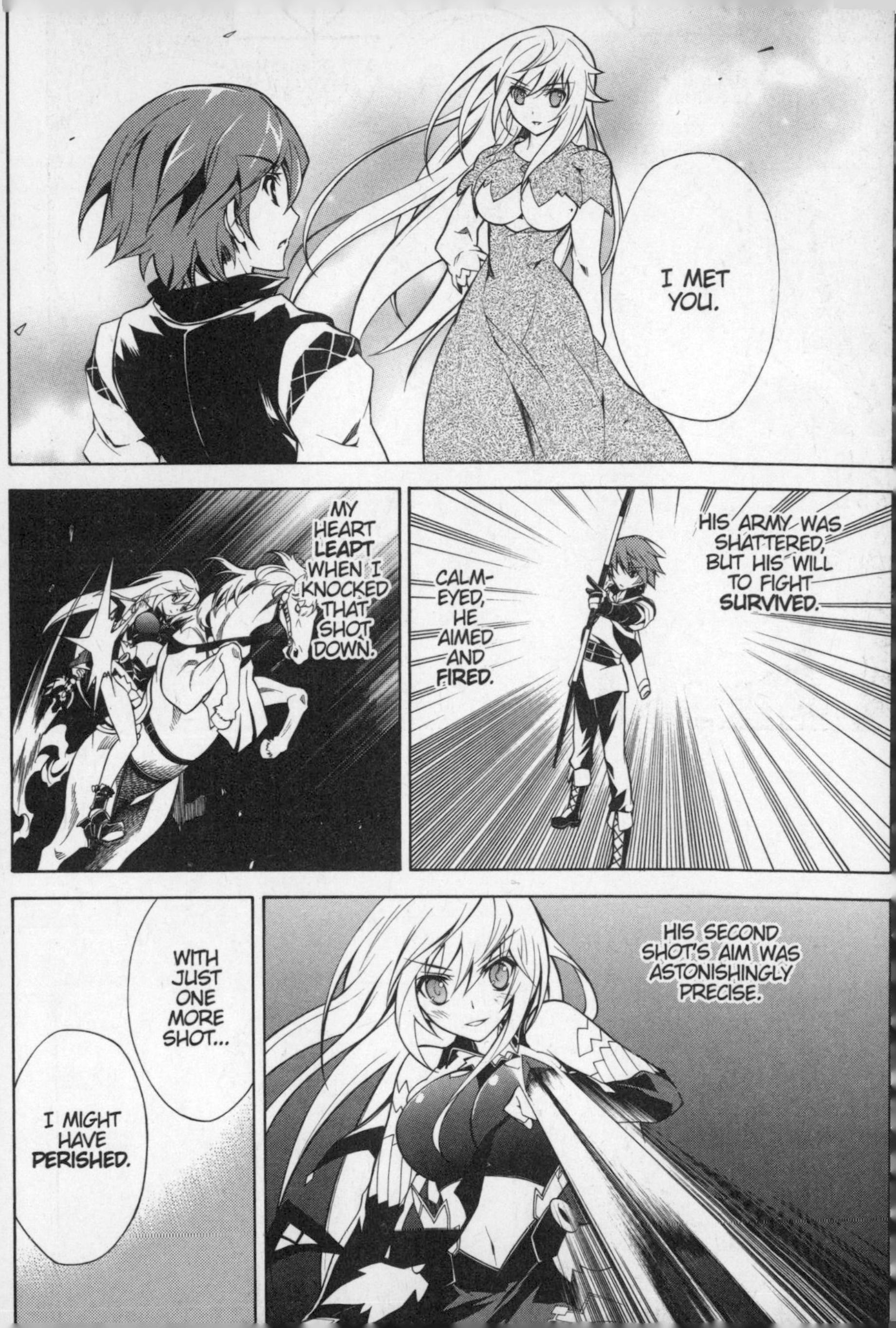
I MET YOU.
HIS ARMY WAS SHATTERED, BUT HIS WILL TO FIGHT SURVIVED.
CALM-EYED, HE AIMED AND FIRED.
MY HEART LEAPT WHEN I KNOCKED THAT SHOT DOWN.
HIS SECOND SHOT'S AIM WAS ASTONISHINGLY PRECISE.
WITH JUST ONE MORE SHOT...
I MIGHT HAVE PERISHED.

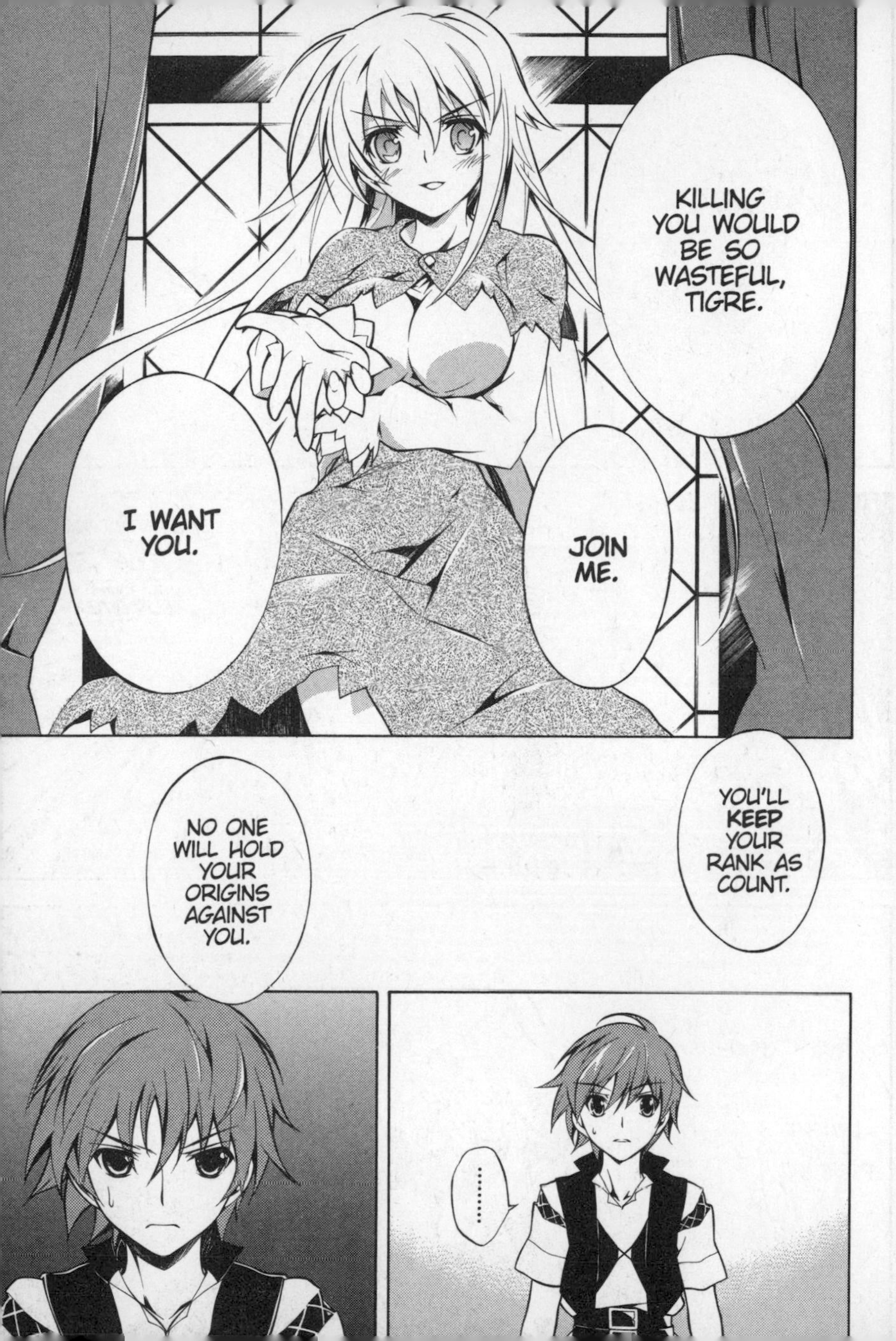
KILLING YOU WOULD BE SO WASTEFUL, TIGRE.
JOIN ME.
I WANT YOU.
YOU'LL KEEP YOUR RANK AS COUNT.
NO ONE WILL HOLD YOUR ORIGINS AGAINST YOU.
......

THANK YOU. NO.

THEN WHY REFUSE?

I DON'T EXPECT IT REPEATED.

IT'S A GRACIOUS OFFER.

IN ZHCTED...

ELEN WOULD ACKNOWLEDGE MY MARKSMANSHIP. STILL...

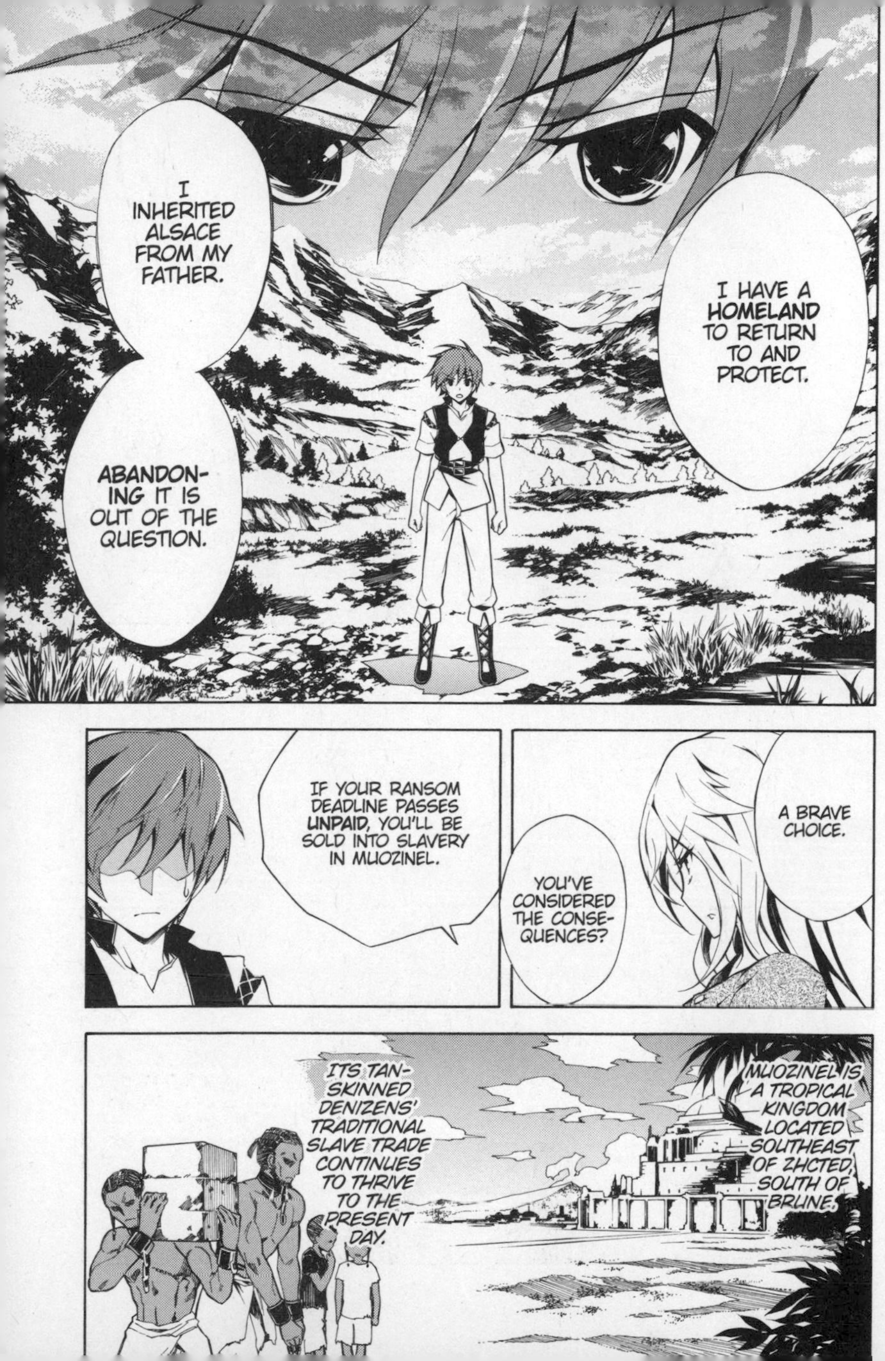
I HAVE A HOMELAND TO RETURN TO AND PROTECT.
I INHERITED ALSACE FROM MY FATHER.
ABANDONING IT IS OUT OF THE QUESTION.
A BRAVE CHOICE.
YOU'VE CONSIDERED THE CONSEQUENCES?
IF YOUR RANSOM DEADLINE PASSES UNPAID, YOU'LL BE SOLD INTO SLAVERY IN MUOZINEL.
MUOZINEL IS A TROPICAL KINGDOM LOCATED SOUTHEAST OF ZHCTED, SOUTH OF BRUNE.
ITS TAN-SKINNED DENIZENS' TRADITIONAL SLAVE TRADE CONTINUES TO THRIVE TO THE PRESENT DAY.

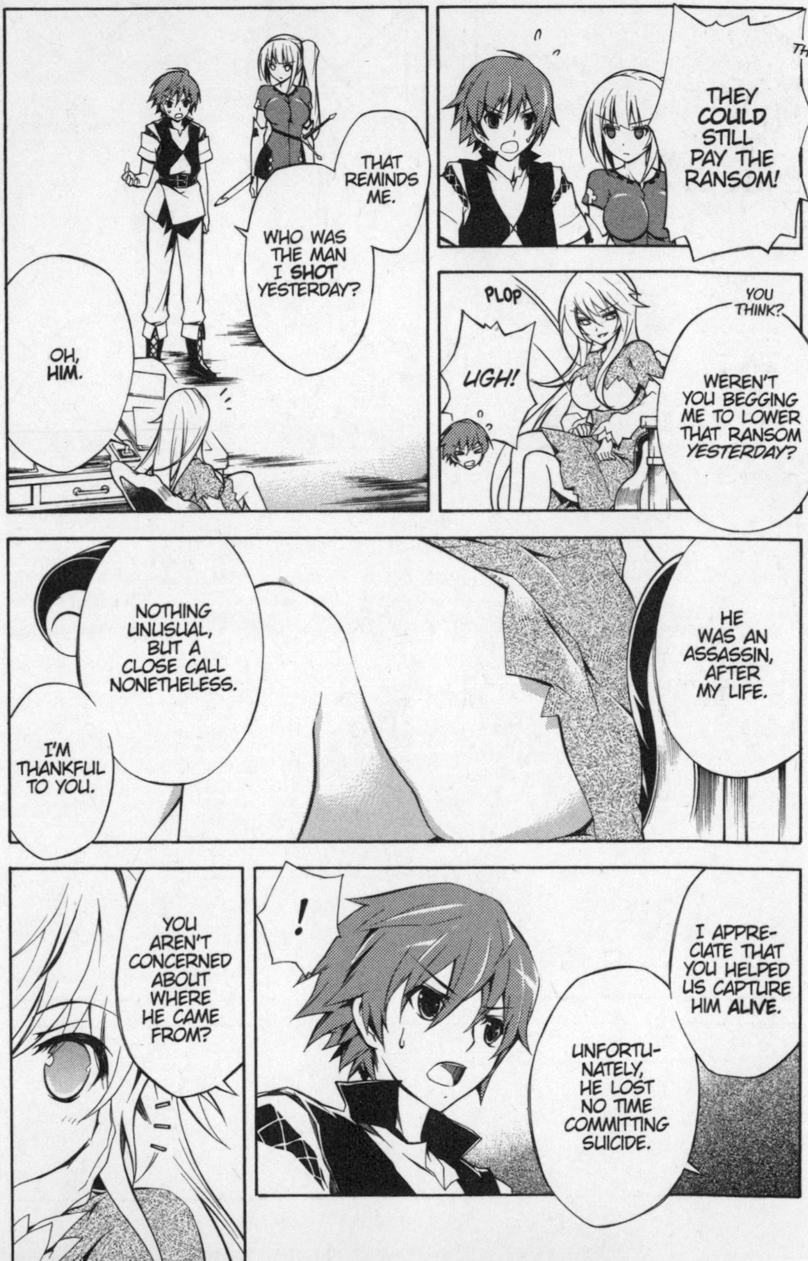
TH-
THEY COULD STILL PAY THE RANSOM!
YOU THINK?
WEREN'T YOU BEGGING ME TO LOWER THAT RANSOM YESTERDAY?
PLOP
UGH!
THAT REMINDS ME.
WHO WAS THE MAN I SHOT YESTERDAY?
OH, HIM.
HE WAS AN ASSASSIN, AFTER MY LIFE.
NOTHING UNUSUAL, BUT A CLOSE CALL NONETHELESS.
I'M THANKFUL TO YOU.
I APPRE-CIATE THAT YOU HELPED US CAPTURE HIM ALIVE.
UNFORTU-NATELY, HE LOST NO TIME COMMITTING SUICIDE.
!
YOU AREN'T CONCERNED ABOUT WHERE HE CAME FROM?

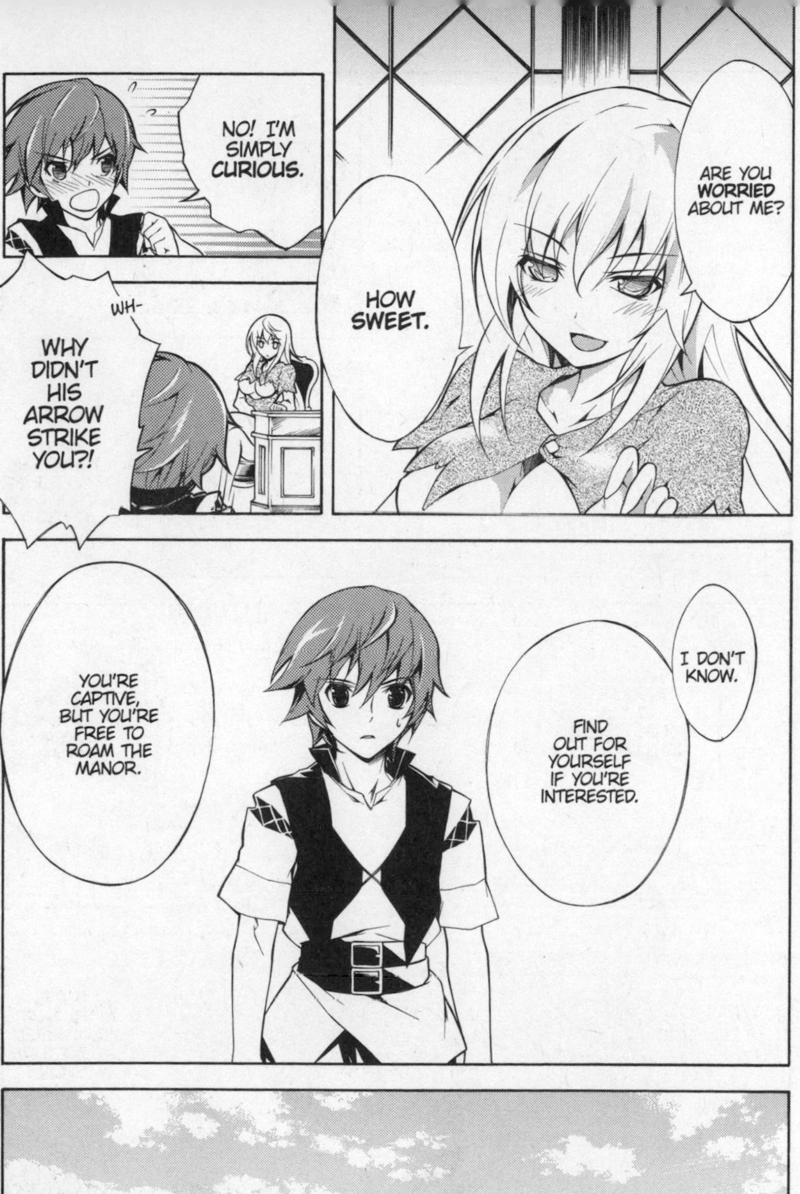
ARE YOU WORRIED ABOUT ME?
HOW SWEET.
NO! I'M SIMPLY CURIOUS.
WH-
WHY DIDN'T HIS ARROW STRIKE YOU?!
I DON'T KNOW.
FIND OUT FOR YOURSELF IF YOU'RE INTERESTED.
YOU'RE CAPTIVE, BUT YOU'RE FREE TO ROAM THE MANOR.

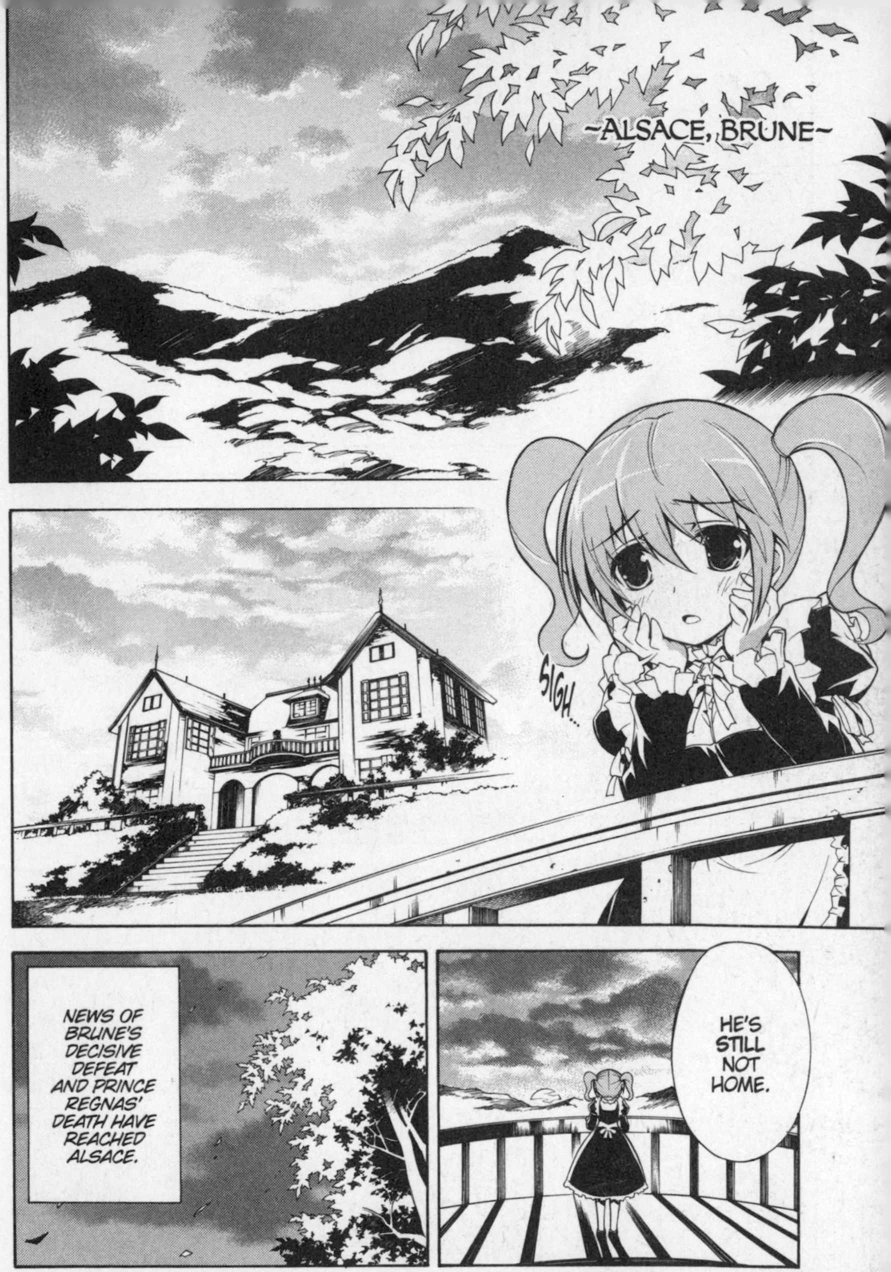
~ALSACE, BRUNE~
SIGH...
HE'S STILL NOT HOME.
NEWS OF BRUNE'S DECISIVE DEFEAT AND PRINCE REGNAS' DEATH HAVE REACHED ALSACE.

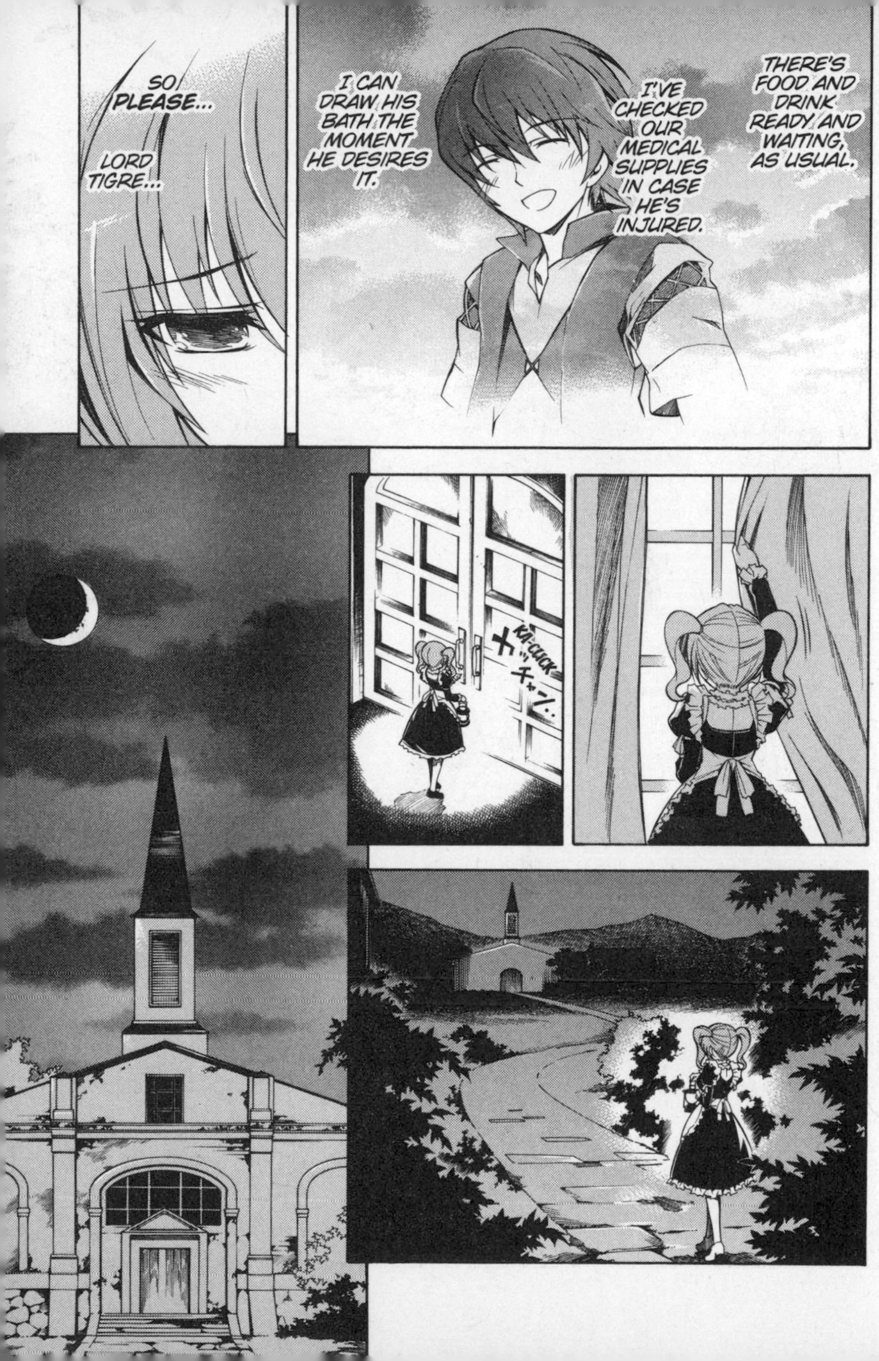
THERE'S FOOD AND DRINK READY AND WAITING, AS USUAL.
I'VE CHECKED OUR MEDICAL SUPPLIES IN CASE HE'S INJURED.
I CAN DRAW HIS BATH THE MOMENT HE DESIRES IT.
SO PLEASE...
LORD TIGRE...
KA-CLICK

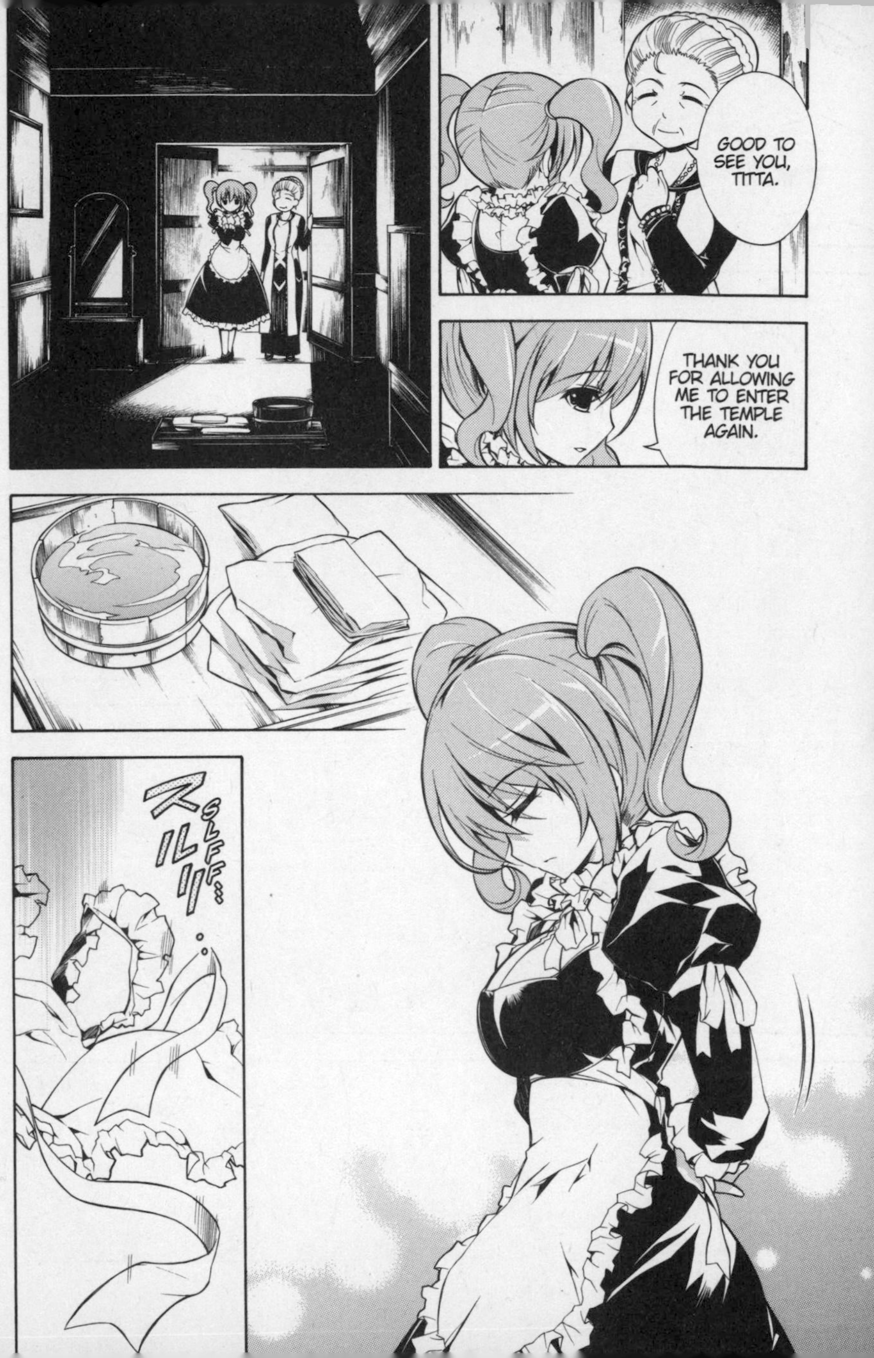
GOOD TO SEE YOU, TITTA.
THANK YOU FOR ALLOWING ME TO ENTER THE TEMPLE AGAIN.
スルッ
SLFF...

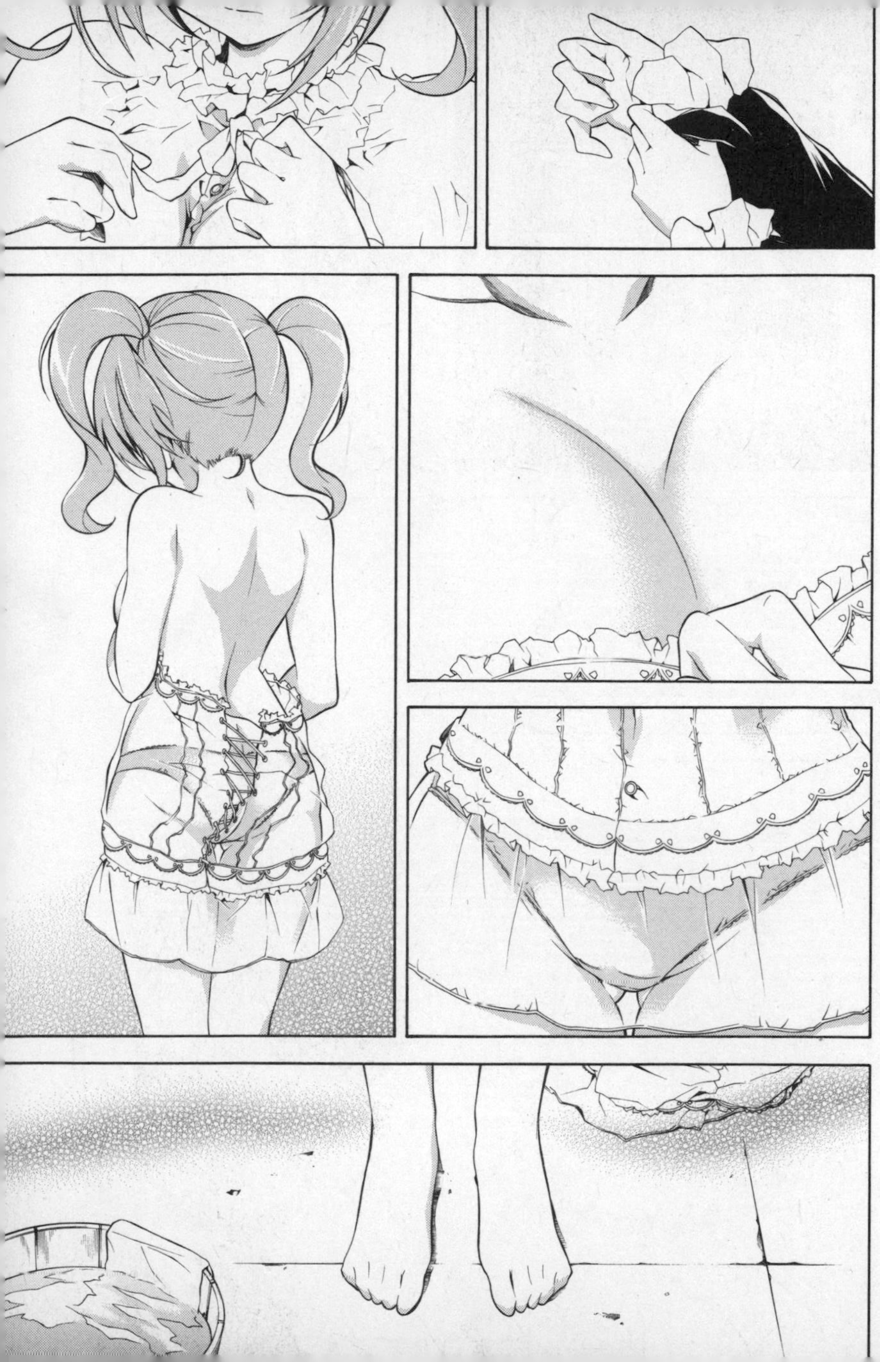

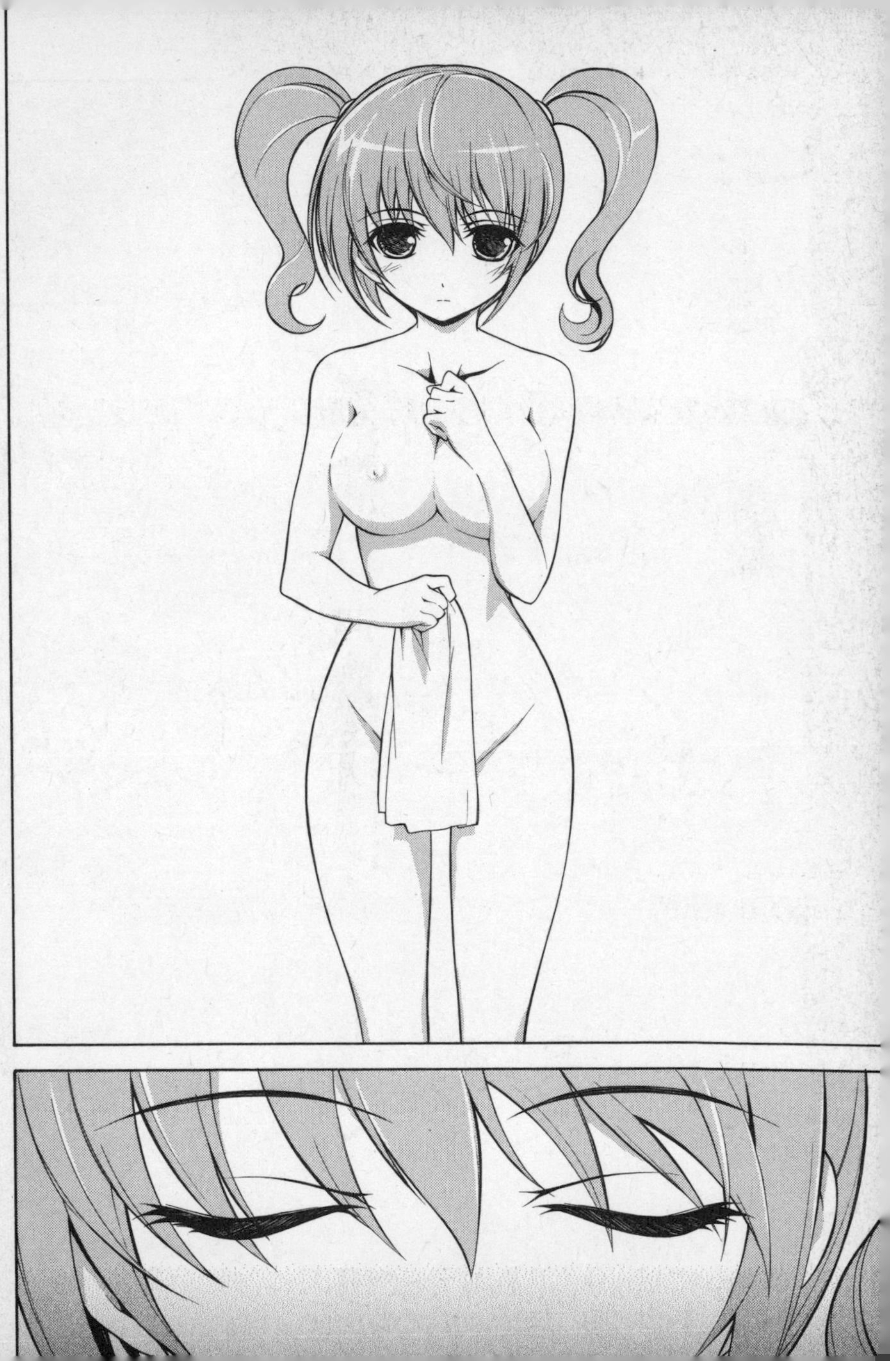

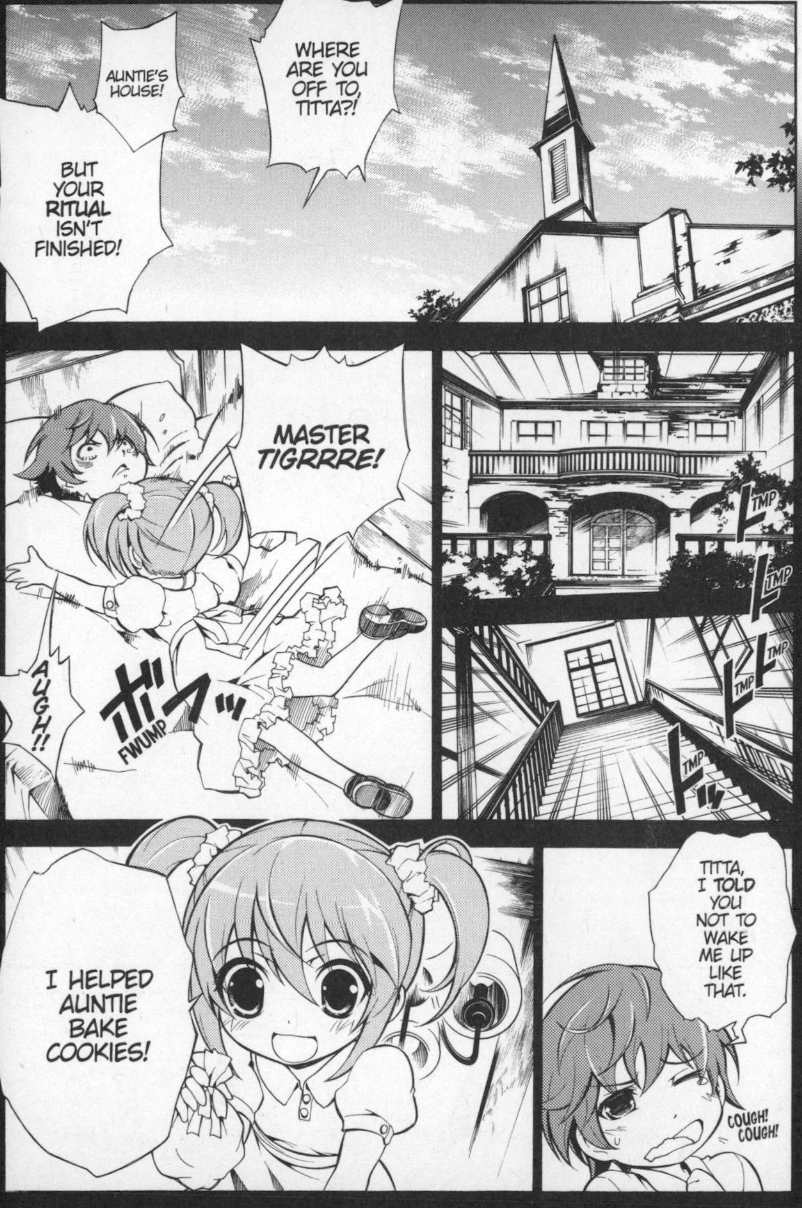

WHERE ARE YOU OFF TO, TITTA?!
AUNTIE'S HOUSE!
BUT YOUR RITUAL ISN'T FINISHED!
TMP
TMP
TMP
TMP
TMP
MASTER TIGRRRE!
FWUMP
AUGH!!
TITTA, I TOLD YOU NOT TO WAKE ME UP LIKE THAT.
COUGH! COUGH!
I HELPED AUNTIE BAKE COOKIES!

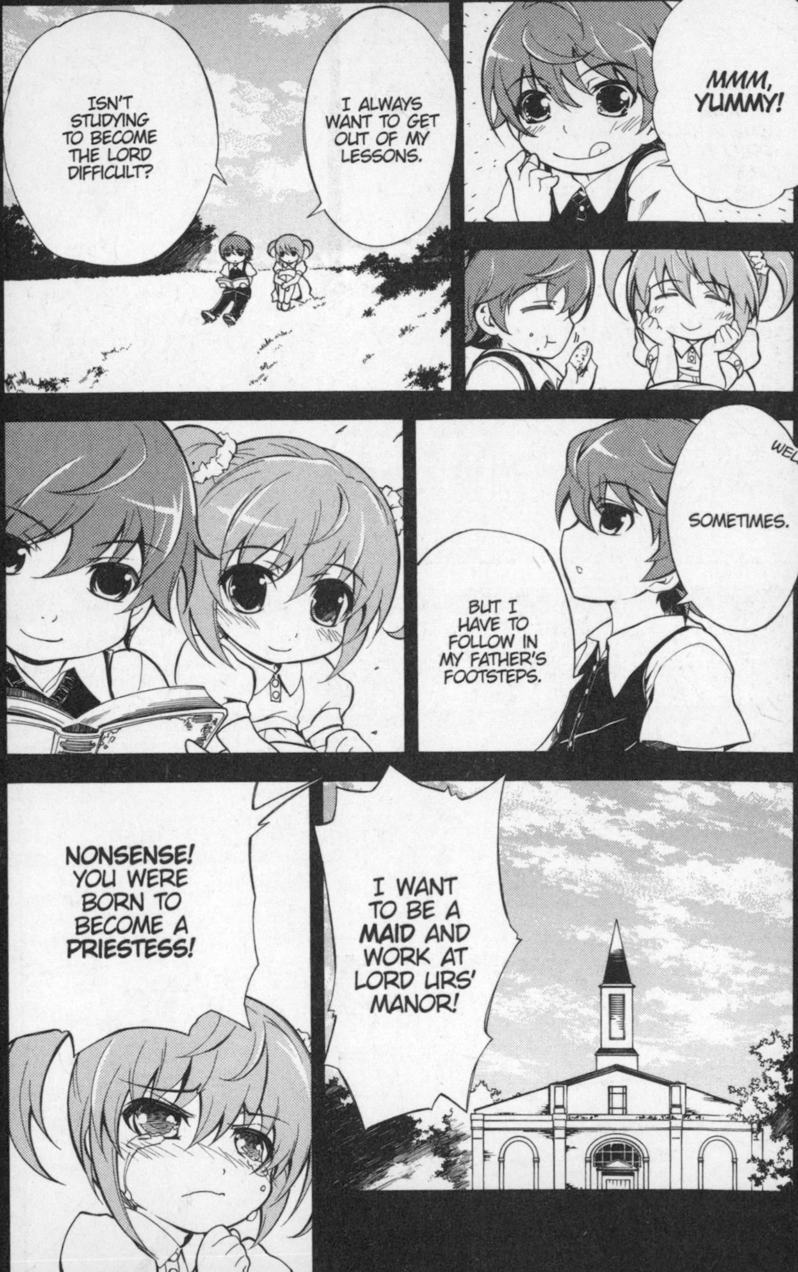
MMM, YUMMY!
I ALWAYS WANT TO GET OUT OF MY LESSONS.
ISN'T STUDYING TO BECOME THE LORD DIFFICULT?
WELL...
SOMETIMES.
BUT I HAVE TO FOLLOW IN MY FATHER'S FOOTSTEPS.
I WANT TO BE A MAID AND WORK AT LORD URS' MANOR!
NONSENSE! YOU WERE BORN TO BECOME A PRIESTESS!

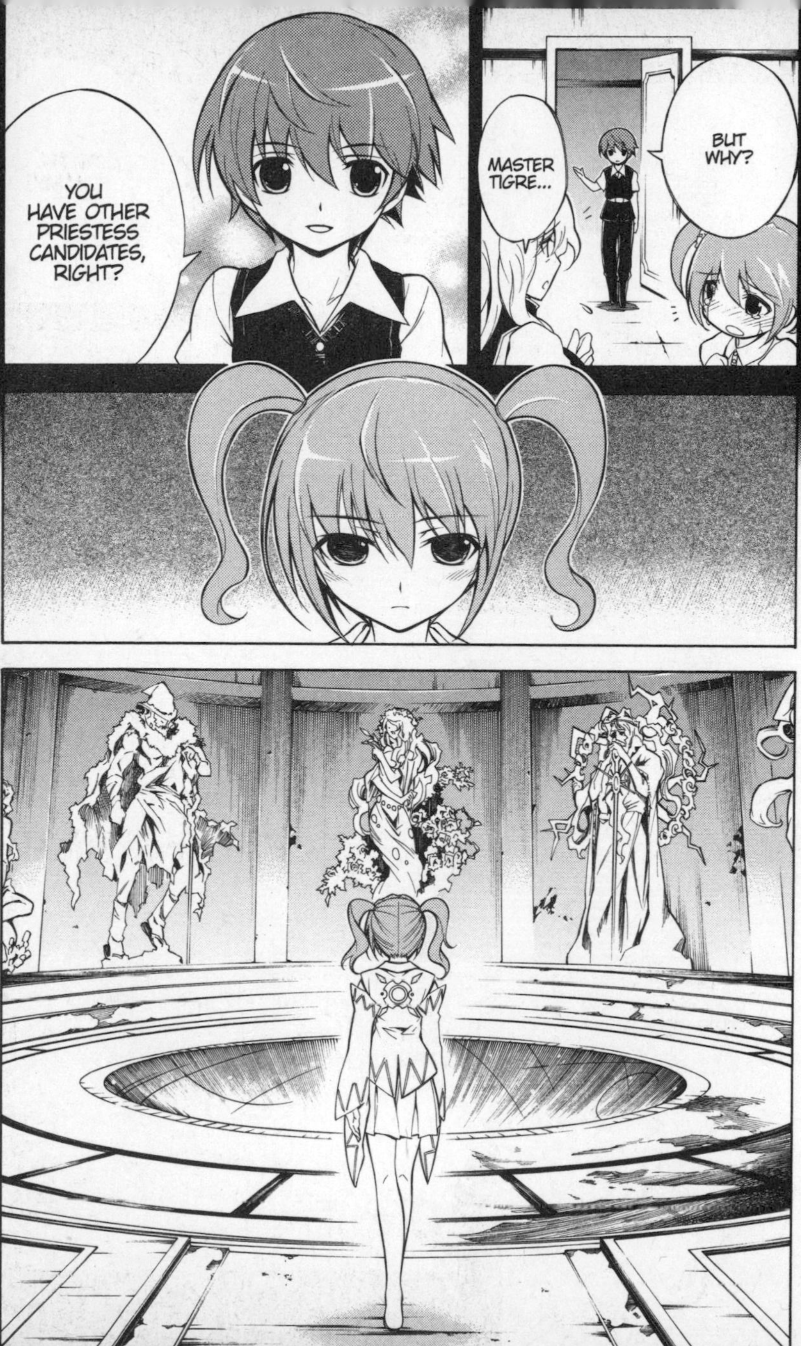
BUT WHY?
MASTER TIGRE...
YOU HAVE OTHER PRIESTESS CANDIDATES, RIGHT?

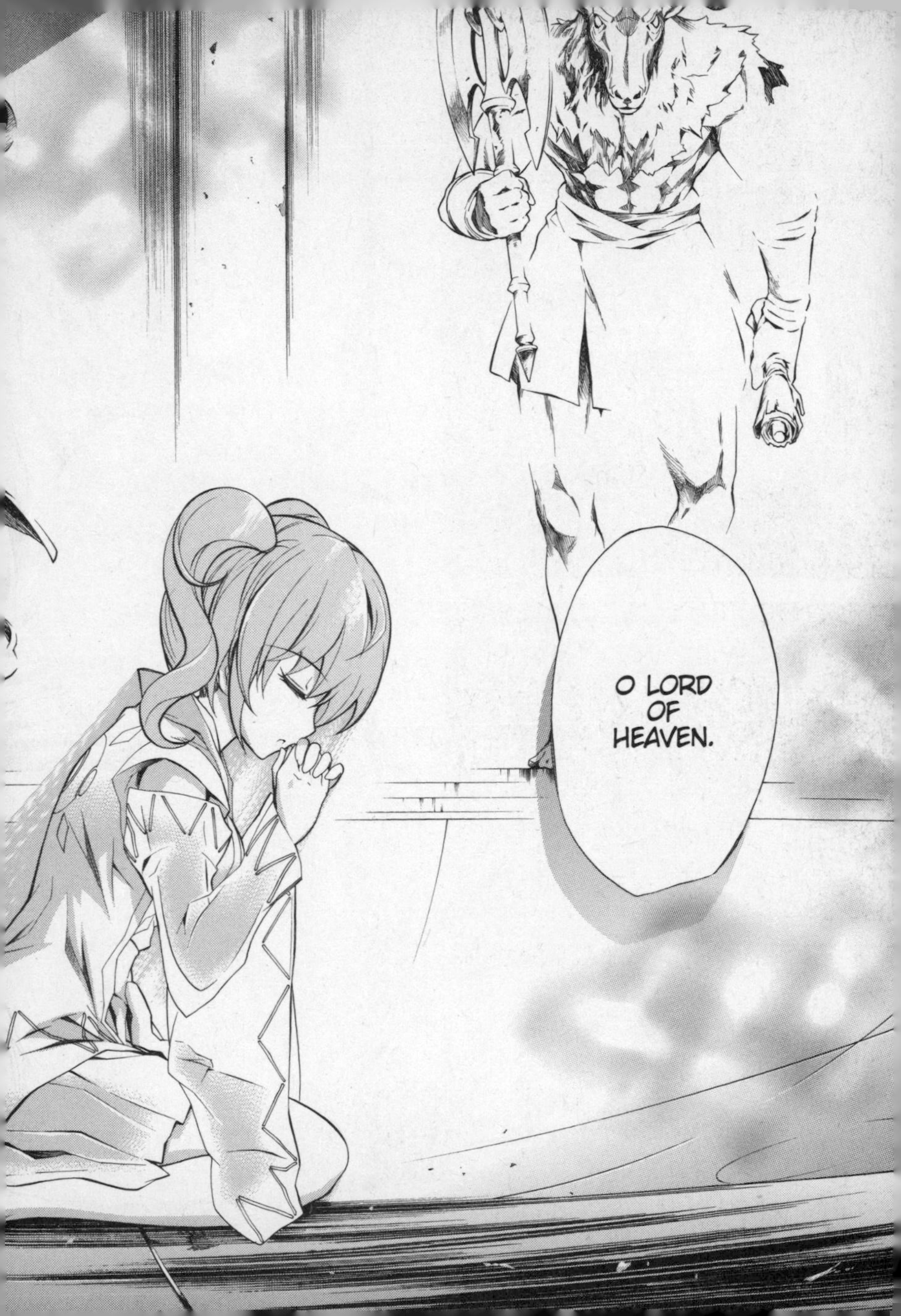
O LORD
OF
HEAVEN.

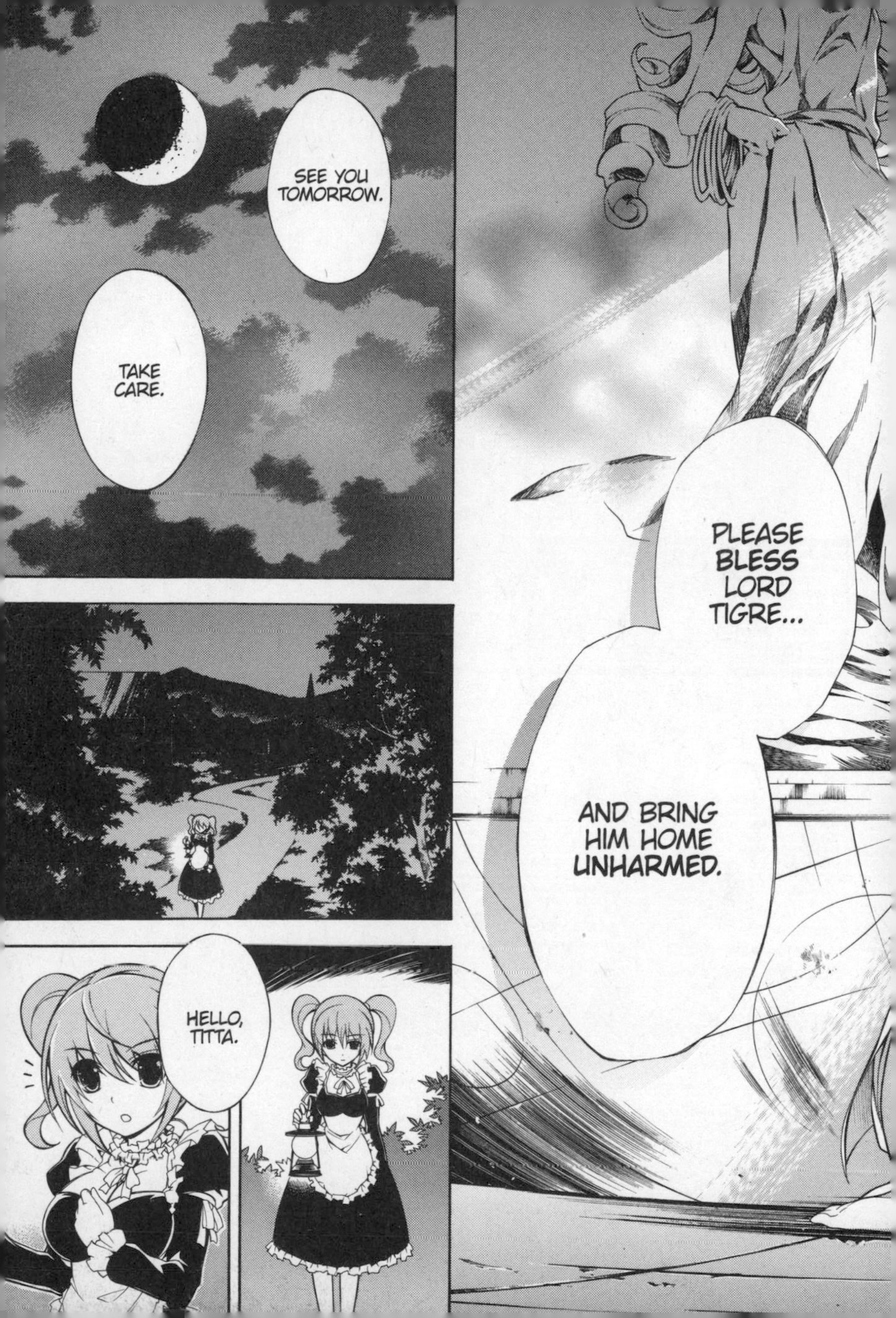
PLEASE BLESS LORD TIGRE...
AND BRING HIM HOME UNHARMED.
SEE YOU TOMORROW.
TAKE CARE.
HELLO, TITTA.

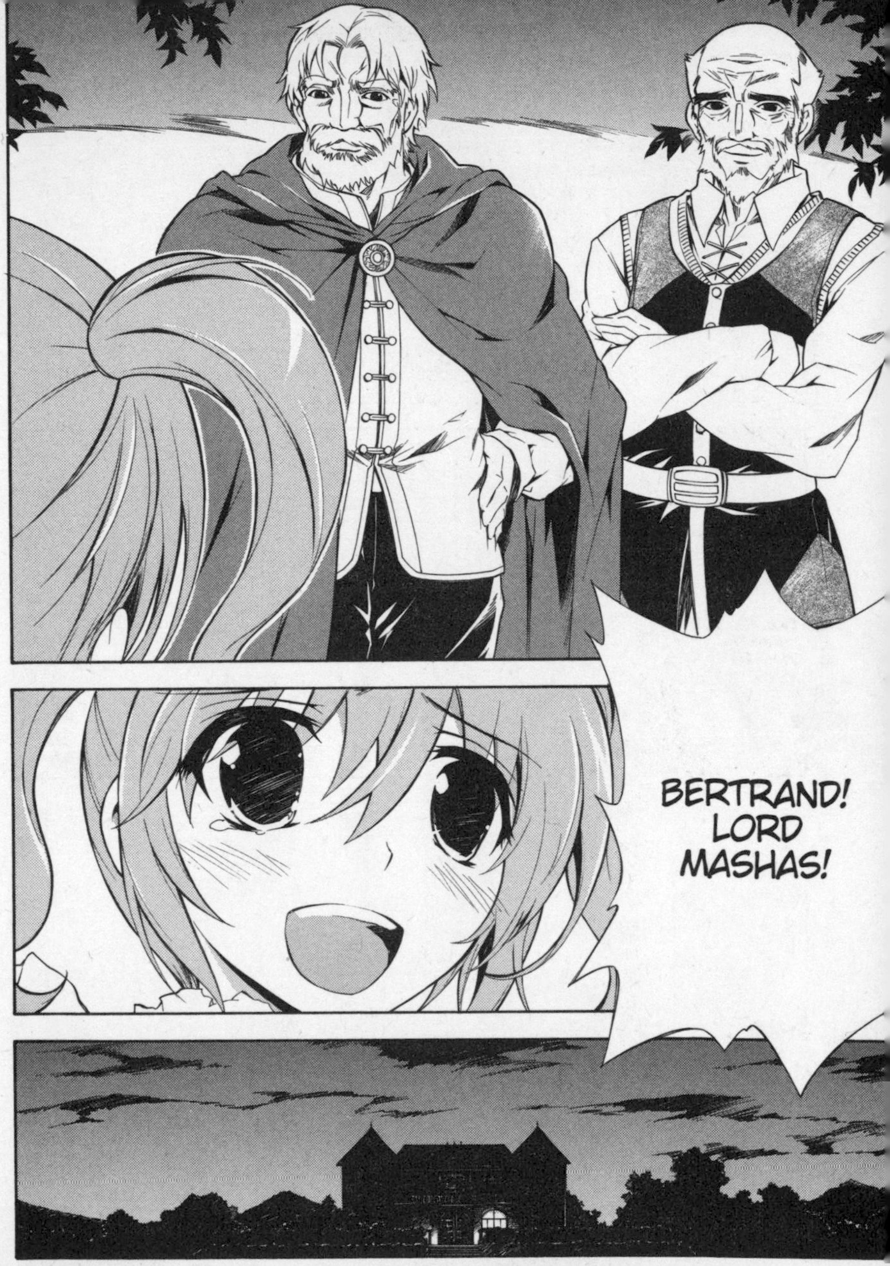
BERTRAND! LORD MASHAS!

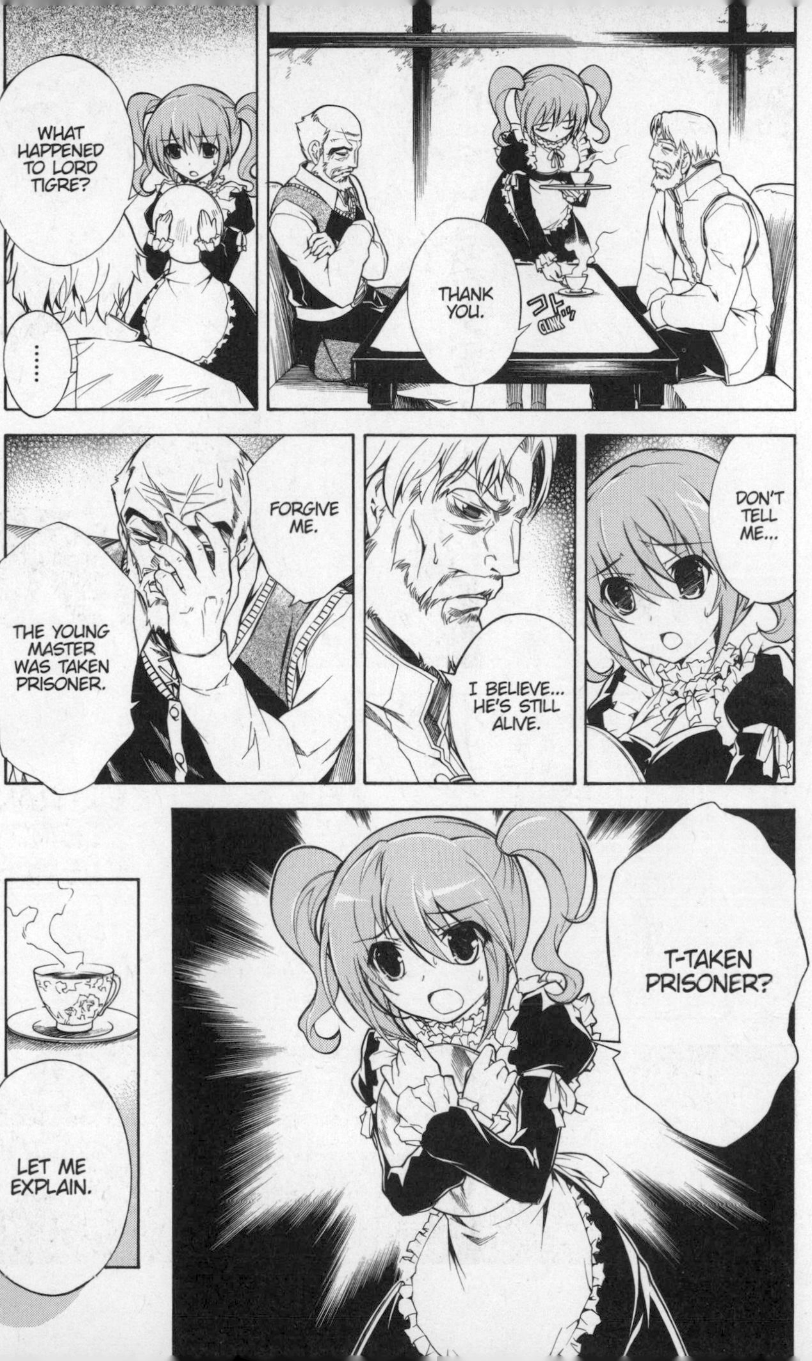
THANK YOU.
CLINK
WHAT HAPPENED TO LORD TIGRE?
......
DON'T TELL ME...
I BELIEVE... HE'S STILL ALIVE.
FORGIVE ME.
THE YOUNG MASTER WAS TAKEN PRISONER.
T-TAKEN PRISONER?
LET ME EXPLAIN.

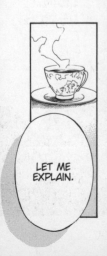

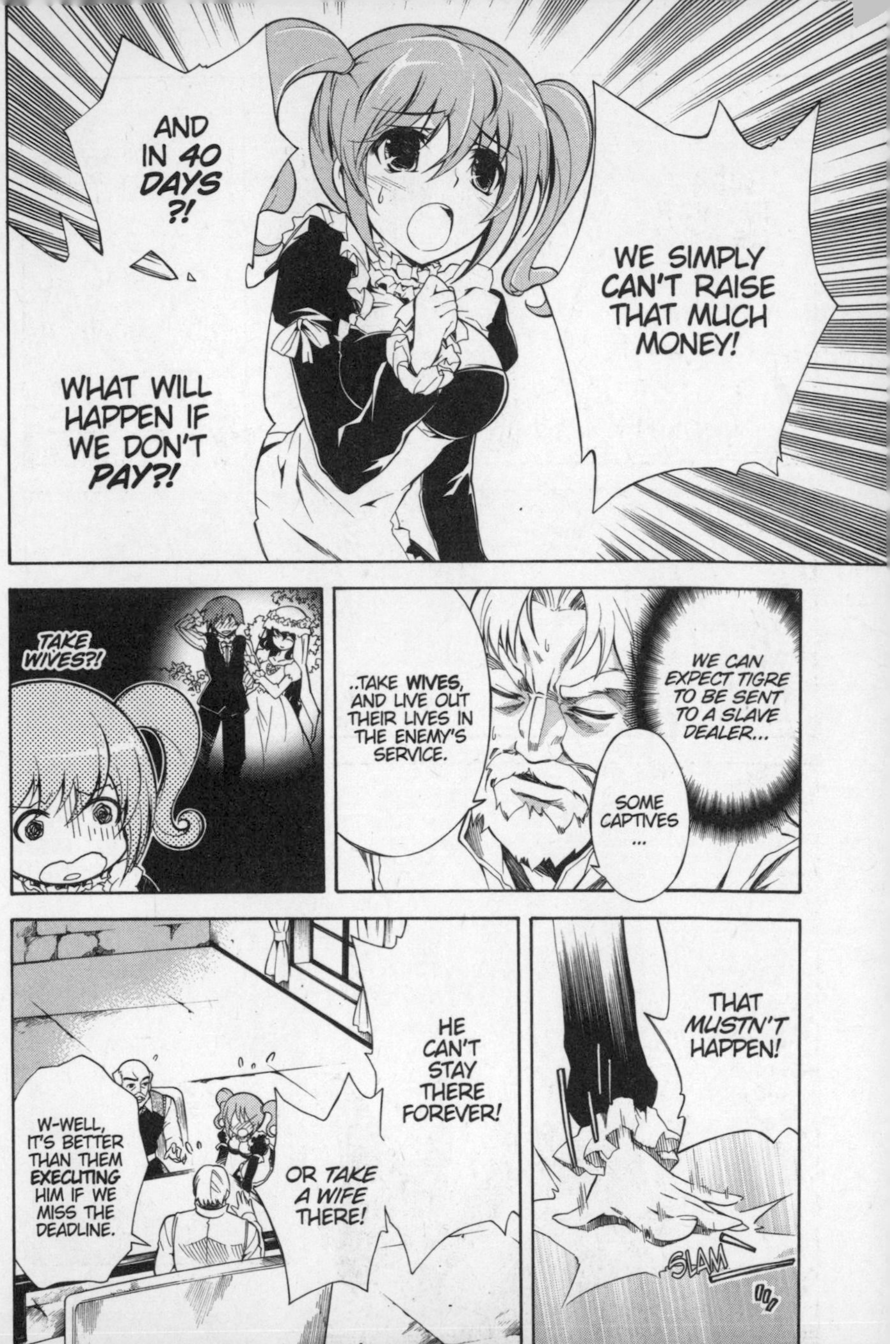
WE SIMPLY CAN'T RAISE THAT MUCH MONEY!
AND IN 40 DAYS?!
WHAT WILL HAPPEN IF WE DON'T PAY?!
WE CAN EXPECT TIGRE TO BE SENT TO A SLAVE DEALER...
SOME CAPTIVES ...
..TAKE WIVES, AND LIVE OUT THEIR LIVES IN THE ENEMY'S SERVICE.
TAKE WIVES?!
THAT MUSTN'T HAPPEN!
SLAM
HE CAN'T STAY THERE FOREVER!
OR TAKE A WIFE THERE!
W-WELL, IT'S BETTER THAN THEM EXECUTING HIM IF WE MISS THE DEADLINE.

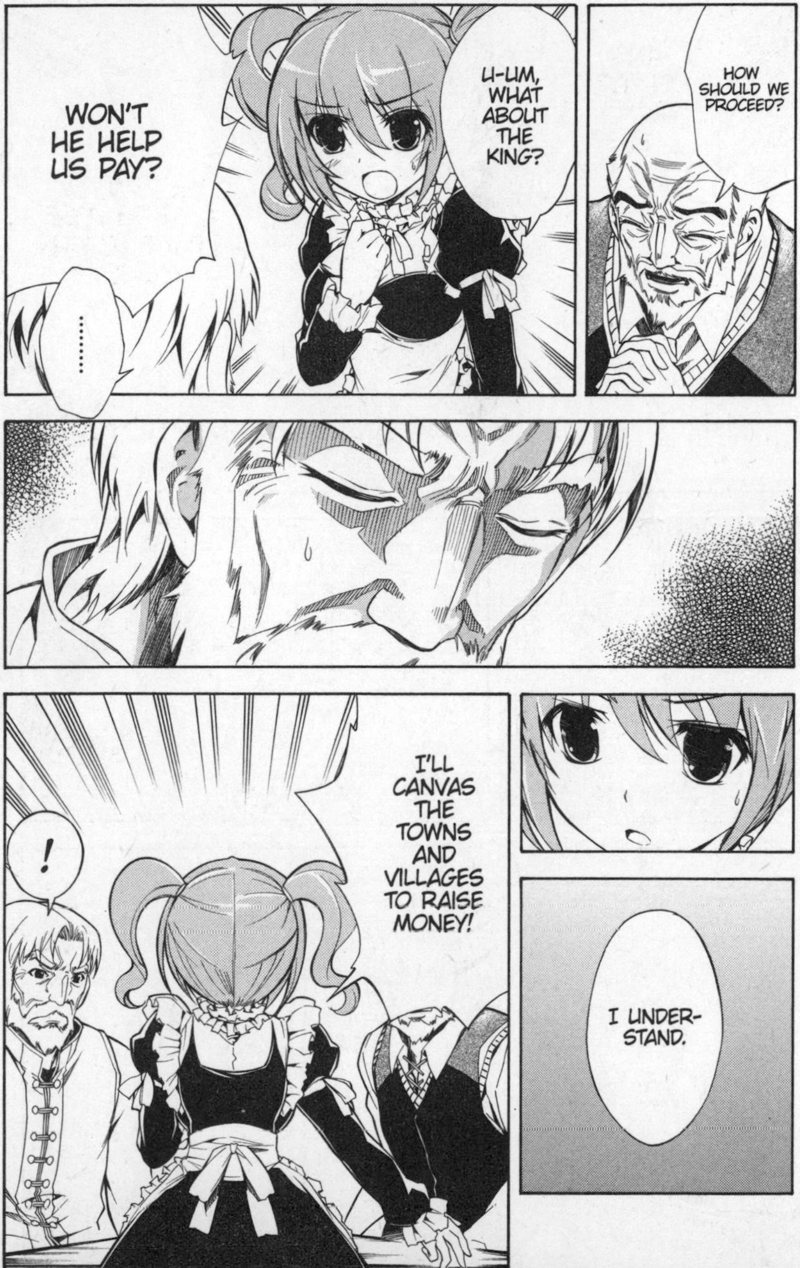
HOW SHOULD WE PROCEED?
U-UM, WHAT ABOUT THE KING?
WON'T HE HELP US PAY?
......
I UNDER-STAND.
I'LL CANVAS THE TOWNS AND VILLAGES TO RAISE MONEY!
!

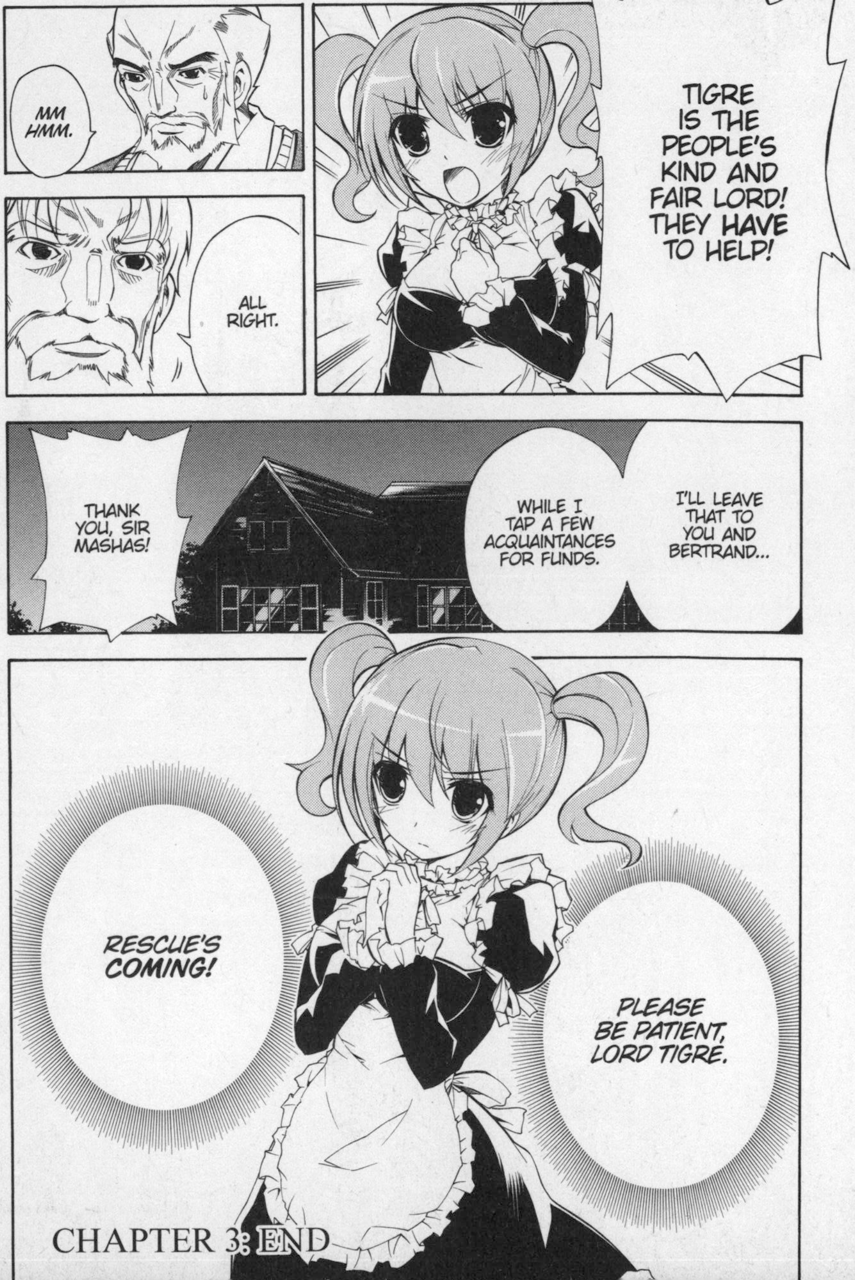
TIGRE IS THE PEOPLE'S KIND AND FAIR LORD! THEY HAVE TO HELP!
MM HMM.
ALL RIGHT.
I'LL LEAVE THAT TO YOU AND BERTRAND...
WHILE I TAP A FEW ACQUAINTANCES FOR FUNDS.
THANK YOU, SIR MASHAS!
PLEASE BE PATIENT, LORD TIGRE.
RESCUE'S COMING!
CHAPTER 3: END

4 ◆ THE TRAINING BEGINS

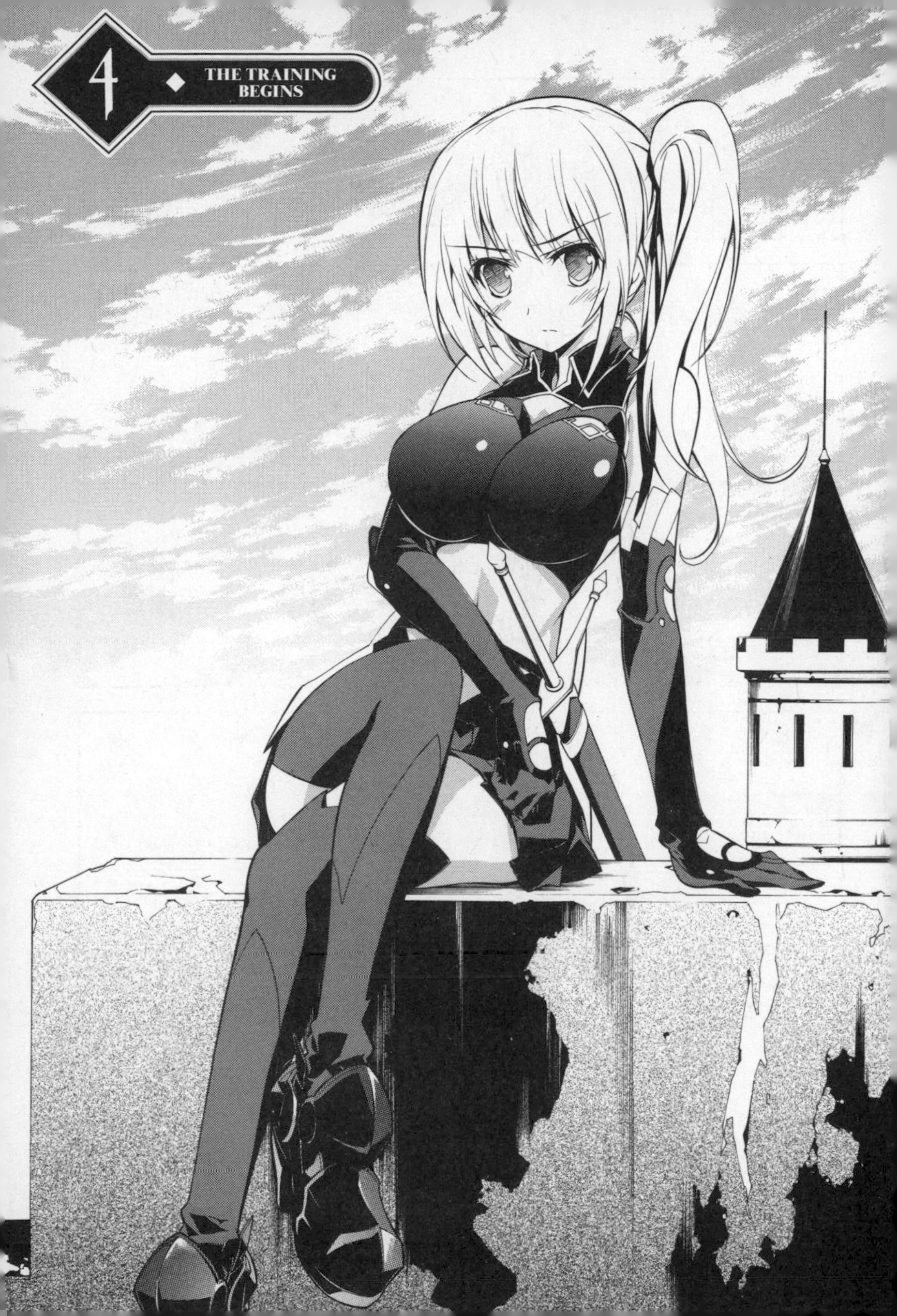

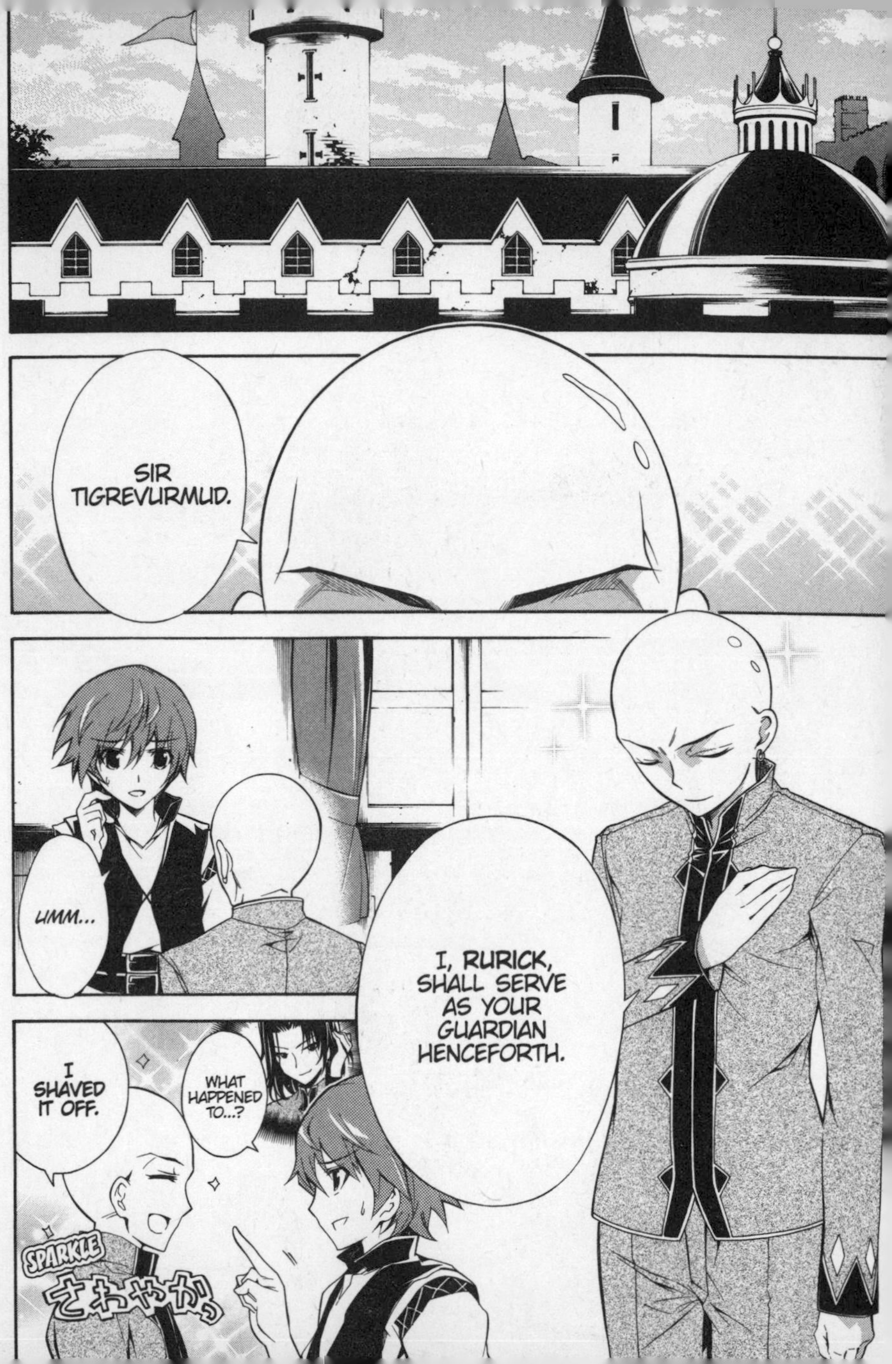
SIR TIGREVURMUD.
I, RURICK, SHALL SERVE AS YOUR GUARDIAN HENCEFORTH.
UMM...
WHAT HAPPENED TO...?
I SHAVED IT OFF.
SPARKLE
さわやかっ

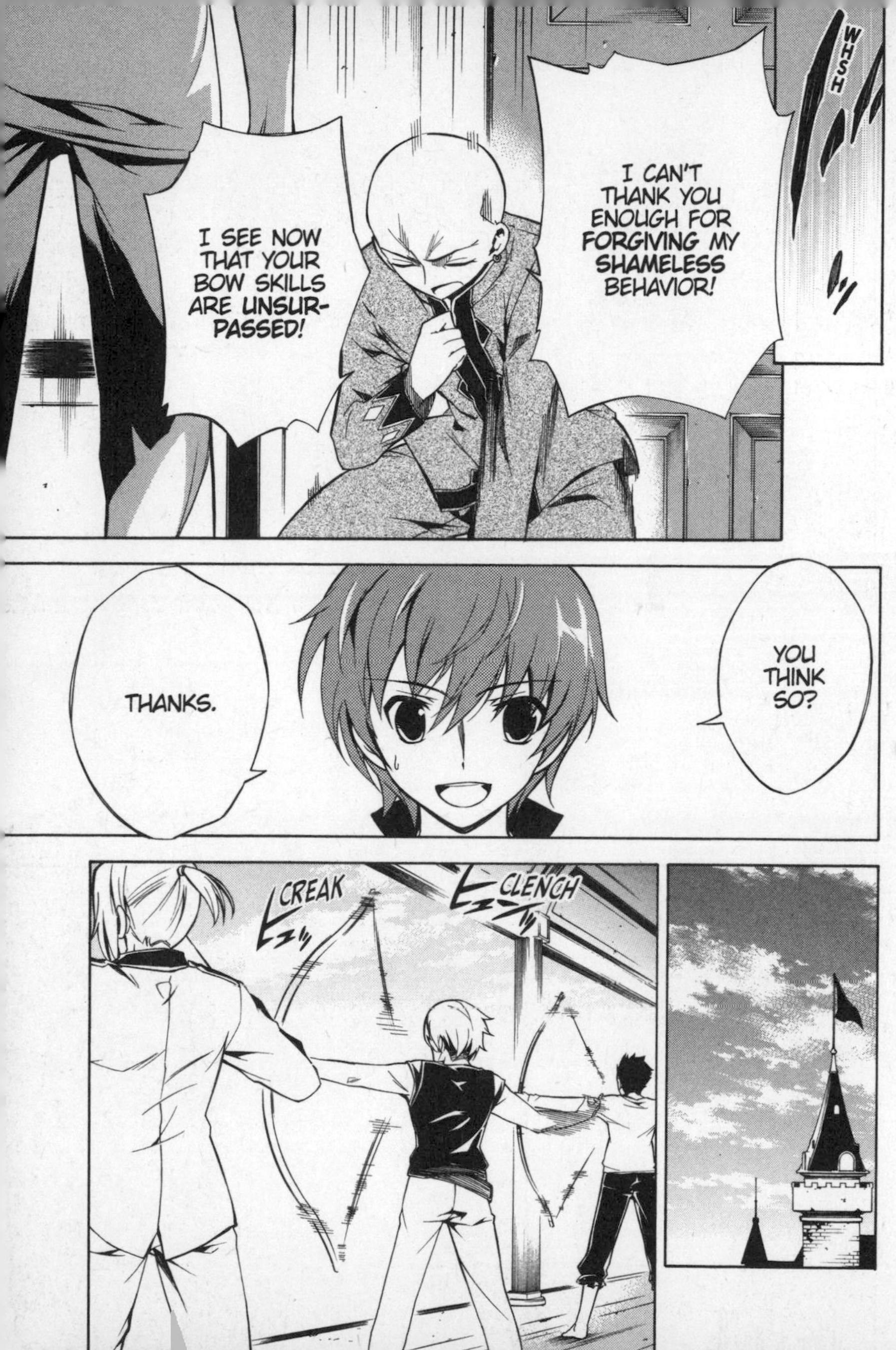
WHSH
I CAN'T THANK YOU ENOUGH FOR FORGIVING MY SHAMELESS BEHAVIOR!
I SEE NOW THAT YOUR BOW SKILLS ARE UNSUR-PASSED!
YOU THINK SO?
THANKS.
CLENCH
CREAK

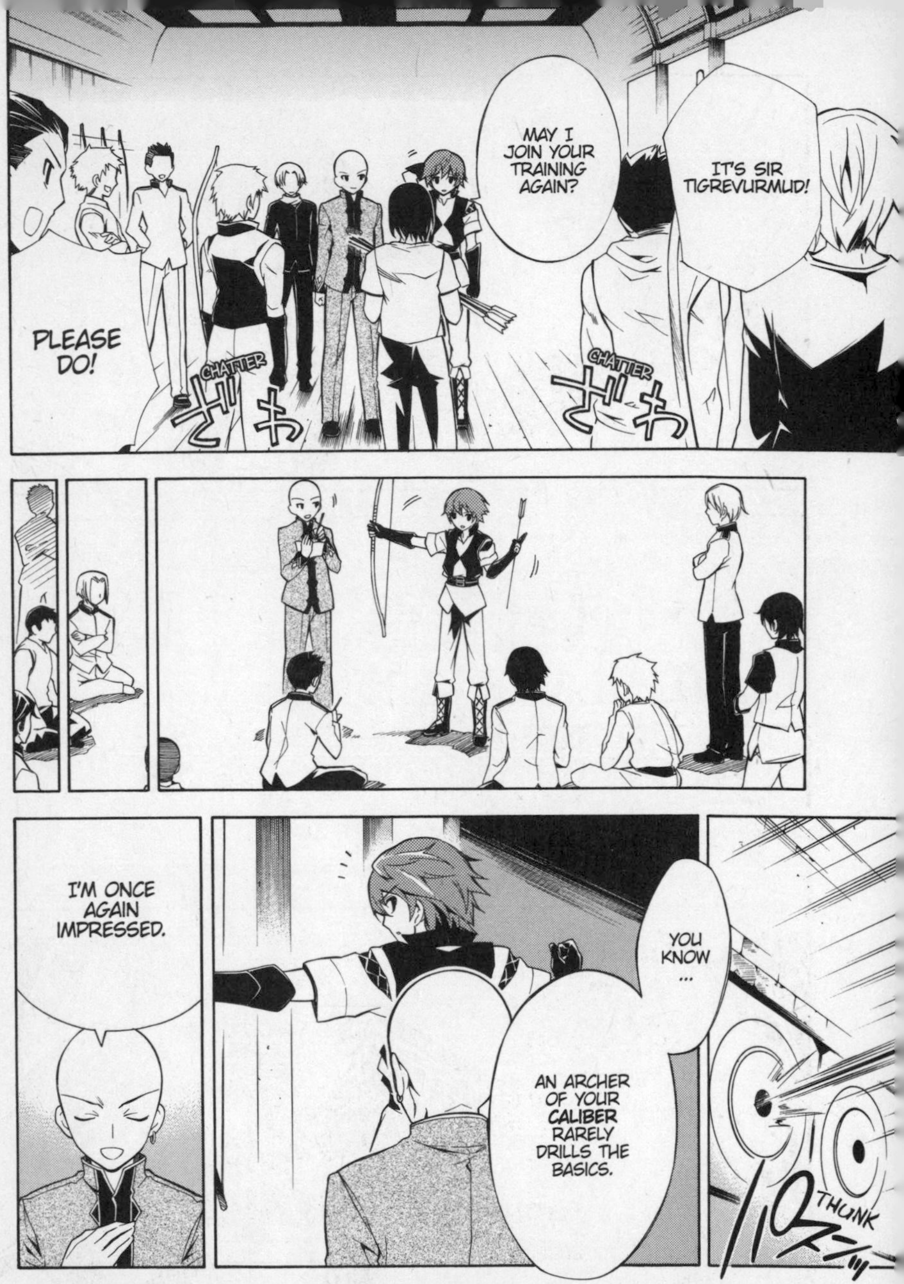
IT'S SIR TIGREVURMUD!
MAY I JOIN YOUR TRAINING AGAIN?
CHATTER
ざわ
CHATTER
ざわ
PLEASE DO!
THUNK
YOU KNOW ...
AN ARCHER OF YOUR **CALIBER** RARELY DRILLS THE BASICS.
I'M ONCE AGAIN IMPRESSED.

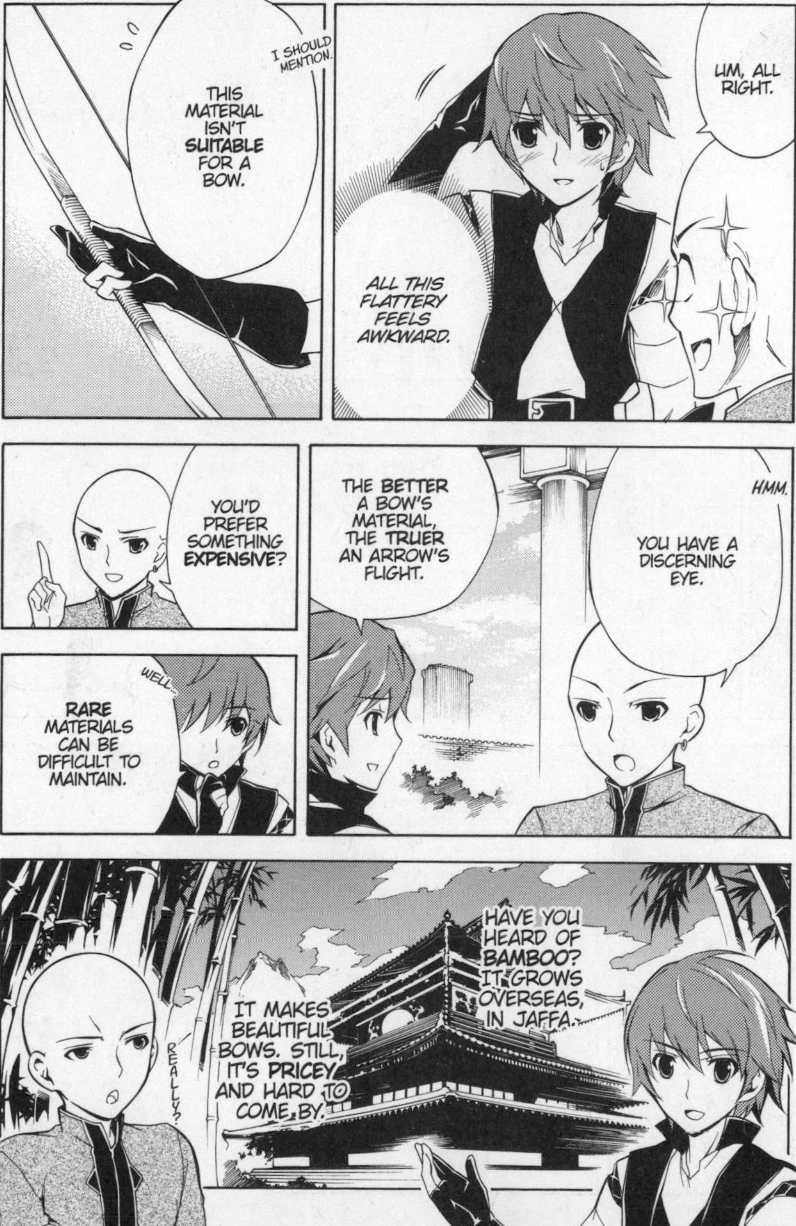
UM, ALL RIGHT.
ALL THIS FLATTERY FEELS AWKWARD.
I SHOULD MENTION.
THIS MATERIAL ISN'T SUITABLE FOR A BOW.
HMM.
YOU HAVE A DISCERNING EYE.
THE BETTER A BOW'S MATERIAL, THE TRUER AN ARROW'S FLIGHT.
YOU'D PREFER SOMETHING EXPENSIVE?
WELL...
RARE MATERIALS CAN BE DIFFICULT TO MAINTAIN.
HAVE YOU HEARD OF BAMBOO? IT GROWS OVERSEAS, IN JAFFA.
IT MAKES BEAUTIFUL BOWS. STILL, IT'S PRICEY AND HARD TO COME BY.
REALLY?

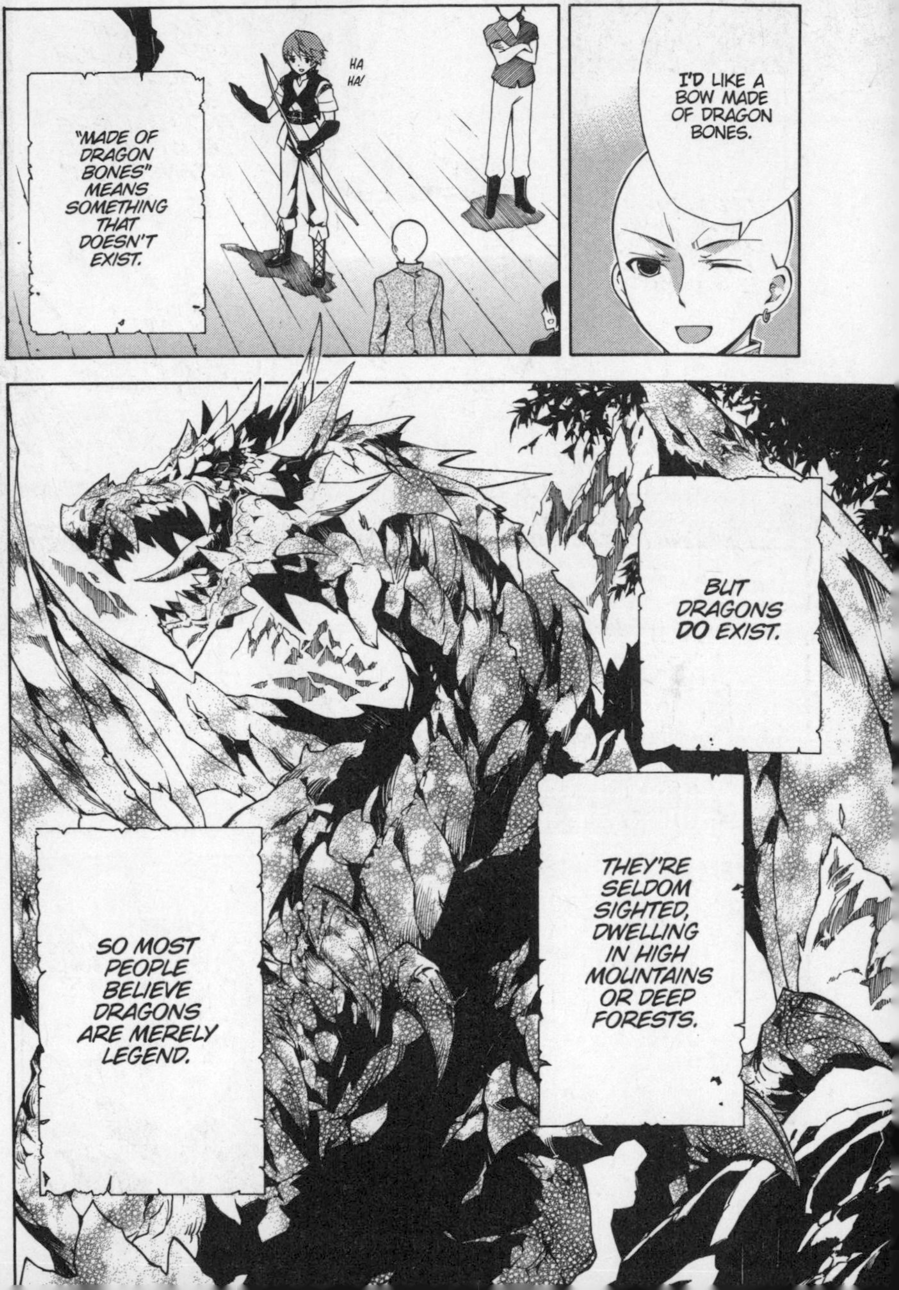
I'D LIKE A BOW MADE OF DRAGON BONES.
HA HA!
"MADE OF DRAGON BONES" MEANS SOMETHING THAT DOESN'T EXIST.
BUT DRAGONS DO EXIST.
THEY'RE SELDOM SIGHTED, DWELLING IN HIGH MOUNTAINS OR DEEP FORESTS.
SO MOST PEOPLE BELIEVE DRAGONS ARE MERELY LEGEND.

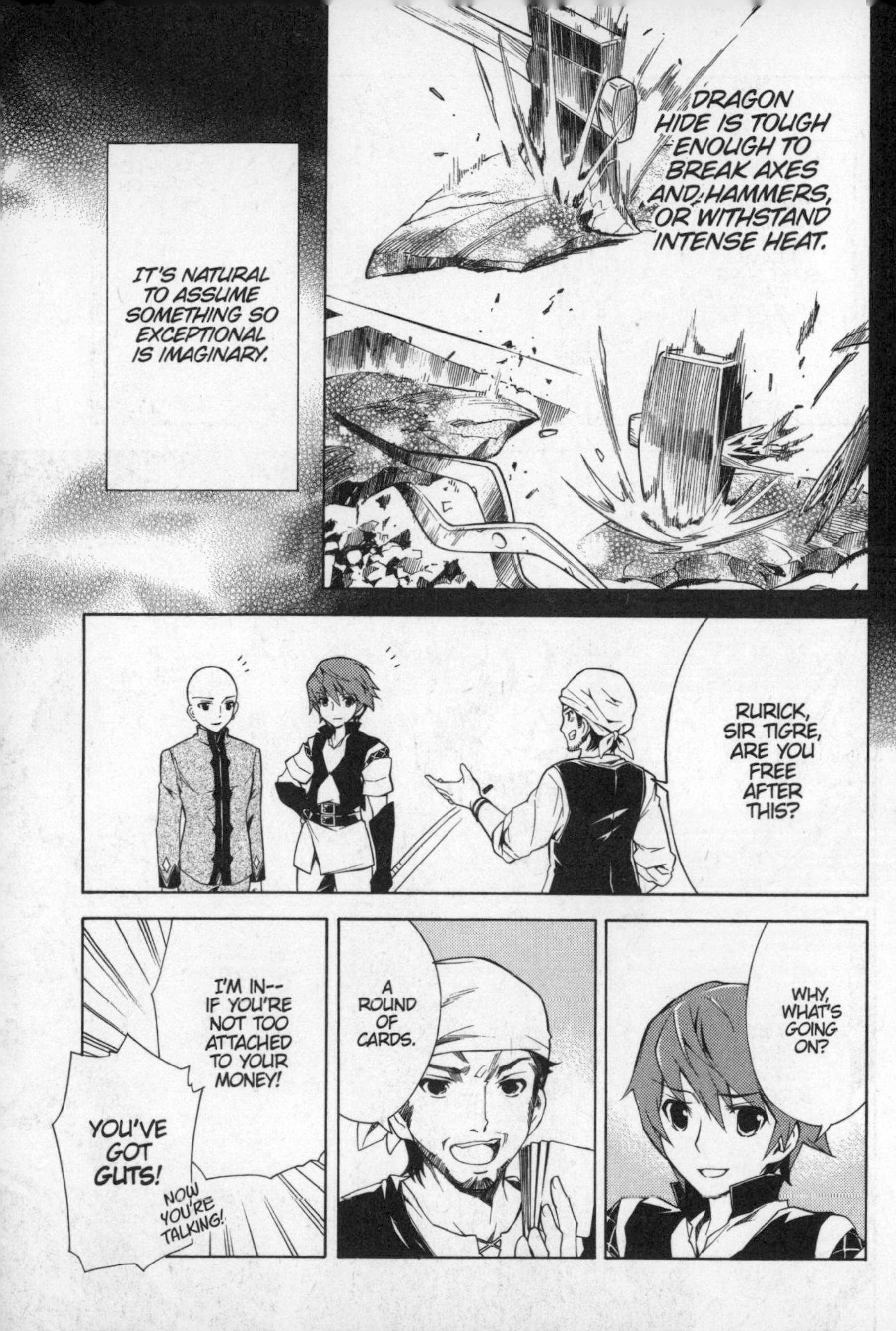
DRAGON HIDE IS TOUGH ENOUGH TO BREAK AXES AND HAMMERS, OR WITHSTAND INTENSE HEAT.
IT'S NATURAL TO ASSUME SOMETHING SO EXCEPTIONAL IS IMAGINARY.
RURICK, SIR TIGRE, ARE YOU FREE AFTER THIS?
WHY, WHAT'S GOING ON?
A ROUND OF CARDS.
I'M IN-- IF YOU'RE NOT TOO ATTACHED TO YOUR MONEY!
YOU'VE GOT GUTS!
NOW YOU'RE TALKING!

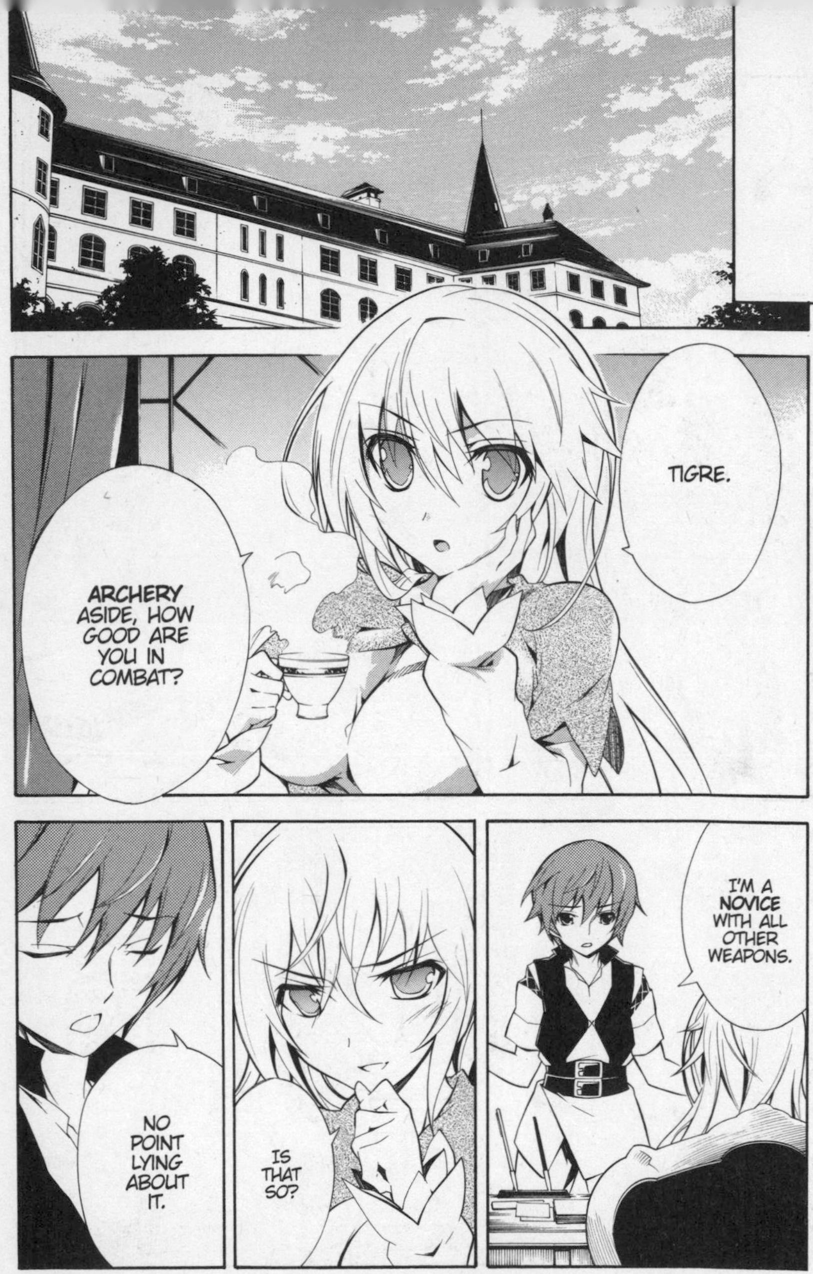
TIGRE.
ARCHERY ASIDE, HOW GOOD ARE YOU IN COMBAT?
I'M A NOVICE WITH ALL OTHER WEAPONS.
IS THAT SO?
NO POINT LYING ABOUT IT.

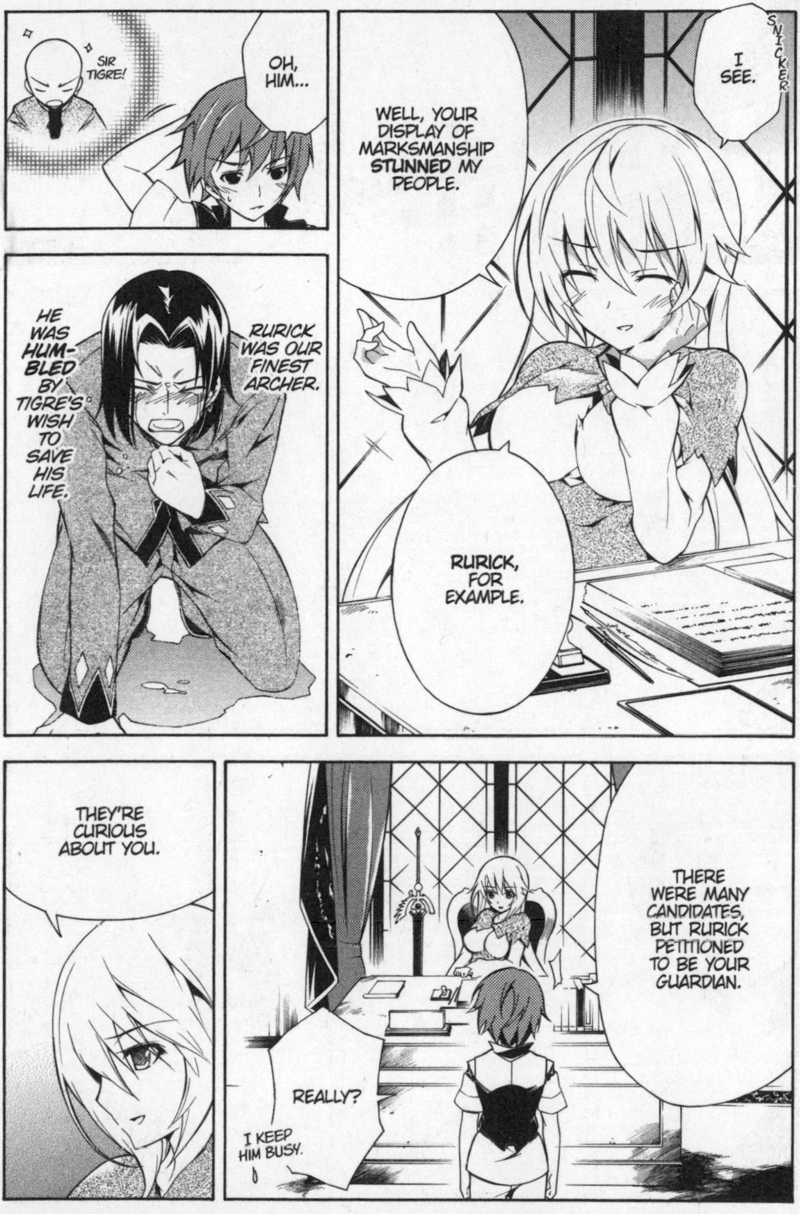
SNICKER
I SEE.
WELL, YOUR DISPLAY OF MARKSMANSHIP STUNNED MY PEOPLE.
RURICK, FOR EXAMPLE.
OH, HIM...
SIR TIGRE!
RURICK WAS OUR FINEST ARCHER.
HE WAS HUMBLED BY TIGRE'S WISH TO SAVE HIS LIFE.
THERE WERE MANY CANDIDATES, BUT RURICK PETITIONED TO BE YOUR GUARDIAN.
REALLY?
I KEEP HIM BUSY.
THEY'RE CURIOUS ABOUT YOU.

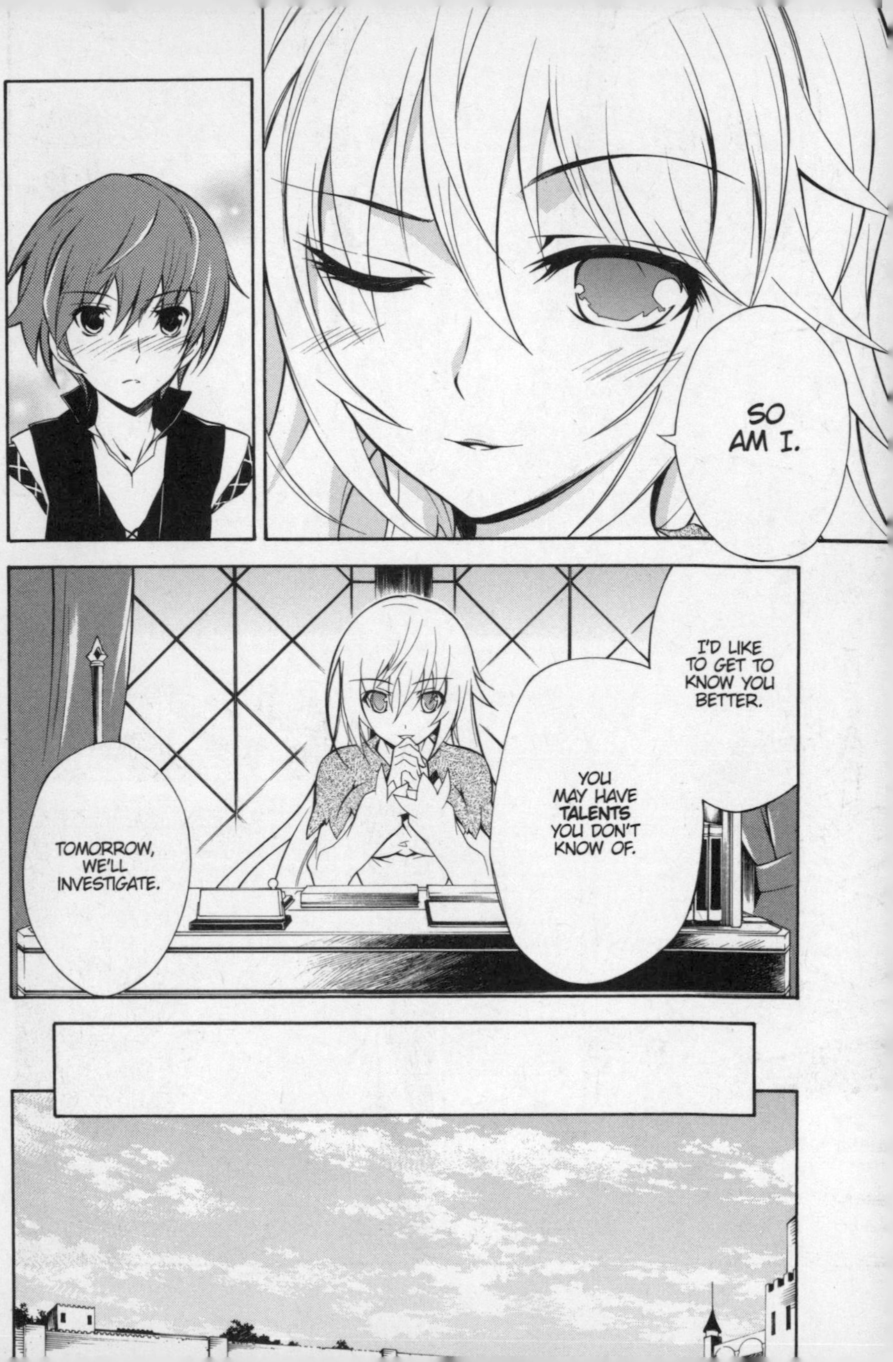
SO AM I.
I'D LIKE TO GET TO KNOW YOU BETTER.
YOU MAY HAVE TALENTS YOU DON'T KNOW OF.
TOMORROW, WE'LL INVESTIGATE.

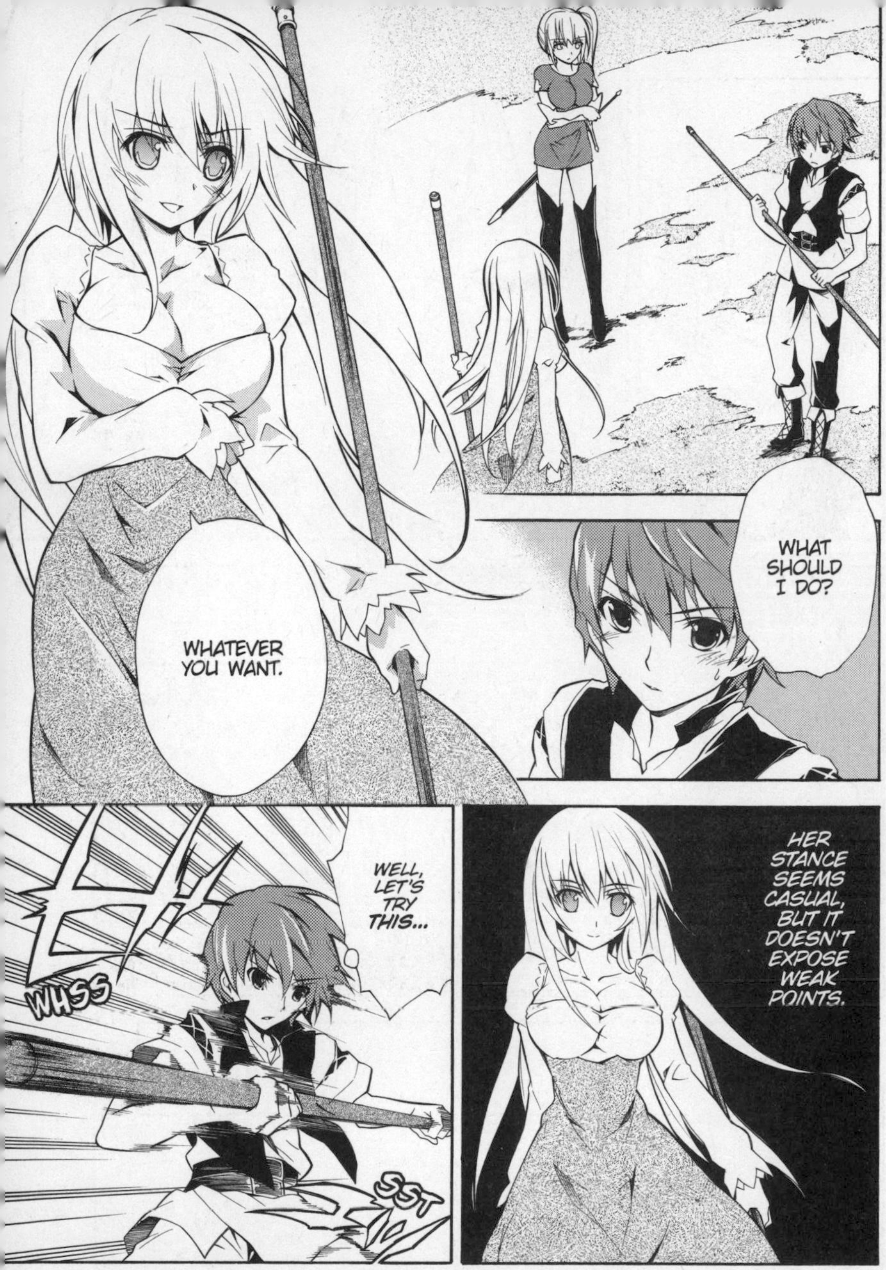
WHAT SHOULD I DO?
WHATEVER YOU WANT.
HER STANCE SEEMS CASUAL, BUT IT DOESN'T EXPOSE WEAK POINTS.
WELL, LET'S TRY THIS...
WHSS
SST

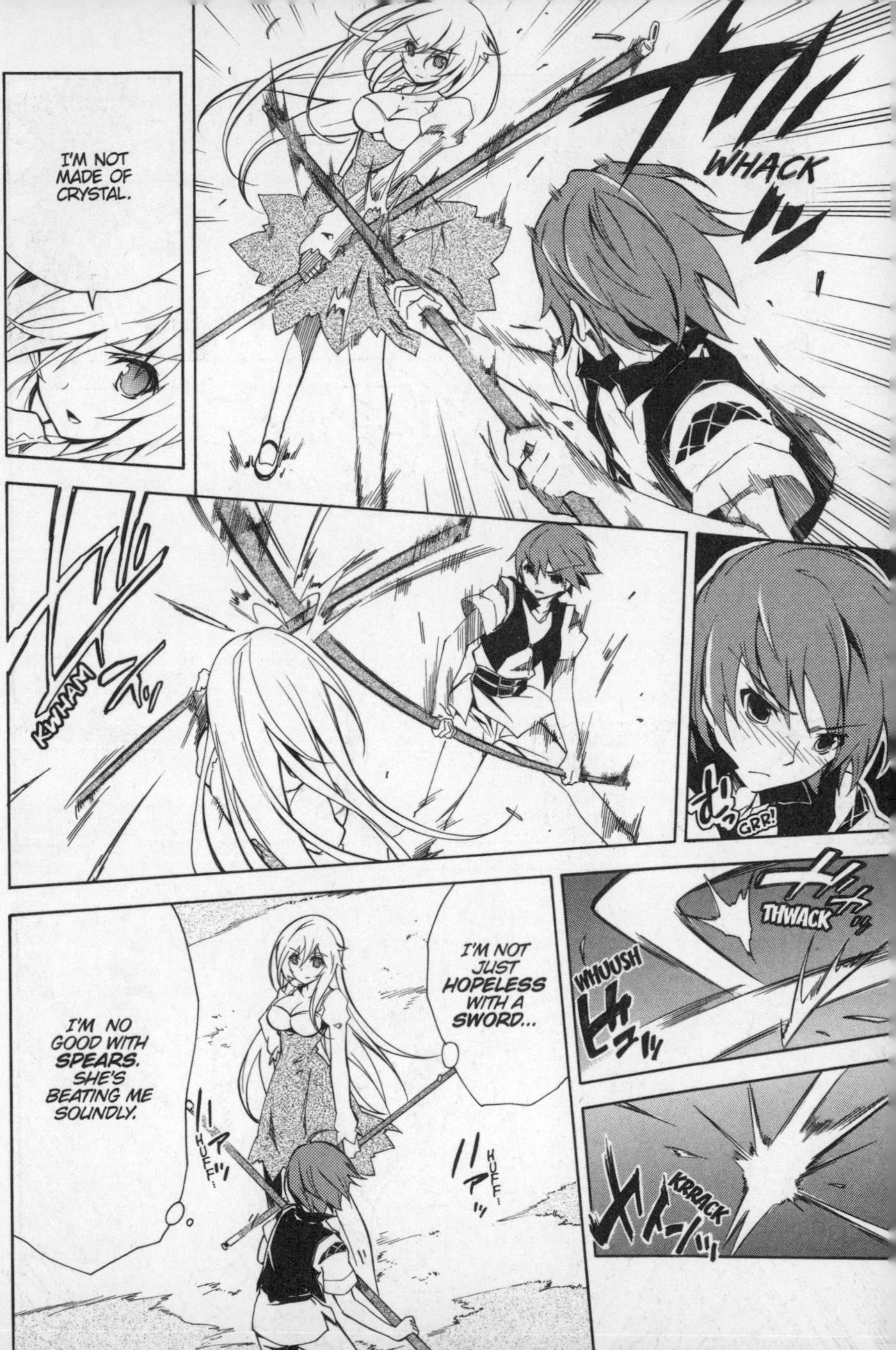
WHACK
I'M NOT MADE OF CRYSTAL.
GRR!
KWHAM
THWACK
WHUUSH
KRRACK
I'M NOT JUST HOPELESS WITH A SWORD...
I'M NO GOOD WITH SPEARS. SHE'S BEATING ME SOUNDLY.
HUFF...
HUFF...

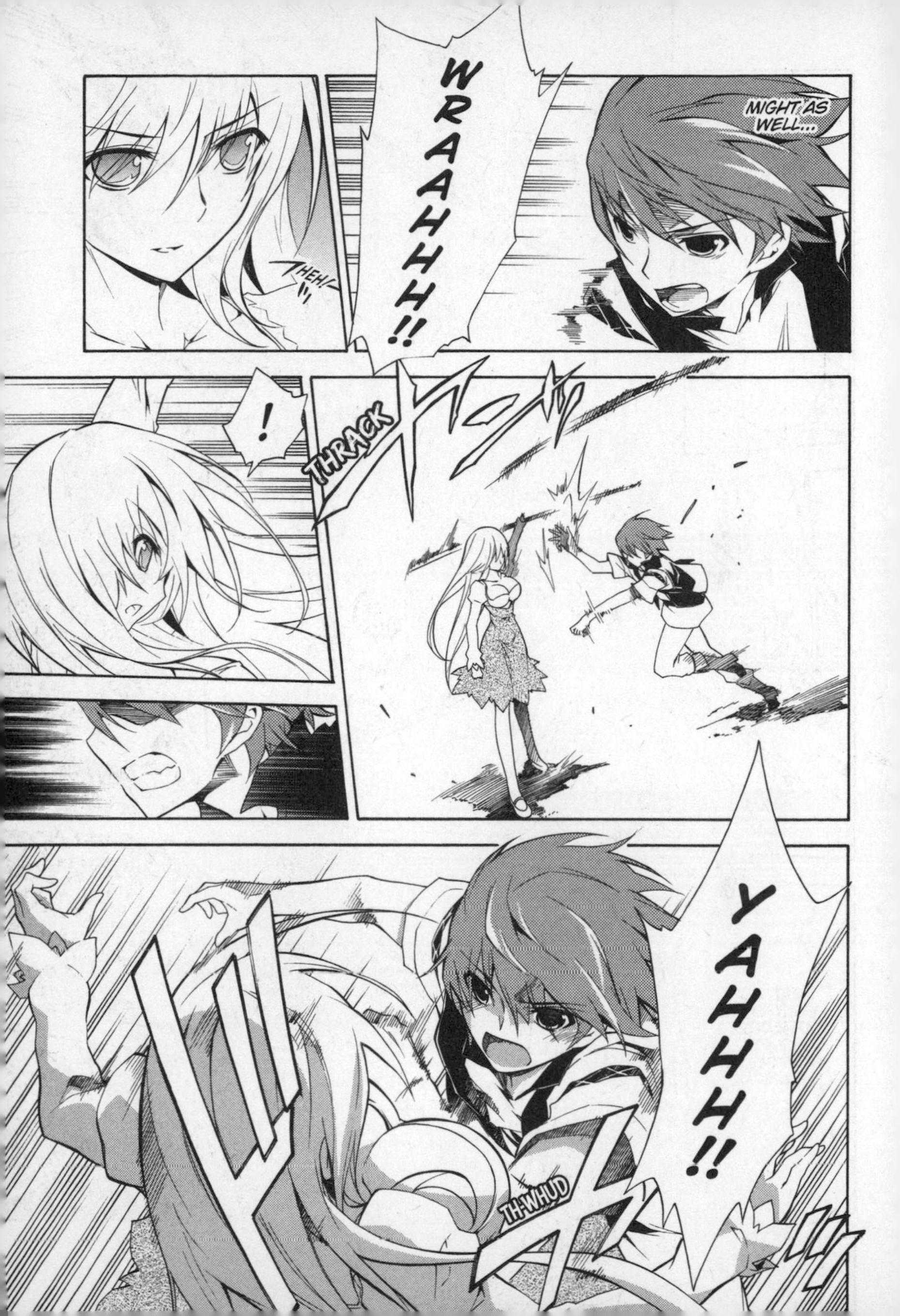
MIGHT AS WELL...
WRAAAHHHH!!
HEH!
THRACK
!
YAHHHH!!
THWHUD

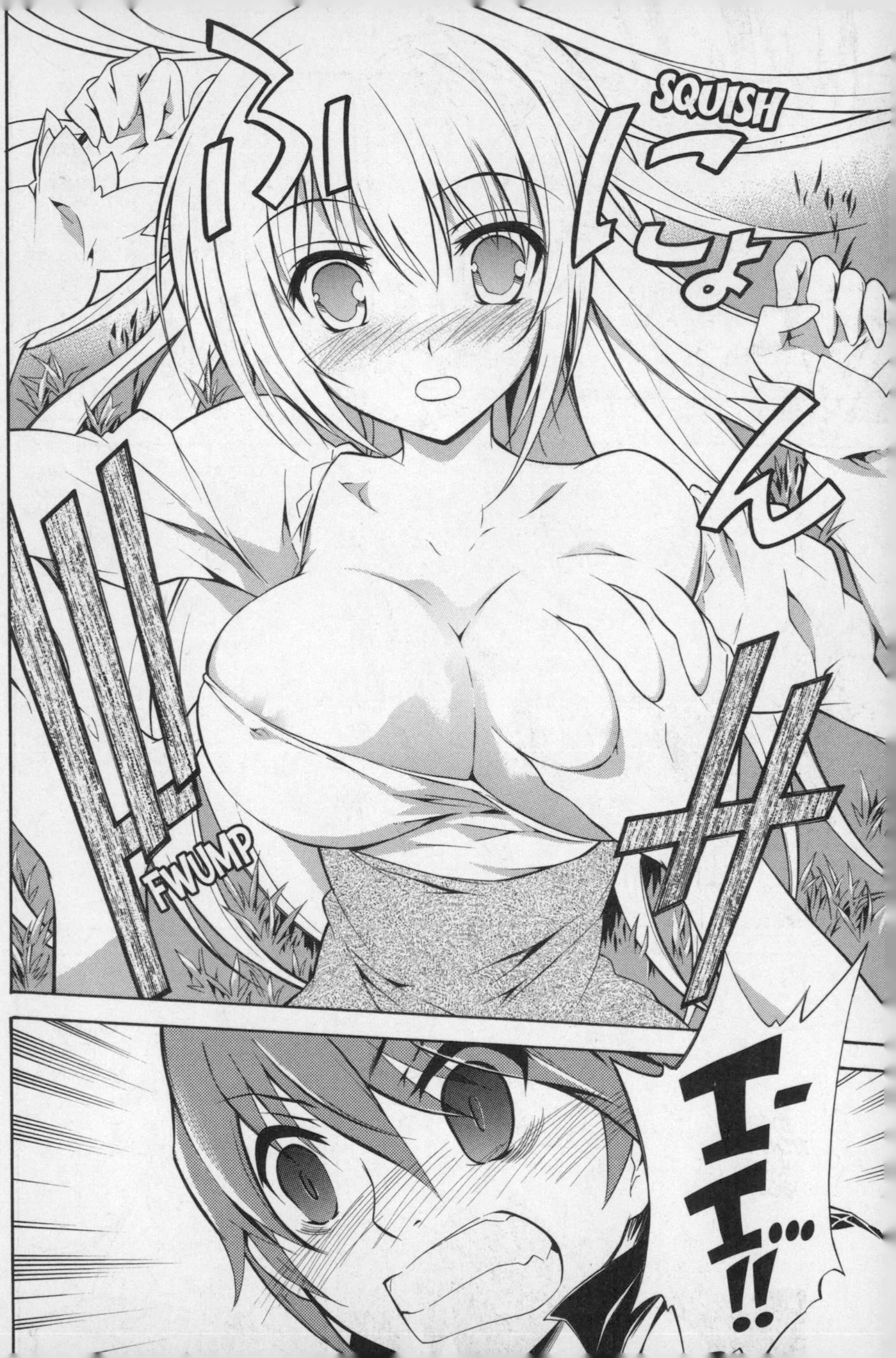
ふにょん
SQUISH
ドサッ
FWUMP
エーエ…!!

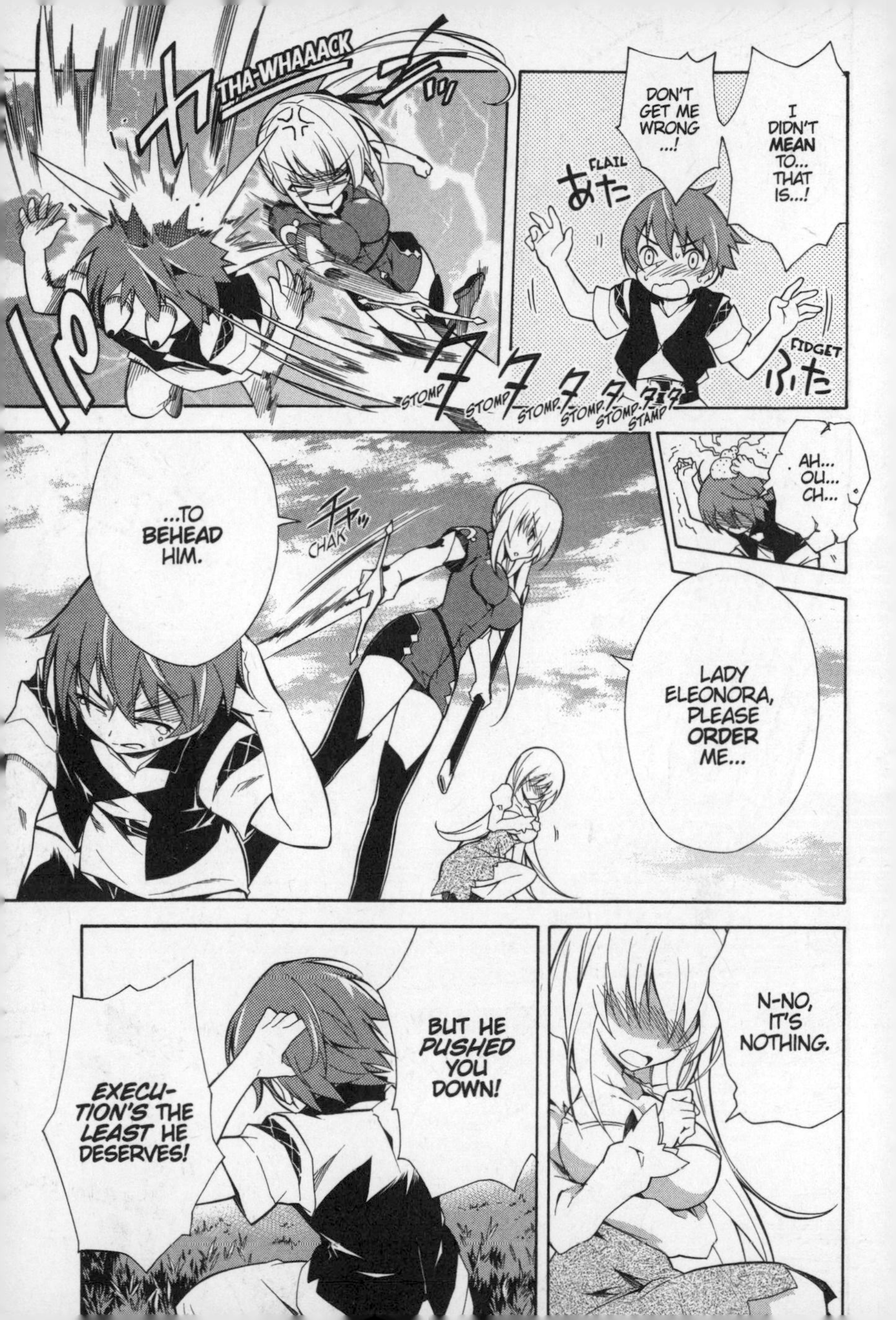
I DIDN'T MEAN TO... THAT IS...!
DON'T GET ME WRONG...!
FLAIL あた
FIDGET ふた
THA-WHAAACK
STOMP STOMP STOMP STOMP STOMP STAMP
AH... OU... CH...
LADY ELEONORA, PLEASE ORDER ME...
CHAK
...TO BEHEAD HIM.
N-NO, IT'S NOTHING.
BUT HE *PUSHED* YOU DOWN!
EXECUTION'S THE *LEAST* HE DESERVES!

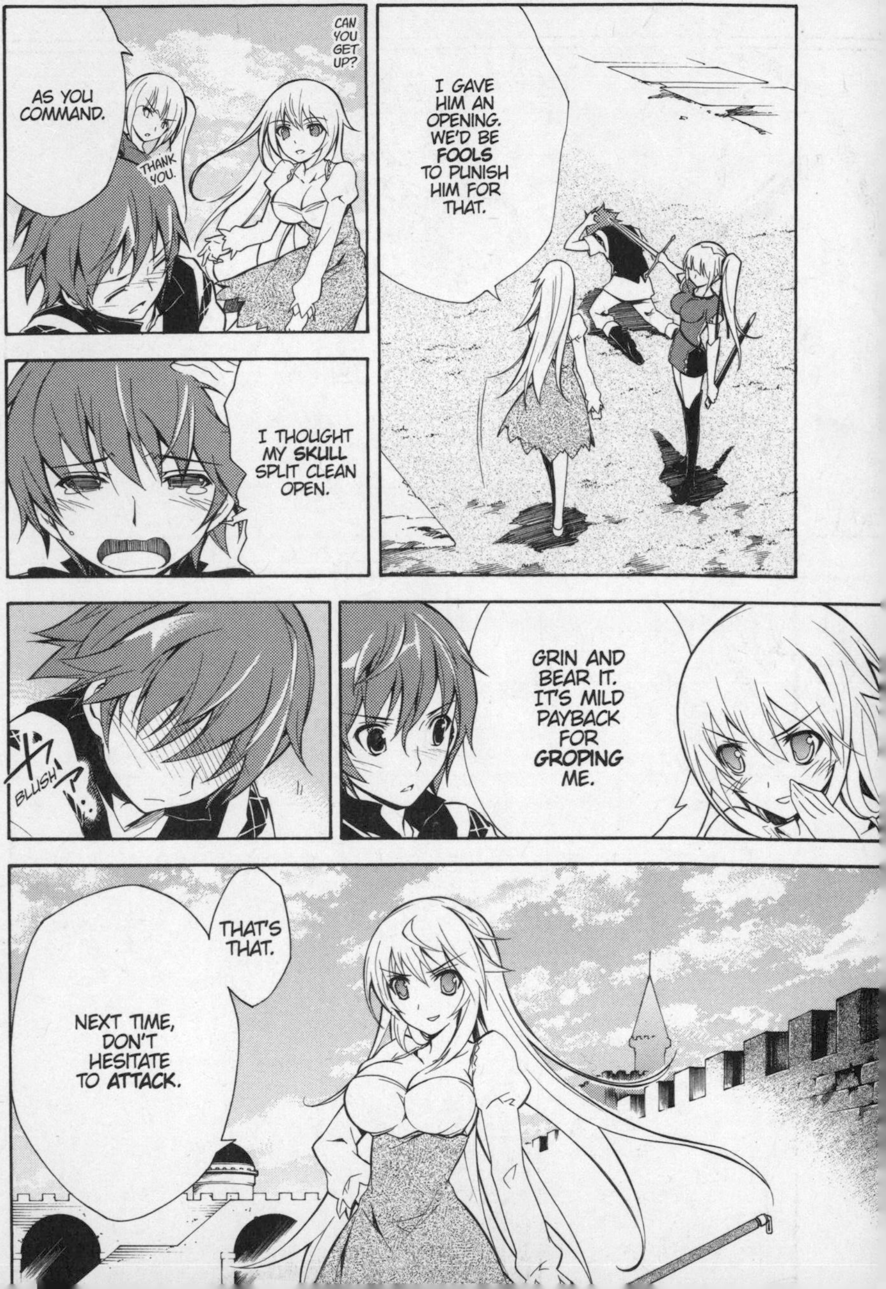
I GAVE HIM AN OPENING. WE'D BE FOOLS TO PUNISH HIM FOR THAT.
CAN YOU GET UP?
AS YOU COMMAND.
THANK YOU.
I THOUGHT MY SKULL SPLIT CLEAN OPEN.
GRIN AND BEAR IT. IT'S MILD PAYBACK FOR GROPING ME.
BLUSH
THAT'S THAT.
NEXT TIME, DON'T HESITATE TO ATTACK.

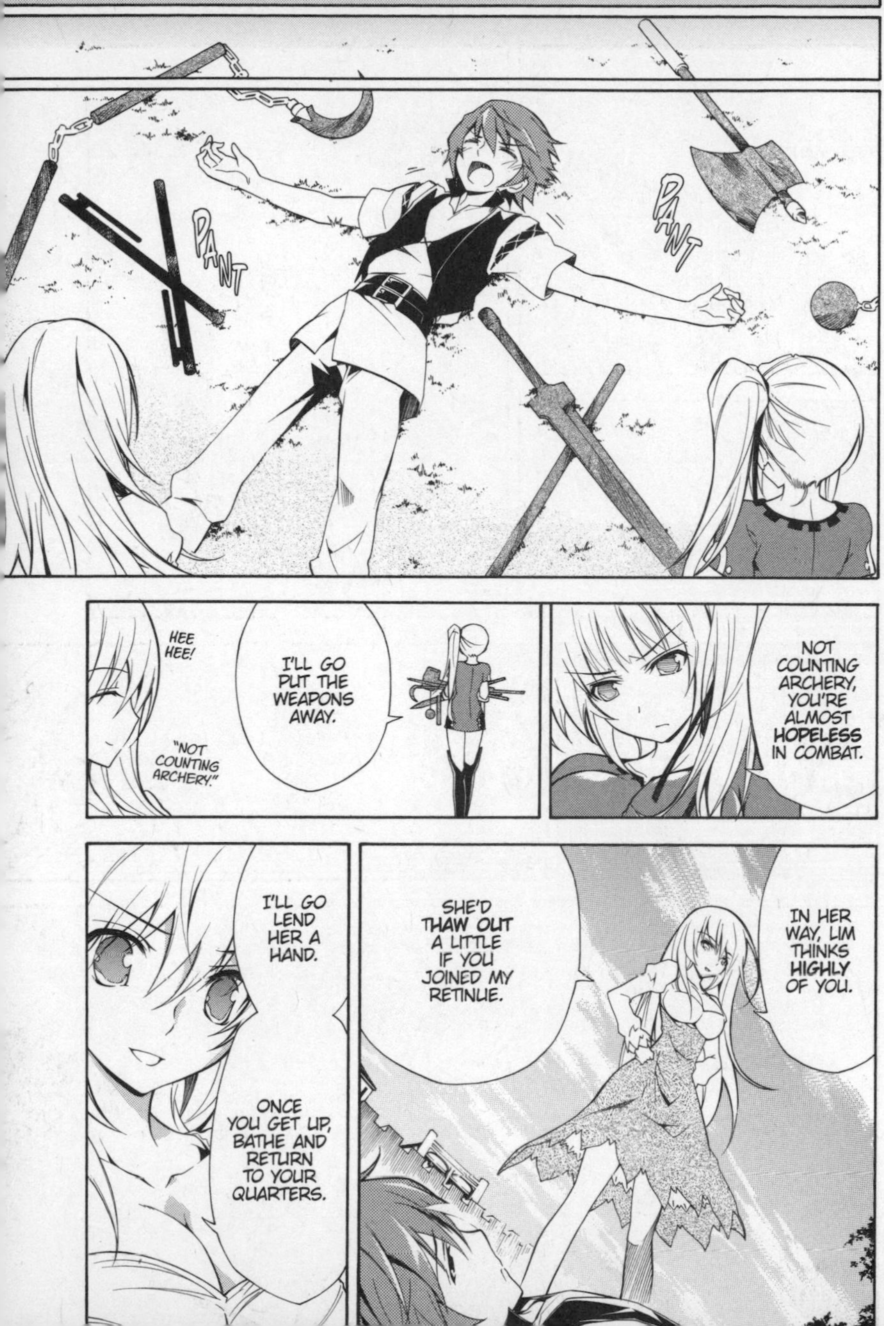
PANT
PANT
NOT COUNTING ARCHERY, YOU'RE ALMOST HOPELESS IN COMBAT.
I'LL GO PUT THE WEAPONS AWAY.
HEE HEE!
"NOT COUNTING ARCHERY."
IN HER WAY, LIM THINKS HIGHLY OF YOU.
SHE'D THAW OUT A LITTLE IF YOU JOINED MY RETINUE.
I'LL GO LEND HER A HAND.
ONCE YOU GET UP, BATHE AND RETURN TO YOUR QUARTERS.

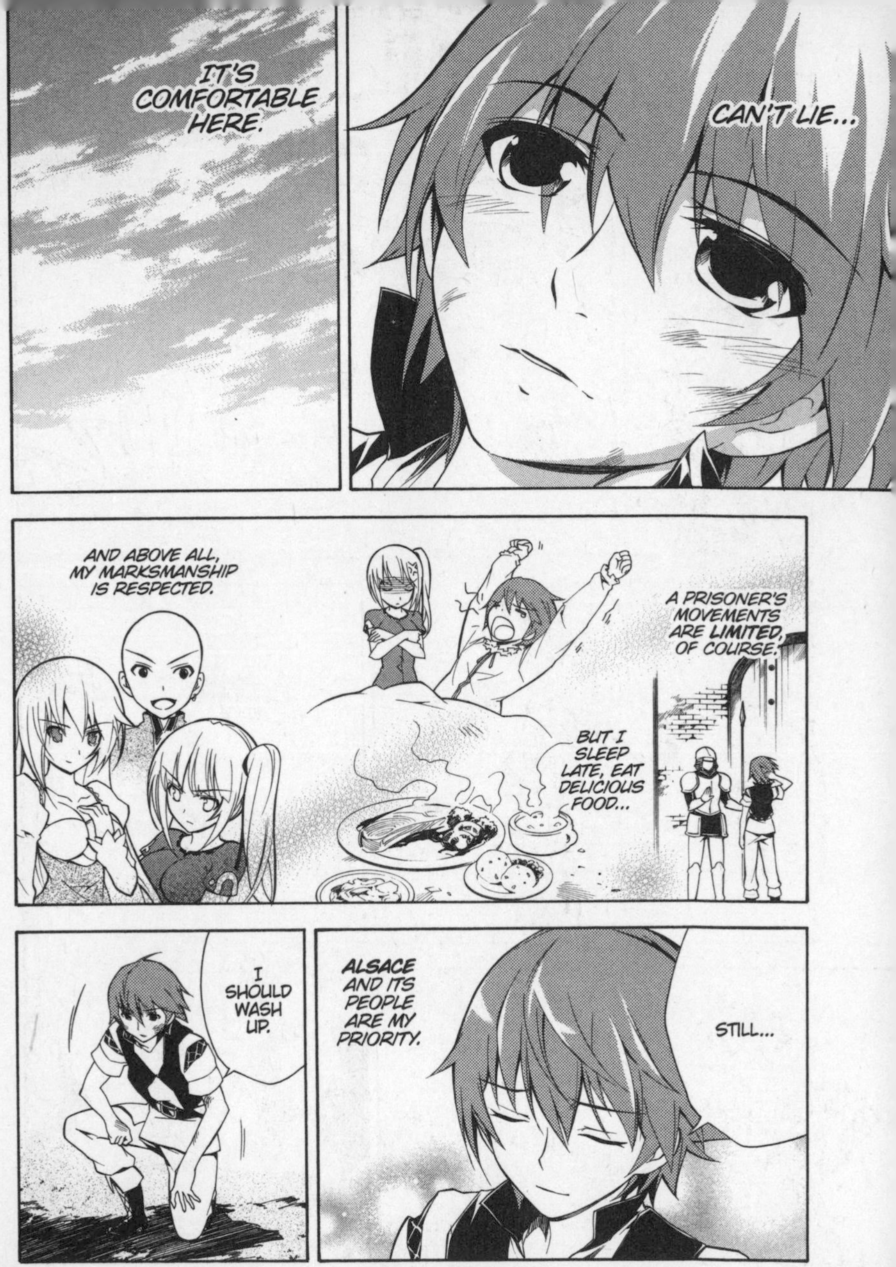
CAN'T LIE...
IT'S COMFORTABLE HERE.
A PRISONER'S MOVEMENTS ARE **LIMITED**, OF COURSE.
BUT I SLEEP LATE, EAT DELICIOUS FOOD...
AND ABOVE ALL, MY MARKSMANSHIP IS RESPECTED.
STILL...
ALSACE AND ITS PEOPLE ARE MY PRIORITY.
I SHOULD WASH UP.

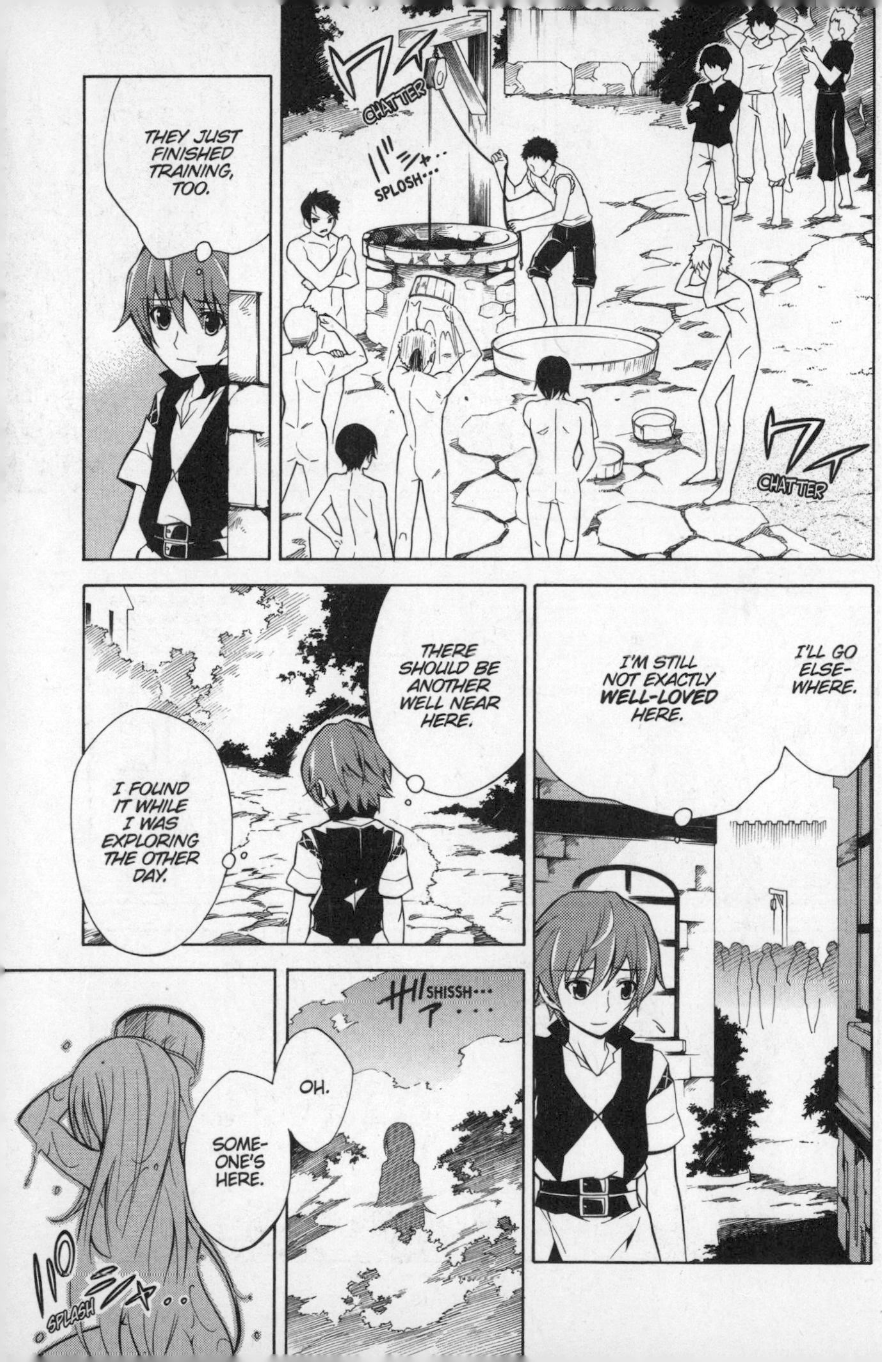
ワイ
CHATTER
バシャ…
SPLOSH…
ワイ
CHATTER
THEY JUST FINISHED TRAINING, TOO.
I'LL GO ELSE-WHERE.
I'M STILL NOT EXACTLY **WELL-LOVED** HERE.
THERE SHOULD BE ANOTHER WELL NEAR HERE.
I FOUND IT WHILE I WAS EXPLORING THE OTHER DAY.
SHISSH…
OH.
SOME-ONE'S HERE.
SPLASH

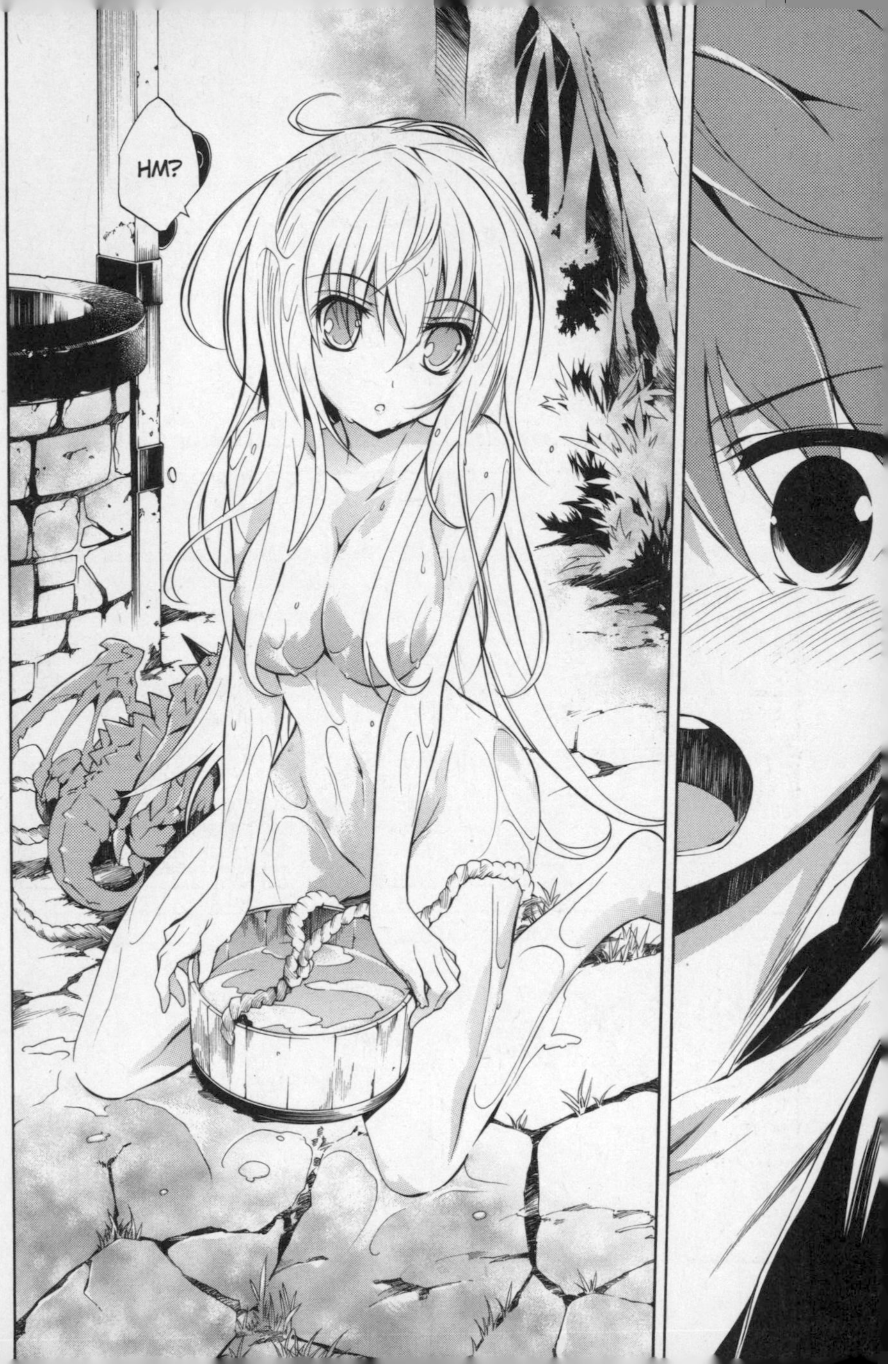
HM?

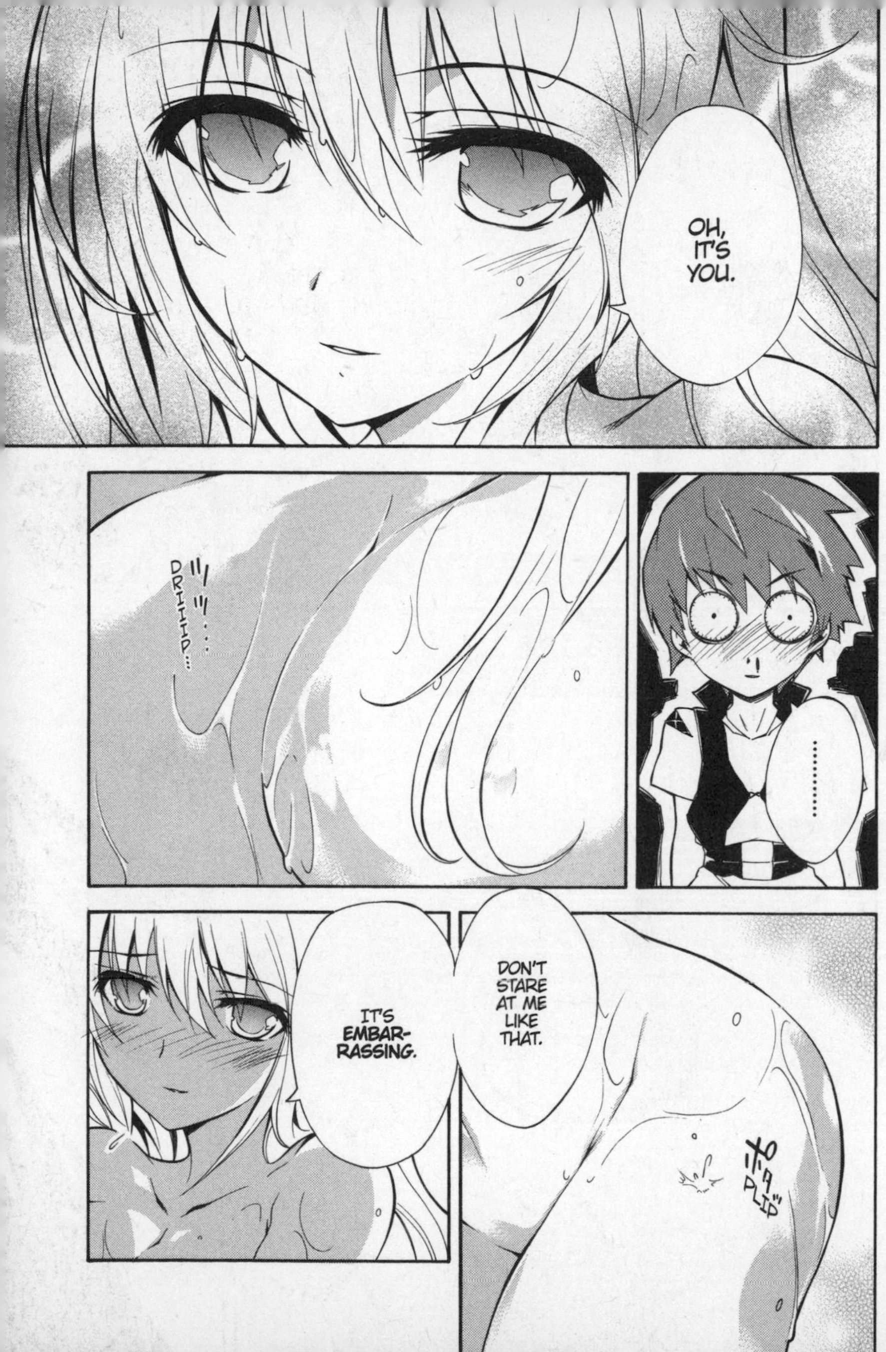
OH, IT'S YOU.
......
DRIIIP...
DON'T STARE AT ME LIKE THAT.
PLIP
IT'S EMBARRASSING.

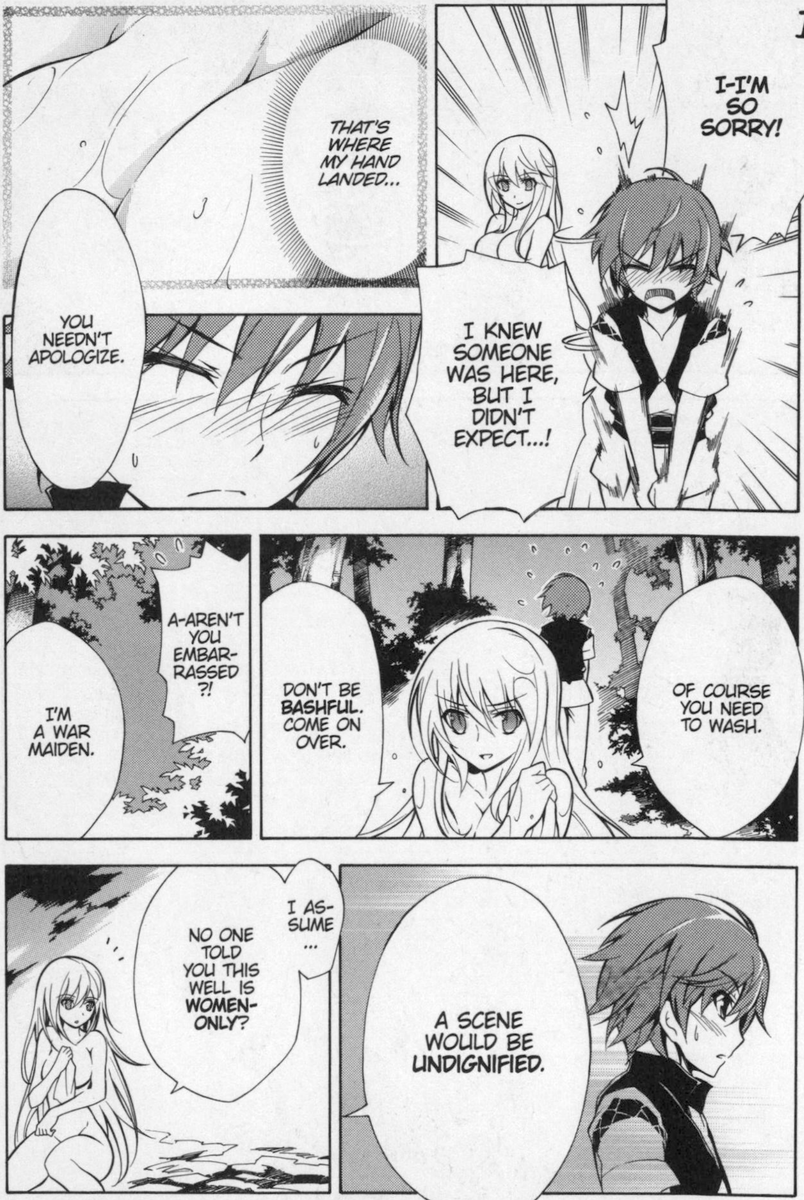
I...
I-I'M SO SORRY!
I KNEW SOMEONE WAS HERE, BUT I DIDN'T EXPECT...!
THAT'S WHERE MY HAND LANDED...
YOU NEEDN'T APOLOGIZE.
OF COURSE YOU NEED TO WASH.
DON'T BE BASHFUL. COME ON OVER.
A-AREN'T YOU EMBARRASSED?!
I'M A WAR MAIDEN.
A SCENE WOULD BE UNDIGNIFIED.
I ASSUME...
NO ONE TOLD YOU THIS WELL IS WOMEN-ONLY?

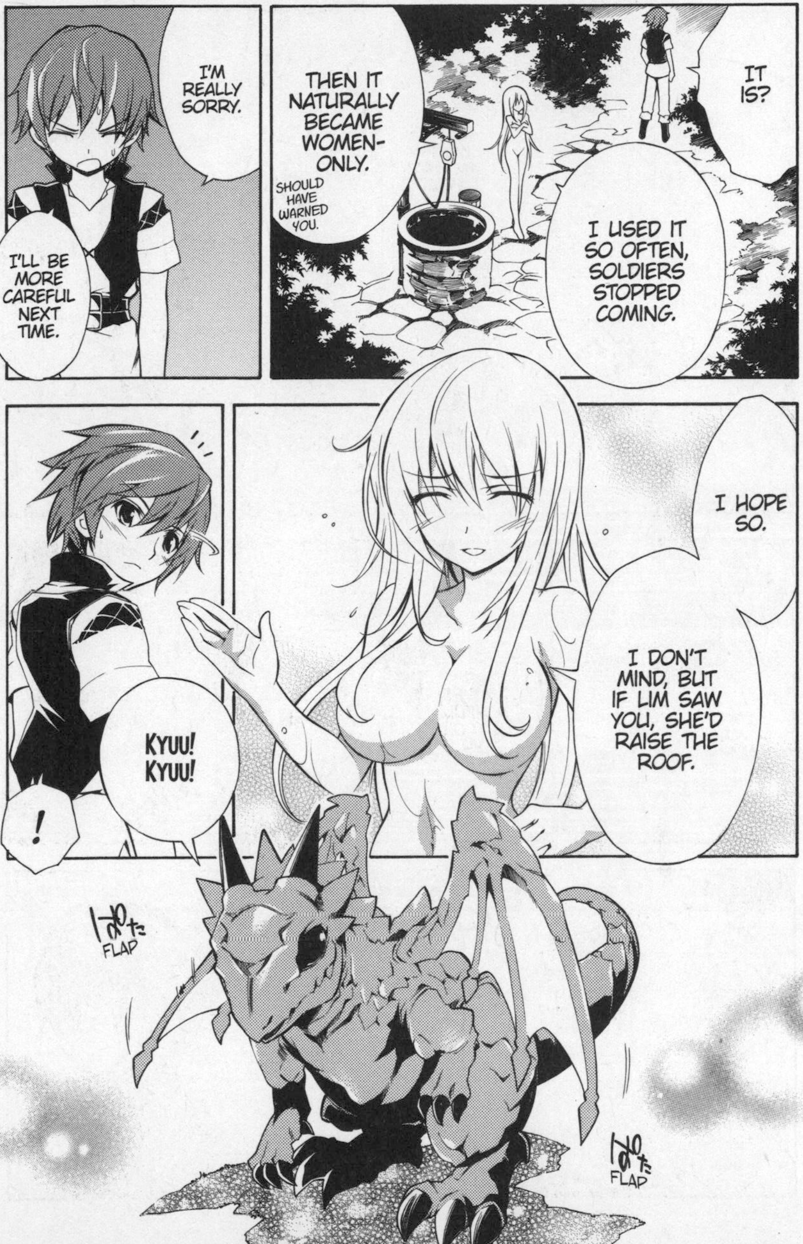
IT IS?
I USED IT SO OFTEN, SOLDIERS STOPPED COMING.
THEN IT NATURALLY BECAME WOMEN-ONLY.
SHOULD HAVE WARNED YOU.
I'M REALLY SORRY.
I'LL BE MORE CAREFUL NEXT TIME.
I HOPE SO.
I DON'T MIND, BUT IF LIM SAW YOU, SHE'D RAISE THE ROOF.
KYUU! KYUU!
!
FLAP
FLAP

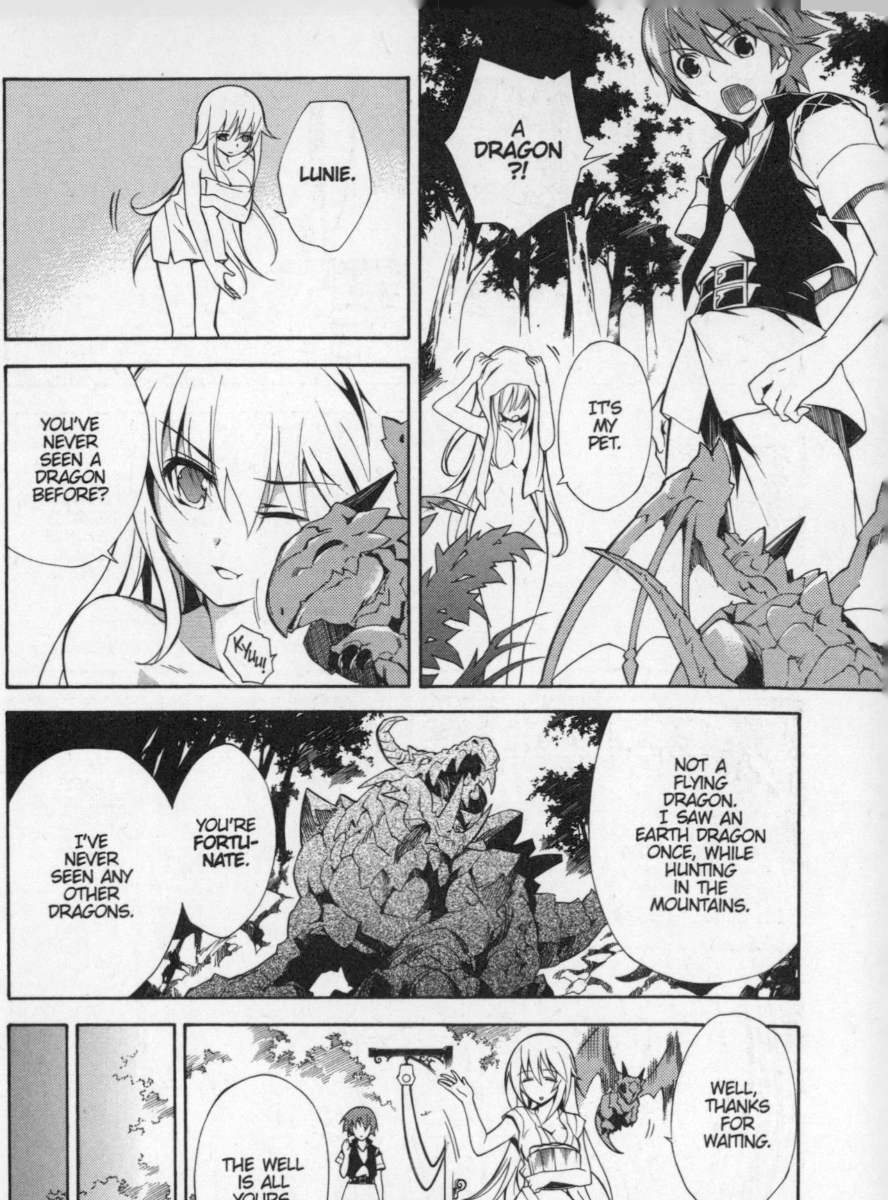
A DRAGON ?!
IT'S MY PET.
LUNIE.
YOU'VE NEVER SEEN A DRAGON BEFORE?
K-YUU!
NOT A FLYING DRAGON. I SAW AN EARTH DRAGON ONCE, WHILE HUNTING IN THE MOUNTAINS.
YOU'RE FORTU-NATE.
I'VE NEVER SEEN ANY OTHER DRAGONS.
WELL, THANKS FOR WAITING.
THE WELL IS ALL YOURS.

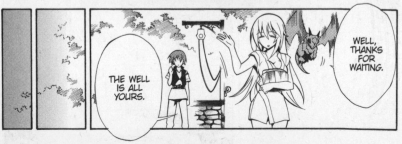

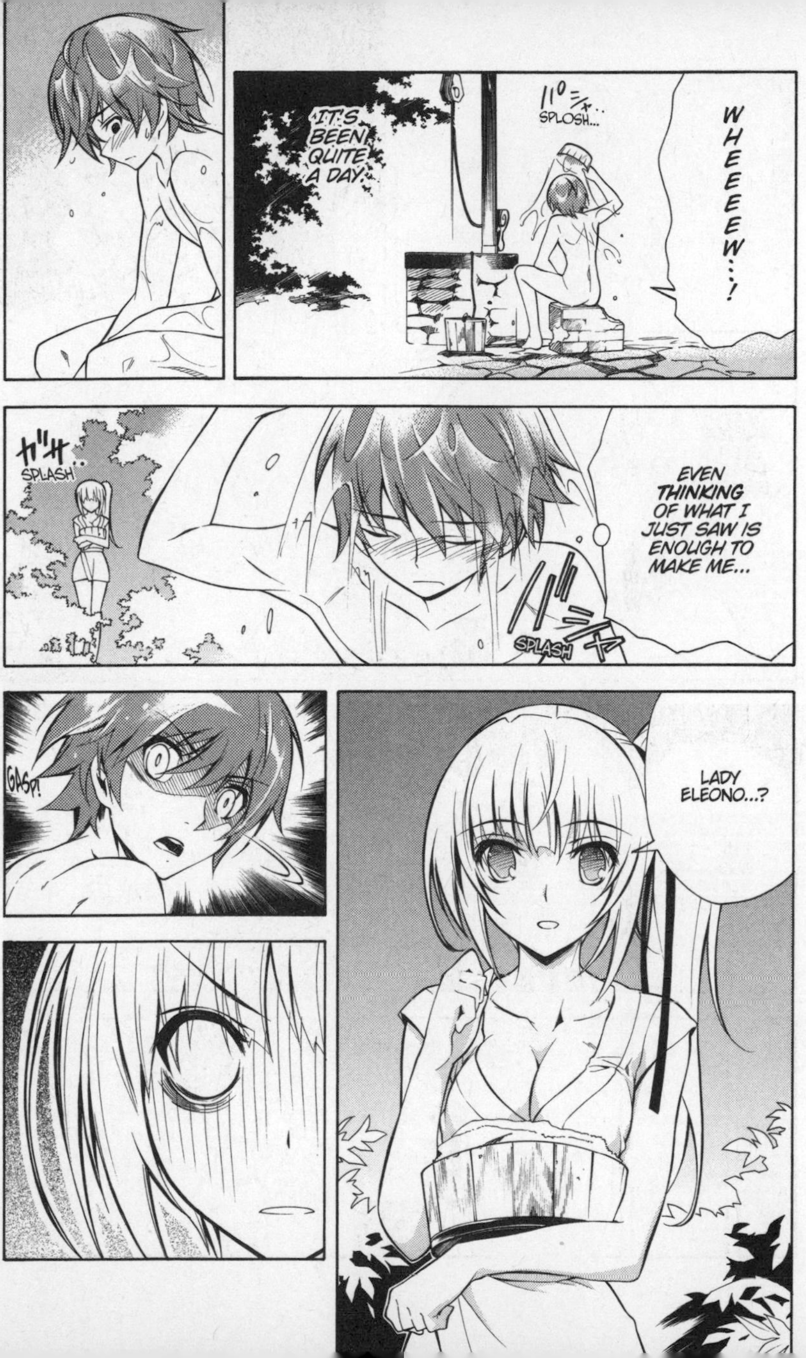
WHEEEEEW...!
パシャ...
SPLOSH...
IT'S BEEN QUITE A DAY.
EVEN THINKING OF WHAT I JUST SAW IS ENOUGH TO MAKE ME...
SPLASH
SPLASH
LADY ELEONO...?
GASP!

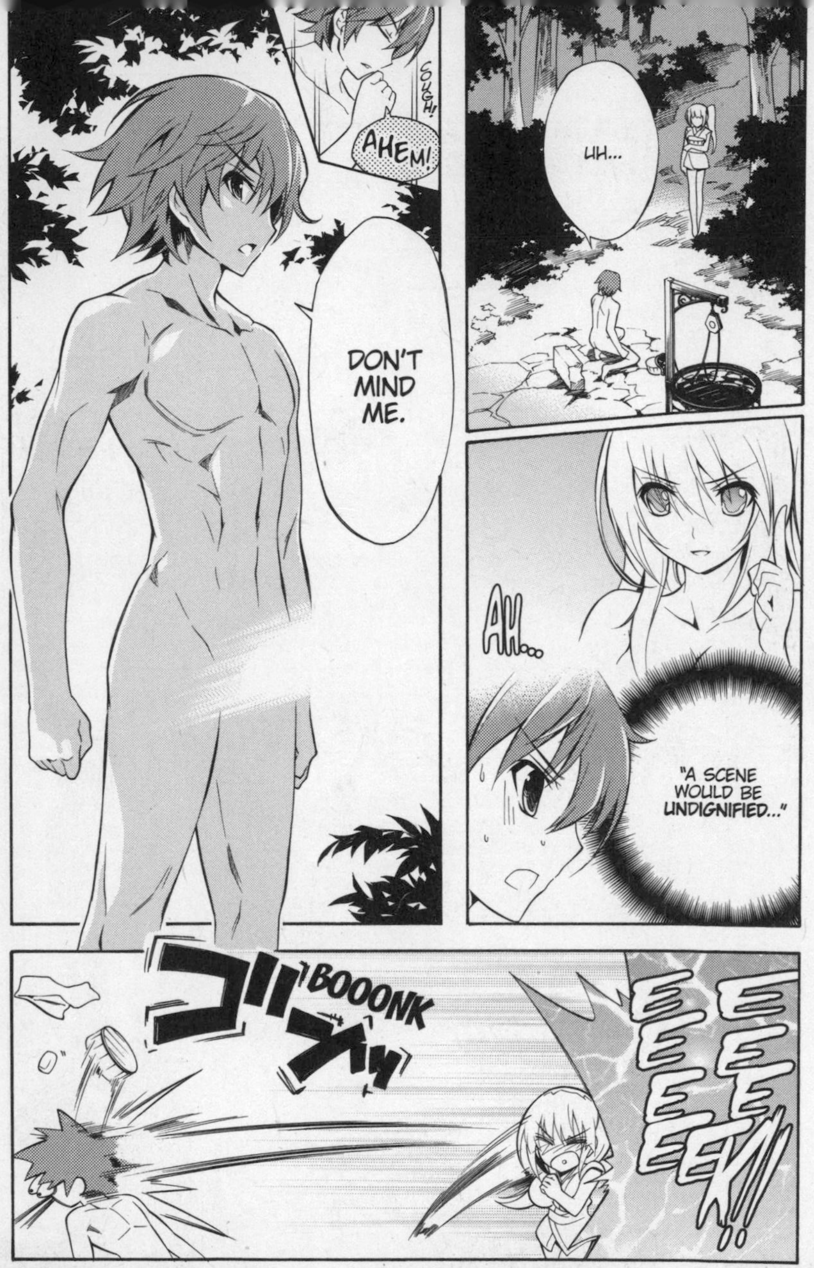
UH...
AH...
"A SCENE WOULD BE UNDIGNIFIED..."
AHEM!
COUGH!
DON'T MIND ME.
EEEEEEEEK!!
BOOOONK

CHAPTER 4: END

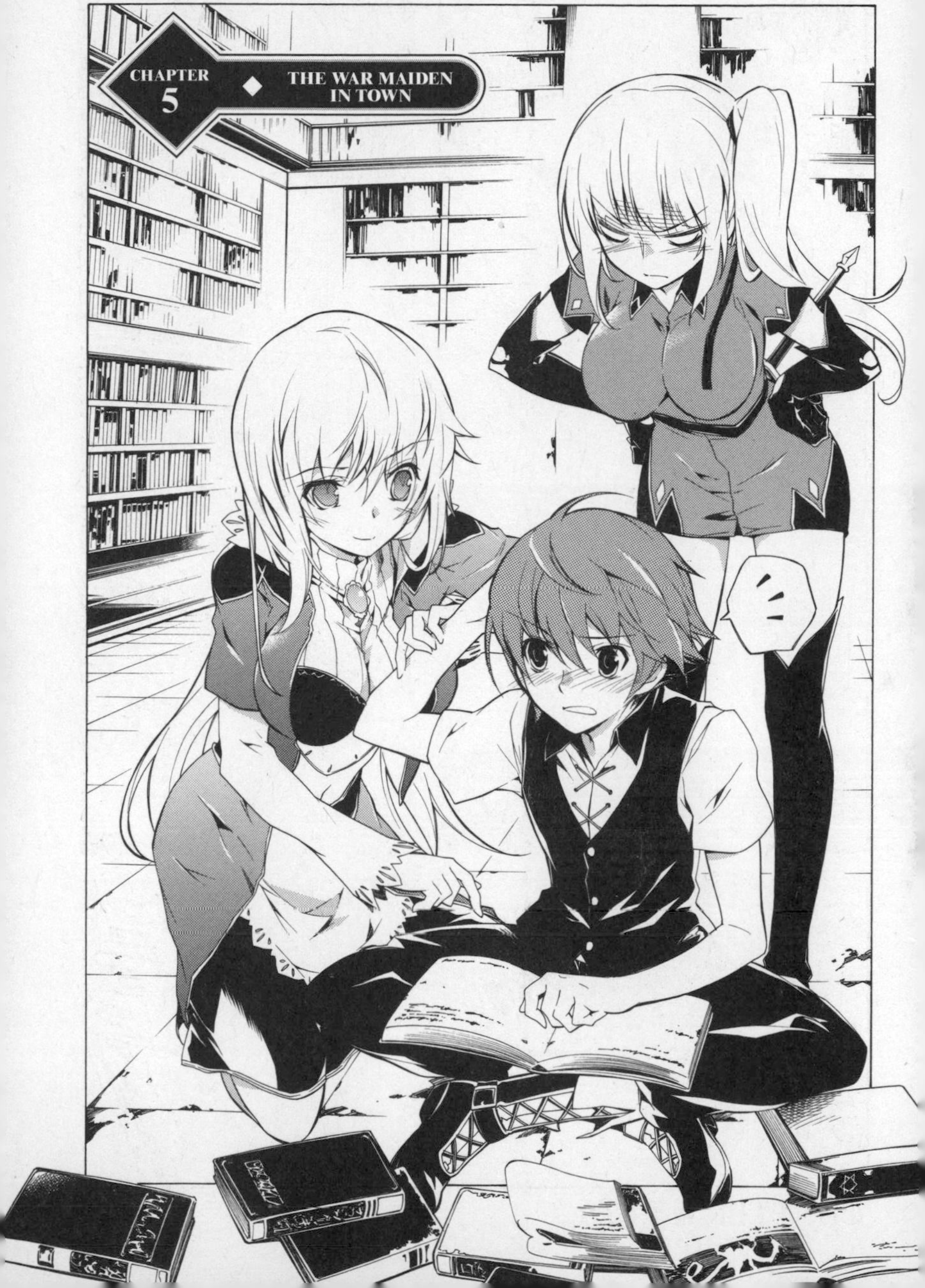
CHAPTER 5
THE WAR MAIDEN IN TOWN

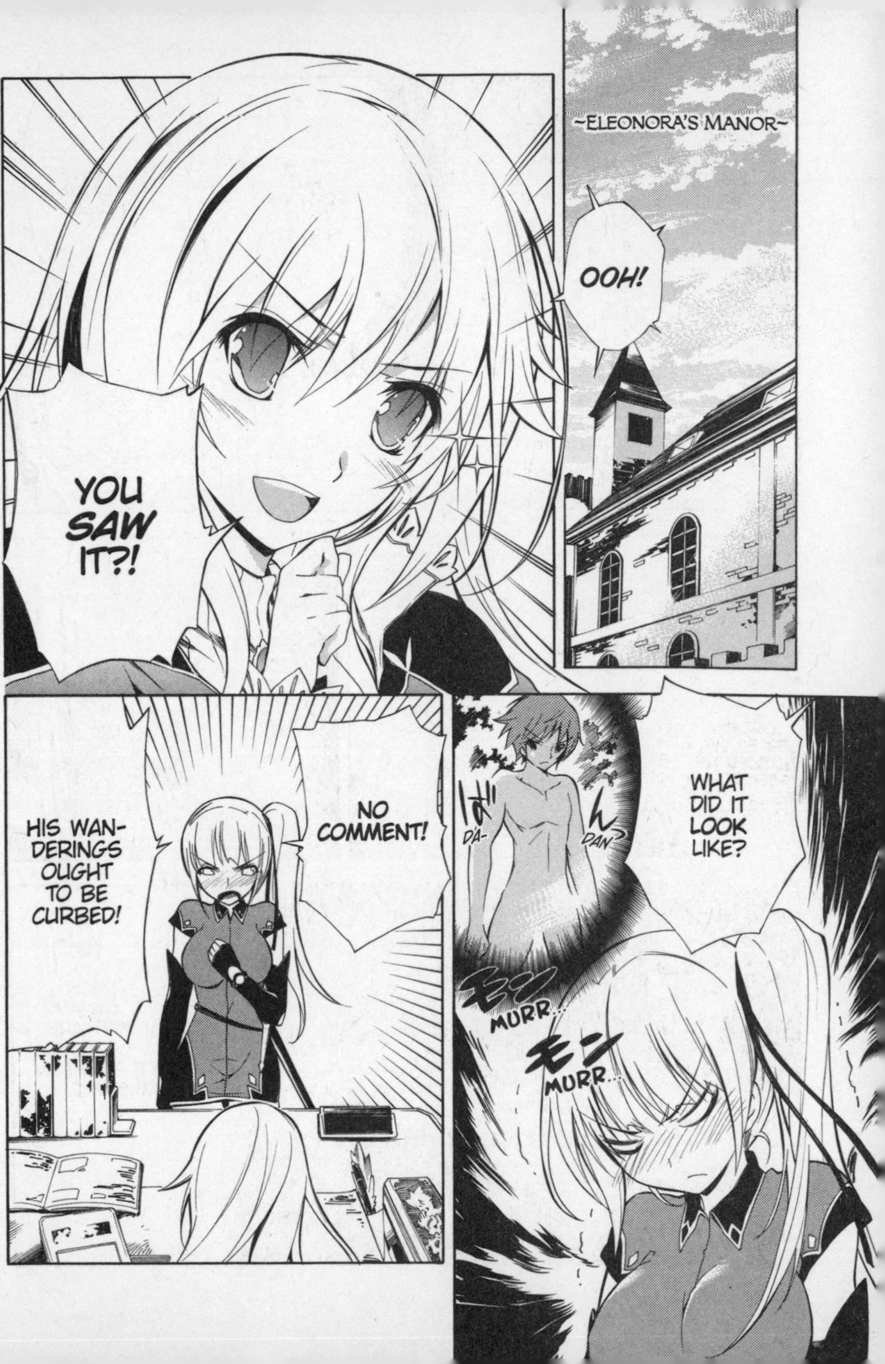
~ELEONORA'S MANOR~
OOH!
YOU SAW IT?!
WHAT DID IT LOOK LIKE?
DA-
DAN
MURR...
MURR...
NO COMMENT!
HIS WAN-DERINGS OUGHT TO BE CURBED!

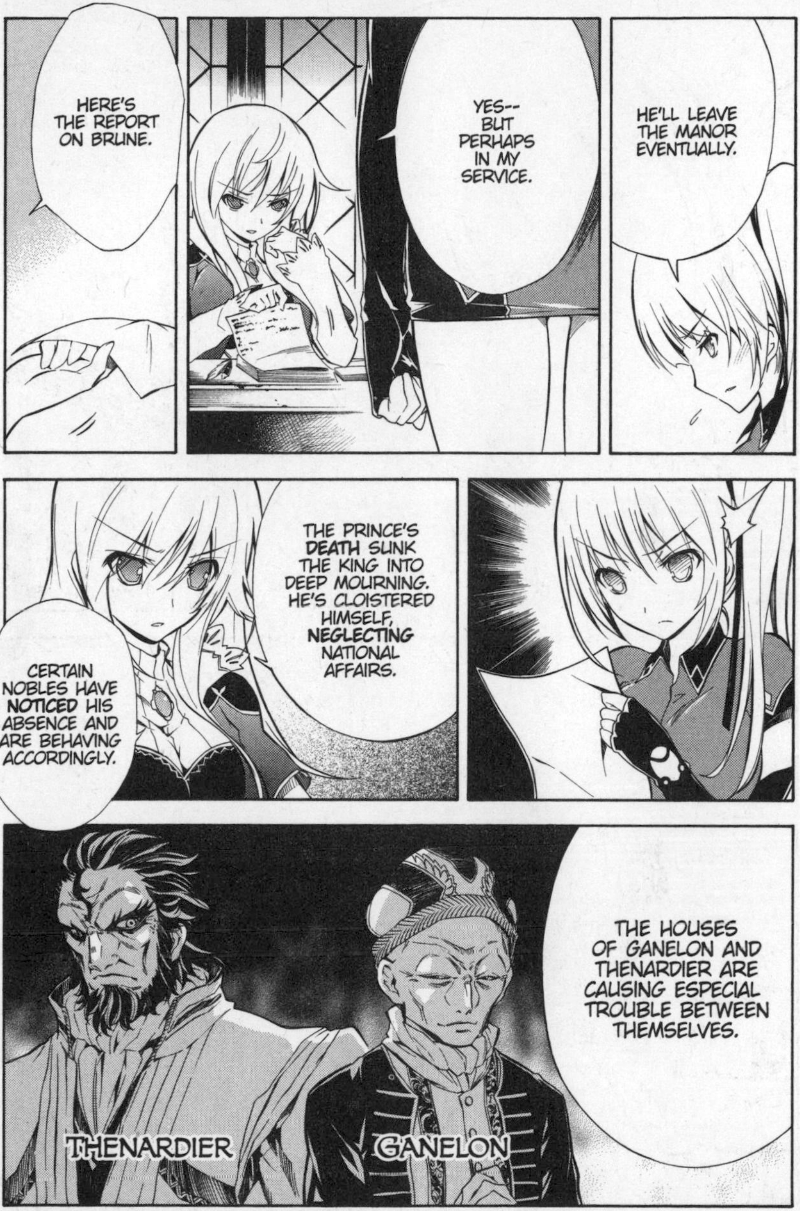
HE'LL LEAVE THE MANOR EVENTUALLY.
YES-- BUT PERHAPS IN MY SERVICE.
HERE'S THE REPORT ON BRUNE.
THE PRINCE'S DEATH SUNK THE KING INTO DEEP MOURNING. HE'S CLOISTERED HIMSELF, NEGLECTING NATIONAL AFFAIRS.
CERTAIN NOBLES HAVE NOTICED HIS ABSENCE AND ARE BEHAVING ACCORDINGLY.
THE HOUSES OF GANELON AND THENARDIER ARE CAUSING ESPECIAL TROUBLE BETWEEN THEMSELVES.
GANELON
THENARDIER

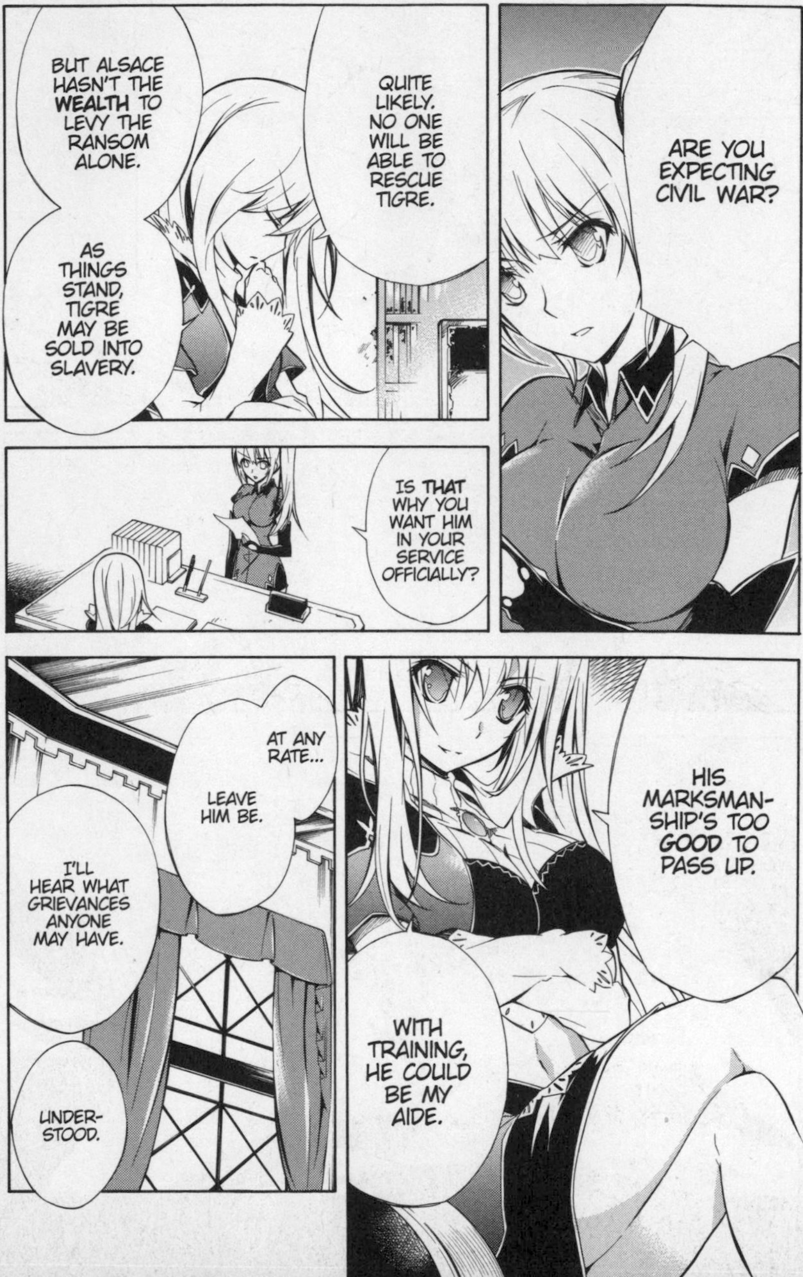
ARE YOU EXPECTING CIVIL WAR?
QUITE LIKELY. NO ONE WILL BE ABLE TO RESCUE TIGRE.
BUT ALSACE HASN'T THE **WEALTH** TO LEVY THE RANSOM ALONE.
AS THINGS STAND, TIGRE MAY BE SOLD INTO SLAVERY.
IS **THAT** WHY YOU WANT HIM IN YOUR SERVICE OFFICIALLY?
HIS MARKSMANSHIP'S TOO **GOOD** TO PASS UP.
WITH TRAINING, HE COULD BE MY AIDE.
AT ANY RATE...
LEAVE HIM BE.
I'LL HEAR WHAT GRIEVANCES ANYONE MAY HAVE.
UNDER-STOOD.

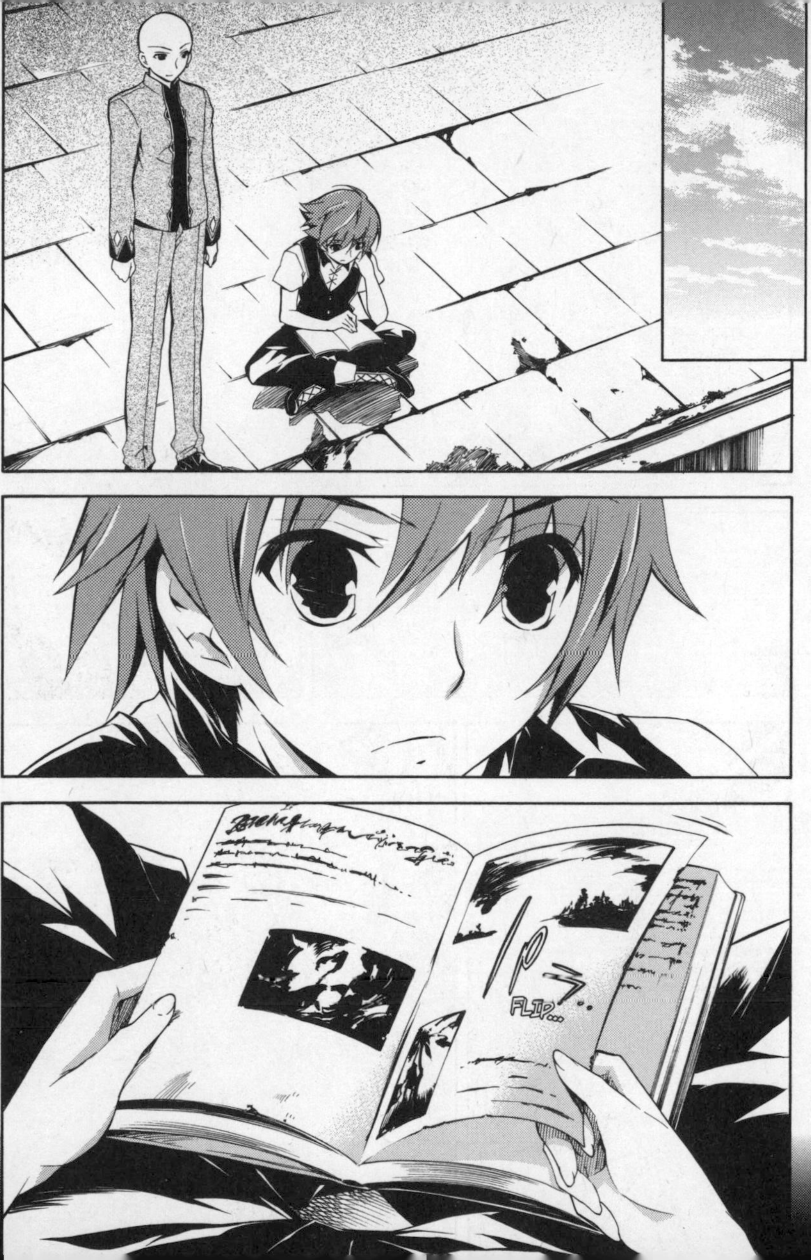
FLIP...

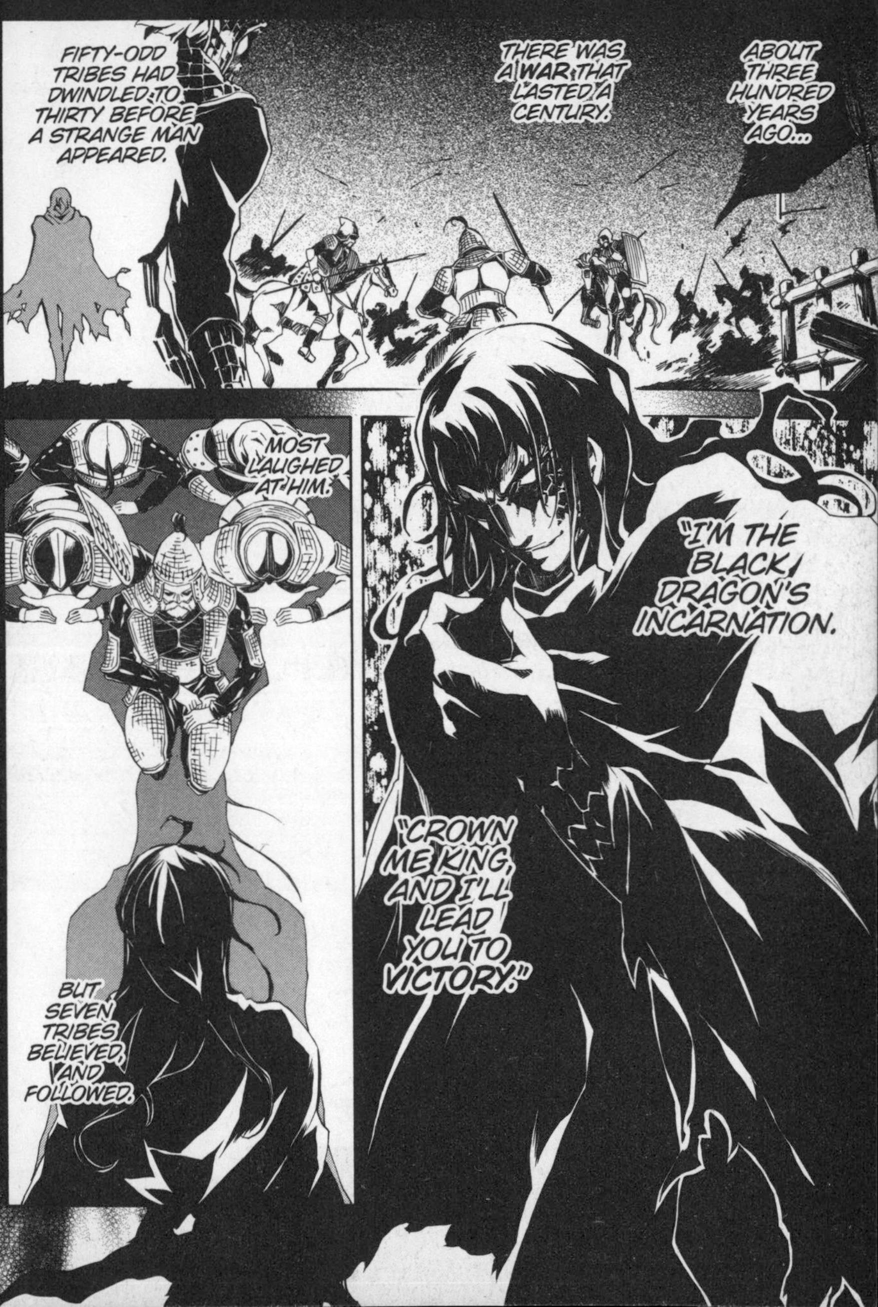
ABOUT THREE HUNDRED YEARS AGO...
THERE WAS A WAR THAT LASTED A CENTURY.
FIFTY-ODD TRIBES HAD DWINDLED TO THIRTY BEFORE A STRANGE MAN APPEARED.
"I'M THE BLACK DRAGON'S INCARNATION.
"CROWN ME KING, AND I'LL LEAD YOU TO VICTORY."
MOST LAUGHED AT HIM.
BUT SEVEN TRIBES BELIEVED, AND FOLLOWED.

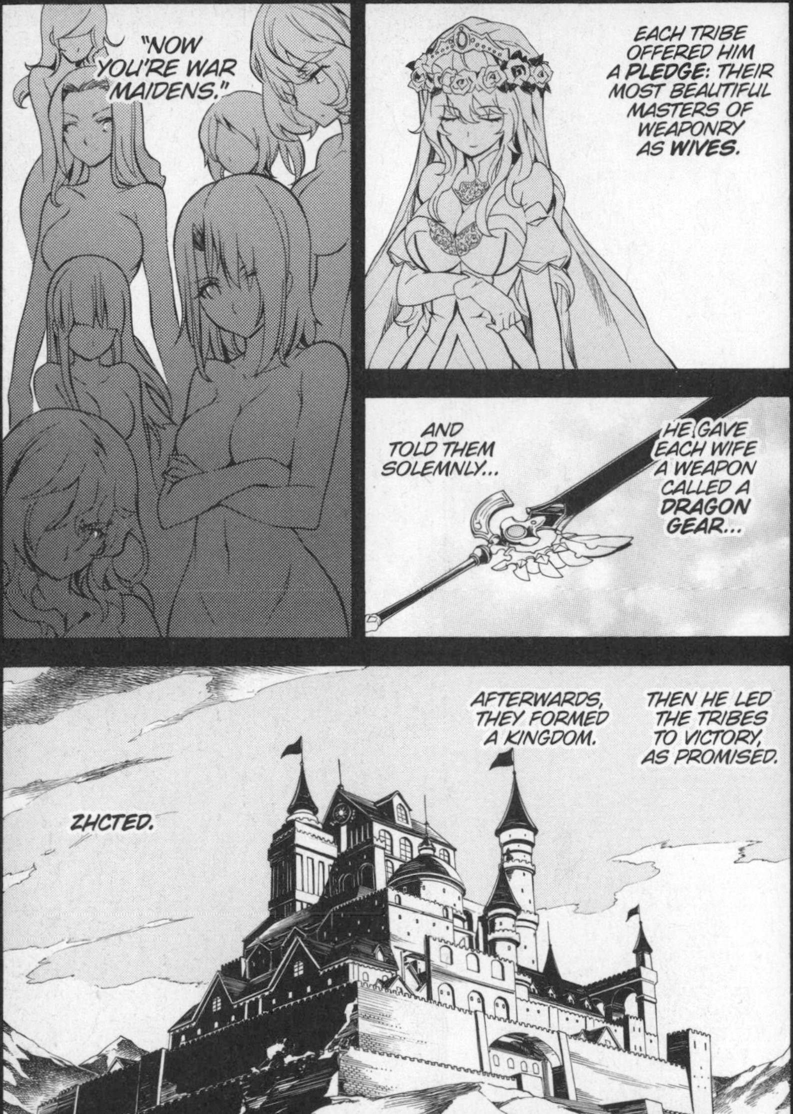
EACH TRIBE OFFERED HIM A PLEDGE: THEIR MOST BEAUTIFUL MASTERS OF WEAPONRY AS WIVES.
HE GAVE EACH WIFE A WEAPON CALLED A DRAGON GEAR...
AND TOLD THEM SOLEMNLY...
"NOW YOU'RE WAR MAIDENS."
THEN HE LED THE TRIBES TO VICTORY, AS PROMISED.
AFTERWARDS, THEY FORMED A KINGDOM.
ZHCTED.

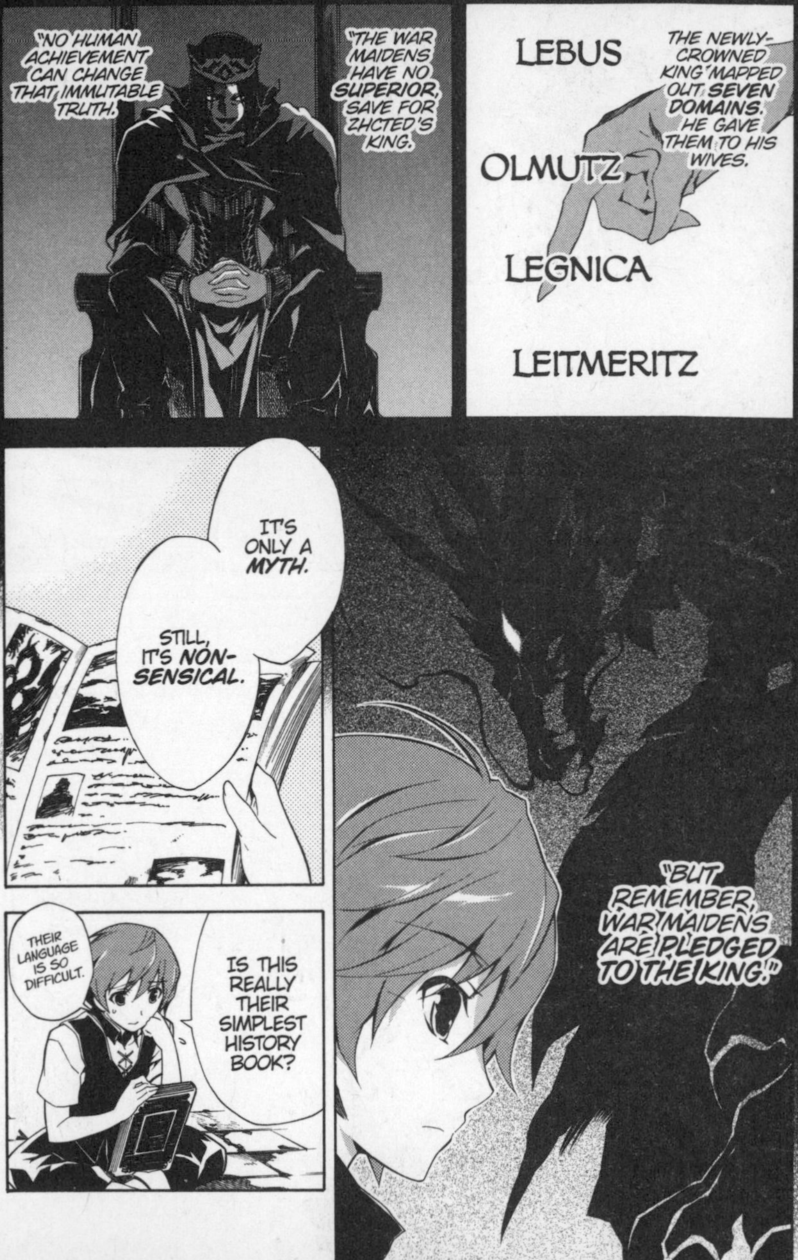
THE NEWLY-CROWNED KING MAPPED OUT SEVEN DOMAINS. HE GAVE THEM TO HIS WIVES.
LEBUS
OLMUTZ
LEGNICA
LEITMERITZ
"THE WAR MAIDENS HAVE NO SUPERIOR, SAVE FOR ZHCTED'S KING.
"NO HUMAN ACHIEVEMENT CAN CHANGE THAT IMMUTABLE TRUTH.
"BUT REMEMBER, WAR MAIDENS ARE PLEDGED TO THE KING."
IT'S ONLY A MYTH.
STILL, IT'S NON-SENSICAL.
IS THIS REALLY THEIR SIMPLEST HISTORY BOOK?
THEIR LANGUAGE IS SO DIFFICULT.

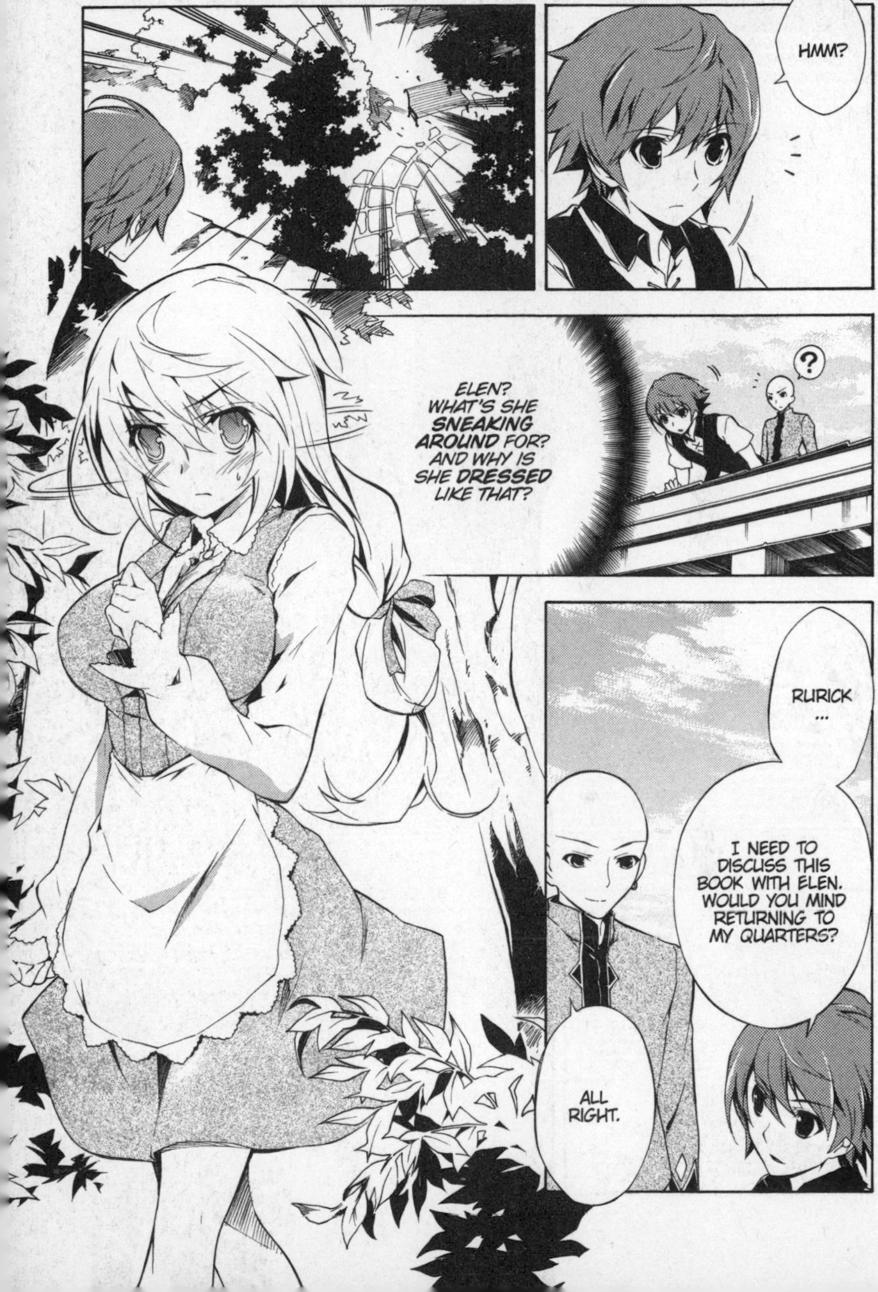
HMM?
?
ELEN? WHAT'S SHE SNEAKING AROUND FOR? AND WHY IS SHE DRESSED LIKE THAT?
RURICK ...
I NEED TO DISCUSS THIS BOOK WITH ELEN. WOULD YOU MIND RETURNING TO MY QUARTERS?
ALL RIGHT.

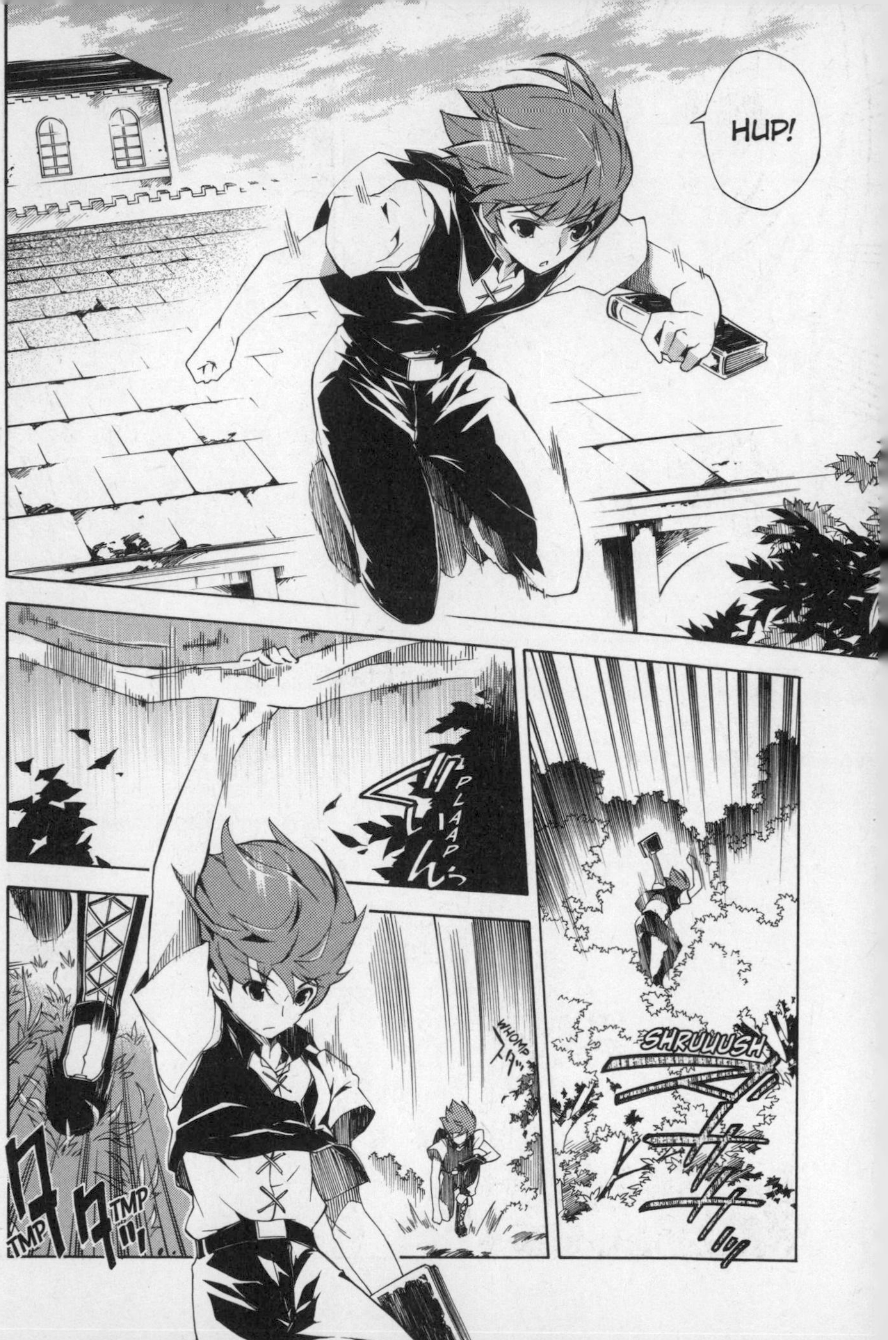
HUP!
SHRUUUSH
PLAAP
WHOMP
TMP
TMP

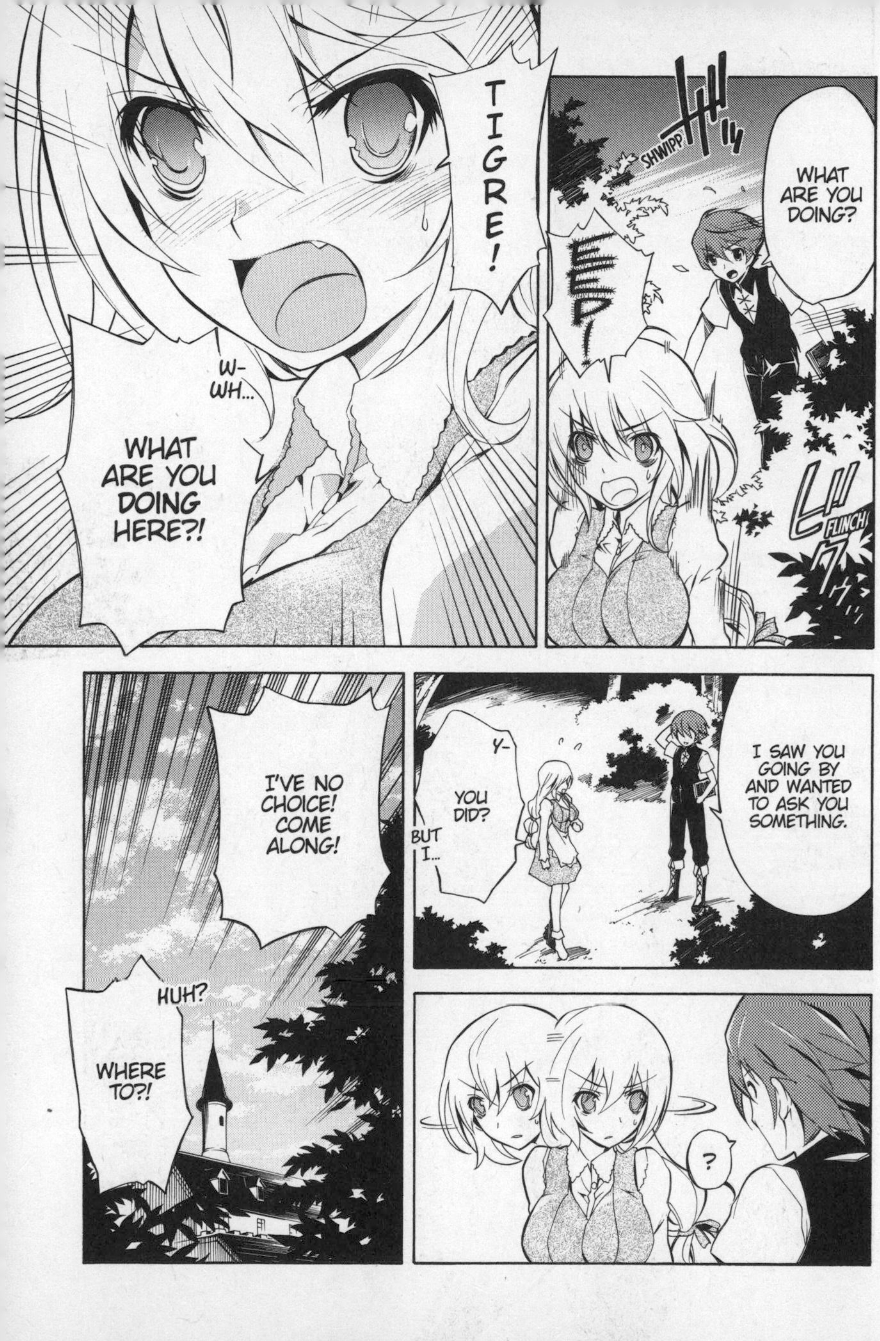
SHWIPP
WHAT ARE YOU DOING?
EEP!
FLINCH
TIGRE!
W-WH...
WHAT ARE YOU DOING HERE?!
I SAW YOU GOING BY AND WANTED TO ASK YOU SOMETHING.
Y-
YOU DID?
BUT I...
?
I'VE NO CHOICE! COME ALONG!
HUH?
WHERE TO?!

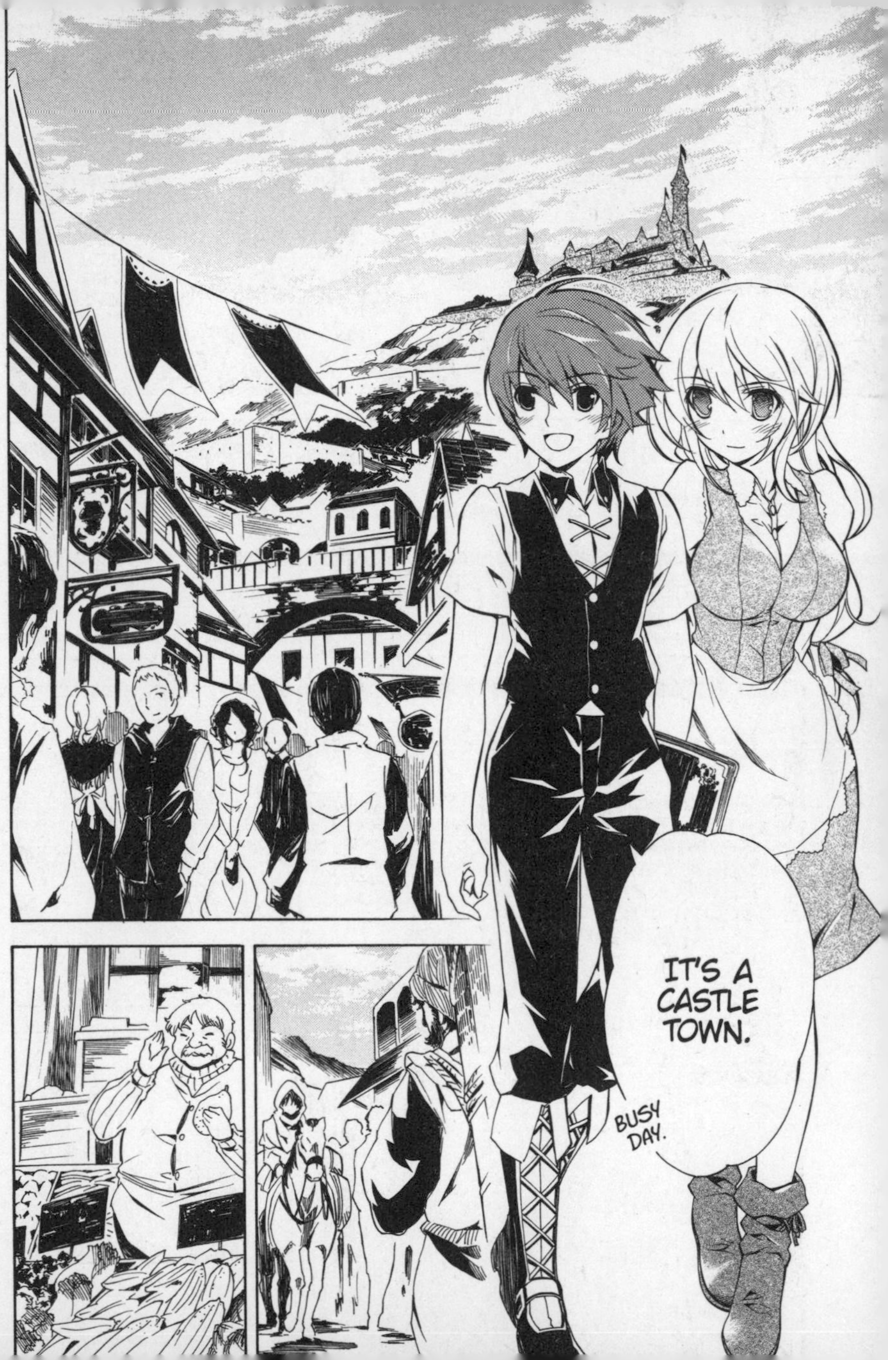
IT'S A CASTLE TOWN.
BUSY DAY.

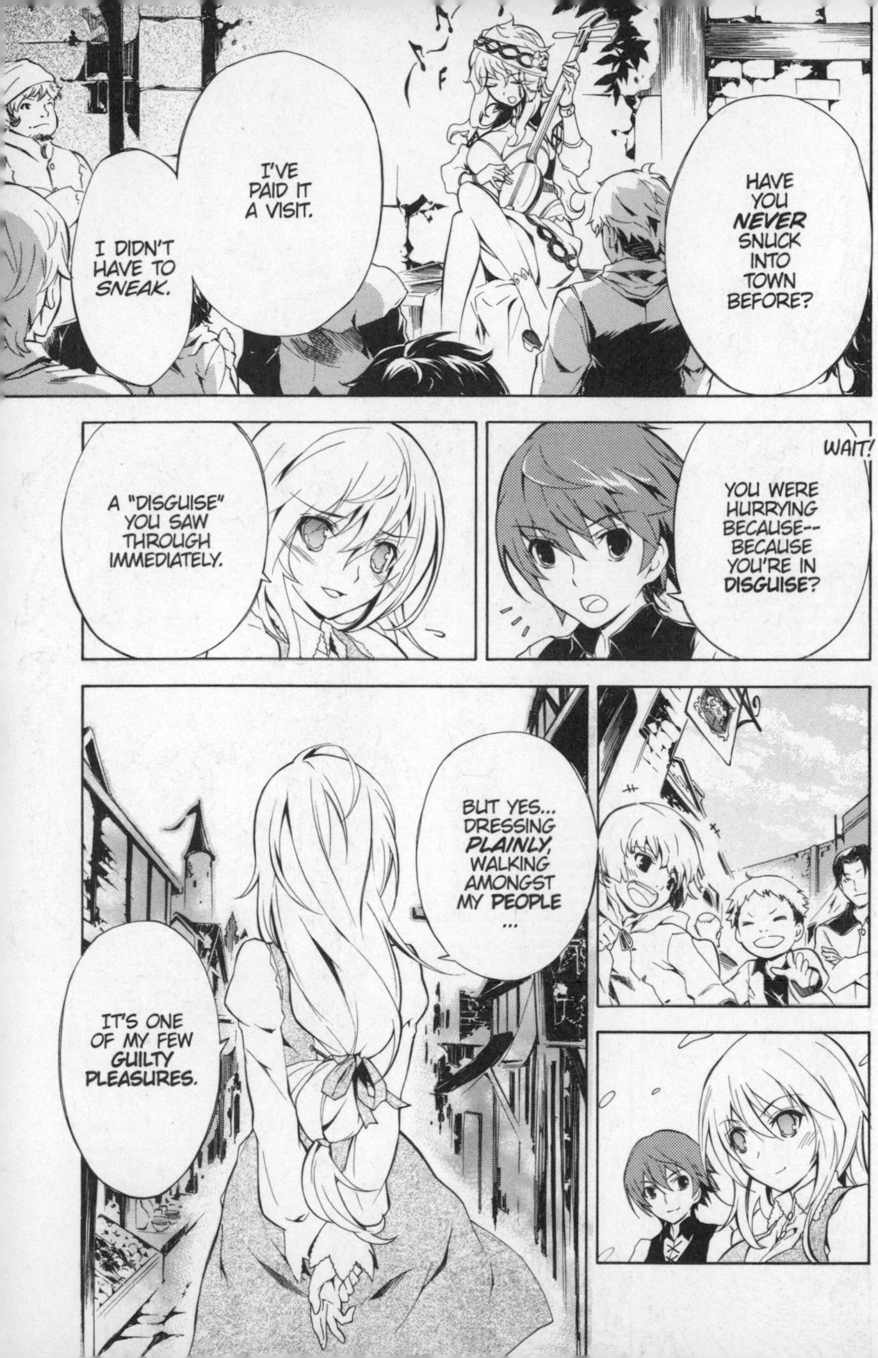
HAVE YOU NEVER SNUCK INTO TOWN BEFORE?
I'VE PAID IT A VISIT.
I DIDN'T HAVE TO SNEAK.
WAIT!
YOU WERE HURRYING BECAUSE-- BECAUSE YOU'RE IN DISGUISE?
A "DISGUISE" YOU SAW THROUGH IMMEDIATELY.
BUT YES... DRESSING PLAINLY, WALKING AMONGST MY PEOPLE ...
IT'S ONE OF MY FEW GUILTY PLEASURES.

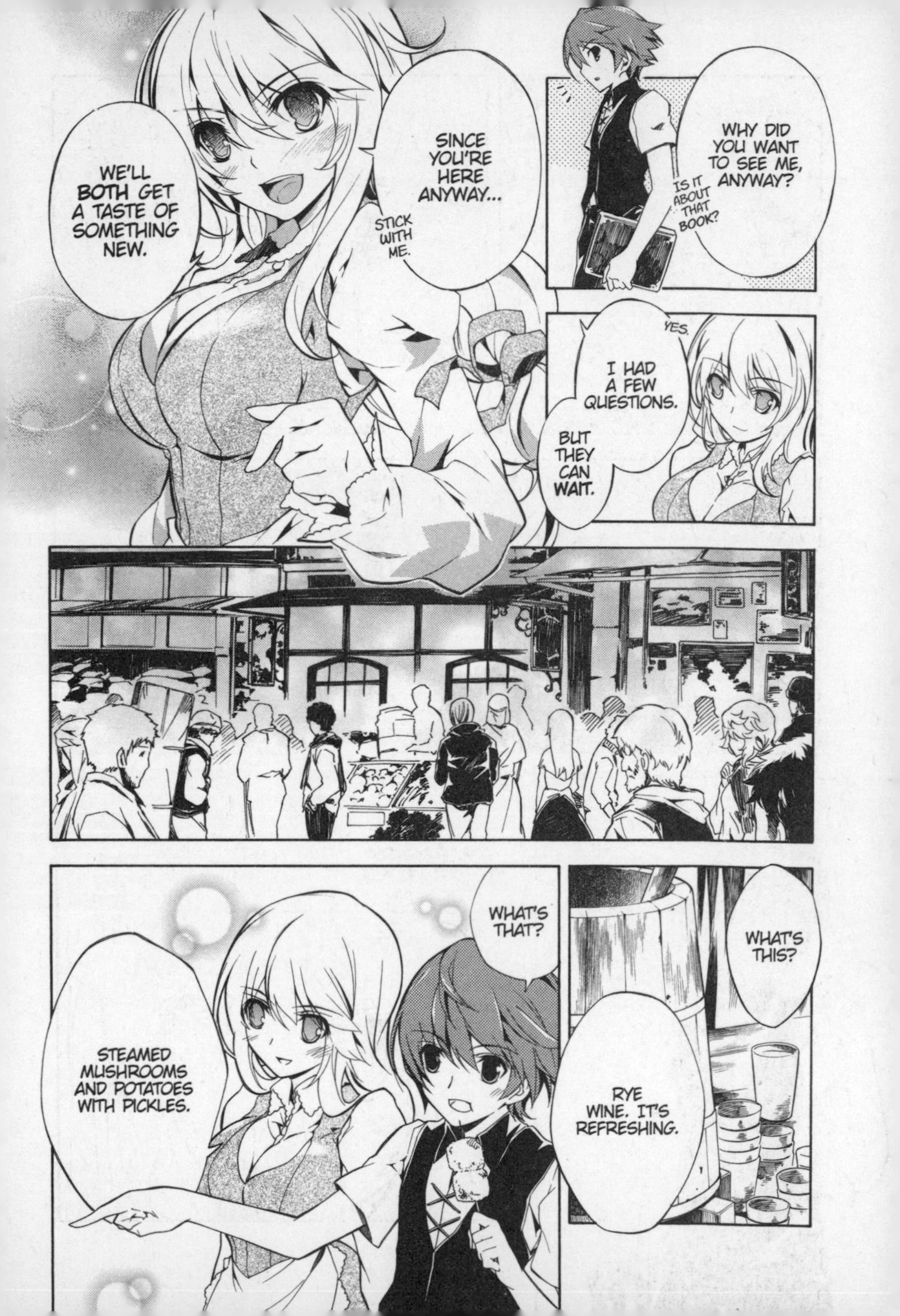
WHY DID YOU WANT TO SEE ME, ANYWAY?
IS IT ABOUT THAT BOOK?
YES.
I HAD A FEW QUESTIONS.
BUT THEY CAN WAIT.
SINCE YOU'RE HERE ANYWAY...
STICK WITH ME.
WE'LL BOTH GET A TASTE OF SOMETHING NEW.
WHAT'S THIS?
RYE WINE. IT'S REFRESHING.
WHAT'S THAT?
STEAMED MUSHROOMS AND POTATOES WITH PICKLES.

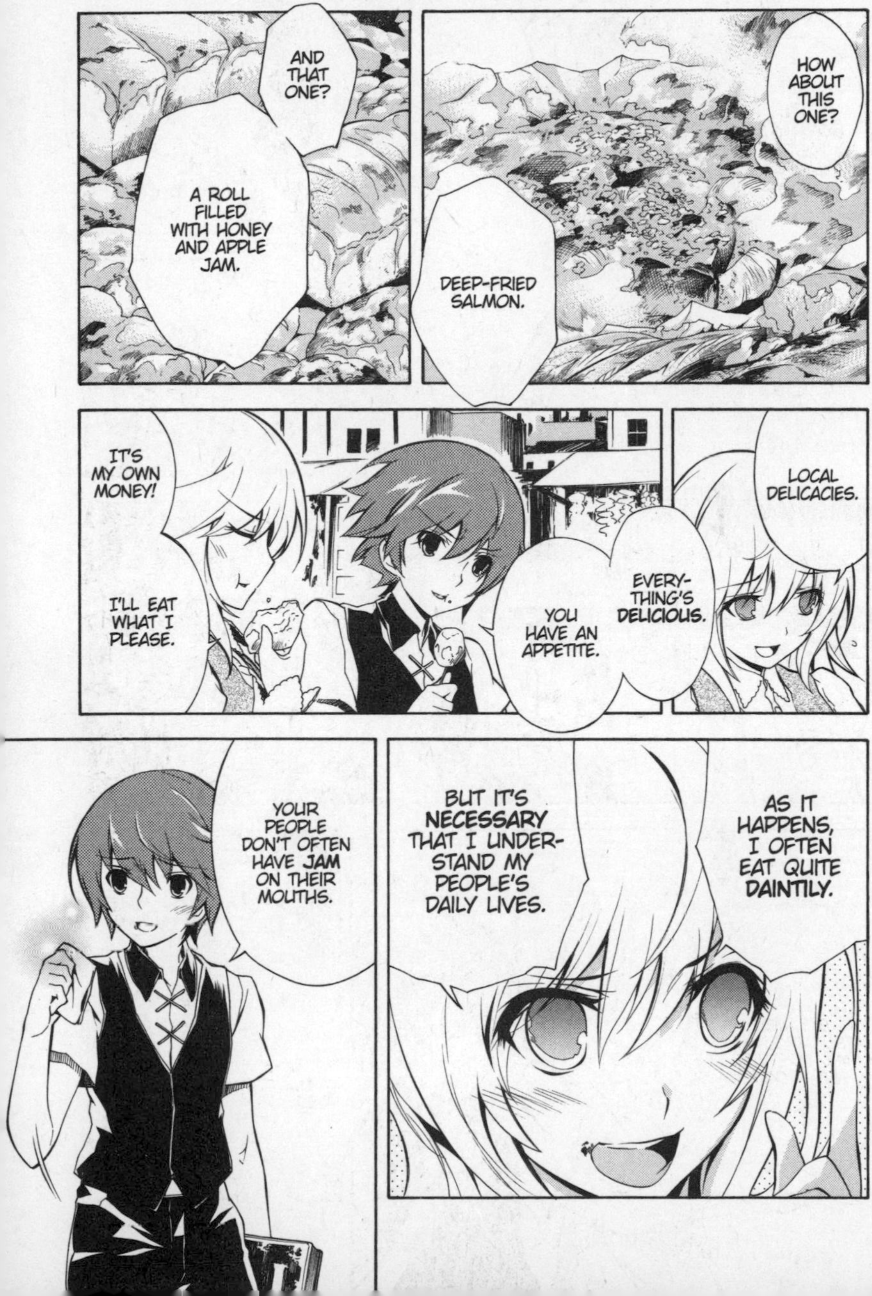
HOW ABOUT THIS ONE?
DEEP-FRIED SALMON.
AND THAT ONE?
A ROLL FILLED WITH HONEY AND APPLE JAM.
LOCAL DELICACIES.
EVERY-THING'S **DELICIOUS.**
YOU HAVE AN APPETITE.
IT'S MY OWN MONEY!
I'LL EAT WHAT I PLEASE.
AS IT HAPPENS, I OFTEN EAT QUITE **DAINTILY.**
BUT IT'S **NECESSARY** THAT I UNDER-STAND MY PEOPLE'S DAILY LIVES.
YOUR PEOPLE DON'T OFTEN HAVE **JAM** ON THEIR MOUTHS.

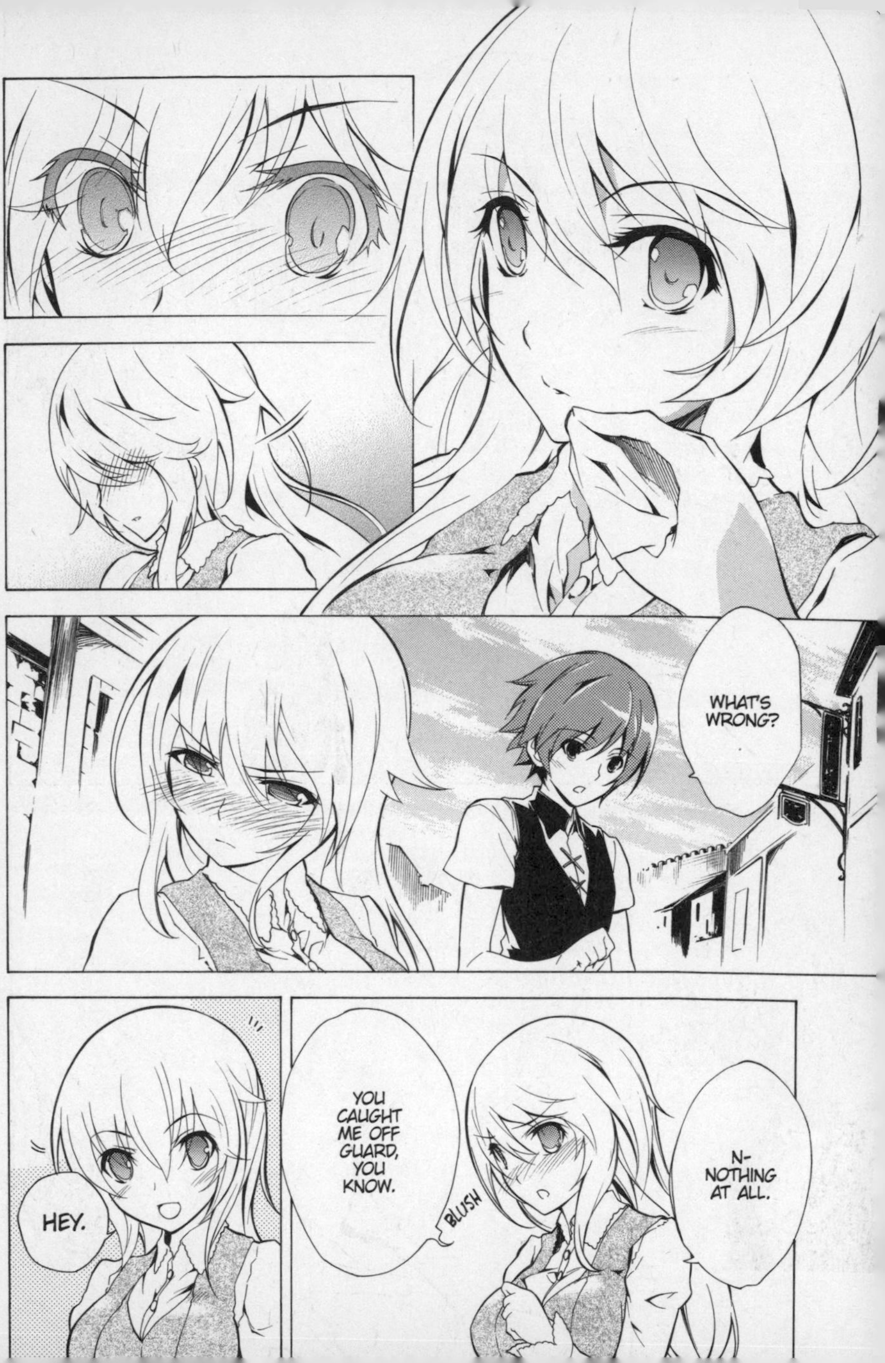
WHAT'S WRONG?
N-NOTHING AT ALL.
YOU CAUGHT ME OFF GUARD, YOU KNOW.
BLUSH
HEY.

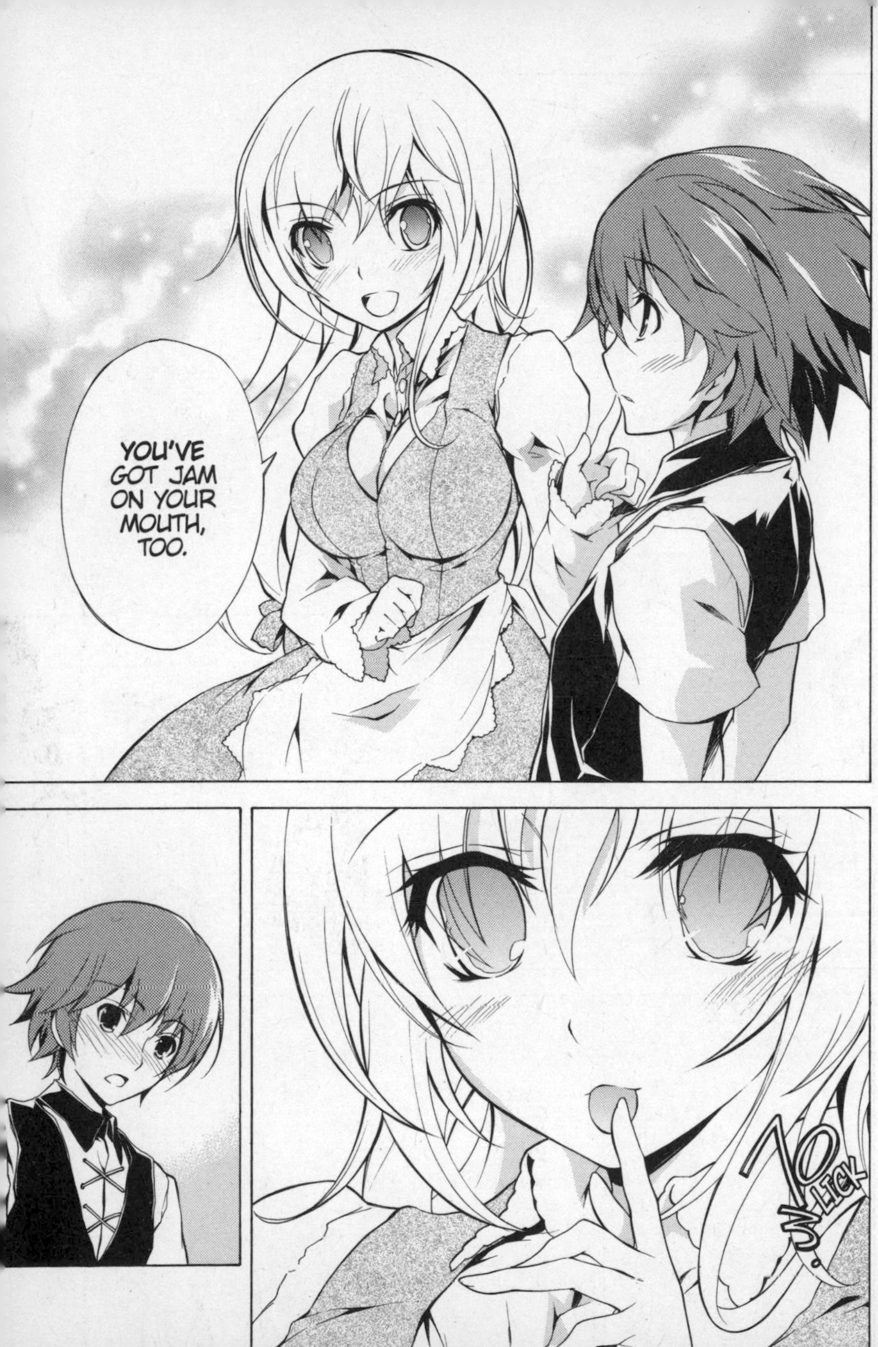
YOU'VE GOT JAM ON YOUR MOUTH, TOO.
LICK

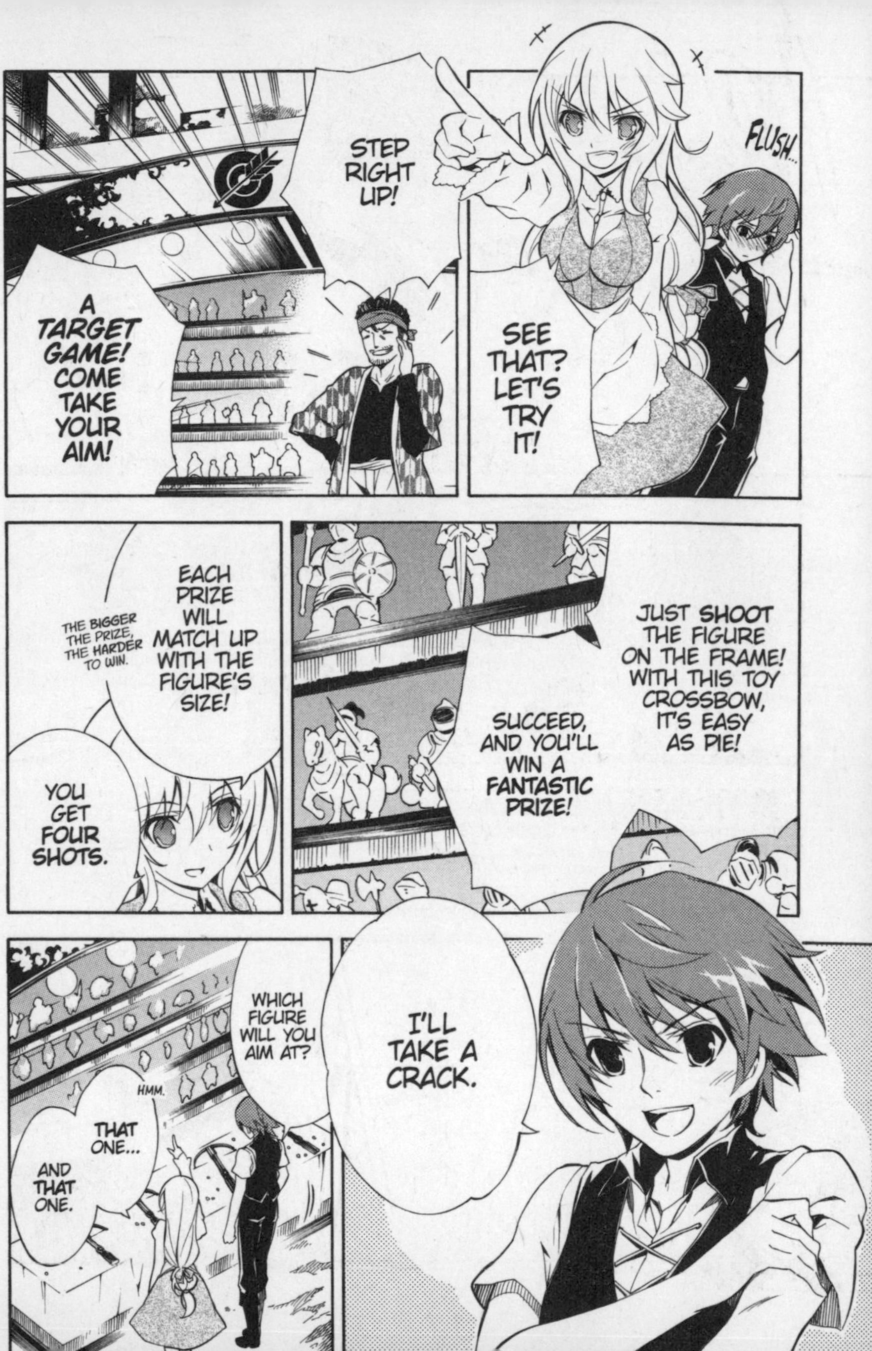
FLUSH...
SEE THAT? LET'S TRY IT!
STEP RIGHT UP!
A TARGET GAME! COME TAKE YOUR AIM!
JUST SHOOT THE FIGURE ON THE FRAME! WITH THIS TOY CROSSBOW, IT'S EASY AS PIE!
SUCCEED, AND YOU'LL WIN A FANTASTIC PRIZE!
EACH PRIZE WILL MATCH UP WITH THE FIGURE'S SIZE!
THE BIGGER THE PRIZE, THE HARDER TO WIN.
YOU GET FOUR SHOTS.
I'LL TAKE A CRACK.
WHICH FIGURE WILL YOU AIM AT?
HMM.
THAT ONE...
AND THAT ONE.

PASHOO

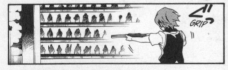

I SEE HOW
THIS BOW
WORKS.

GRIP

THOINK

BOIING

PASHOO

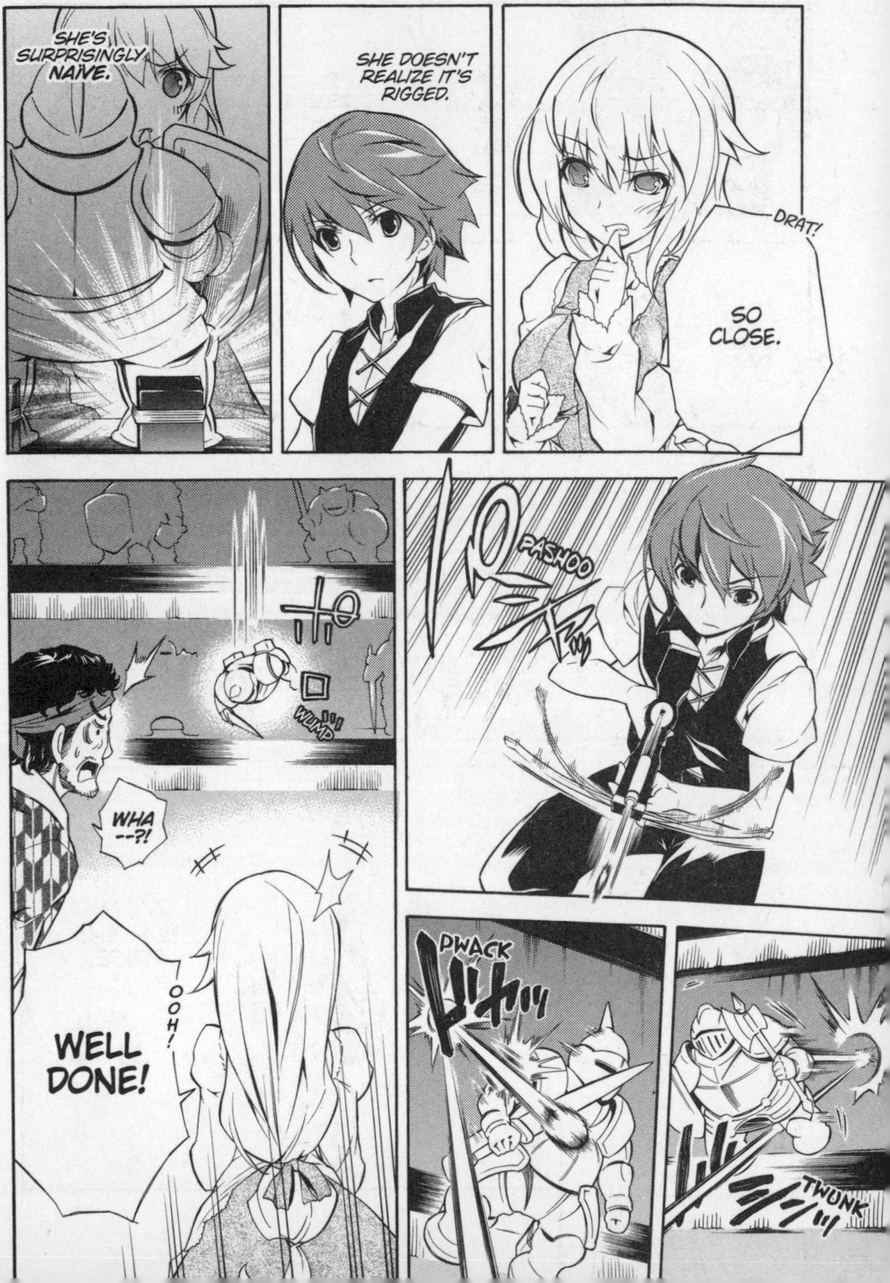
DRAT!
SO CLOSE.
SHE DOESN'T REALIZE IT'S RIGGED.
SHE'S SURPRISINGLY NAÏVE.
PASHOO
TWONK
PWACK
WUMP
WHA --?!
OOH!
WELL DONE!

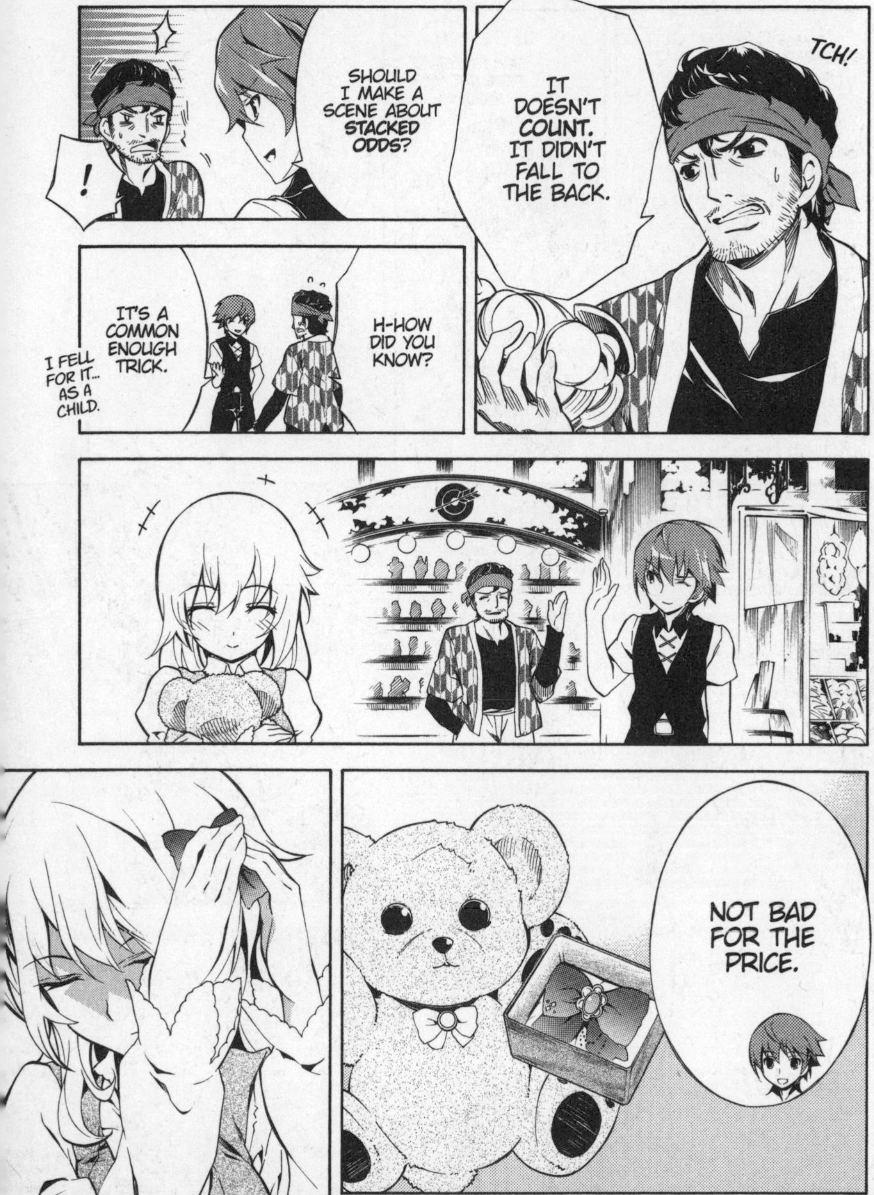
TCH!
IT DOESN'T COUNT. IT DIDN'T FALL TO THE BACK.
SHOULD I MAKE A SCENE ABOUT STACKED ODDS?
!
H-HOW DID YOU KNOW?
IT'S A COMMON ENOUGH TRICK.
I FELL FOR IT... AS A CHILD.
NOT BAD FOR THE PRICE.

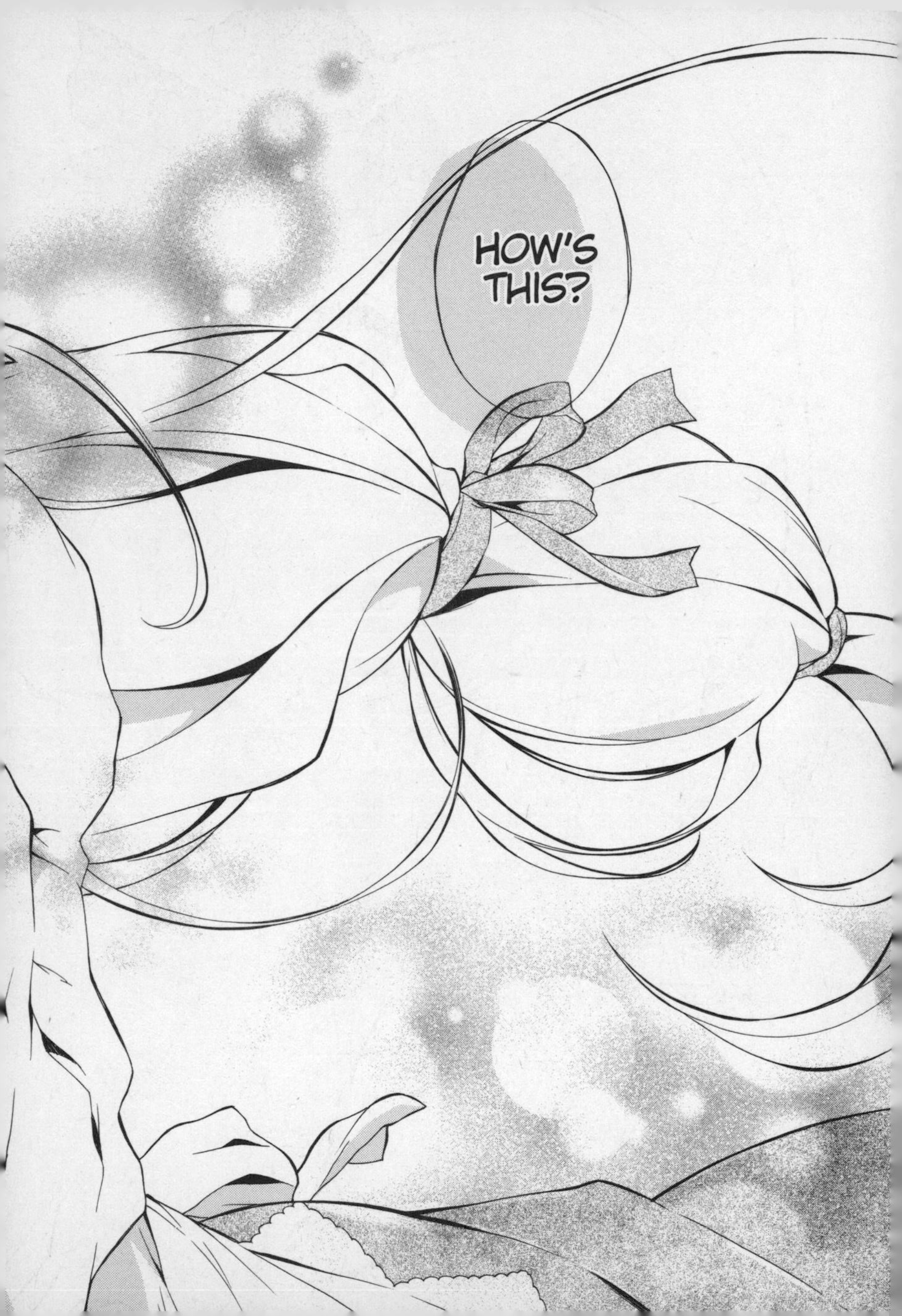
HOW'S THIS?

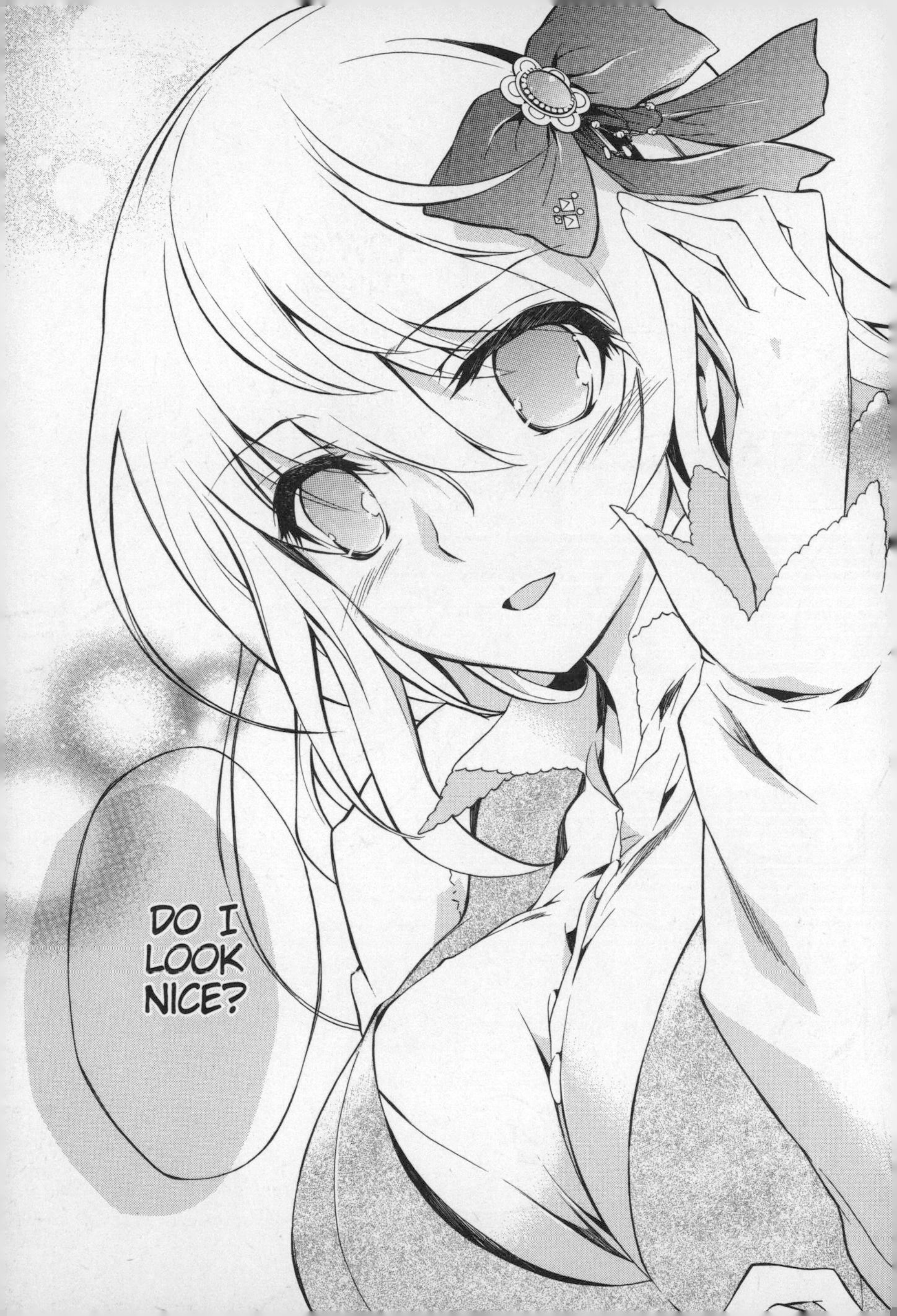
DO I LOOK NICE?

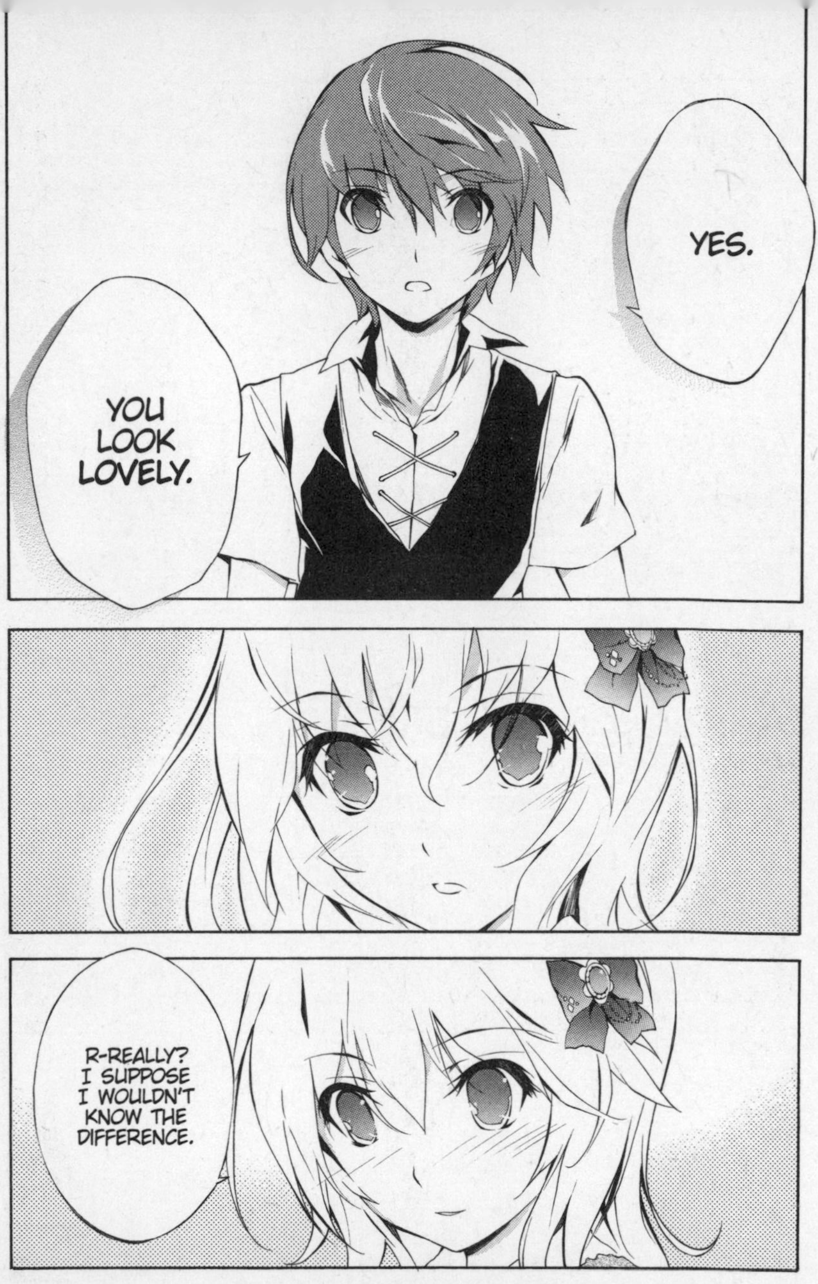
YES.
YOU LOOK LOVELY.
R-REALLY? I SUPPOSE I WOULDN'T KNOW THE DIFFERENCE.

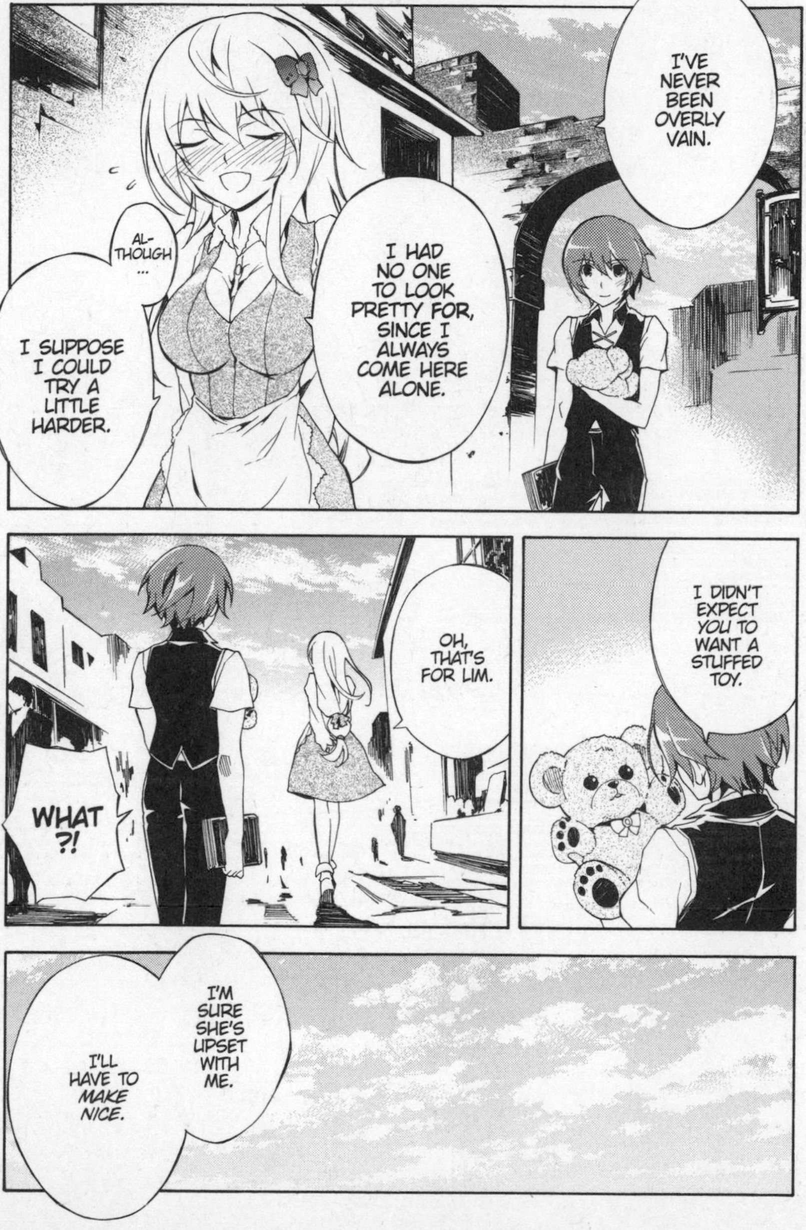
I'VE NEVER BEEN OVERLY VAIN.
I HAD NO ONE TO LOOK PRETTY FOR, SINCE I ALWAYS COME HERE ALONE.
AL-THOUGH...
I SUPPOSE I COULD TRY A LITTLE HARDER.
I DIDN'T EXPECT *YOU* TO WANT A STUFFED TOY.
OH, THAT'S FOR LIM.
WHAT?!
I'M SURE SHE'S UPSET WITH ME.
I'LL HAVE TO *MAKE NICE*.

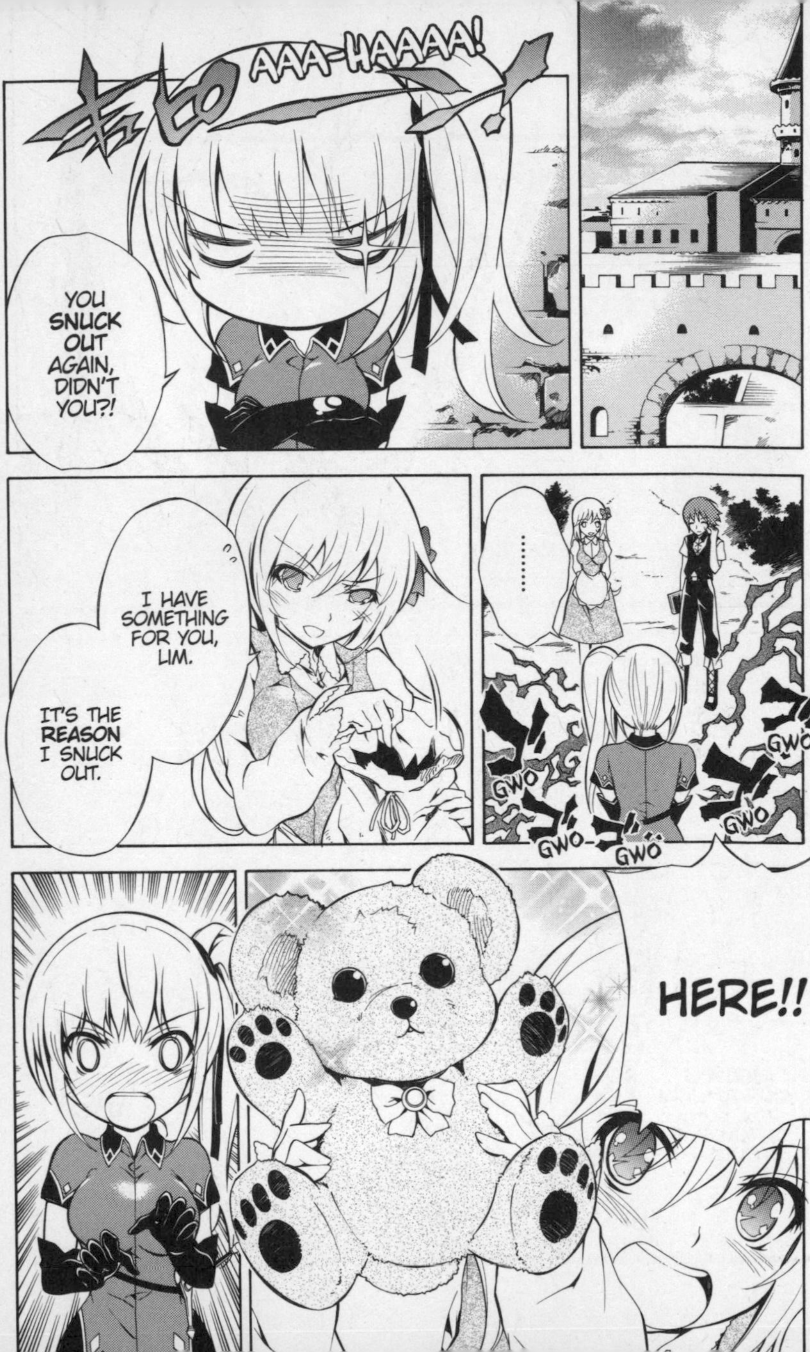
AAA-HAAAA!
YOU SNUCK OUT AGAIN, DIDN'T YOU?!
......
GWO
GWO
GWO
GWO
GWO
I HAVE SOMETHING FOR YOU, LIM.
IT'S THE REASON I SNUCK OUT.
HERE!!

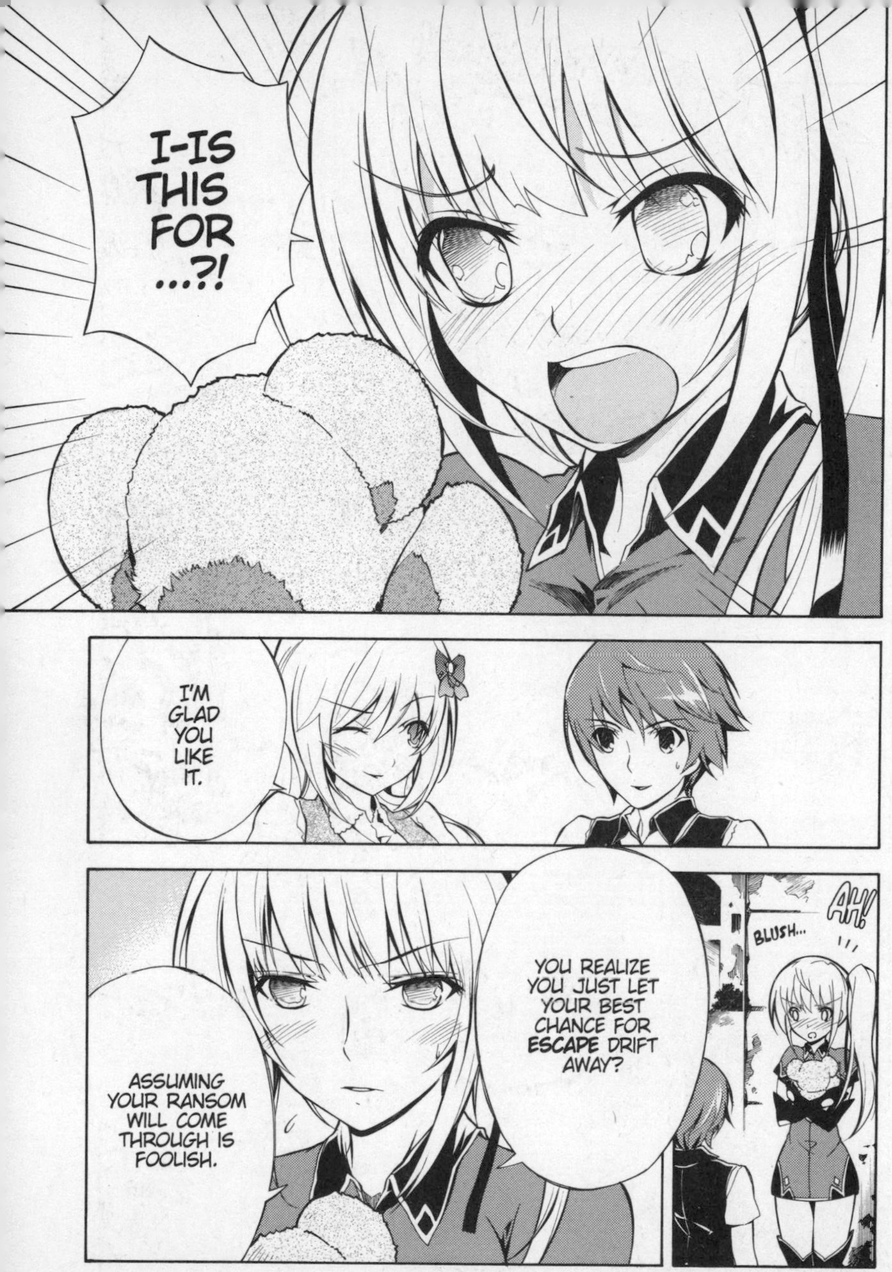
I-IS THIS FOR...?!
I'M GLAD YOU LIKE IT.
AH!
BLUSH...
YOU REALIZE YOU JUST LET YOUR BEST CHANCE FOR ESCAPE DRIFT AWAY?
ASSUMING YOUR RANSOM WILL COME THROUGH IS FOOLISH.

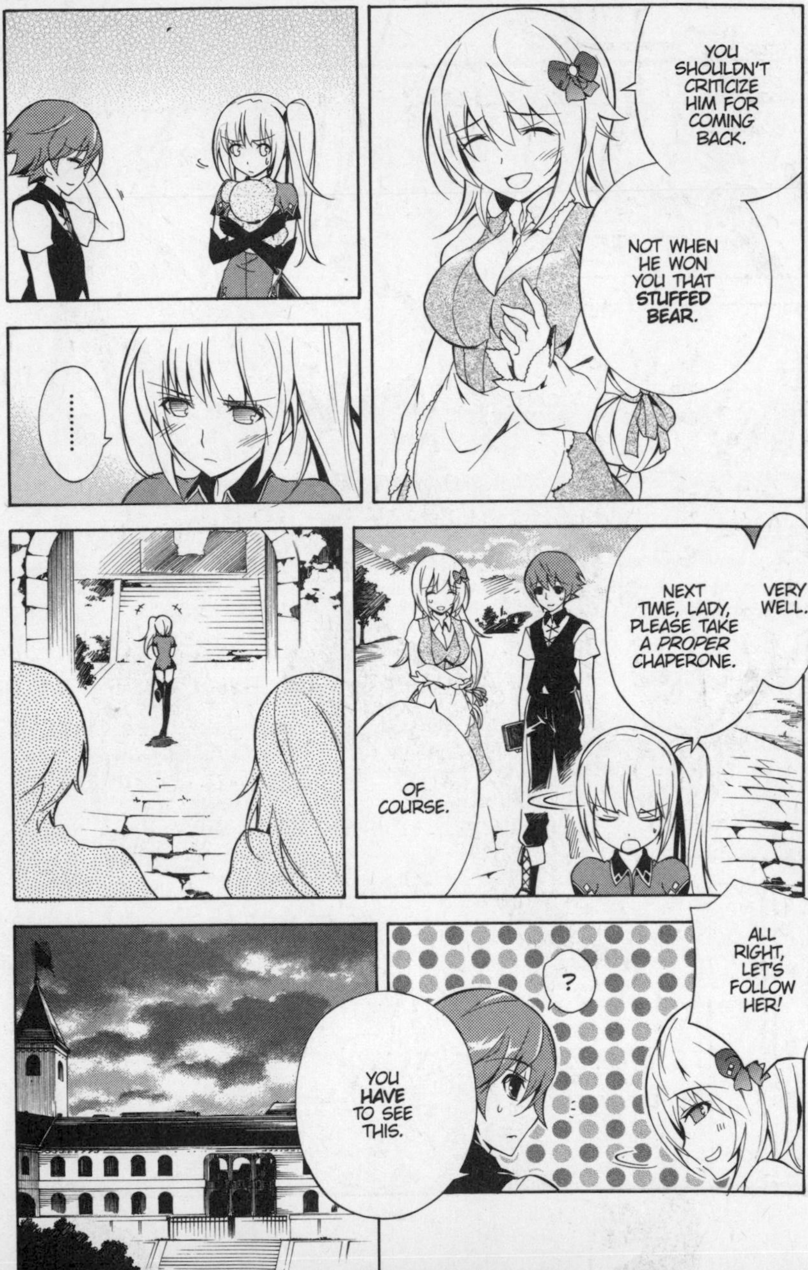

YOU SHOULDN'T CRITICIZE HIM FOR COMING BACK.
NOT WHEN HE WON YOU THAT STUFFED BEAR.
......
VERY WELL.
NEXT TIME, LADY, PLEASE TAKE A *PROPER* CHAPERONE.
OF COURSE.
ALL RIGHT, LET'S FOLLOW HER!
?
YOU HAVE TO SEE THIS.

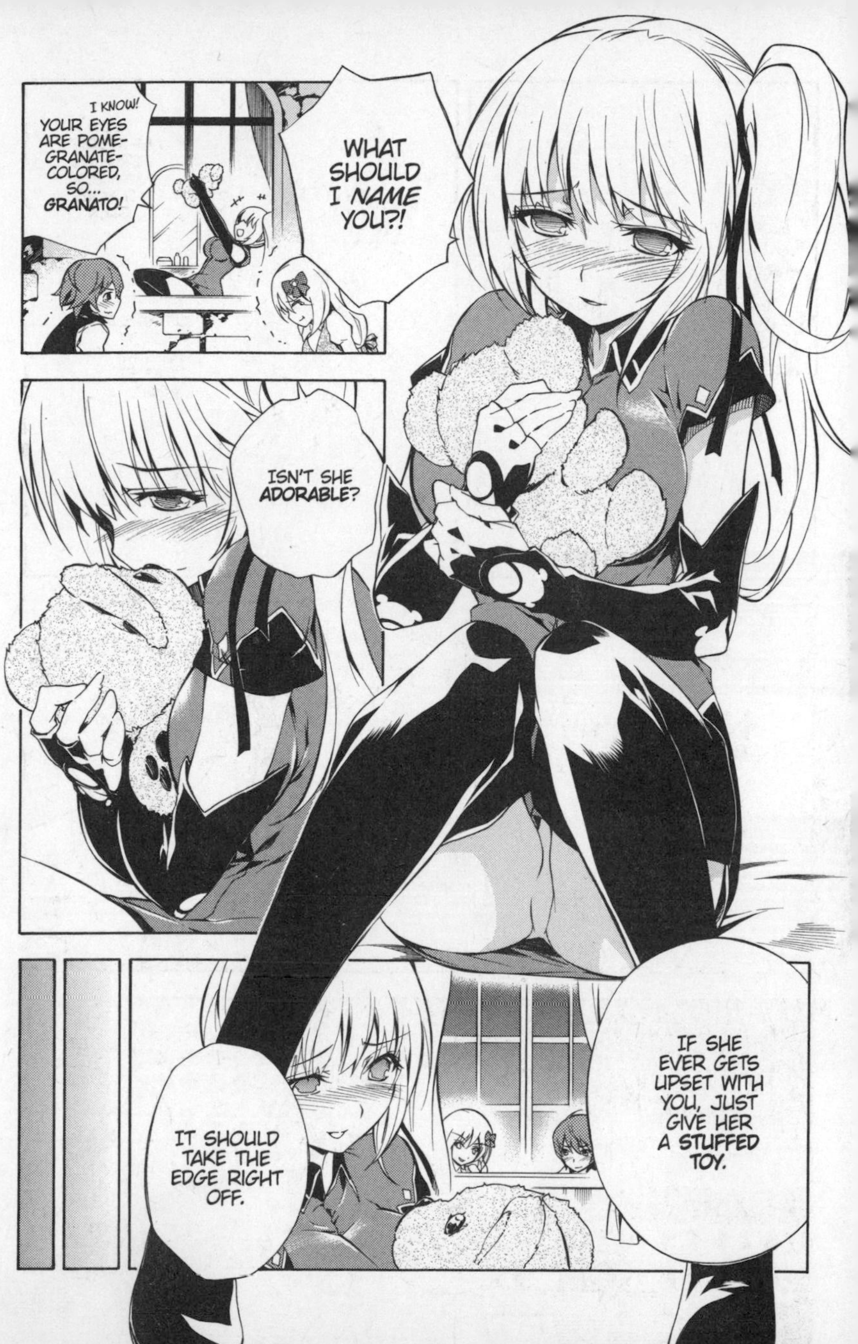
WHAT SHOULD I *NAME* YOU?!
I KNOW! YOUR EYES ARE POME-GRANATE-COLORED, SO... GRANATO!
ISN'T SHE ADORABLE?
IF SHE EVER GETS UPSET WITH YOU, JUST GIVE HER A STUFFED TOY.
IT SHOULD TAKE THE EDGE RIGHT OFF.

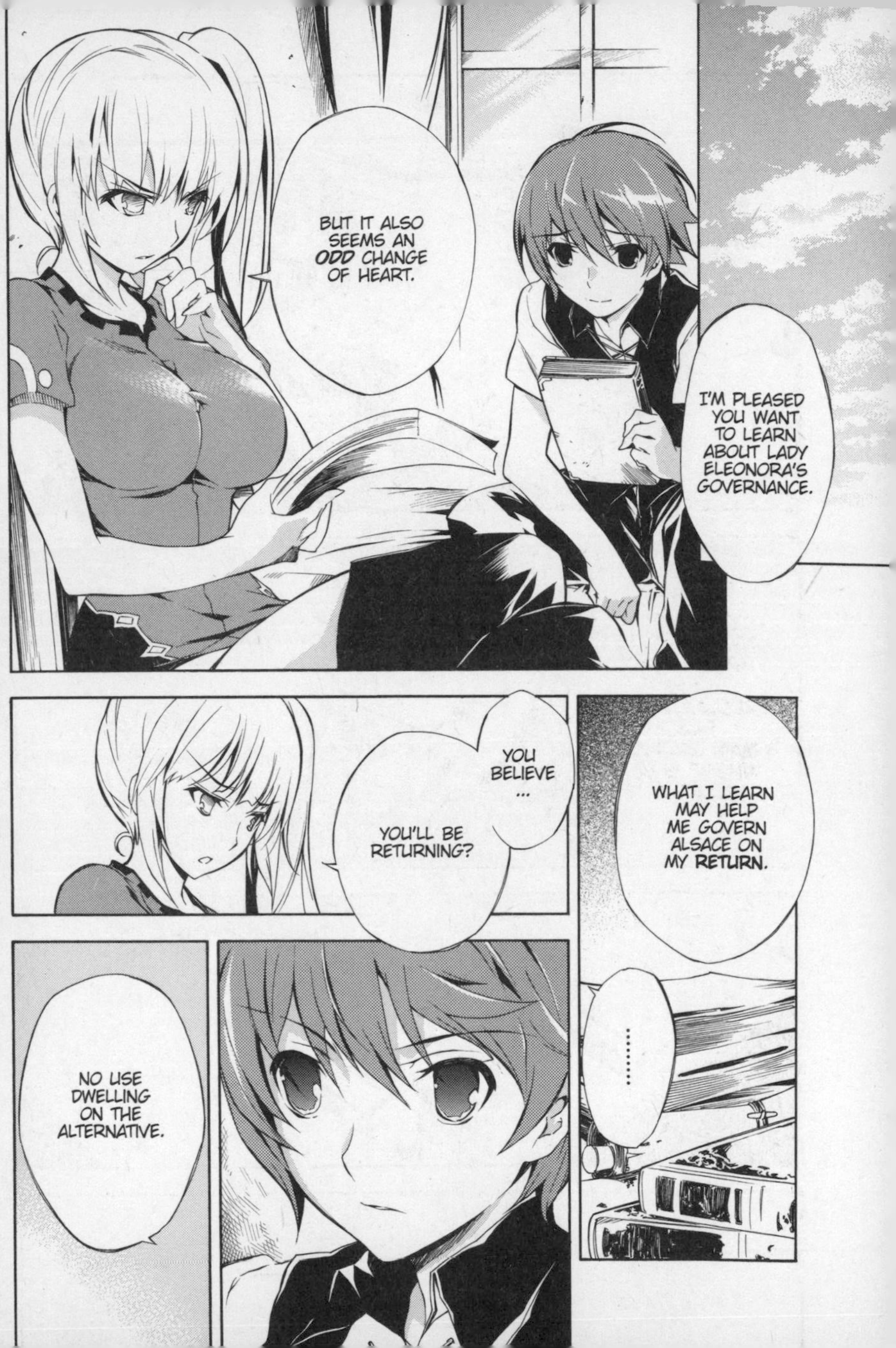
I'M PLEASED YOU WANT TO LEARN ABOUT LADY ELEONORA'S GOVERNANCE.
BUT IT ALSO SEEMS AN ODD CHANGE OF HEART.
WHAT I LEARN MAY HELP ME GOVERN ALSACE ON MY RETURN.
YOU BELIEVE ...
YOU'LL BE RETURNING?
……
NO USE DWELLING ON THE ALTERNATIVE.

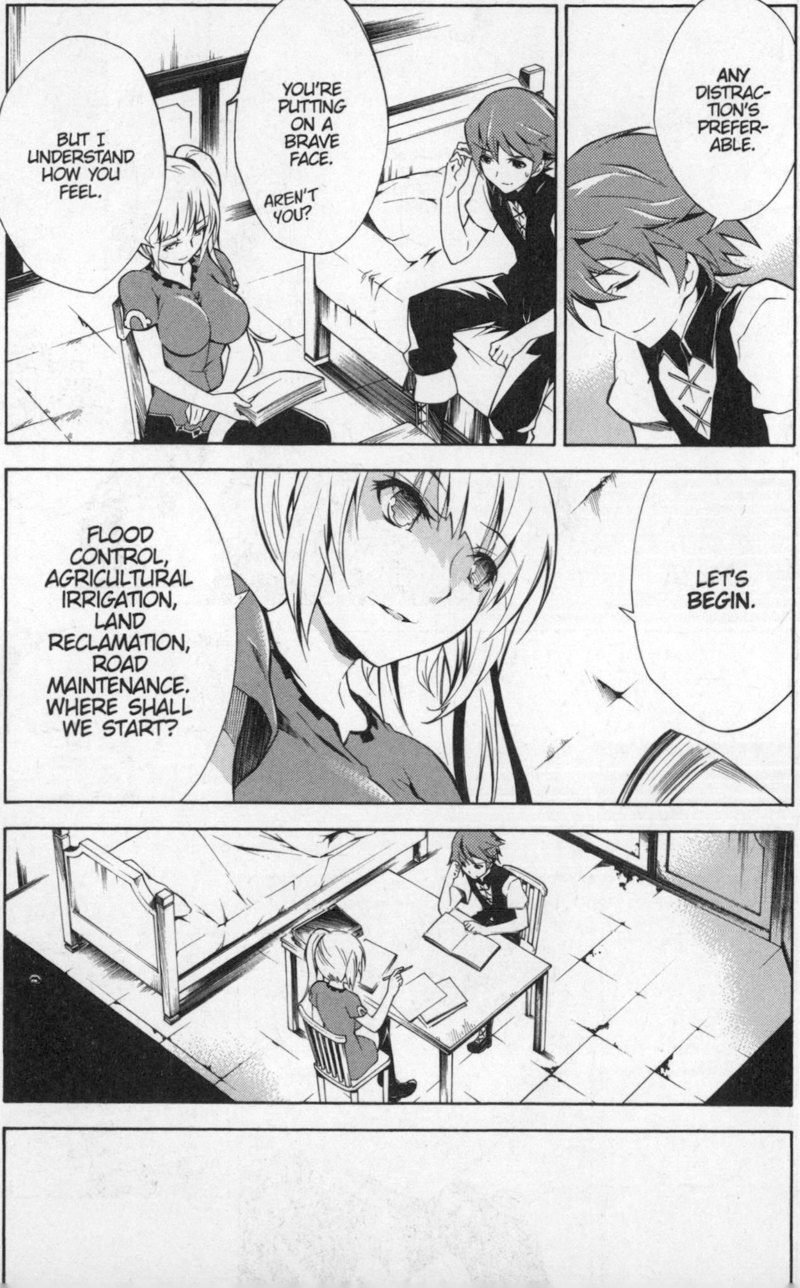
ANY DISTRACTION'S PREFERABLE.
YOU'RE PUTTING ON A BRAVE FACE.
AREN'T YOU?
BUT I UNDERSTAND HOW YOU FEEL.
LET'S BEGIN.
FLOOD CONTROL, AGRICULTURAL IRRIGATION, LAND RECLAMATION, ROAD MAINTENANCE. WHERE SHALL WE START?

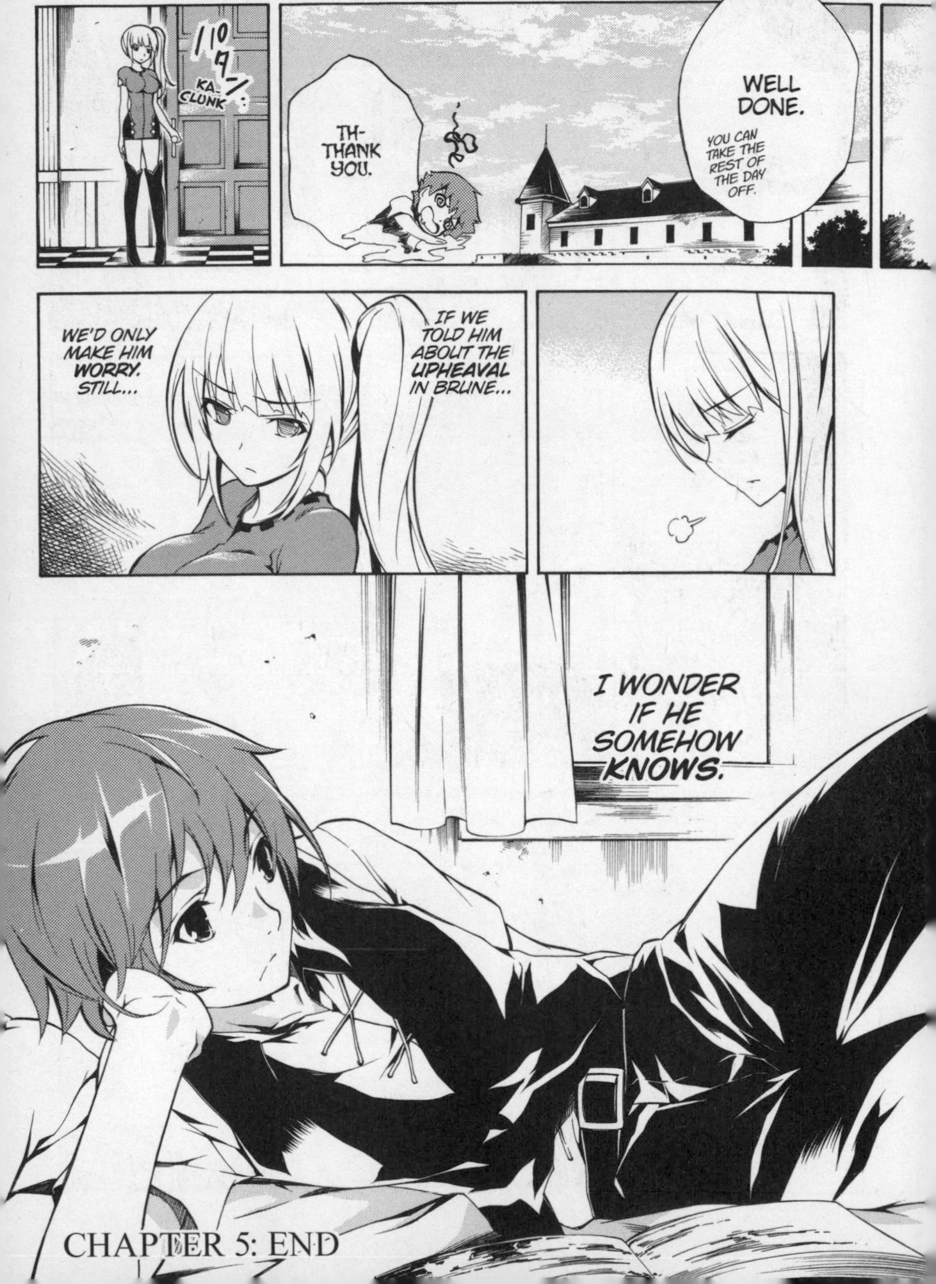
WELL DONE.
YOU CAN TAKE THE REST OF THE DAY OFF.
TH-THANK YOU.
KA-CLUNK
IF WE TOLD HIM ABOUT THE UPHEAVAL IN BRUNE...
WE'D ONLY MAKE HIM WORRY. STILL...
I WONDER IF HE SOMEHOW KNOWS.
CHAPTER 5: END

FOR ANY CONTRIBUTION!

WE'RE DESPERATE ...

FIVE VISITS. ALL *FRUITLESS.* NO ONE LEFT TO ASK.

COUNT VORN'S LATE FATHER WAS MY BEST FRIEND! I *MUST* PROTECT HIS CHILD!

I NATURALLY REGRET THAT I CAN'T BE OF MORE ASSISTANCE.

STILL, YOU'RE AWARE OF THE STATE OF THINGS IN BRUNE.

MY APOLOGIES.

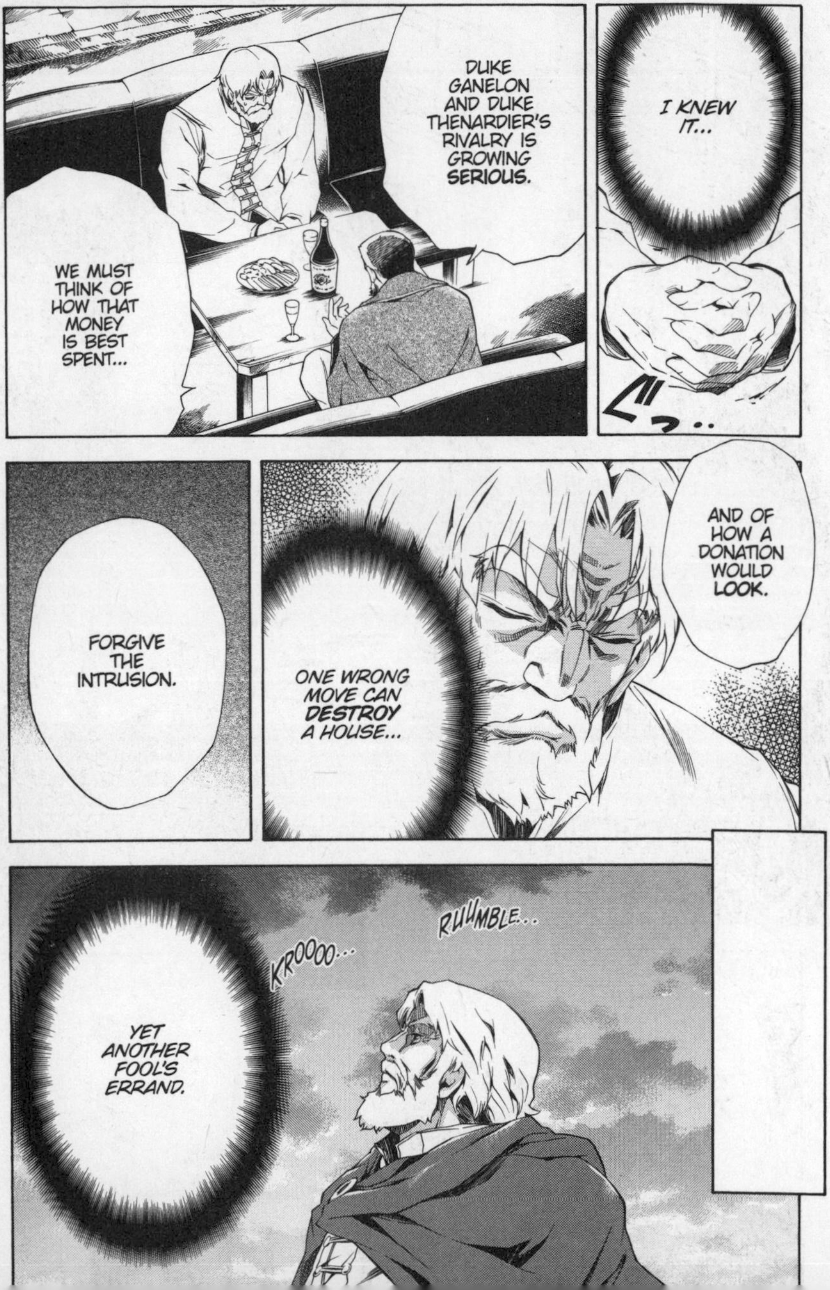
I KNEW IT...
DUKE GANELON AND DUKE THENARDIER'S RIVALRY IS GROWING SERIOUS.
WE MUST THINK OF HOW THAT MONEY IS BEST SPENT...
AND OF HOW A DONATION WOULD LOOK.
ONE WRONG MOVE CAN DESTROY A HOUSE...
FORGIVE THE INTRUSION.
RUUMBLE...
KROOOO...
YET ANOTHER FOOL'S ERRAND.

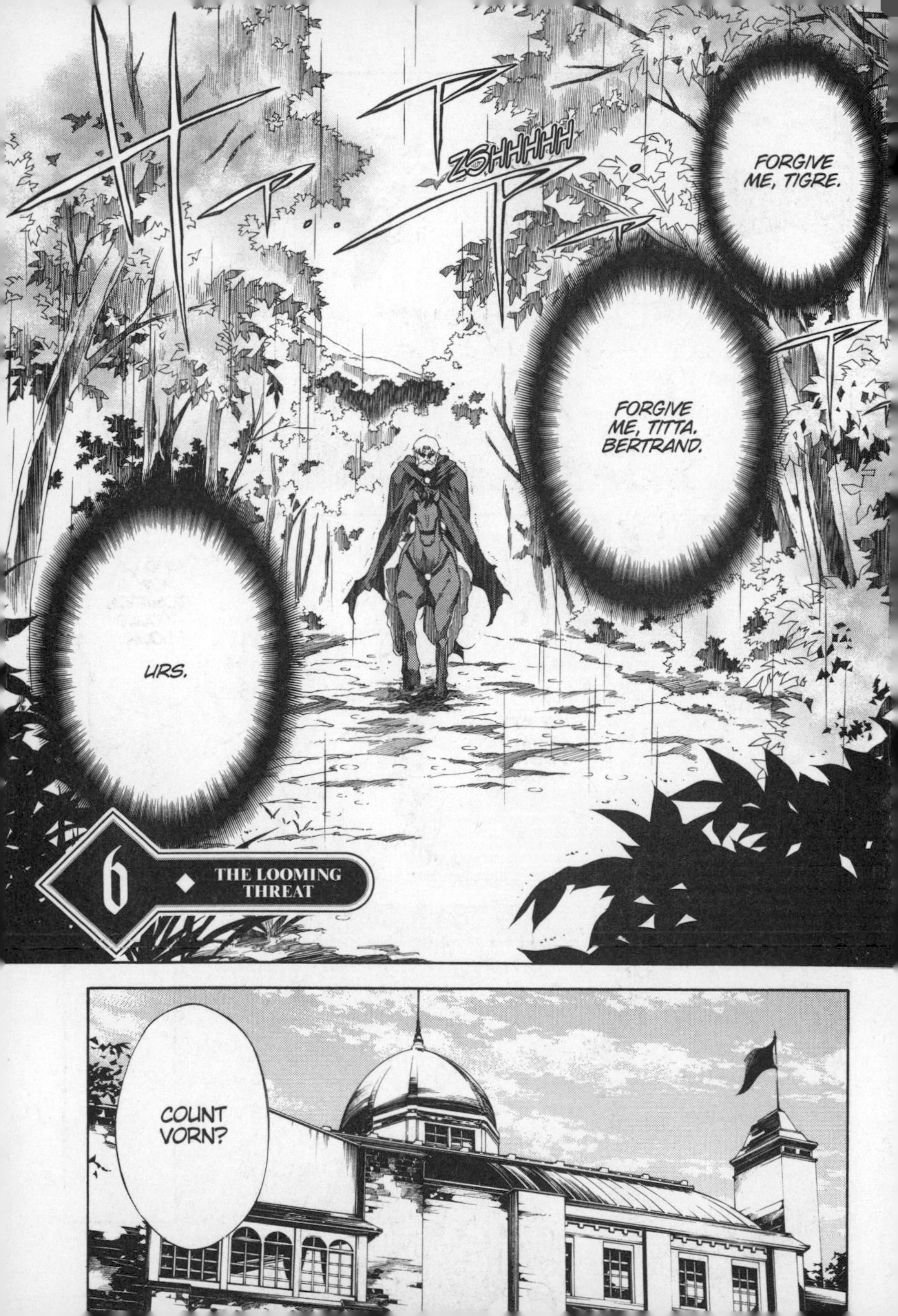
FORGIVE ME, TIGRE.
ZSHHHHH
FORGIVE ME, TITTA. BERTRAND.
URS.
6
THE LOOMING THREAT
COUNT VORN?

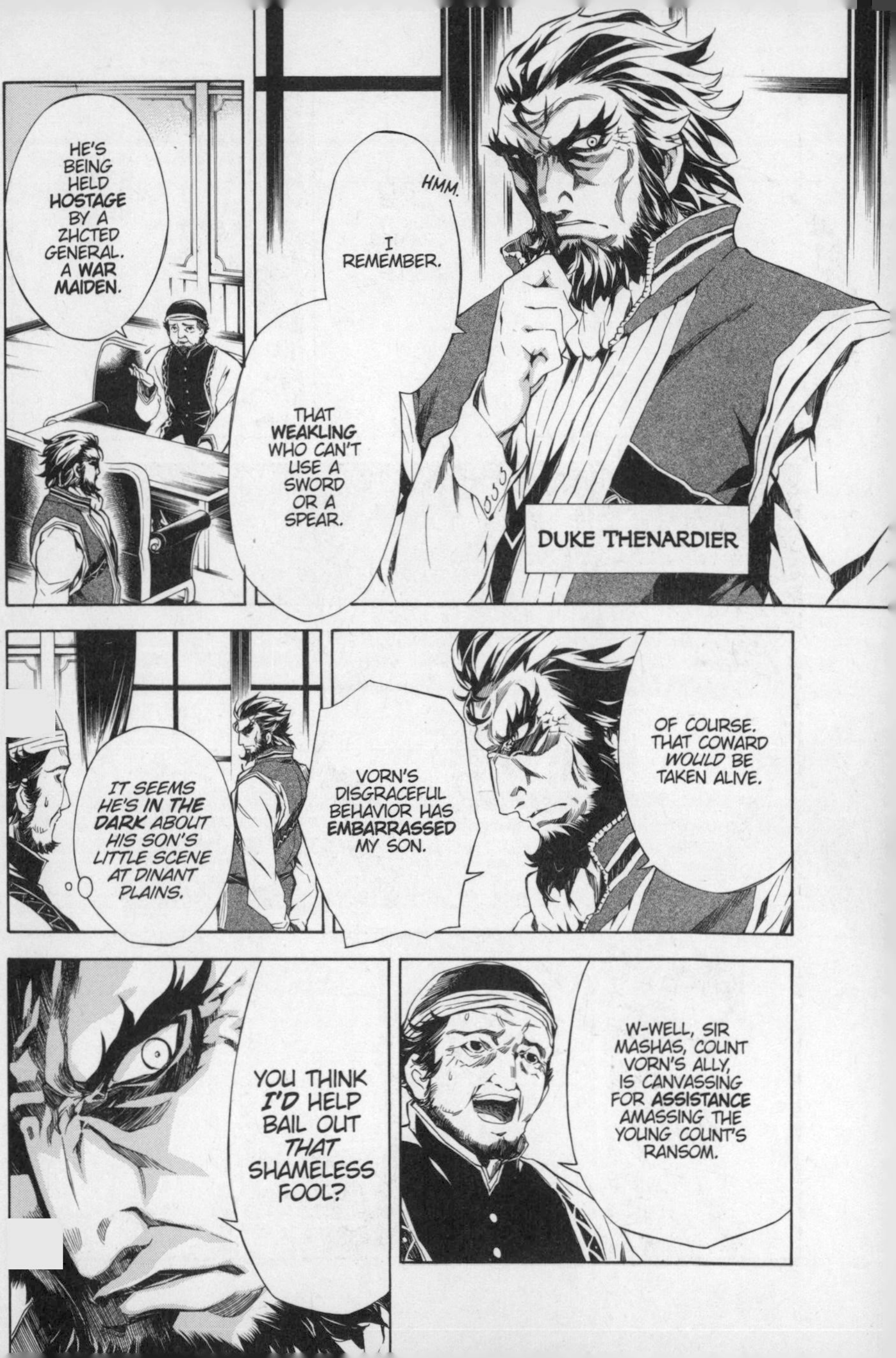
HMM.
I REMEMBER.
THAT WEAKLING WHO CAN'T USE A SWORD OR A SPEAR.
DUKE THENARDIER
HE'S BEING HELD HOSTAGE BY A ZHCTED GENERAL. A WAR MAIDEN.
OF COURSE. THAT COWARD WOULD BE TAKEN ALIVE.
VORN'S DISGRACEFUL BEHAVIOR HAS EMBARRASSED MY SON.
IT SEEMS HE'S IN THE DARK ABOUT HIS SON'S LITTLE SCENE AT DINANT PLAINS.
W-WELL, SIR MASHAS, COUNT VORN'S ALLY, IS CANVASSING FOR ASSISTANCE AMASSING THE YOUNG COUNT'S RANSOM.
YOU THINK I'D HELP BAIL OUT THAT SHAMELESS FOOL?

N-NOT IN SO MANY WORDS, YOUR EXCELLENCY.
VORN'S MINOR NOBILITY, GRANTED, BUT HIS RESCUE...
...MIGHT **BENEFIT YOUR EFFORTS** AGAINST DUKE GANELON.
THE **POWER STRUGGLE** BETWEEN THENARDIER AND GANELON IS NO SHOCK TO THE BRUNISH NOBILITY.
THENARDIER'S **WIFE** IS THE KING'S **NIECE**. THE KING'S **NEPHEW** IS GANELON'S **BROTHER-IN-LAW**.
THE KING NOW HAS NO SIBLINGS OR CHILDREN.
THEREFORE, HIS NIECE AND NEPHEW ARE **NEXT IN LINE** FOR THE **THRONE**.

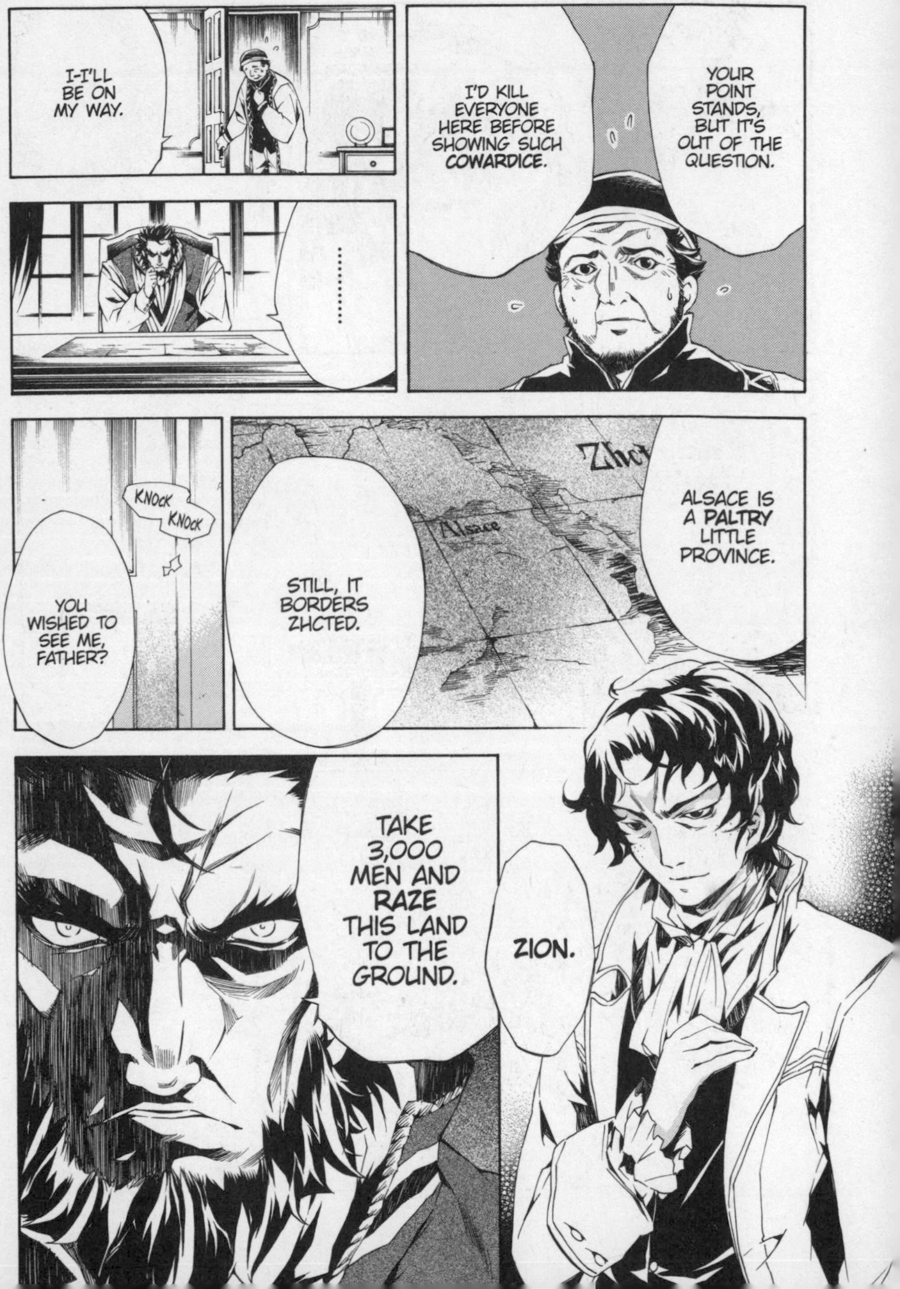
YOUR POINT STANDS, BUT IT'S OUT OF THE QUESTION.
I'D KILL EVERYONE HERE BEFORE SHOWING SUCH **COWARDICE.**
I-I'LL BE ON MY WAY.
......
Zhct
Alsace
ALSACE IS A **PALTRY** LITTLE PROVINCE.
STILL, IT BORDERS ZHCTED.
KNOCK
KNOCK
YOU WISHED TO SEE ME, FATHER?
ZION.
TAKE 3,000 MEN AND RAZE THIS LAND TO THE GROUND.

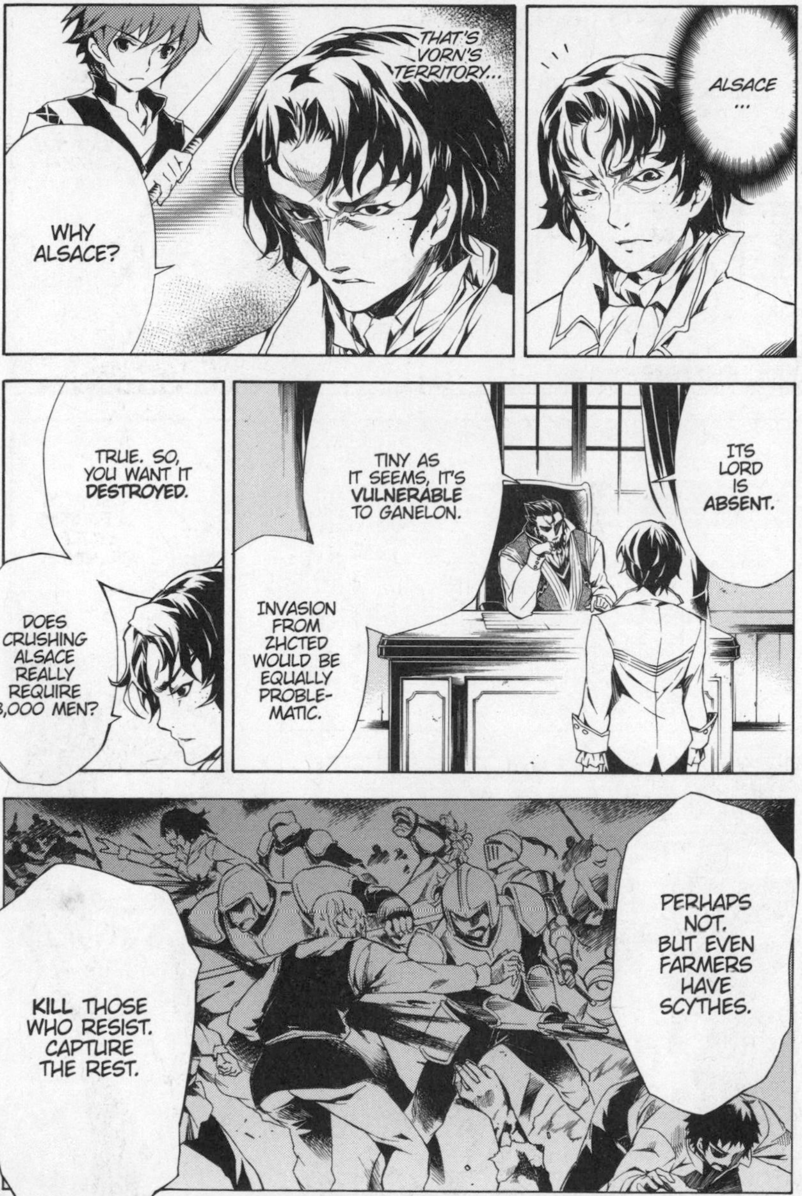
ALSACE ...
THAT'S VORN'S TERRITORY...
WHY ALSACE?
ITS LORD IS ABSENT.
TINY AS IT SEEMS, IT'S VULNERABLE TO GANELON.
INVASION FROM ZHCTED WOULD BE EQUALLY PROBLEMATIC.
TRUE. SO, YOU WANT IT DESTROYED.
DOES CRUSHING ALSACE REALLY REQUIRE 3,000 MEN?
PERHAPS NOT. BUT EVEN FARMERS HAVE SCYTHES.
KILL THOSE WHO RESIST. CAPTURE THE REST.

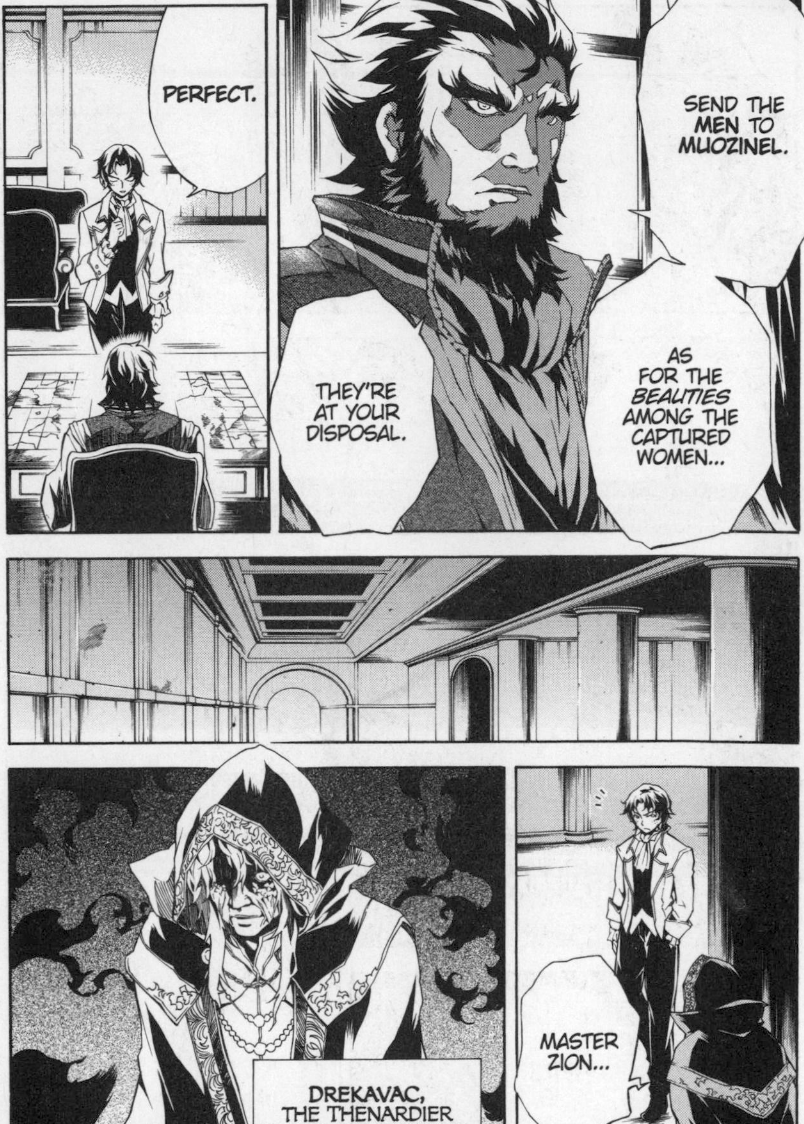
SEND THE MEN TO MUOZINEL.
AS FOR THE *BEAUTIES* AMONG THE CAPTURED WOMEN...
THEY'RE AT YOUR DISPOSAL.
PERFECT.
MASTER ZION...
DREKAVAC, THE THENARDIER CLAN'S SOOTHSAYER.

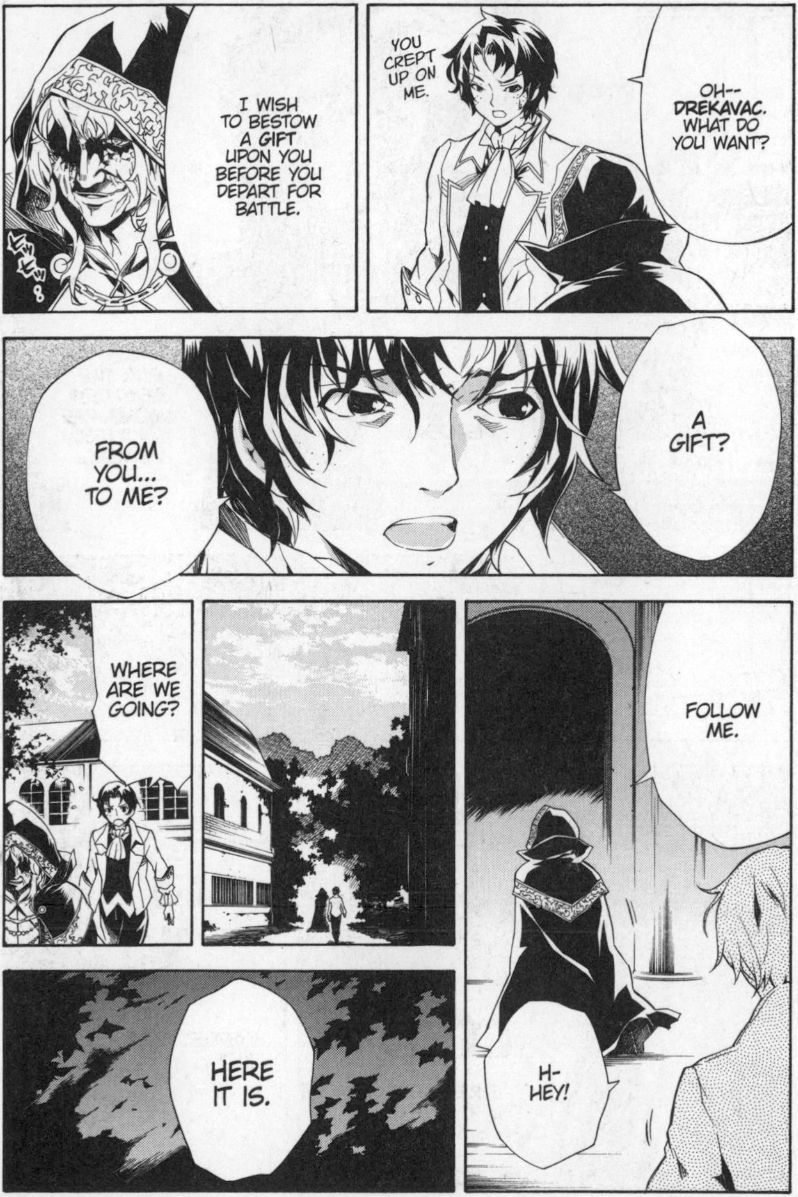
OH-- DREKAVAC. WHAT DO YOU WANT?
YOU CREPT UP ON ME.
I WISH TO BESTOW A GIFT UPON YOU BEFORE YOU DEPART FOR BATTLE.
A GIFT?
FROM YOU... TO ME?
FOLLOW ME.
H- HEY!
WHERE ARE WE GOING?
HERE IT IS.

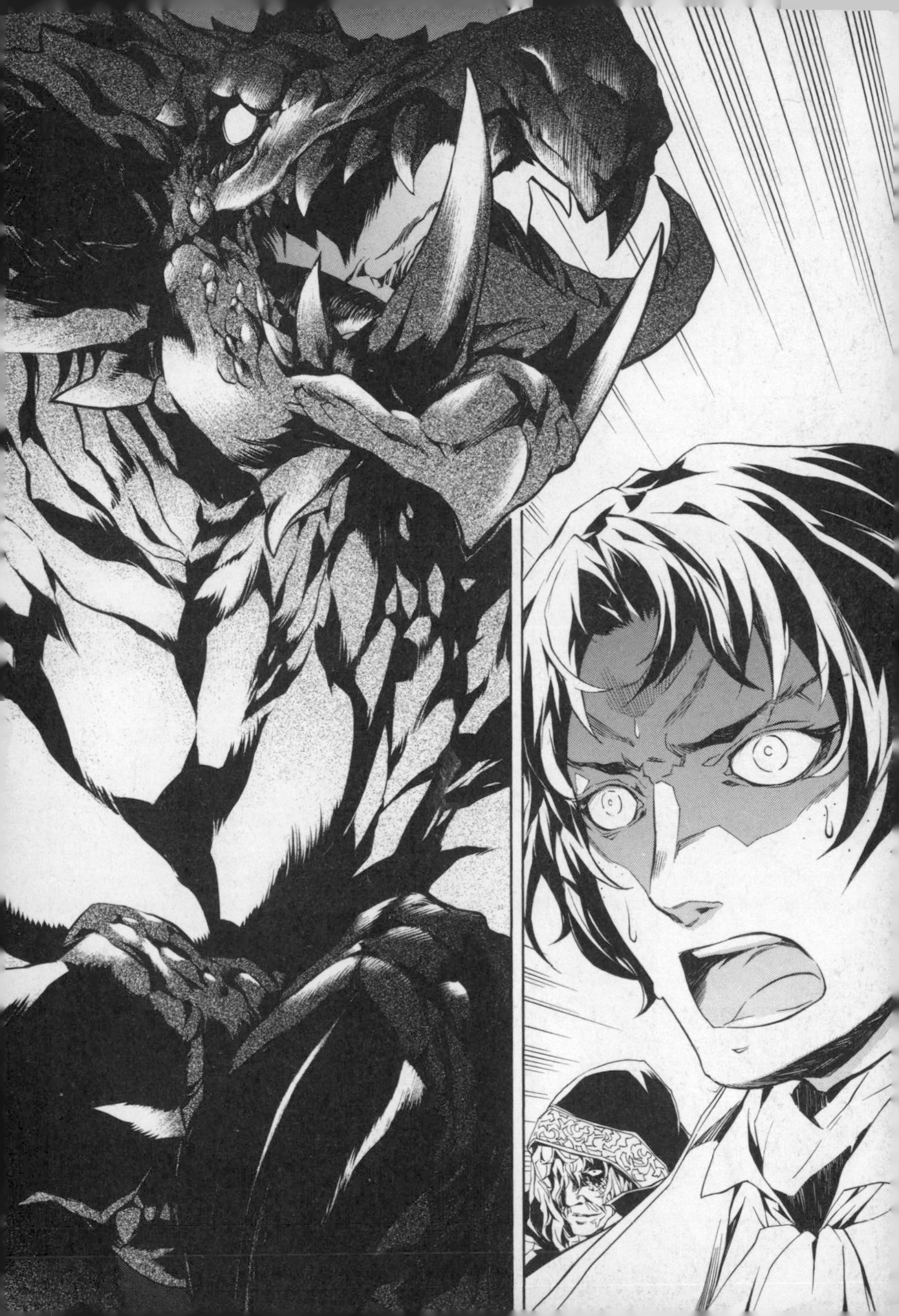

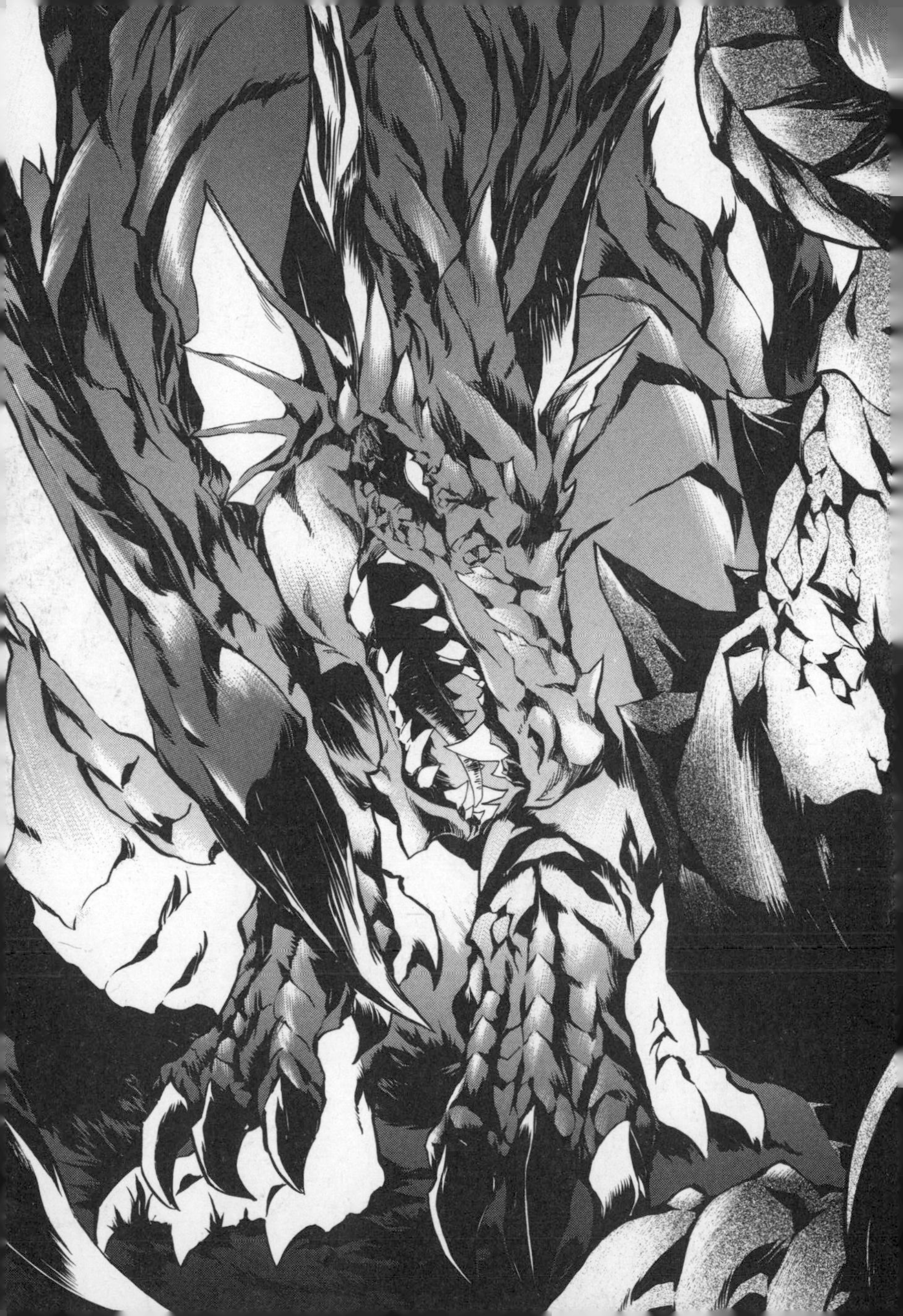

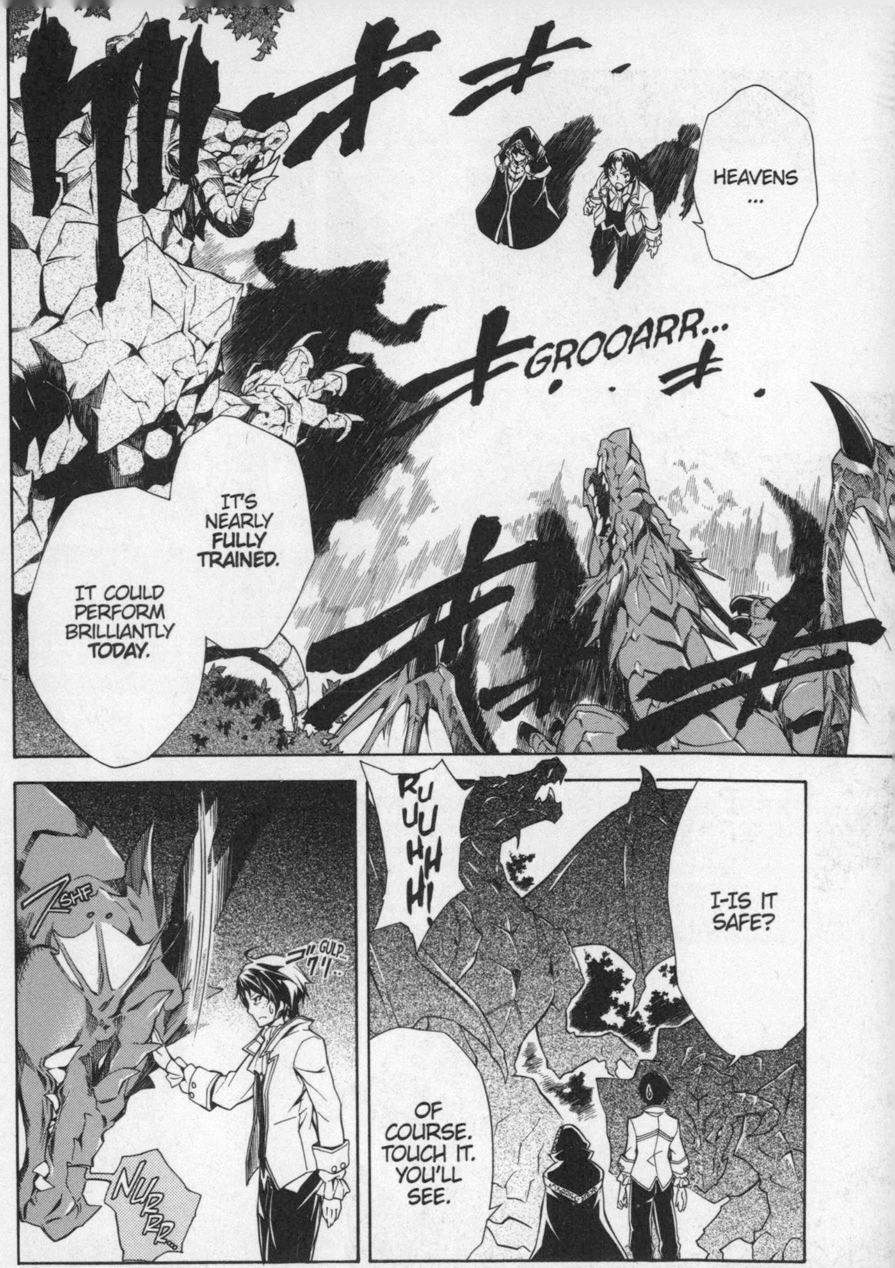
HEAVENS ...
GROOARR...
IT'S NEARLY FULLY TRAINED.
IT COULD PERFORM BRILLIANTLY TODAY.
RUUUHHHHI!
I-IS IT SAFE?
OF COURSE. TOUCH IT. YOU'LL SEE.
SHF
GULP...
NURRR...

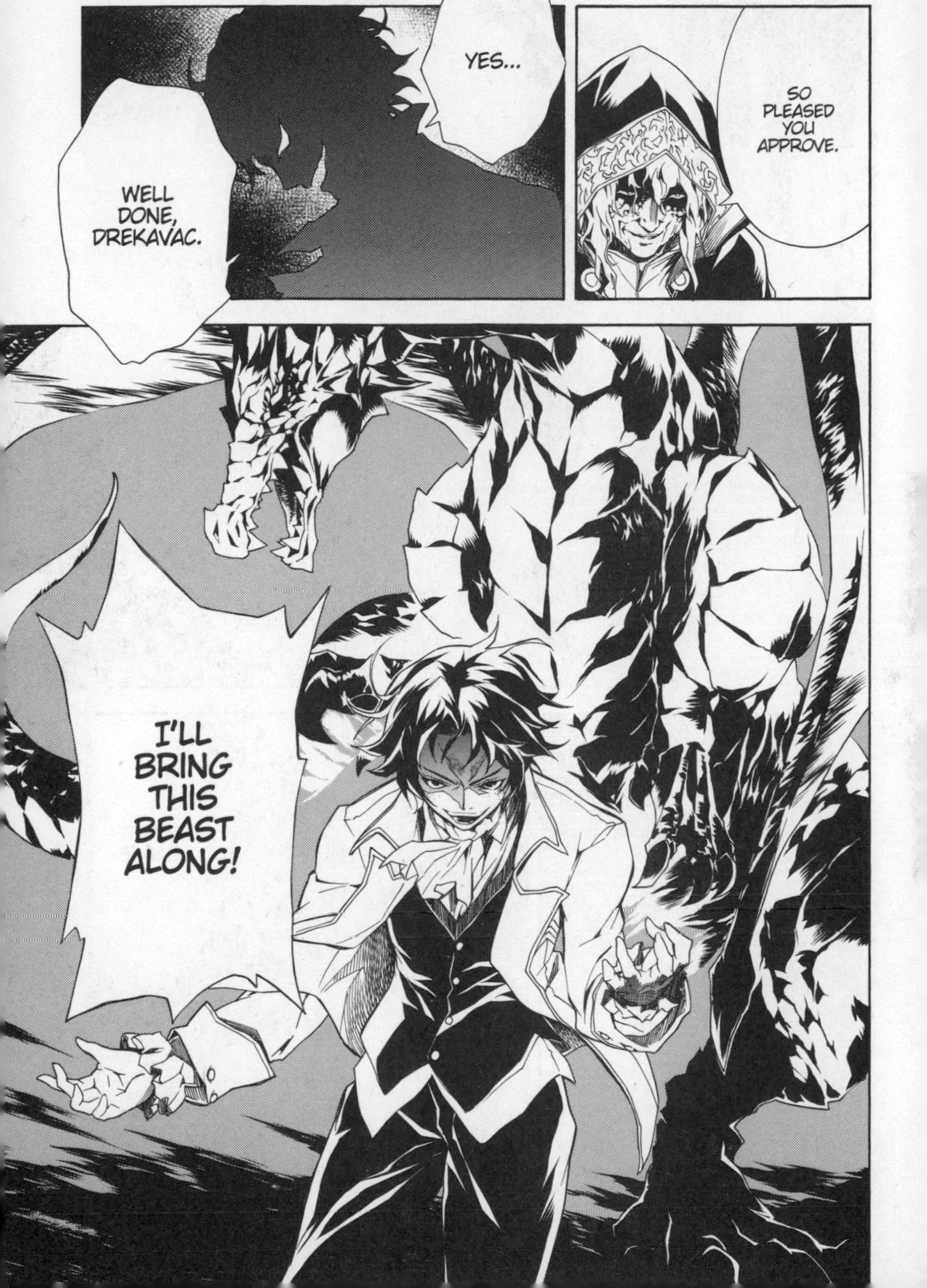
SO PLEASED YOU APPROVE.
YES...
WELL DONE, DREKAVAC.
I'LL BRING THIS BEAST ALONG!

MY RANSOM IS DUE IN TWO DAYS.

KNOCK KNOCK

BUT THERE'S NOTHING TO DO BUT WAIT.

I DON'T THINK IT'S COMING.

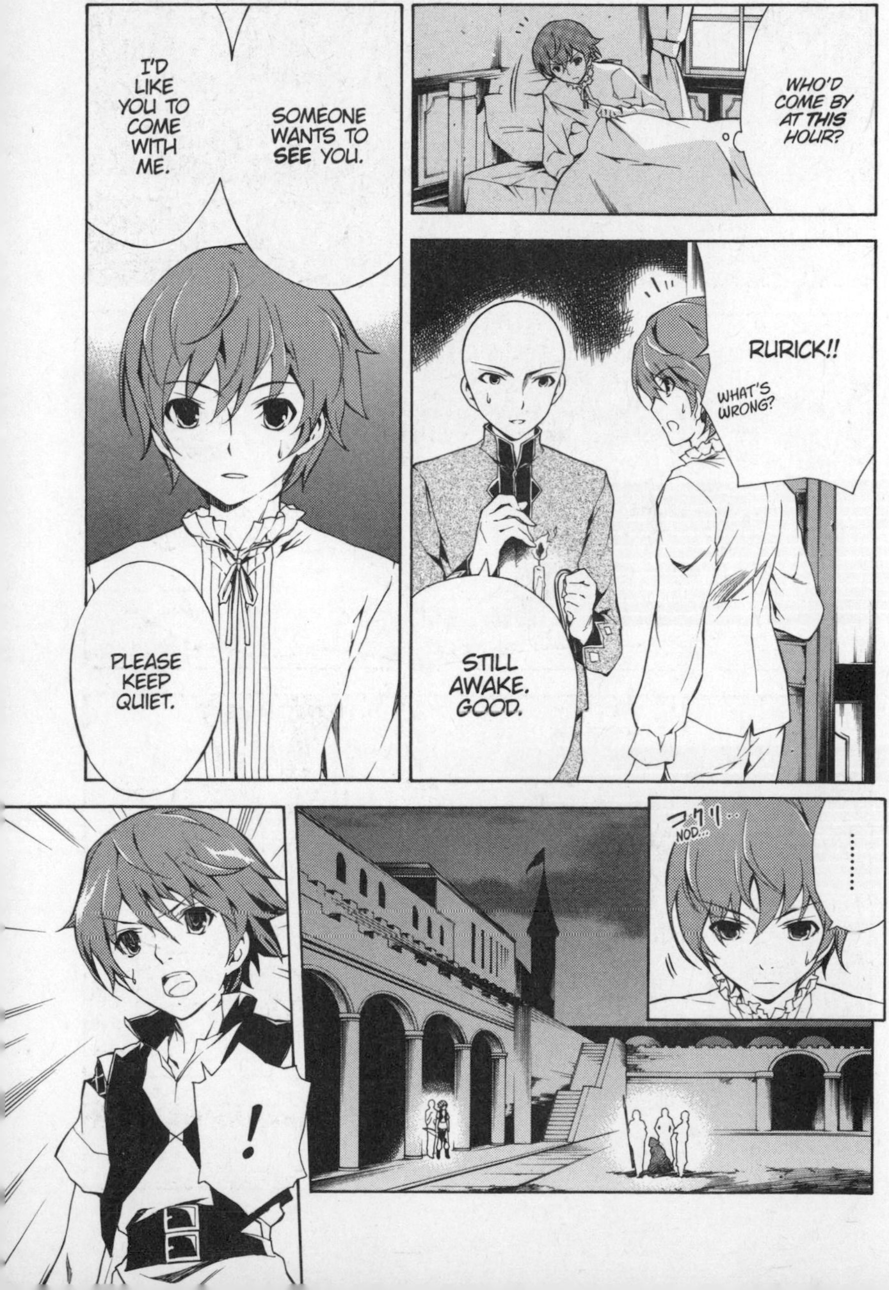
WHO'D COME BY AT THIS HOUR?
RURICK!!
WHAT'S WRONG?
STILL AWAKE. GOOD.
SOMEONE WANTS TO SEE YOU.
I'D LIKE YOU TO COME WITH ME.
PLEASE KEEP QUIET.
コクリ..
NOD...
......
!

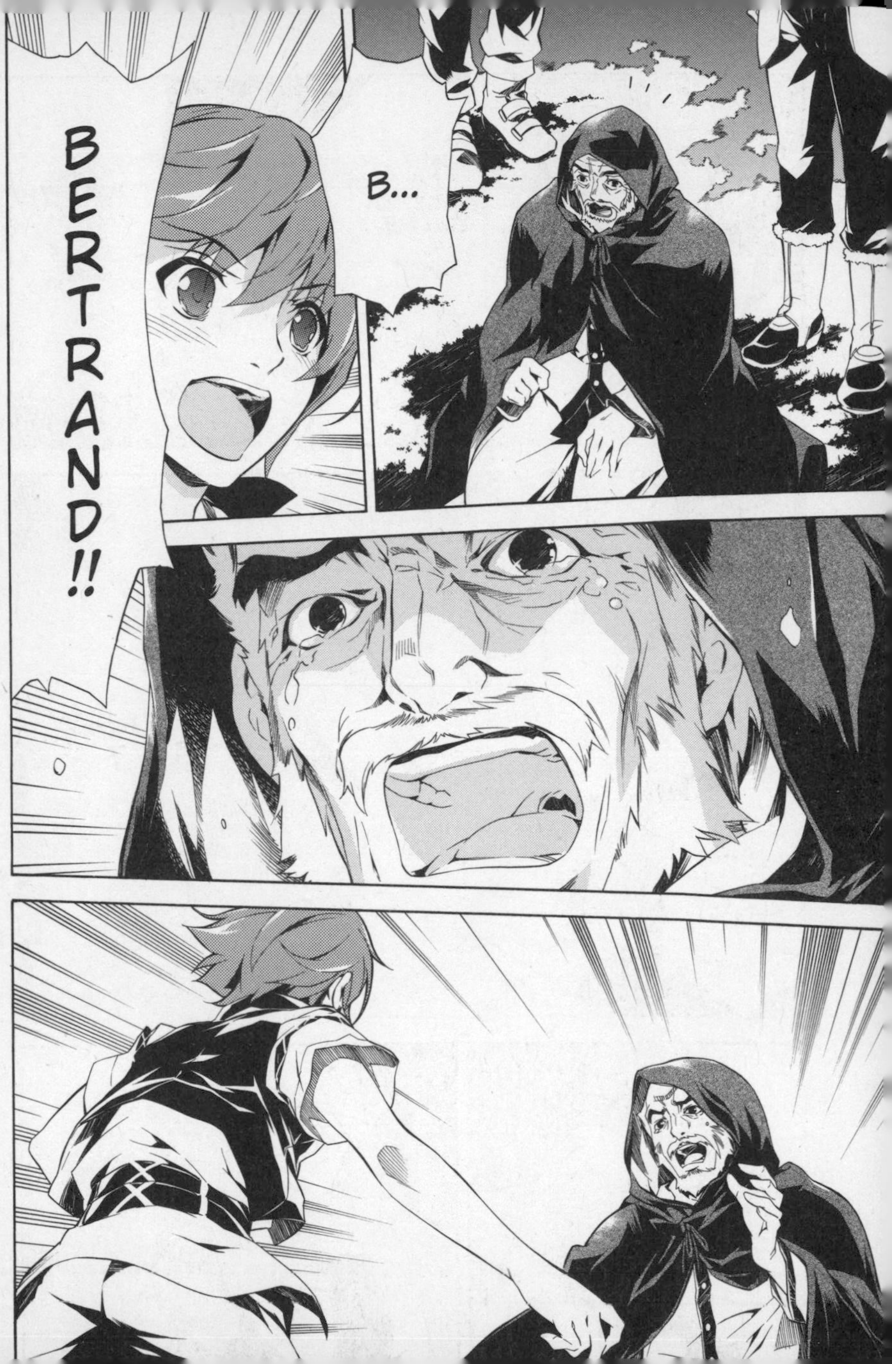
B...
BERTRAND!!

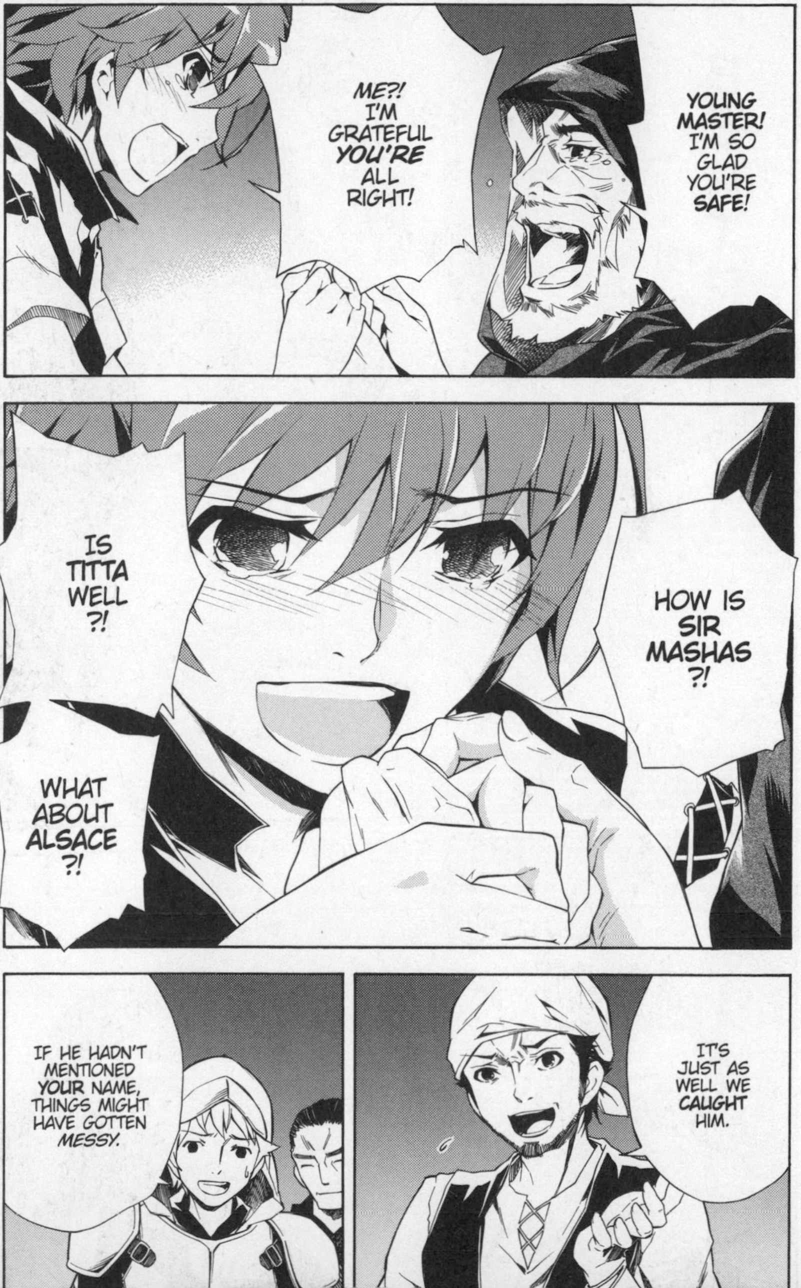
YOUNG MASTER! I'M SO GLAD YOU'RE SAFE!
ME?! I'M GRATEFUL YOU'RE ALL RIGHT!
HOW IS SIR MASHAS ?!
IS TITTA WELL ?!
WHAT ABOUT ALSACE ?!
IT'S JUST AS WELL WE CAUGHT HIM.
IF HE HADN'T MENTIONED YOUR NAME, THINGS MIGHT HAVE GOTTEN MESSY.

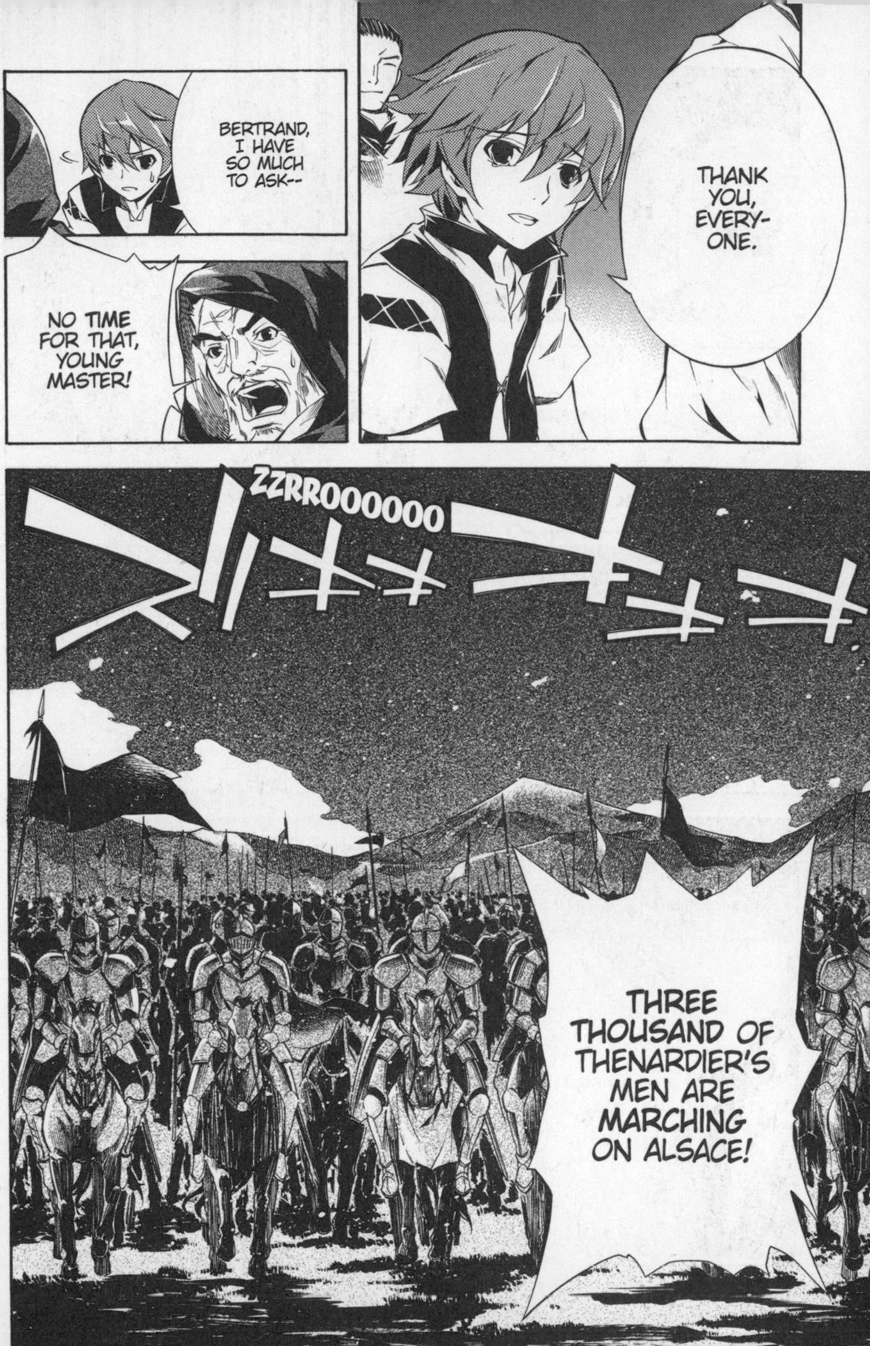
THANK YOU, EVERYONE.
BERTRAND, I HAVE SO MUCH TO ASK--
NO TIME FOR THAT, YOUNG MASTER!
ZZRROOOOOO
THREE THOUSAND OF THENARDIER'S MEN ARE MARCHING ON ALSACE!

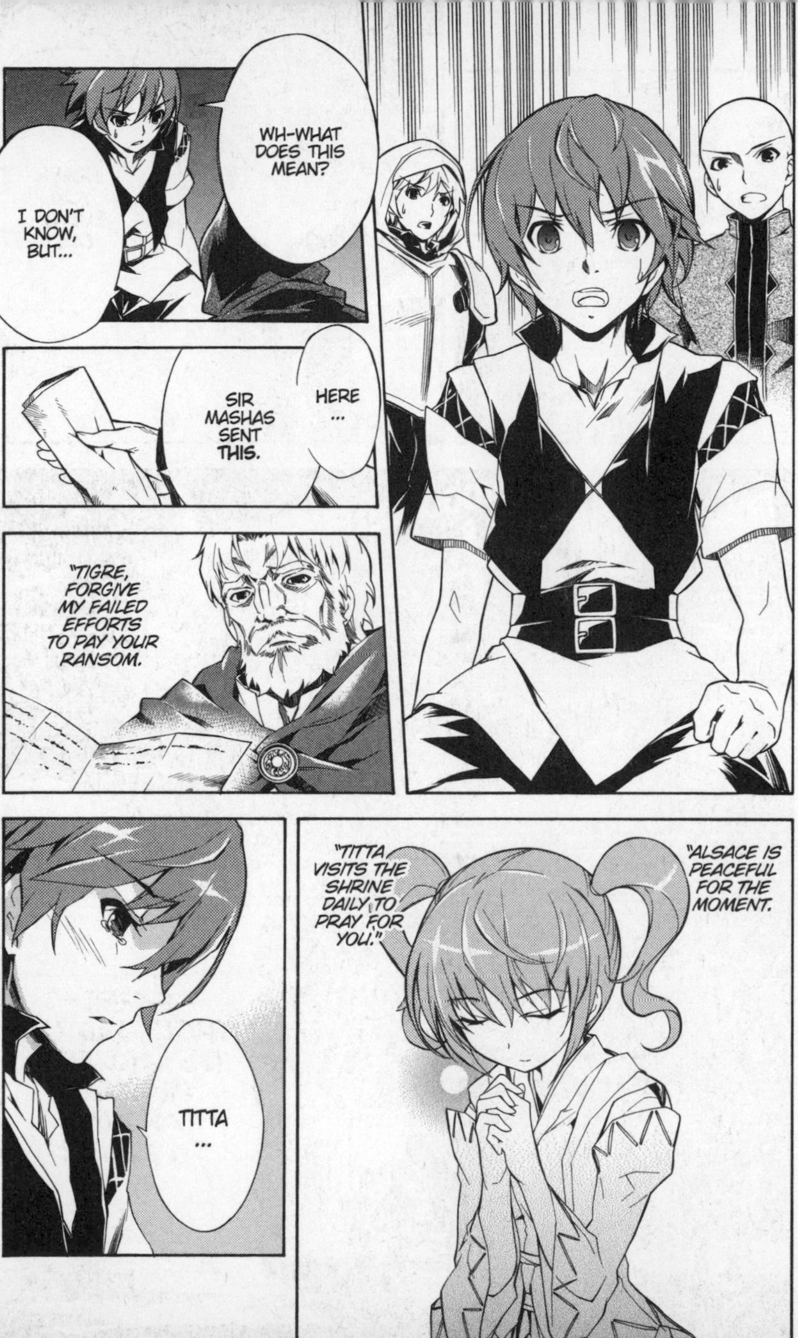
WH-WHAT DOES THIS MEAN?
I DON'T KNOW, BUT...
HERE...
SIR MASHAS SENT THIS.
"TIGRE, FORGIVE MY FAILED EFFORTS TO PAY YOUR RANSOM.
"ALSACE IS PEACEFUL FOR THE MOMENT.
"TITTA VISITS THE SHRINE DAILY TO PRAY FOR YOU."
TITTA...

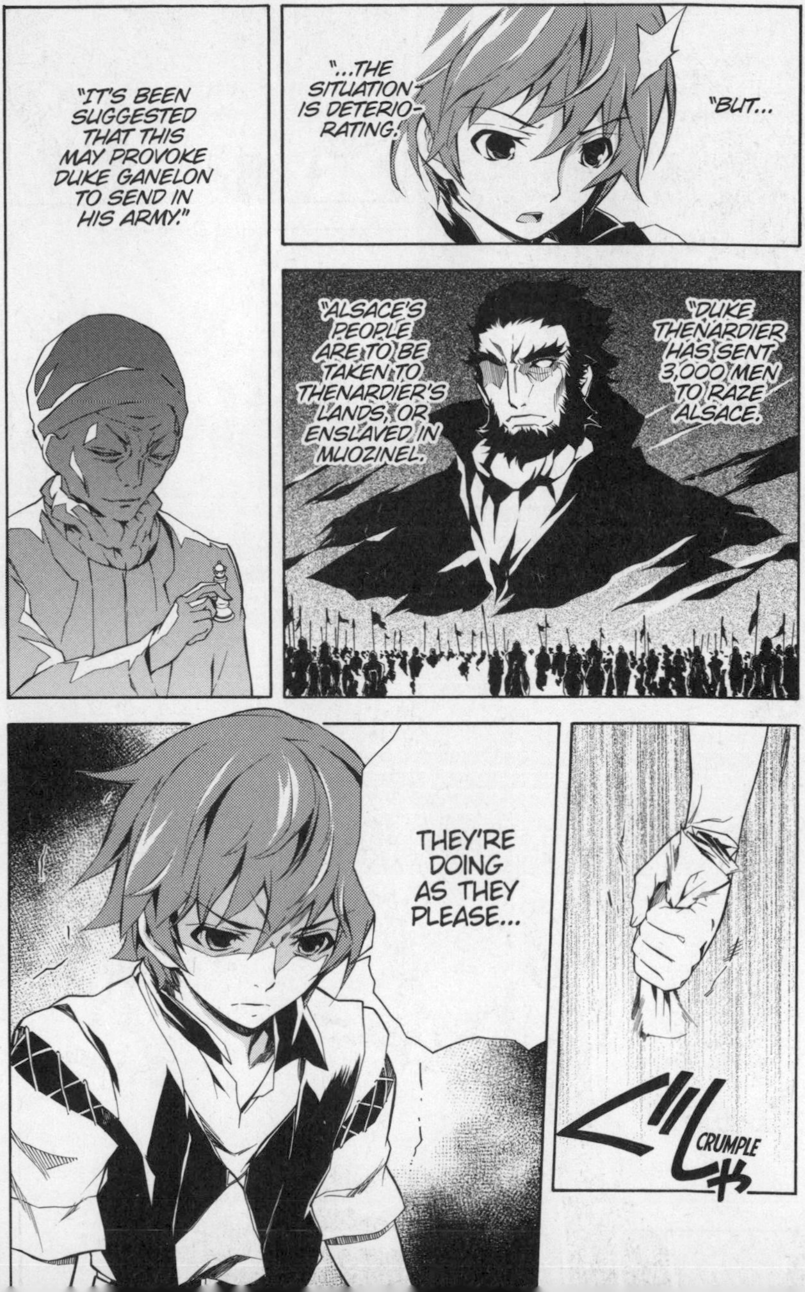
"BUT...
"...THE SITUATION IS DETERIORATING."
"DUKE THENARDIER HAS SENT 3,000 MEN TO RAZE ALSACE.
"ALSACE'S PEOPLE ARE TO BE TAKEN TO THENARDIER'S LANDS, OR ENSLAVED IN MUOZINEL.
"IT'S BEEN SUGGESTED THAT THIS MAY PROVOKE DUKE GANELON TO SEND IN HIS ARMY."
CRUMPLE
THEY'RE DOING AS THEY PLEASE...

I'M SORRY, BUT I CAN'T.

I UNDER-STAND YOUR FEELINGS, BUT PLEASE RETURN TO YOUR QUARTERS.

SIR TIGRE-VURMUD...

PLEASE GO BACK!

REMEMBER THE WAR MAIDEN'S WARNING! APPROACH THE WALL, AND YOU'LL BE EXECUTED!

ガシャン CLANNK!.

SHWIPP

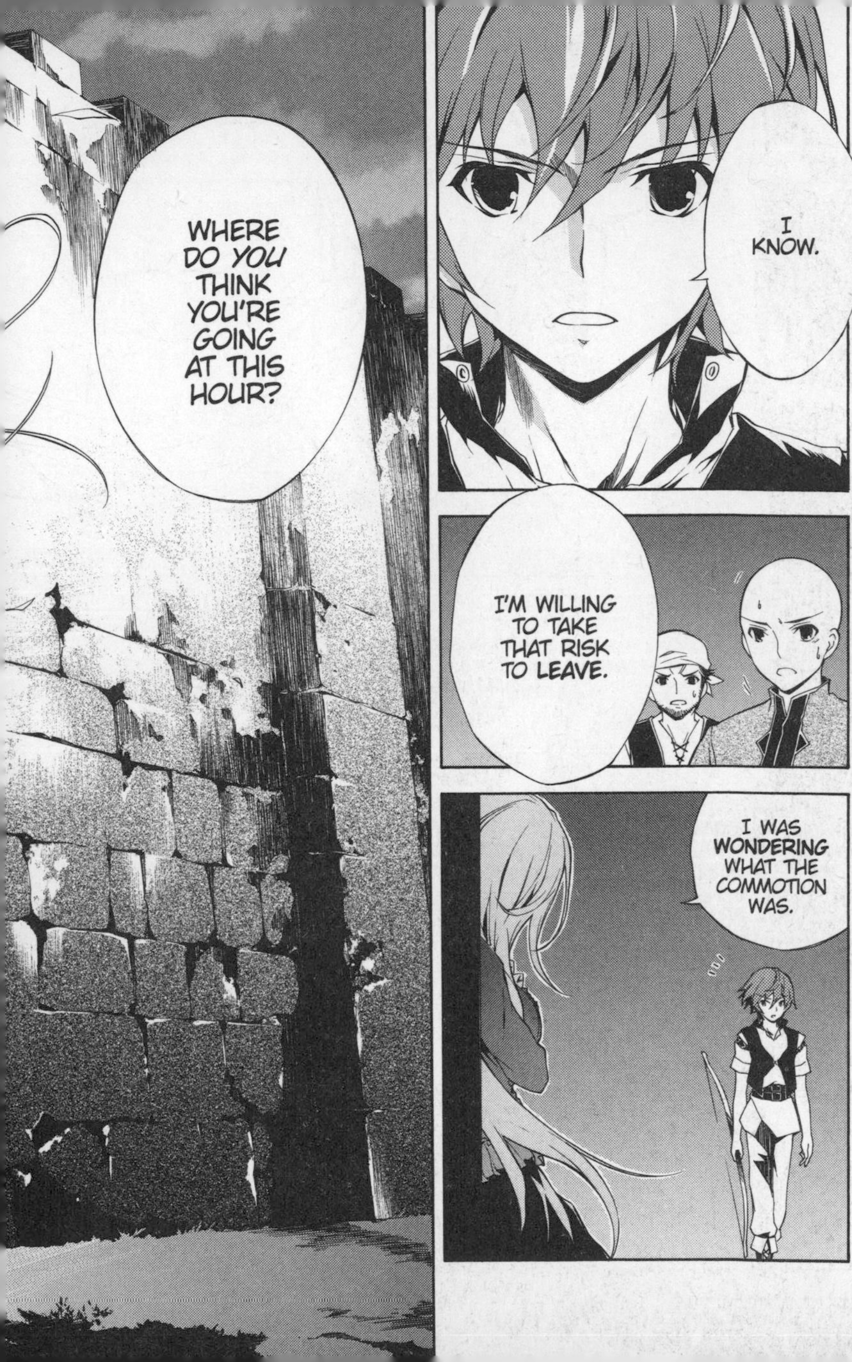
I KNOW.
I'M WILLING TO TAKE THAT RISK TO LEAVE.
I WAS WONDERING WHAT THE COMMOTION WAS.
WHERE DO *YOU* THINK YOU'RE GOING AT THIS HOUR?

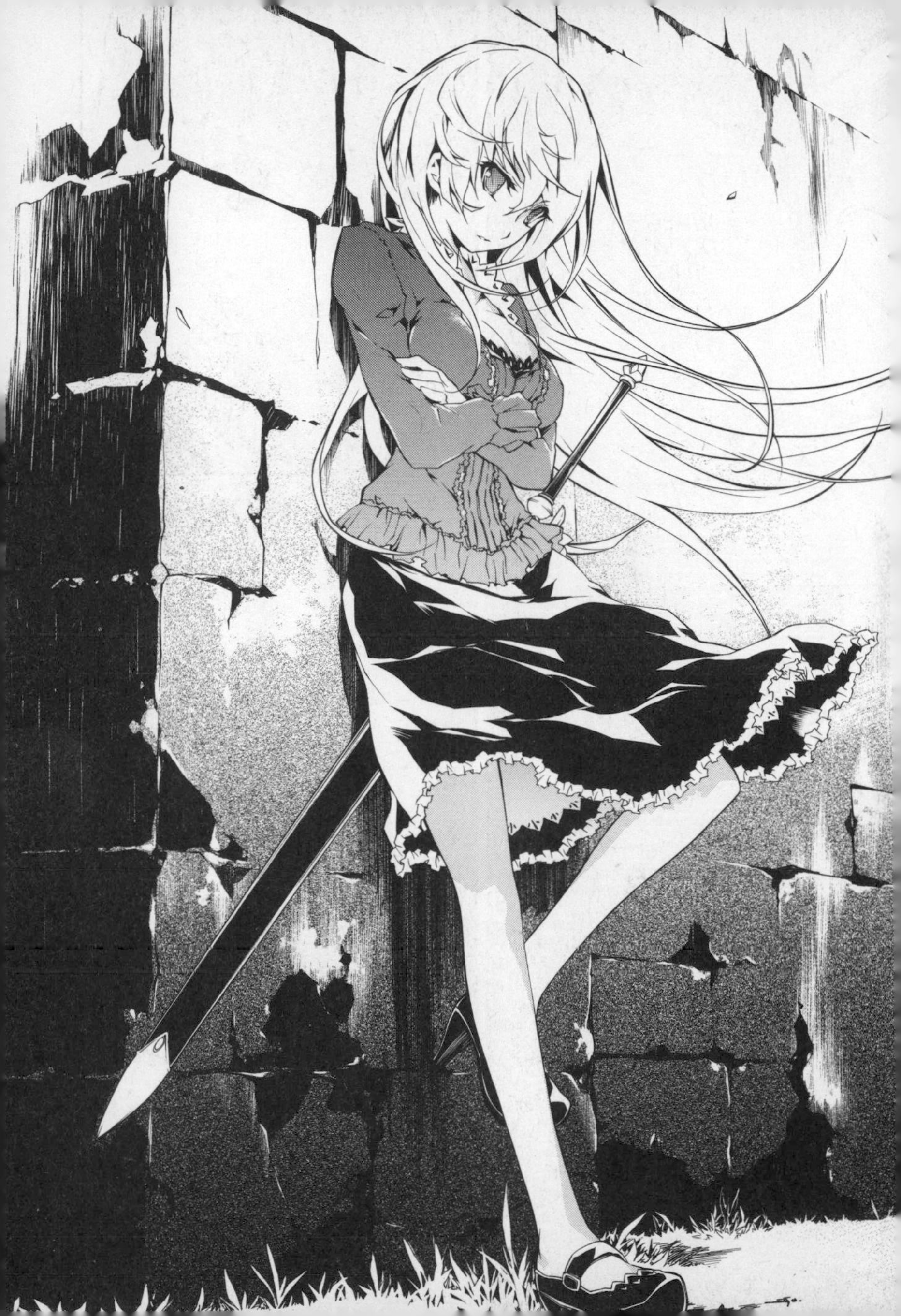

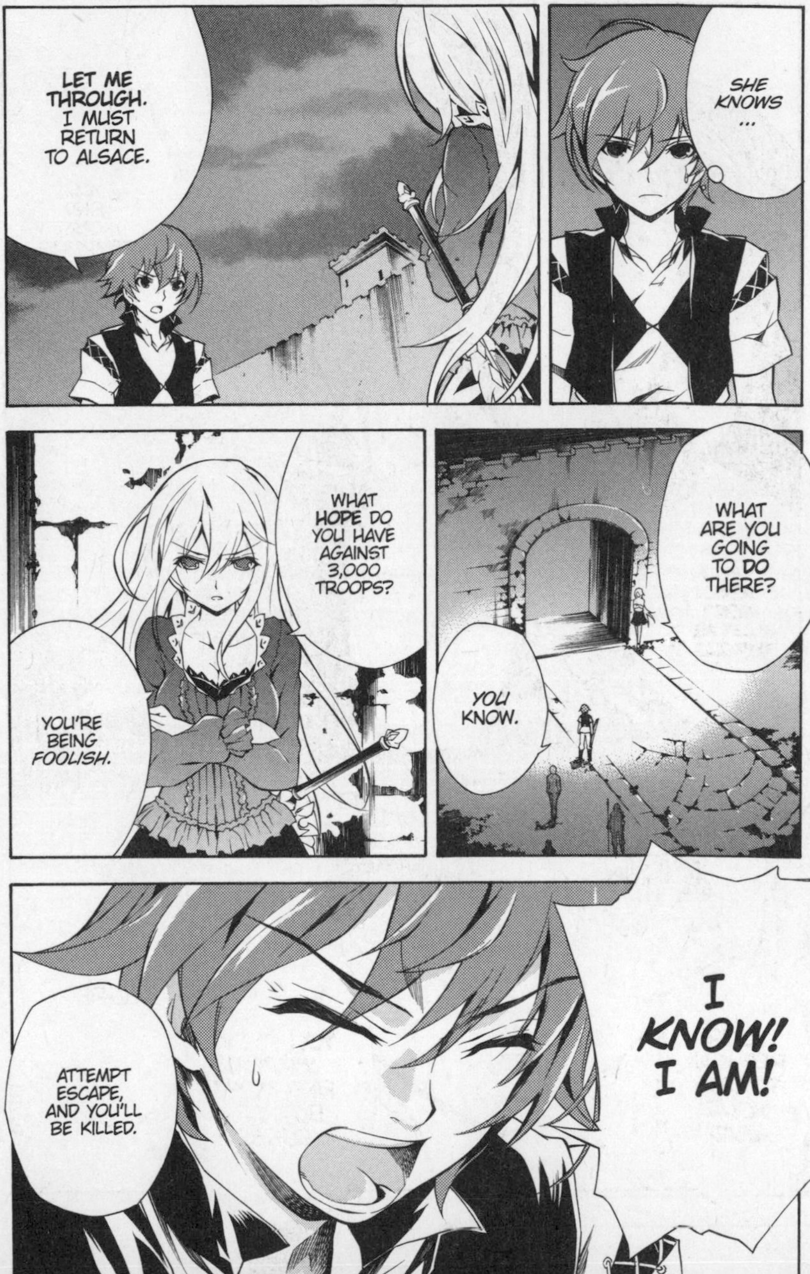
SHE KNOWS ...
LET ME THROUGH. I MUST RETURN TO ALSACE.
WHAT ARE YOU GOING TO DO THERE?
YOU KNOW.
WHAT HOPE DO YOU HAVE AGAINST 3,000 TROOPS?
YOU'RE BEING FOOLISH.
I KNOW! I AM!
ATTEMPT ESCAPE, AND YOU'LL BE KILLED.

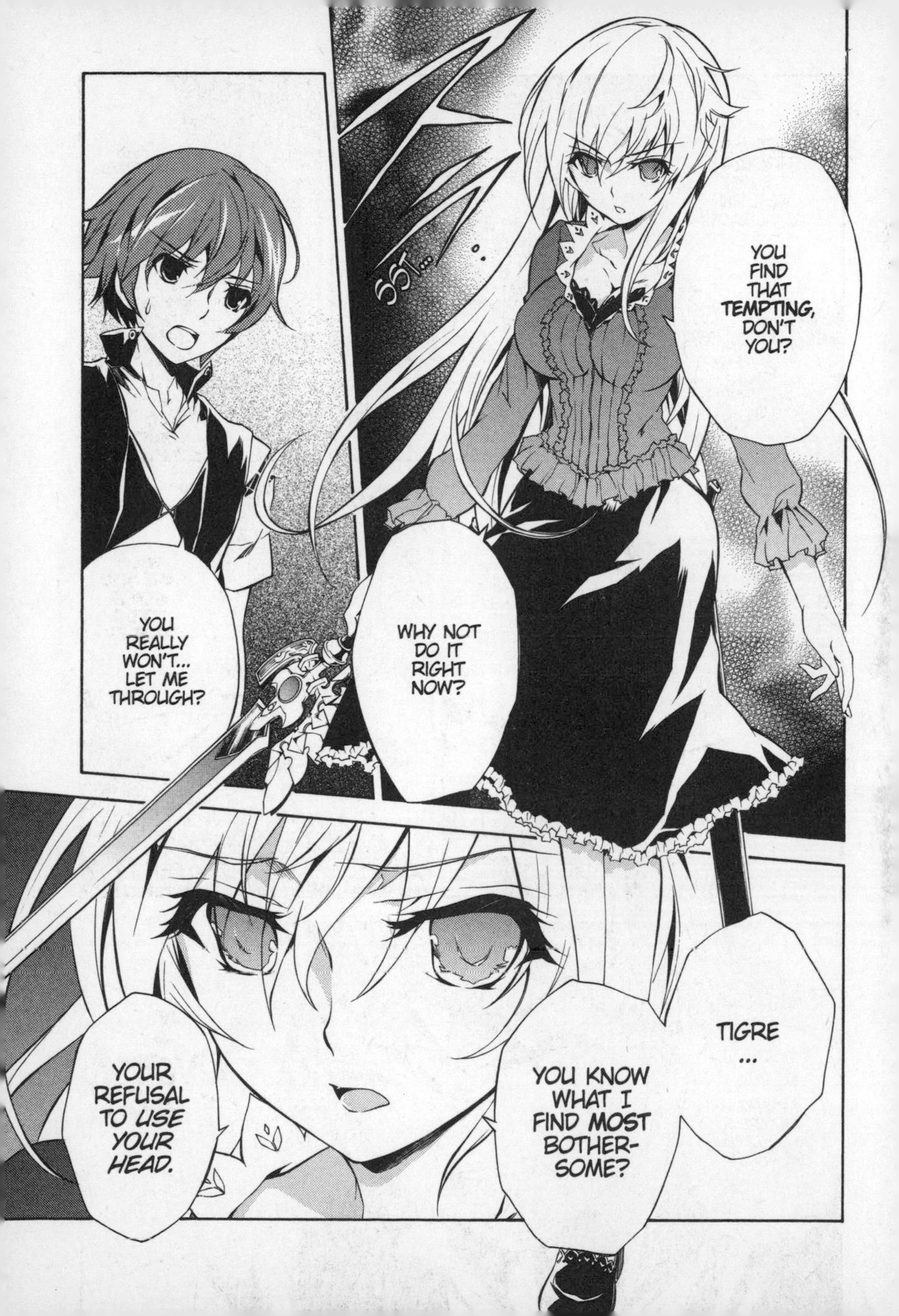
YOU FIND THAT TEMPTING, DON'T YOU?
SST...
WHY NOT DO IT RIGHT NOW?
YOU REALLY WON'T... LET ME THROUGH?
TIGRE ...
YOU KNOW WHAT I FIND MOST BOTHER-SOME?
YOUR REFUSAL TO USE YOUR HEAD.

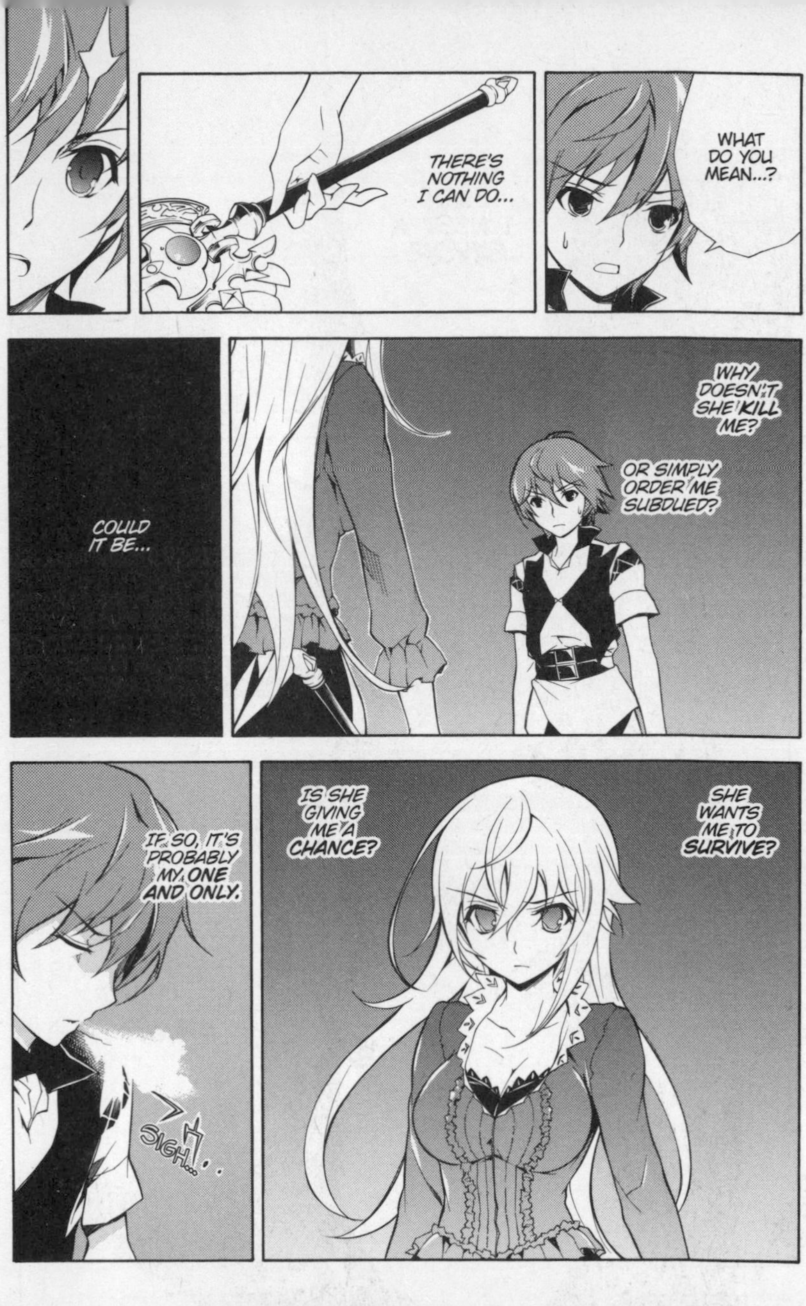
WHAT DO YOU MEAN...?
THERE'S NOTHING I CAN DO...
WHY DOESN'T SHE KILL ME?
OR SIMPLY ORDER ME SUBDUED?
COULD IT BE...
SHE WANTS ME TO SURVIVE?
IS SHE GIVING ME A CHANCE?
IF SO, IT'S PROBABLY MY ONE AND ONLY.
SIGH...

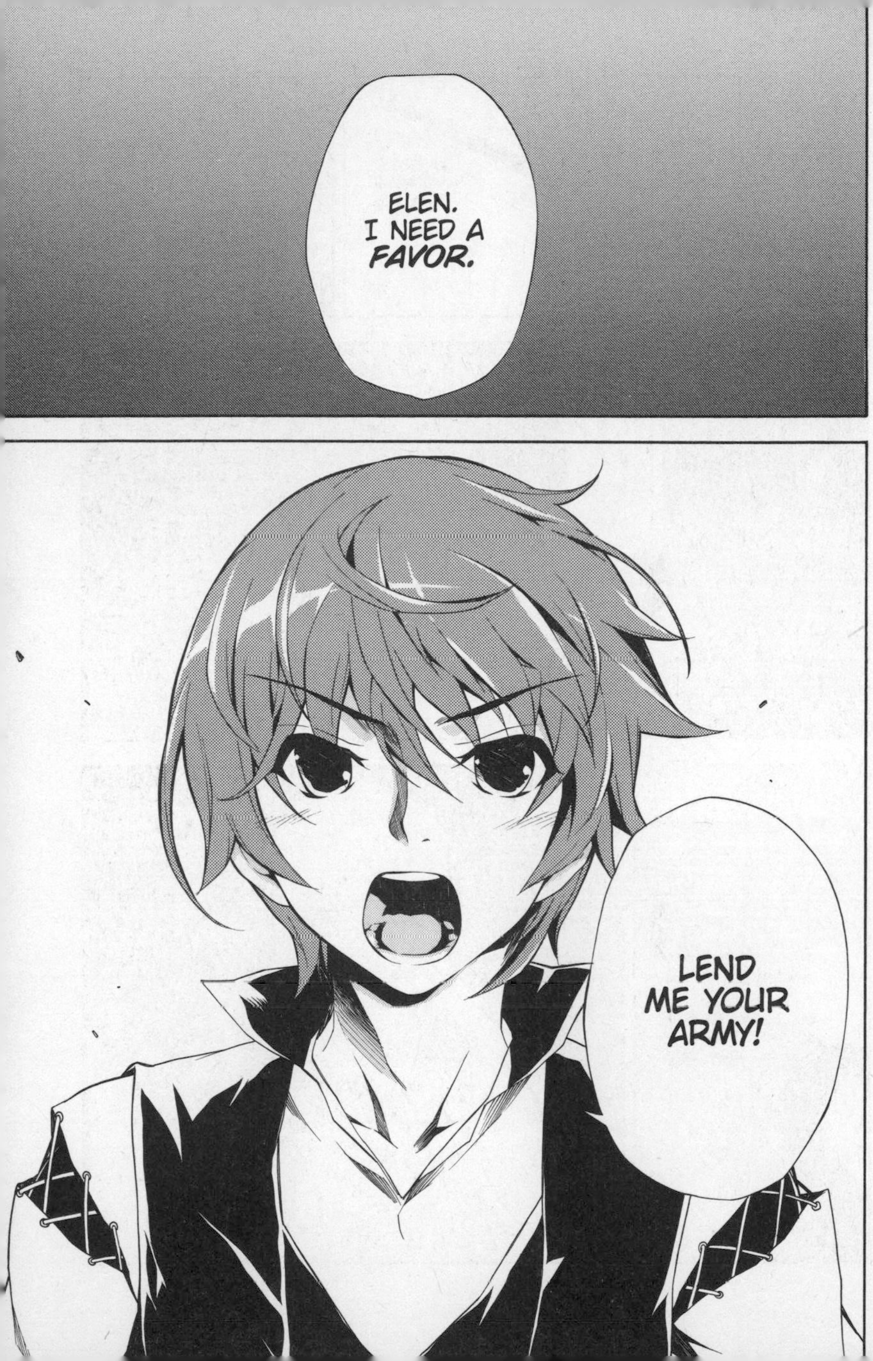
ELEN. I NEED A *FAVOR.*
LEND ME YOUR ARMY!

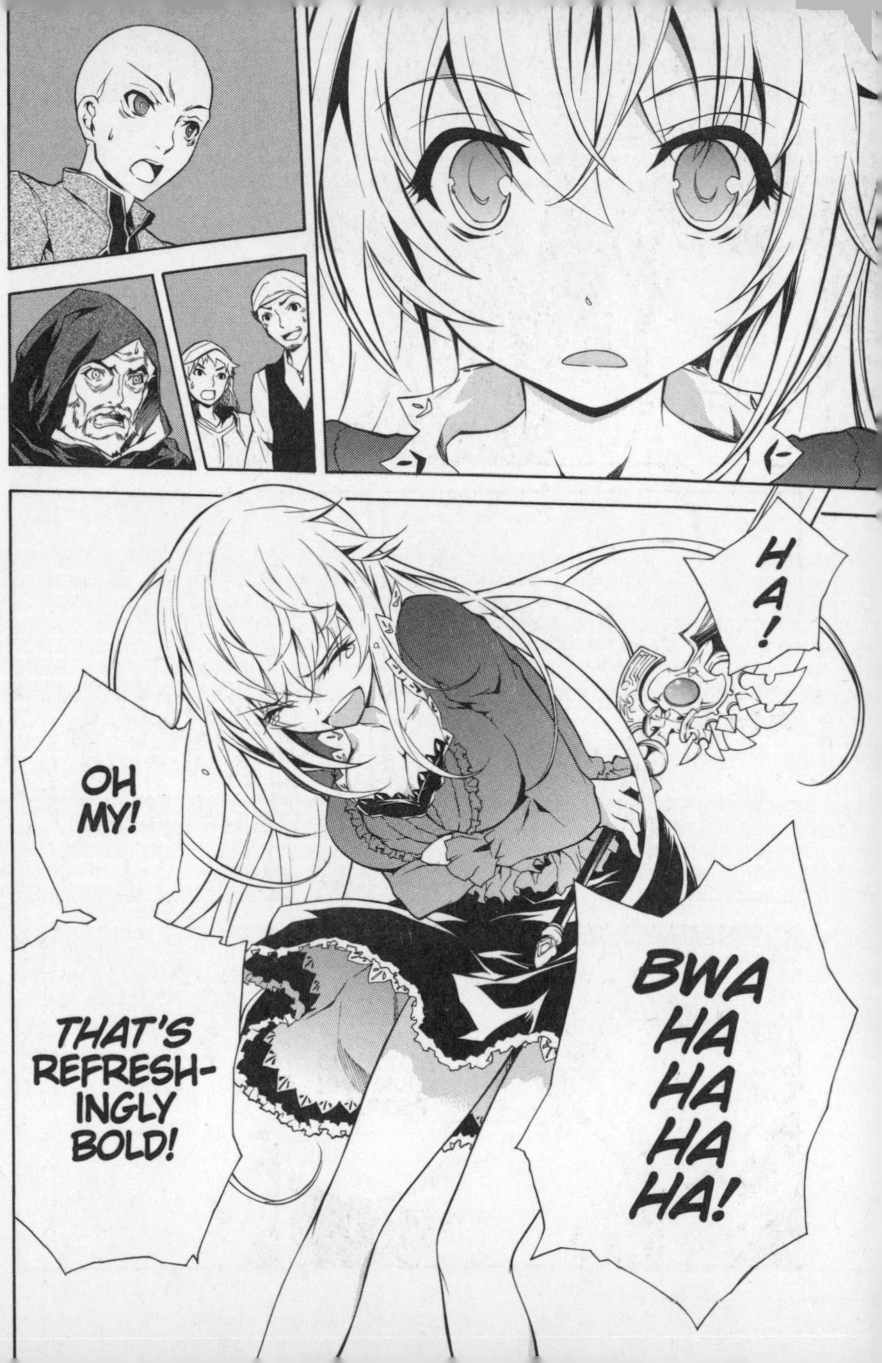
HA!
BWA HA HA HA HA!
OH MY!
THAT'S REFRESH-INGLY BOLD!

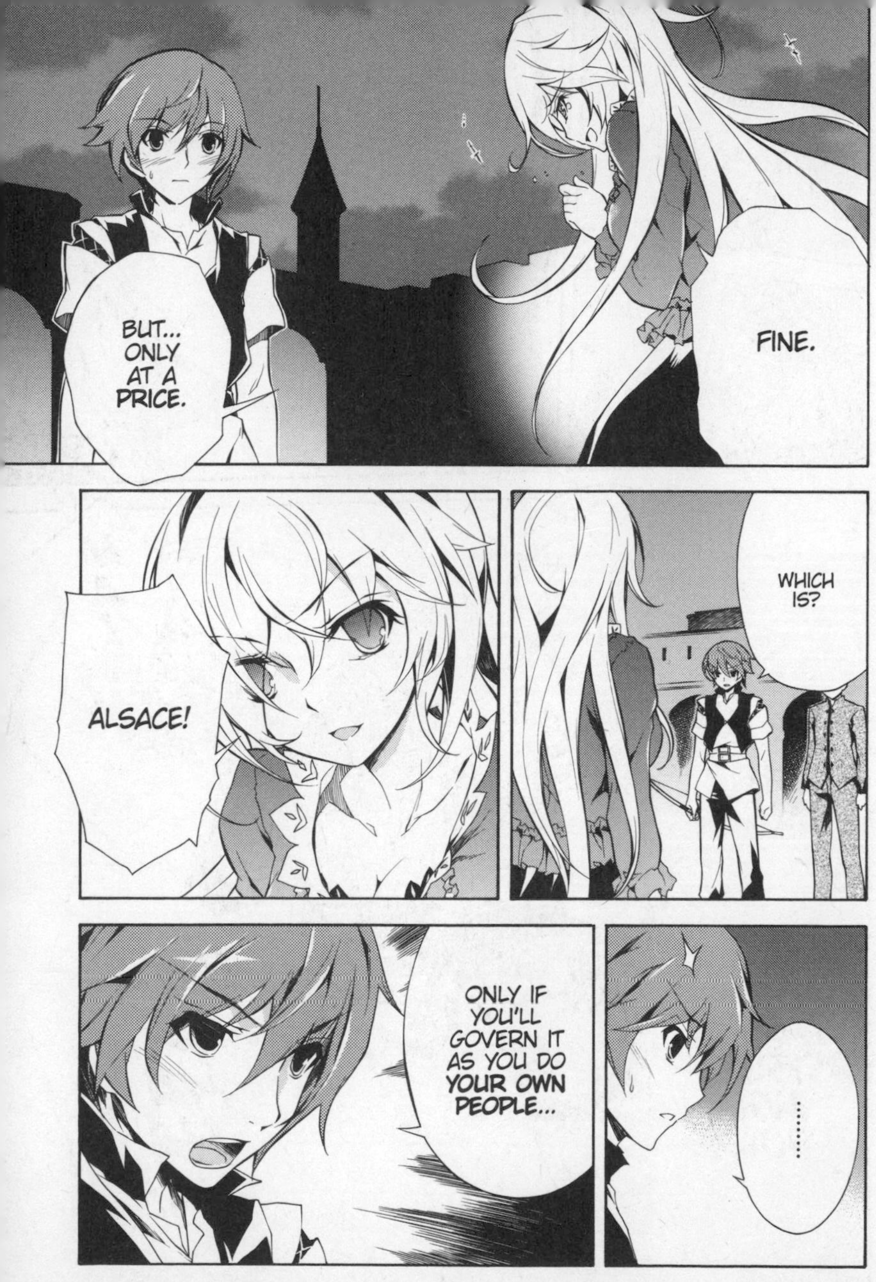
FINE.
BUT... ONLY AT A PRICE.
WHICH IS?
ALSACE!
......
ONLY IF YOU'LL GOVERN IT AS YOU DO YOUR OWN PEOPLE...

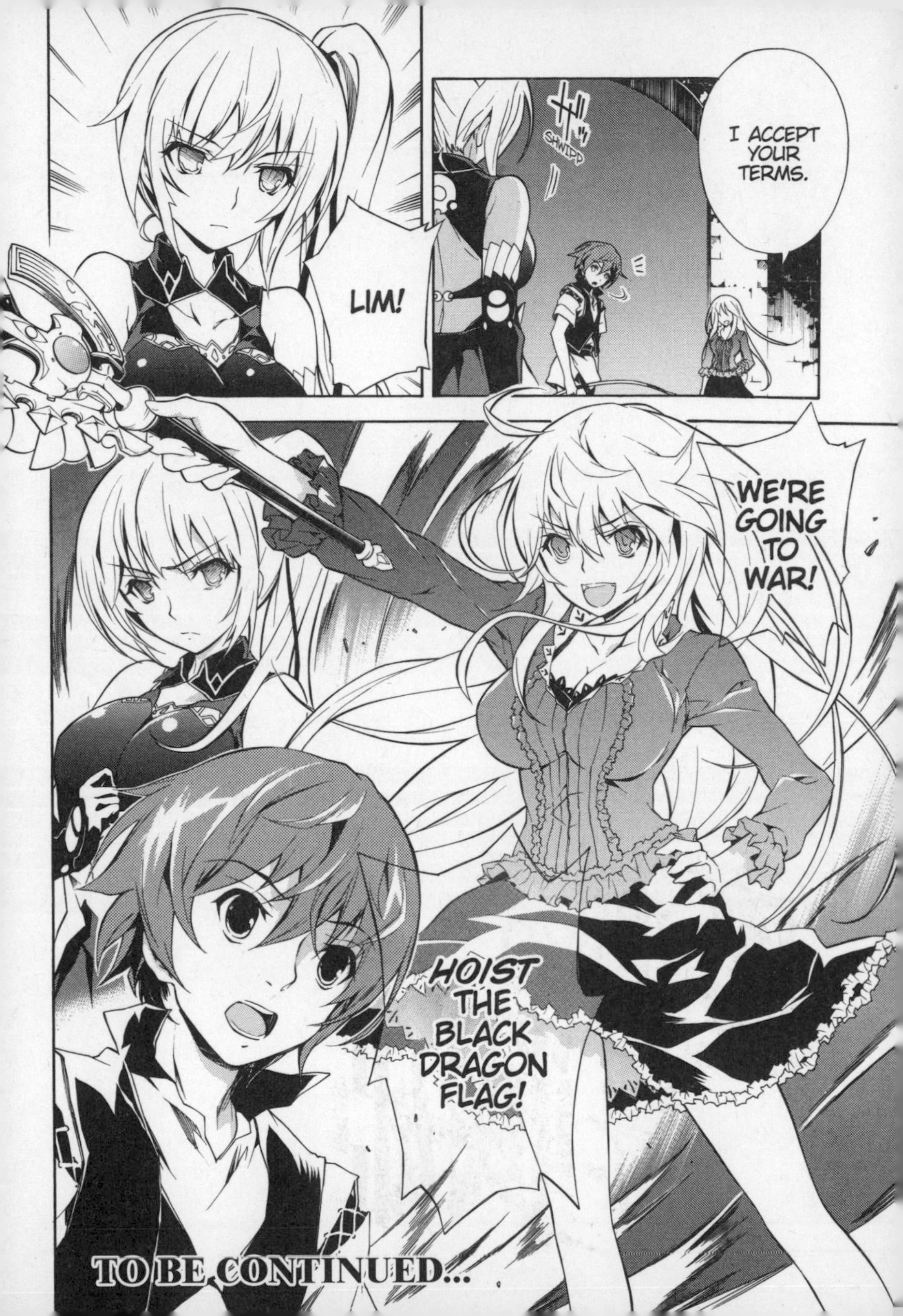
I ACCEPT YOUR TERMS.
SHWIPP
LIM!
WE'RE GOING TO WAR!
HOIST THE BLACK DRAGON FLAG!
TO BE CONTINUED...

魔弾の王と戦姫
ヴァナディース

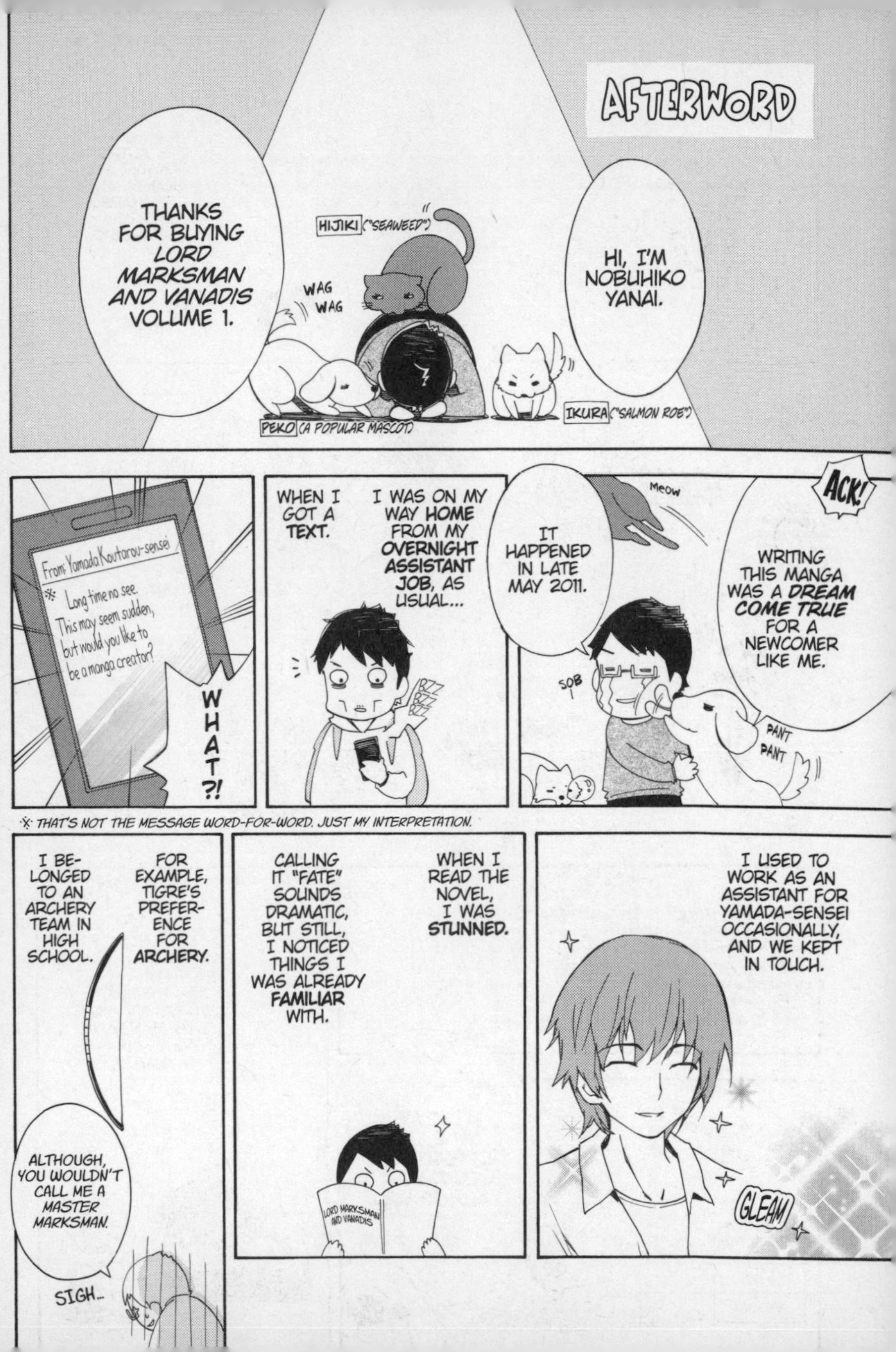
AFTERWORD
HI, I'M NOBUHIKO YANAI.
THANKS FOR BUYING LORD MARKSMAN AND VANADIS VOLUME 1.
HIJIKI ("SEAWEED")
WAG WAG
IKURA ("SALMON ROE")
PEKO (A POPULAR MASCOT)
ACK!
Meow
WRITING THIS MANGA WAS A DREAM COME TRUE FOR A NEWCOMER LIKE ME.
IT HAPPENED IN LATE MAY 2011.
SOB
PANT PANT
I WAS ON MY WAY HOME FROM MY OVERNIGHT ASSISTANT JOB, AS USUAL...
WHEN I GOT A TEXT.
BZZ BZZ BZZ
From: Yamada Koutarou-sensei
※ Long time no see. This may seem sudden, but would you like to be a manga creator?
WHAT?!
※ THAT'S NOT THE MESSAGE WORD-FOR-WORD. JUST MY INTERPRETATION.
I USED TO WORK AS AN ASSISTANT FOR YAMADA-SENSEI OCCASIONALLY, AND WE KEPT IN TOUCH.
GLEAM
WHEN I READ THE NOVEL, I WAS STUNNED.
CALLING IT "FATE" SOUNDS DRAMATIC, BUT STILL, I NOTICED THINGS I WAS ALREADY FAMILIAR WITH.
LORD MARKSMAN AND VANADIS
FOR EXAMPLE, TIGRE'S PREFERENCE FOR ARCHERY.
I BELONGED TO AN ARCHERY TEAM IN HIGH SCHOOL.
ALTHOUGH, YOU WOULDN'T CALL ME A MASTER MARKSMAN.
SIGH...

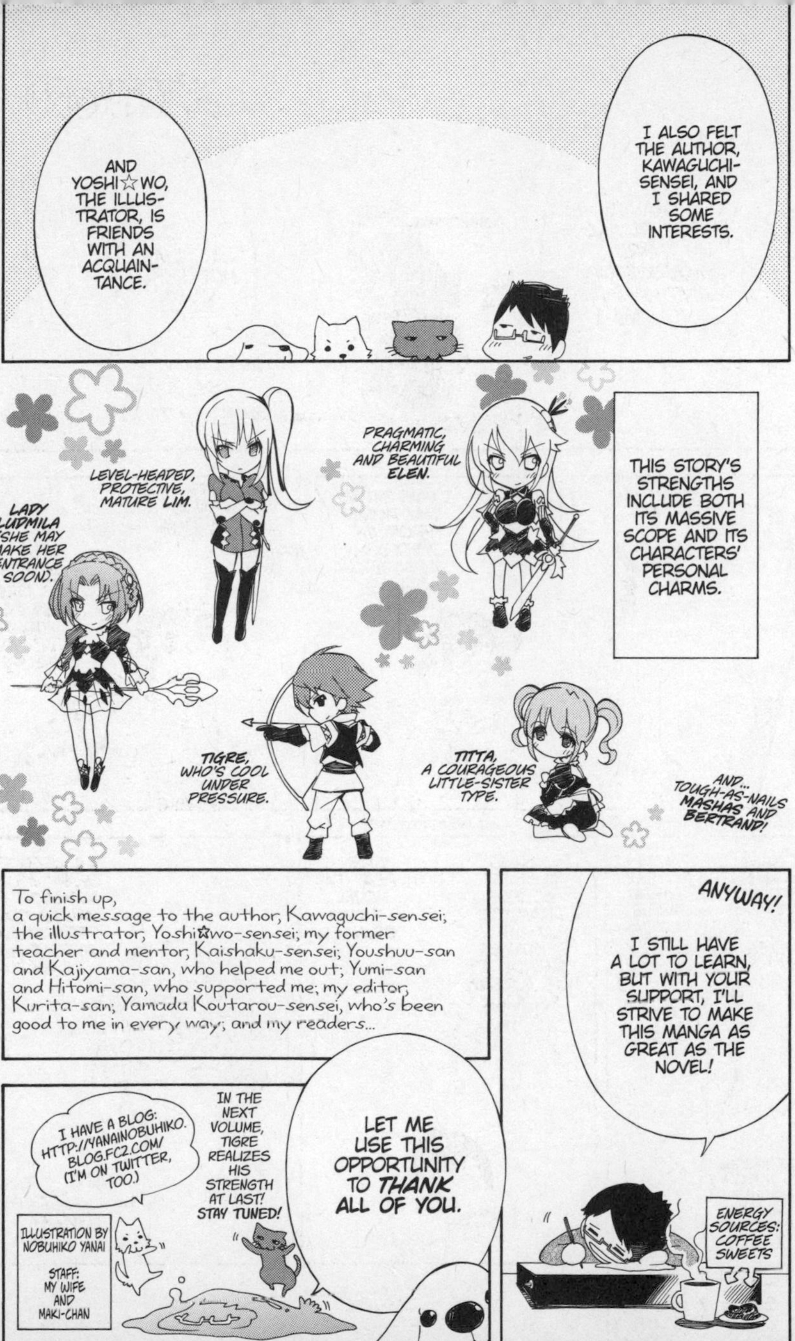
I ALSO FELT THE AUTHOR, KAWAGUCHI-SENSEI, AND I SHARED SOME INTERESTS.
AND YOSHI☆WO, THE ILLUSTRATOR, IS FRIENDS WITH AN ACQUAINTANCE.
THIS STORY'S STRENGTHS INCLUDE BOTH ITS MASSIVE SCOPE AND ITS CHARACTERS' PERSONAL CHARMS.
PRAGMATIC, CHARMING AND BEAUTIFUL ELEN.
LEVEL-HEADED, PROTECTIVE, MATURE LIM.
LADY LUDMILA (SHE MAY MAKE HER ENTRANCE SOON).
AND... TOUGH-AS-NAILS MASHAS AND BERTRAND!
TITTA, A COURAGEOUS LITTLE-SISTER TYPE.
TIGRE, WHO'S COOL UNDER PRESSURE.
ANYWAY!
I STILL HAVE A LOT TO LEARN, BUT WITH YOUR SUPPORT, I'LL STRIVE TO MAKE THIS MANGA AS GREAT AS THE NOVEL!
ENERGY SOURCES: COFFEE SWEETS
To finish up, a quick message to the author, Kawaguchi-sensei; the illustrator, Yoshi☆wo-sensei; my former teacher and mentor, Kaishaku-sensei; Youshuu-san and Kajiyama-san, who helped me out; Yumi-san and Hitomi-san, who supported me; my editor, Kurita-san; Yamada Koutarou-sensei, who's been good to me in every way; and my readers...
LET ME USE THIS OPPORTUNITY TO THANK ALL OF YOU.
IN THE NEXT VOLUME, TIGRE REALIZES HIS STRENGTH AT LAST! STAY TUNED!
I HAVE A BLOG: HTTP://YANAINOBUHIKO.BLOG.FC2.COM/ (I'M ON TWITTER, TOO.)
ILLUSTRATION BY NOBUHIKO YANAI
STAFF: MY WIFE AND MAKI-CHAN

Hi, I'm Tsukasa Kawagachi, the original author
of *Lord Marksman and Vanadis*. Although I see the
storyboards each month, having my story adapted into
manga is still exciting and hard to believe. The adaptation's
quality is amazing. So are Yoshi☆wo-san's illustrations.
I'm deeply moved by the interpretations of Tigre and Elen, as well as
Mashas and Bertrand, who are rarely illustrated in the novels.
I'd like to use this opportunity to thank Yanai-sensei, the editor,
and the editorial staff. I hope you continue to support
Lord Marksman and Vanadis!

Tsukasa Kawaguchi
Light Novel Author

Supporting Comments from the Author and Character Designer

☆*｡･･*♡　　♡　　♡*･･｡*☆
Hello, hello! ☆ It's April. (ˆ ω ˆ)
The warm spring weather is on its way!
Mmm! ♡ It's so lovely.♡
I love the gentle weather!
It makes me want to go outside!
I want to relax somewhere nice. ♡♡
☆*　　*　　*° ° * *° ° *☆

Yoshi☆wo's Twitter account:
http://twitter.com/yoshi_wo

Yoshi☆wo
Character Designer

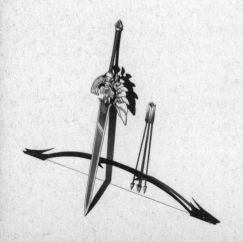

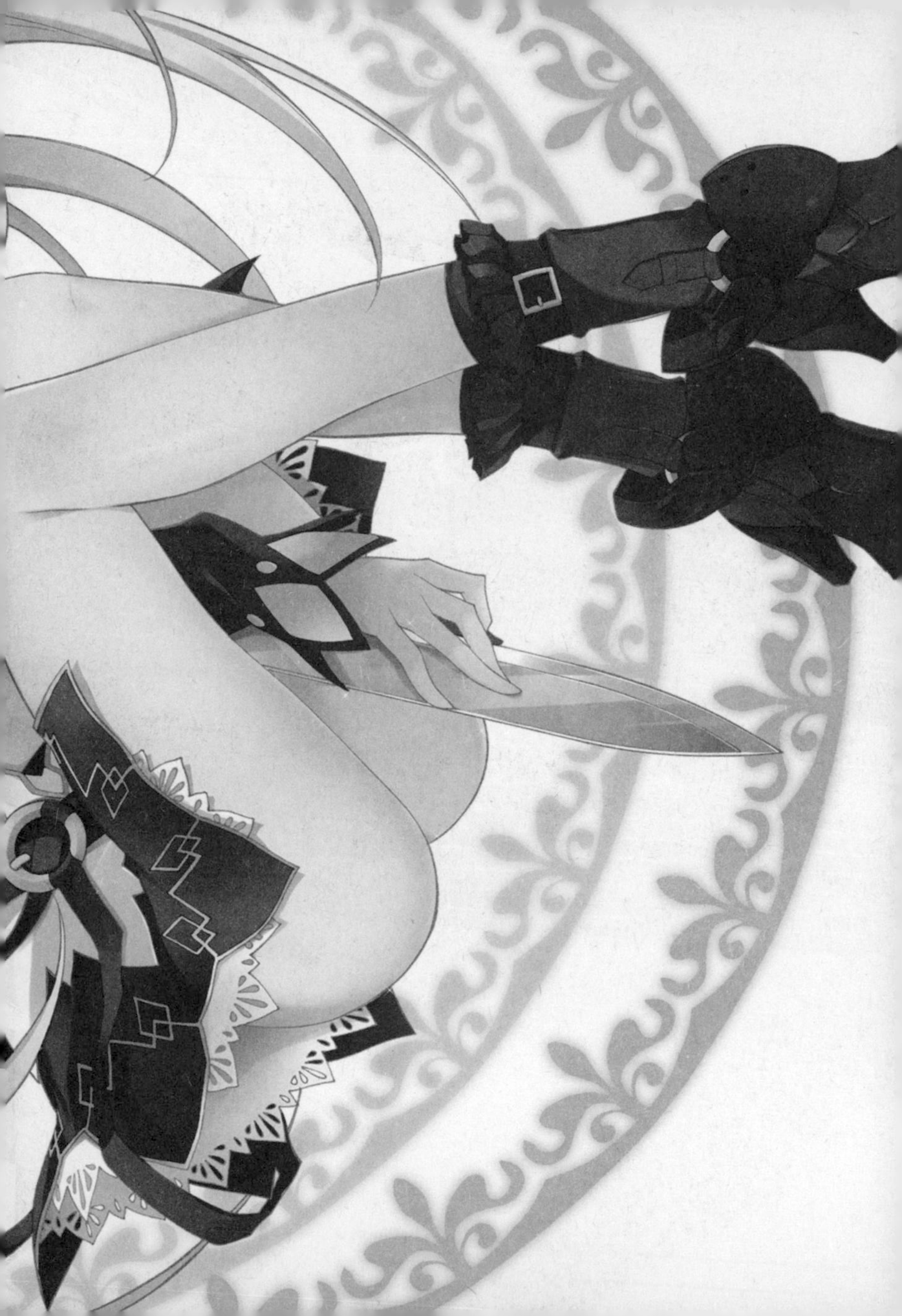

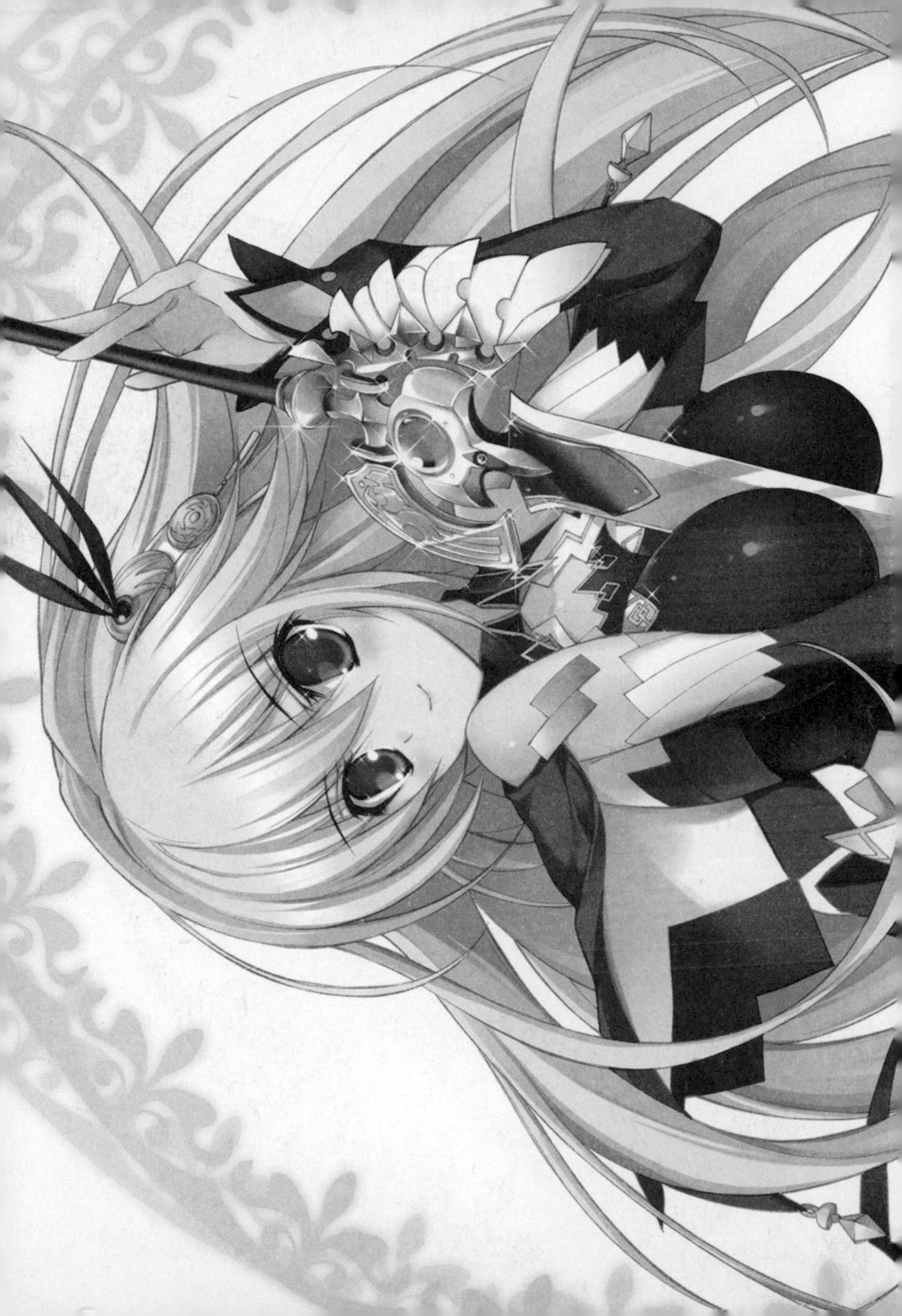

Lord Marksman and Vanadis

SEVEN SEAS ENTERTAINMENT PRESENTS

Lord Marksman and Vanadis VOL. 1

original story by **TSUKASA KAWAGUCHI** / art by **NOBUHIKO YANAI** / character design by **YOSHI☆WO**

TRANSLATION
Elina Ishikawa

ADAPTATION
Rebecca Schneider

LETTERING
James Gaubatz

COVER DESIGN
Nicky Lim

PROOFREADER
Danielle King
Tom Roddy

PRODUCTION MANAGER
Lissa Pattillo

EDITOR-IN-CHIEF
Adam Arnold

PUBLISHER
Jason DeAngelis

ISBN: 978-1-626924-03-1

Printed in Canada

First Printing: September 2016

10 9 8 7 6 5 4 3 2 1

FOLLOW US ONLINE: **www.gomanga.com**

READING DIRECTIONS

This book reads from *right to left*, Japanese style.
If this is your first time reading manga, you start
reading from the top right panel on each page and
take it from there. If you get lost, just follow the
numbered diagram here. It may seem backwards at
first, but you'll get the hang of it! Have fun!!

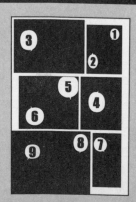